V O G U E
COMPLETE BEAUTY

VOGUE
COMPLETE BEAUTY

Deborah Hutton

CRESCENT BOOKS
NEW YORK

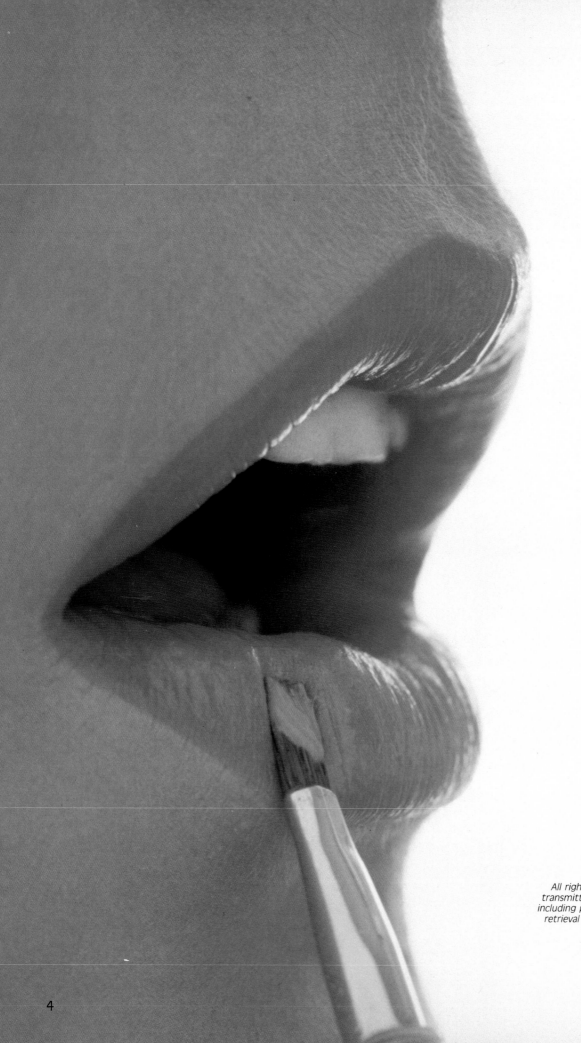

Published 1985 by Crescent Books,
Distributed by Crown Publishers, Inc.

© text: The Condé Nast Publications Ltd
® illustrations: Octopus Books Ltd

Printed in Hong Kong

1098765432

C O N T E N T S

Author's acknowledgments

It is, sadly, impossible to acknowledge all the help and advice that I have received while compiling this book. There are, however, a few people who have played a significant part in its production and to whom I am especially indebted.

First, my thanks to Beatrix Miller, Editor-in-Chief of British *Vogue*, who gave me the idea for the book, the opportunity of writing it and her absolute support whenever obstacles presented themselves; to Alex Kroll, Editor of *Vogue* Books, for his help and advice at every stage of the writing; and to Felicity Clark, Beauty Editor of *Vogue*, for lending an experienced eye to the photography and her expertise to the make-up pages. Thanks, too, to Georgina Boosey, Jennifer Harman and Richard Askwith for enabling my life as Health Editor of *Vogue* to proceed as smoothly as it has done, and to Penny Summers and Marie-Louise Avery of Octopus Books for the considerable time and trouble they have taken over the manuscript and its illustration.

More specific thanks go to Barbara Dale for devising the exercises for the Shape chapter and the pregnancy section at the back of the book, to Maxine Tobias for her guidance in compiling the yoga section and to Arabella Boxer for her recipes, which do more than justice to the premise that it is possible to eat healthily and deliciously. Help, comments and criticisms were also gratefully received at the various stages of research, writing and proof checking from Dr Wilfred Barlow, who introduced me to the Alexander Technique, Neville Bass, Dr Malcolm Carruthers, Professor J W Dickerson, Daniel Galvin, Dr Jeremy Gilkes, Dr Ruth Gould, Maggie Hunt, Dr Jonathan Kersley, Dr Veronica Kirton, Dr Patricia Last of BUPA, Mr Phillip Lebon, FRCS, Alastair Murray of London's City Gym, Mr Frederick Nicolle, FRCS, Dr Barbara Pickard, John Reuter, Hugh Rushton of the Philip Kingsley Trichology Clinic and Dr Nichol Thin. If, after all their comments, any inaccuracies remain in the text, they are entirely my own.

Two final and special thank yous to Patrick Collister whose affectionate bullying led me to *Vogue* in the first place and to my family who rescued me from my typewriter on innumerable occasions and sustained me in every way until the book was written.

THE ARTIST'S EYE VIEW

This page

Legendary beauty (right). The exquisite features, perfect bones and long elegant neck of Queen Nefertiti of the eighteenth Egyptian dynasty cast in limestone by an anonymous sculptor, circa 1,500 BC.

Beauty undressed (far right). Cranach's Venus depicts a medieval ideal: pale and slender, nubile and pear-shaped with long thighs low waistline and ears and hands that are disproportionately large. The model who posed for this Venus would almost certainly have been male – hence, perhaps, her slightly androgynous quality. Later painters were to endow her with more opulent charms.

Archetypal beauty (below left). Botticelli's Venus is free and unrestrained – expressive of the values of a new enlightened age and evocative of the memory of an old and golden one. She is very close to our own contemporary idea of beauty, too.

Sultry beauty (below right). Botticelli revived in the shape of Jane Morris, wife of the painter and designer William Morris, posing for Rossetti's study of Proserpine. Her heavy hair, chiselled features, swanlike neck and full expressive mouth convey the strangely sorrowful sensuality of the Pre-Raphaelite ideal.

Opposite page

Society beauty (above). Consuelo Vanderbilt, the turn of the century American heiress who became Duchess of Marlborough and, later, Madame Balsan, here painted by Boldini. Her dark eyes, small heart-shaped face and slim figure were much admired.

Ugly beauty (below). The strong, forthright profile of Lady Ottoline Morrell, in striking caricature by Bussy. A remarkable woman of decided opinions, versatile talents and considerable vanity, Lady Ottoline took 'the utmost pains to set off her beauty,' noted friend and contemporary Virginia Woolf, 'as though it were some rare object picked up in a dusty Florentine back street.'

what is beauty?

Beauty yesterday – historical perspectives

To the ancient Greeks, the secret of beauty lay in the proportions of the face. They divided it into three equal parts — hairline to eyebrow, eyebrow to upper lip, upper lip to chin — and called it the golden section. For them, beauty was a straightforward matter of mathematics.

Renaissance painters kept to mathematics but divided the face into seven. Beauty became the face of a Botticelli angel (later revived by the Pre-Raphaelite artists of the late nineteenth century). Cranach's Venus, with her long white limbs and slender, slightly pear-shaped figure meanwhile celebrated the medieval ideal of bodily perfection. Other artists, dissatisfied with both the classical and the Renaissance lineaments of physical perfection, joined the proportional pursuit of beauty. One of the most notable was Reynolds who plundered features from a number of different sitters and reassembled them to create what he considered to be the perfectly harmonious and absolutely beautiful face. That he could not find it in real life suggests that beauty is not a mathematical equation. It also suggests that perfection, which belongs to art not life, has little to do with it.

The twentieth century has separated the ideal and the actual. Leaving the arena of physical, figurative beauty, art has turned to the abstract — the faceless figures of Brancusi, the huge forms of Moore — that embody subjective ideals rather than present specific examples. Early in the century, the 'real life' image of beauty transferred from canvas and stone to celluloid, the relatively new mediums of still photography and moving film. The idea of beauty, perfect and permanent, was exchanged for that of momentary beauty captured in a single frame — inseparable from the instant that had created it.

Although the instant may have been curiously timeless, the attitude and the style were firmly rooted in their time. Beauty and ideals of beauty are reflections of the age that creates them, however studied or mannered the style, however removed from real life the setting. Whole decades can be summed up by a single image. A 1937 *Vogue* retrospective is enlightening: 'The Great War left a race of nerve-shattered, disillusioned creatures and that type, engendered by hardship and suffering, persisted into beauty's currency. It was *de rigueur* not to look innocent or unravaged.' In such a context, beauty became a decadent, raffish, weary, longer-than-life creature with bobbed hair, dark eyes and heavy drop earrings, hanging, as Cecil Beaton recalled,

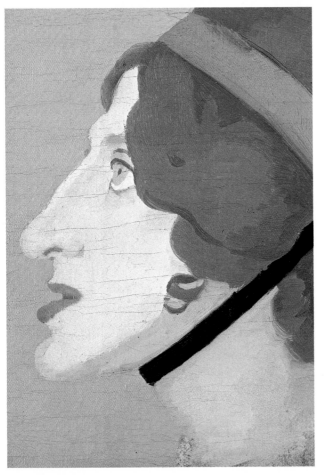

TWENTIETH CENTURY BEAUTIES

From left

Paula Gellibrand (above), 1920s flapper and model, combined a fashionable langour with suitably decadent behaviour, wearing hats trailing with wistaria for luncheon appointments and dressing as a nun for her wedding. Cecil Beaton, however, remembered her as: 'a completely unaffected somewhat hearty schoolgirl type…'

Greta Garbo (below). Her Scandinavian looks had an eloquence of expression that had no need for words. Her influence reached its height in the 1930s and persisted for 20 years. Her simple style of dress and sparing use of cosmetics – for many years just a black line across the lid – were endlessly imitated.

Marilyn Monroe (centre), the first of the great sex symbols. Sensuous in red satin or wholesome in checked gingham, Marilyn was America… 'a natural phenomenon like Niagara Falls or the Grand Canyon,' said Nunally Johnson, 'You can't talk to it. It can't talk to you. All you can do is stand back and be awed by it…'

Henrietta Tiarks (below), society beauty, debutante and later successful fashion model, photographed in the year of her coming out (1957).

Penelope Tree (above) and Jean Shrimpton (inset above), two of the great British models of the 1960s… long and leggy with weeping willow hair, elfin faces and black-rimmed eyes. Jean Shrimpton's out-of-doors naturalness presaged the health revival of the next decade.

Margaux Hemingway (below), one of the first of a new generation of American models, took New York by storm in 1975. Her naturally good looks – blue eyes beneath untamed eyebrows, corn blonde hair and sleek, six foot body – made her the highest paid model of the day.

Katharine Hepburn (right), photographed in 1975 at the age of 59, still in enviable possession of the beauty she once dismissed as 'the good fortune to have been born with a set of the characteristics in the public vogue…'

'like fuchsias'. His own portrait of Paula Gellibrand describes the look exactly.

The twentieth century provides new insights. Through photography and written records we can see how images and attitudes towards beauty have changed. From 1916 onwards, *Vogue* gives an unbroken monthly commentary on how women wanted to look and who they wanted to look like. During the 30s and 40s there was an absolute passion for imitation. Garbo, Dietrich, Hepburn … these were the originals. Many of those who followed were confections rather than beauties, created by film producers and publicity managers for a public that craved new idols. Entire looks were 'lifted', gestures imitated, intonations of speech adopted. The cues came from Hollywood and its influence was enormous. In November 1941, *Life* magazine pin-pointed the forty-ninth minute of the film *I Wanted Wings* as one of the historic moments of the cinema. What happened? 'It was the moment at which an unknown young actress named Veronica Lake walked into camera range and waggled a head of long blonde hair at a suddenly enchanted public…' The article continues by describing the cut exactly ('eight inches at the front, 10 inches at the back, it falls straight from the scalp and then begins to wave slowly') and finishes with the wry observation that her hair 'catches fire fairly often when she is smoking'. The fire risk deterred no-one, and Veronica Lake's hairstyle was copied on both sides of the Atlantic for several years.

Whether women created their own idols and ideals of beauty or simply concurred with those created for them is debatable. The general inference, however, is the same — the greatest misfortune was to be born out of one's era, with

features appropriate for some undiscovered style but hopelessly inappropriate for the one of the day. As one of the imitated, Joan Crawford could afford to be scornful and coolly independent: 'Everyone imitated my fuller mouth, darker eyebrows, but I wouldn't copy anybody . . . If I can't be me, I don't want to be anybody . . .' Vogue was infinitely more sympathetic — 'If we can't be beauties in our period,' it commiserated, 'let's forget it and have fun.' —and concluded with the consoling thought that changing tastes might yet provide the chance of being discovered as an unappreciated star among savages in the centuries to come.

While an appreciation of the idiosyncratic or unusual in beauty was still some way away, ideas and attitudes were changing by the end of World War II. By the mid-1940s, women had secured a new independence for themselves, perhaps as a result of their involvement in the war effort, or perhaps as a culmination of a natural evolution in attitudes that had started a century earlier. They were beginning to disassociate themselves from standards of beauty set up 'on their behalf'. Although women had always been able to choose new modes of dress, make-up or hairstyles, theories of beauty had mainly been left to men — male philosophers, male painters, male poets, male film producers, husbands, boyfriends and admirers. Few had asked women what they thought beauty was, much less what it actually felt like to be beautiful. And few women volunteered such information. These questions would be asked and answered, at least in part, in future years when an energetic spirit of inquiry, born out of the women's movement, would address itself to the whole business of beauty, to woman as object and woman as subject and to the psychology behind it.

But even by the 1950s, women were thinking and talking about beauty in a different way. Nancy Astor, the first woman to break the male-dominated bastion of British politics, is quoted in a Vogue feature on the 'Beauty Behaviour of Five Moving Women'. 'Basic beauty,' she said, 'lies in the way a woman walks; it is health and an attitude to life.' This has a modern ring to it. The beauty pages of Vogue reflected the new attitudes — beauty as a means to an end, not an end in itself. For women everywhere, beauty was becoming more practical. The attitude of indefinite leisure parodied by Vogue in 1916 ('Art is long, and time is fleeting — and that's the reason so many women are late to the opera. It takes time to mix the correct purple for one's cheekbones, to go into details of mauve chin and lips of tender blue ....') had disappeared entirely. Women's lives were too busy to allow them to spend hours on their beauty routines. A feature in 1958, simply entitled 'The Busy Beauties' cuts skincare and make-up routines to a matter of minutes and seconds: one minute 35 seconds for the quickest morning make-up and a maximum of 19 minutes and 20 seconds for the most elaborate evening one, which uses 10 different cosmetics and glows with rouge.

The 1960s was a paradoxical decade, being both a throwback to the 20s, with the exhausted stylized look of models such as Penelope Tree — bony bodies, stork-like legs, pale faces and huge, black-rimmed eyes — and an anticipation of the seventies, with models such as Jean Shrimpton and Veruschka moving, jumping, striding out

energetically, and looking well. Beauty and wellbeing were becoming inextricably linked. By the 1970s, any woman concerned about her beauty was also concerned about her health, seeing beauty, not as something to be created from the outside, but something to be nurtured from within. From the beginning of the decade, a revival of interest in natural health, natural beauty and natural remedies reflected a disillusionment with the old order and, more positively, a growing spirit of scrutiny and criticism. The advertisements in the classified pages of Vogue reflected the new mood — 'Does concern for your body go deeply enough?' 'Moisturizer alone can't keep skin looking its very best.'

The early 80s have seen a move away from mere 'naturalness'. Beauty retains its interest in natural resources, but now looks to the laboratory as much as to the garden or hedgerow. It is no longer a game of 'let's pretend'. Women, more scientific in their approach, want to be sure that new routines will work and to know how and why they work. In addition, there is a wider appreciation of what beauty entails. The way we live is now recognized to have as much to do with the way we look as any of the more traditional details. Today, a positive outlook counts for more than inherited good looks and a healthy lifestyle for more than the most exotic make-up or elaborate beauty treatment.

Beauty today – towards a new definition

To ask 'what is beauty?' produces many answers, but few conclusions. The small slice of history and the 15 beautiful women illustrated on these pages demonstrate two things. First, ideas of beauty, like ideals of beauty, are highly idiosyncratic. Second, they usually say more about the individual or the society expressing them than about the quality itself.

On canvas or on camera, 1883 or 1983, beauty lies in the eye of the beholder. Beauty is to be looked at, admired, copied, painted, photographed, even disputed. Appreciation of it lies with the onlooker not the owner, and the onlooker is usually a man. Not only is a woman beheld, she also tends to see herself as beheld, looking at herself through other people's eyes and applying other people's standards to what she sees. Art critic John Berger, in an essay taken from a television series which looked at the representation of women in art, maintains that tradition, culture and sexual stereotyping have been responsible for creating an atmosphere of uneasy self-surveillance: 'A woman... is almost continually accompanied by her own image of herself. Whilst she is walking across a room or whilst she is weeping at the death of her father, she can scarcely avoid envisaging herself walking or weeping... One might simplify this by saying : men act and women appear. Men look at women. Women watch themselves being looked at. This determines not only most relations between men and women but also the relation of women to themselves.'

Perhaps. But, while a woman may be 'almost continually accompanied' by an image of herself, it is not really her own image. It is an image pieced together from other people's judgements or, to be more accurate, the judgements she expects other people to make of her. Women become their own critics, measuring themselves against standards that do not apply and ideals that do not exist, just as surely as the arithmetically perfect ideal of beauty created by the ancient Greeks did not exist. Women see a graceful slender girl and then they turn to the mirror and look at themselves. The gap between the image and the reflection does not make for beauty, it detracts from it because it generates so much misery and anxiety. If, in the future, a context and a manner of thinking could be created in which every woman, liberated from the apprehension of her own 'imperfections', were free to recognize and so to realize her own beauty potential, a much greater contribution would have been made to the field of beauty than any amount of diets or make-up tips.

For the great majority of women, beauty, as a purely abstract quality, is something that happens to other people. But beauty as an inward feeling is something that can and does happen to them. Most women not only feel beautiful at times but will also be able to ascribe that feeling to a particular mood, situation or set of circumstances. The details differ from woman to woman but the emphasis is the same. Feeling beautiful has to do with the feeling that everything is right. It is a total experience — emotional and psychological, as well as physical and aesthetic. It is summed up as 'being in control', 'feeling really well', 'being challenged', 'feeling rested and relaxed', 'liking oneself', 'liking the person one is with'. Beauty lies no longer in the eye of the beholder but in the heart of the possessor. Although appearance is undoubtedly important to these moments of beauty, it is not beauty itself. It is instead a precursor, a part and a natural consequence of the feeling that you are beautiful. This point is brought expressively to life in a short story by Virginia Woolf, when her timid, anxious, heroine tries on her new dress: 'When she put the glass in her hand, and she looked at herself with the dress on, finished, an extraordinary bliss shot through her heart. Suffused with light, she sprang into existence. Rid of cares and wrinkles, what she dreamed of herself was here — a beautiful woman. Just for a second (she had dared not look longer), there looked at her, framed in the scrolloping mahogany, a grey-white, mysteriously smiling, charming girl, the core of herself, the soul of herself...'

Beauty tomorrow – a question of commitment

Feel beautiful and you will look beautiful. But how do you go about feeling beautiful? The answer is a circular one. You must start by looking good. Beauty and appearances matter, not because we are naturally vain or frivolous, but because, as Scott Fitzgerald once said, only when you have attended to the smaller details of your appearance can you then 'go to town on the charm'. Looking good means making space for beauty in your life, taking the time to exercise and to follow simple skincare and haircare routines, eating healthily and losing weight if necessary, and revising certain aspects of your lifestyle. All these are liberating not constricting because, once you have got these aspects 'right', you will then be freed from all the smaller anxieties that interfere with your ability to concentrate on the things that you really want to do and consider to be worthwhile.

The commitment is less to a new way of life than to a new

way of thinking. Broaden your outlook. Beauty encompasses every part of you. So be aware of yourself, of how you feel in and about yourself. Be aware of the way you treat your body, the way you hold yourself, the way you react under stress, the 'props' you reach out for and the way your body responds to influences inside as well as out.

While each of these aspects is examined in the following pages, this book does not pretend to give the total answer. Books and beauty articles may give you the know-how, but commitment and motivation are the two most important factors and these you must find for yourself. Only the very optimistic or the very beautiful expect to look good without working at it. Everyone can have good health and good looks, provided they look after them. And looking after them depends not so much on what you did not do yesterday or what you intend to do tomorrow as on what you do today.

Today's beauty is radiant, healthy and entirely natural with a clear complexion, shining hair, sparkling eyes, slim figure and positive outlook – qualities epitomized by the Princess of Wales...

personal profile

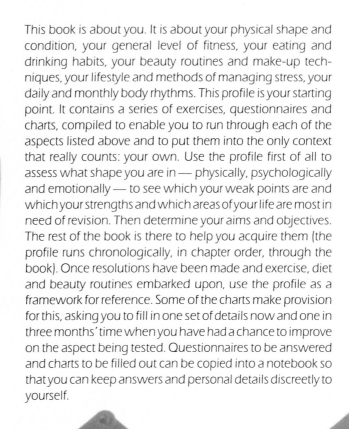

**' "Would you tell me, please, which way I ought to go from here?"
"That depends a good deal on where you want to get to," said the Cat . . .'**

Lewis Carroll

This book is about you. It is about your physical shape and condition, your general level of fitness, your eating and drinking habits, your beauty routines and make-up techniques, your lifestyle and methods of managing stress, your daily and monthly body rhythms. This profile is your starting point. It contains a series of exercises, questionnaires and charts, compiled to enable you to run through each of the aspects listed above and to put them into the only context that really counts: your own. Use the profile first of all to assess what shape you are in — physically, psychologically and emotionally — to see which your weak points are and which your strengths and which areas of your life are most in need of revision. Then determine your aims and objectives. The rest of the book is there to help you acquire them (the profile runs chronologically, in chapter order, through the book). Once resolutions have been made and exercise, diet and beauty routines embarked upon, use the profile as a framework for reference. Some of the charts make provision for this, asking you to fill in one set of details now and one in three months' time when you have had a chance to improve on the aspect being tested. Questionnaires to be answered and charts to be filled out can be copied into a notebook so that you can keep answers and personal details discreetly to yourself.

How do you shape up?

Before embarking on any of the more specific tests for shape and weight detailed below and in the next chapter, check your attitudes to your body.

YOUR BODY IMAGE: how accurate is it?

Your body image has to do with the way you <u>think</u> you look. It may actually have very little to do with your real size and shape. Having a healthy body image means accepting your fundamental frame and body type and feeling happy about the way you look – or, if you do not, analyzing your appearance objectively, the good points along with the bad, and setting yourself <u>realistic</u> goals of change. A less-than-healthy body image means being obsessive about the way you look and what you feel is 'wrong' with your appearance – the image usually distorting in direct proportion to the degree of criticism levelled at it. The way to a better body image lies in altering your outlook, not in trying to alter yourself.

1. Draw a quick sketch of yourself.

2. Answer the following:
a) When people compliment you on your appearance how do you react? Do you tend to disbelieve them?
b) Do you avoid looking at yourself in mirrors?
c) Do you wish you looked like someone else?
d) When you meet people, do you assess them first in terms of fatness and thinness and only then by other aspects of their appearance or personality?
e) Do you feel more at ease with other women if they are 'fatter' than you are?
f) Do you have a 'fat' wardrobe and a 'thin' wardrobe?
g) Do you tend to turn first to the diet pages in a magazine?
h) Do you diet more than once every six months?

3. Write down a list of all your features (hair, eyes, nose, mouth, skin, arms, hands, breasts, stomach, hips, thighs, bottom, etc) and award yourself marks from 3 to 0 for each. 3 is 'marvellous'; 2 is 'not perfect, but I'm happy with it'; 1 is 'I wish I could do something to change it', and 0 is 'terrible'.

1. The Freehand Sketch. Examine it. Is it a fairly accurate reproduction of your general body shape or is it noticeably thinner or fatter? (Ask a friend for her assessment too.) If you made yourself noticeably thinner than you are and, in addition, tend to avoid full-length mirrors and scales, you could be evading the inescapable fact that you are overweight. If you made yourself noticeably fatter, where have you exaggerated? Analyze it. This should help you to understand where you think 'fat'. Now try to discover why.
2. The Questionnaire. All 'Yes' answers indicate that your body image may be bruised. 'Yes' answers to the last five questions indicate that your body image is almost entirely determined by what you weigh. Try to work out why being 'thin' is so important to you. It is essential that you try to answer this if you are to see your relative size and shape in their proper perspective. You may also find the compulsive eating/dieting questionnaire in the nutrition section of the profile helpful. Check your weight against the table given here. If you are overweight, try to lose the extra – but gradually not fanatically. Record your progress on the graph, opposite.
3. The Feature List. Add up all the marks you awarded yourself and divide the total by the number of features listed to get an average. An average of 2 indicates that you are basically happy with the way you look, aware of your imperfections but not obsessed by them and have a realistic and healthy body image. A lower score of between 0 and 2 suggests that you are unhappy with the way you look, have a less-than-healthy body image and are over-exaggerating your bad points. Everyone has good features as well as bad. Cultivate a healthier body image by recognizing which these are.

YOUR BODY WEIGHT: do you need to lose or gain?

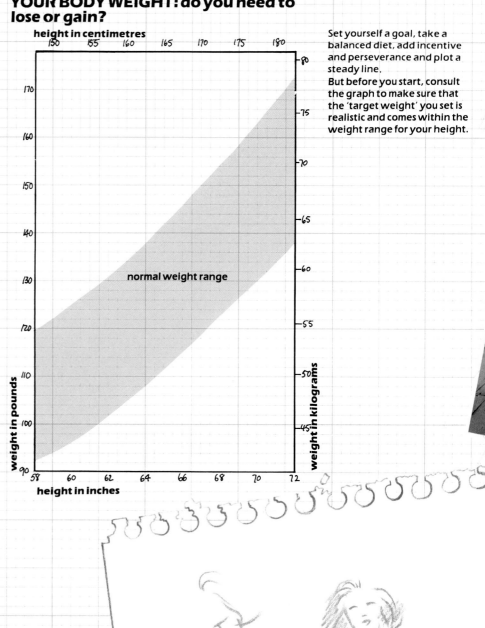

height in centimetres

normal weight range

weight in pounds

weight in kilograms

height in inches

Set yourself a goal, take a balanced diet, add incentive and perseverance and plot a steady line.
But before you start, consult the graph to make sure that the 'target weight' you set is realistic and comes within the weight range for your height.

YOUR PROPORTIONS: how do you measure up?

When getting into shape, measuring yourself can be just as useful a gauge to how you are doing as weighing yourself. The key is to look at your body as an integrated whole: consider your measurements in relation to each other, not just independently.

Measure yourself at bust when breathing in, at waist at its narrowest part and at hips, thighs and calves all at their widest parts. Enter them in the table below. Now subtract each from the hip measurement (your 'base') and enter these too. See page 31 for 'ideal' proportions so you can see how well you measure up and, if there is a significant discrepancy, what you should be working towards. Fill in the second set of details in three months' time when you have had time to work at improving your shape.

	Measurement	Differences more/less than hips	
Bust			now
			three months time
Waist			now
			three months time
Hips			now
			three months time
Thighs			now
			three months time
Calves			now
			three months time

The graph, right, is designed to enable you to plot your weight loss or gain, week by week, as you follow a specially-tailored eating programme (find a diet on page 74), and to see how you are progressing at a glance. What to do: fill in your present weight, together with the kilograms or pounds above and below it, where indicated along the vertical side of the graph. If aiming to lose, enter your present weight slightly below the top so that minor fluctuations and moments of weakness do not cause you to abandon the exercise, and probably the diet, altogether. Enter today's date at the axis. Plot your weight loss by weighing yourself on the same day at the same time each week and entering it up. Aim for an average weight loss of 1 kg (2 lb) a week. If you are aiming to put on weight, enter your weight towards the bottom of the graph, as indicated, and plot your line upwards.

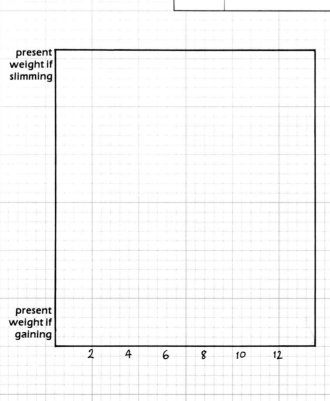

present weight if slimming

present weight if gaining

2   4   6   8   10   12

What shapes do the spaces between your legs make when you stand with feet together and knees facing forwards? Ideally, you should be able to see a diamond at the top followed by three longish ovals between thighs and knees, knees and calves and calves and ankles respectively. Four distinct patches of daylight. Any less and your thigh muscles need toning, you are standing incorrectly or you are under or overweight. Which?

YOUR POSTURE: how much do bad habits affect your wellbeing?

Weaknesses in posture generate strain — residual tensions in the muscle, stiff 'locked' joints, pinched blood vessels that restrict circulation, compressed respiratory and digestive systems where the front of the body has slumped in on itself. Such a wide range of strains can produce an equally wide range of ill effects, both vague and specific. Answer the following questions and the next time that any of the problems listed present themselves, or indeed any others that have been puzzling you, consider your posture. There may well be a connection.

1. Do you frequently stand on one leg while 'resting' the other?
2. Do you slump?
3. Do you usually sit with your knees crossed?
4. When you bend down to pick something up, do you bend your back rather than your knees?
5. Do you have a job that entails bending over a desk for extended periods of time?
6. Are you overweight?
7. Do you suffer from backache?
8. Do you suffer from sore, strained neck muscles?
9. Do you frequently get cramp?
10. Do you frequently get headaches – in particular headaches that get worse as the day wears on?
11. Do you have poor circulation? Do your toes and fingers sometimes tingle and feel numb?
12. Do you suffer from indigestion or is your digestion generally poor?

'Yes' answers to any of the above indicate that you are holding and using your body incorrectly. Questions 1 to 4 are concerned with common bad habits that undermine the natural line of the body. They are often aggravated by a sedentary lifestyle (question 5) and, if allowed to persist, may lead to aches, pains and other more specific problems (questions 7 to 12). If you answered yes to question 6, your extra weight is adding extra strain to muscles and joints. Use the next two tests to help you to identify where you are going wrong.

YOUR POSTURE: how symmetrical are you?

We get so used to standing incorrectly, that it is difficult to assess faults in posture simply by looking in a mirror. Ask a friend to take three, full-length photographs of you – back, front and profile. Wear a leotard (no tights) or pants and a bra so that you will be able to see the line of your body quite clearly. Stand straight, but not stiff, so that you feel comfortable and relaxed. Make sure that the edge of the viewfinder is lined up with a vertical plane such as the edge of a door.

Once the photographs are developed, you will need a pen and a ruler. Taking the profile view first, line up the ruler against the side of the photograph and draw a single, vertical line, starting from just behind your ears. Then take the back and front views and, again aligning the ruler against the parallel edge of the photograph – not against the line of your body – draw two horizontal lines, the first at shoulder level and the second at mid-thigh (front) or just beneath the buttocks (back). Add two vertical lines passing along the outer edge of each shoulder straight down to the ground and you now have a set of geometrical reference points that will show you how symmetrically you are standing.

Profile. The line should pass behind your shoulder, down through your knee and out just in front of your ankle. If it does not, try to identify what is causing your body to be out of line, by using the two back and front views as your reference points.
Back and front. Look at the following:
● Your head: is it centrally balanced or is it closer to one vertical line than the other?
● Your shoulders: does the first of the horizontal lines connect to the shoulders at both sides? Is one shoulder some way above or below the other one?
● Your hips and buttocks: are they positioned in the centre of the grid or is one higher than the other or rotated to one side so that one vertical line passes through a hip or a buttock, while the other goes quite wide of it?
● Your fingertips: are they level or does one hand appear to be lower than the other?
● Your knees: are they level?
● Your feet: do you appear to be standing with your weight evenly distributed?
● Can you see any lines of tension along the sides of your neck, back and buttocks? Are your fists clenched?

YOUR POSTURE: how well are you standing?

Now that you are aware of imbalances in the way you stand and hold yourself that may not be immediately apparent when looking into a mirror, try this second test of body alignment, adapted from a technique developed by Matthias Alexander, founder of the Alexander principle, and used by teachers of the principle in order to detect faults in posture – and to correct them too (page 34). This should enable you to pinpoint specific causes for any imbalances you might have noticed earlier and is worth repeating regularly as a useful check on yourself.

Stand with your heels about 5 cm (2 inches) away from a wall and your feet hip-width apart. Now, keeping your heels where they are, sway gently backwards. Which parts of your body touch the wall first?

16

- If your buttocks and shoulder blades touched the wall simultaneously: you are standing symmetrically and holding your body correctly.
- If one side touched the wall first: you are not holding your body centrally. One side is rotated further round than the other. Return to the starting position and try to adjust the way you are standing so that you are facing absolutely towards the front. Now repeat the exercise.
- If your buttocks touched the wall first: you are carrying your chest too far forwards and your pelvis tilted downwards towards the floor, creating an exaggerated arch in the small of your back. Repeat the test, bringing your shoulders to the wall and placing your hand under this arch. If there is a gap between your spine and the wall such that your hand can slide easily in and out, your spine is too arched. Bend your knees, drop your buttocks and tilt your pelvis slightly upwards. Feel your spine straighten and extend, note how it feels and move up the wall again with your back in this position. Repeat this exercise daily and practise rotating your shoulders too, to bring them back and down.
- If your shoulders touched the wall first: your pelvis is either thrust too far forwards or your back is too rigid (the spine should always be flexible while extended) and your shoulders too far back. Come forward again, and look at yourself side-view in a mirror. Can you see your shoulder blades sticking out? If so, you are almost certainly holding your shoulders too far back. (When standing correctly they should lie flat across your back.) Rotate your shoulders, relax them and let them drop and try the spine extension exercise detailed above.
- If your head was touching the wall: you are holding it too far back, helping to create an exaggerated arch between the back of your head and the base of your neck. This can lead to tense, painful neck muscles and, over the years, a 'dowager's' hump at the base of the neck where these vertebrae join those of the upper back. Free your neck by lengthening it upwards. ·

HOW FIT ARE YOU?

Fitness is a combination of things and they are all important. If you can touch your toes, but cannot climb two flights of stairs without getting breathless, you are not fit. Nor are you fit if you can run a mile in under five minutes, but cannot do a press-up. You must be able to combine the three essential components of fitness – strength, suppleness and stamina. This important trio is tested in the following chapter. Turn to pages 36-9, carry out the exercises there and then enter your rating in the chart, right. Once you have run through the daily exercise programme for three months (also outlined in the next chapter), repeat the tests. You should find that you are able to do significantly better in every area. In addition to these specific aspects, your general degree of activity makes a very important contribution to your state of fitness. This is tested here.

YOUR GENERAL FITNESS: how active are you?

1. Put a pedometer in your pocket or clip it on to your belt in the morning. In the evening, note down how far you walked over the course of the day. Was it
a) more than 6 km (4 miles) **b)** 3 to 6 km (2 to 4 miles) **c)** less than 3 km (2 miles)?

2. Do you take some form of active exercise
a) nearly every day **b)** two or three times a week **c)** once a week or less?

3. When going to offices or apartment buildings, do you use the stairs instead of the lift?
a) always **b)** usually **c)** rarely, if ever

4. When going to work, do you
a) walk or cycle **b)** walk some way to and from the bus stop or the station **c)** drive or take the bus door-to-door?

5. When not in any particular hurry, what is the point in terms of distance at which you decide to take an alternative means of transport in preference to walking?
a) 3 km (2 miles) or more **b)** between ½-3 km (1-2 miles) **c)** less than 1½ km (1 mile)

a answers indicate a very good general level of fitness, **b** answers a fair level and **c** answers a poor one. If your answers were predominantly **c**, think laterally when organizing the details of your day, so that you increase the amount of time you spend on the move. You will find that it is surprisingly easy to double a walking distance of 3 km (2 miles) over the day. So easy, in fact, that you probably will not be aware of any extra effort.

SUPPLENESS, STRENGTH AND STAMINA: how well did you do?

		POOR	FAIR	GOOD	
SUPPLENESS	Deep knee bend				now
					3 months time
	Shoulder grasp				now
					3 months time
	Spinal stretch				now
					3 months time
	Ankle exercise				now
					3 months time
STRENGTH	Wall sit*				now
					3 months time
	Table press-up*				now
					3 months time
STAMINA	Skip test*				now
					3 months time
	Jog test*				now
					3 months time

* Keep a more precise record by noting down details, such as how long you managed to control the exercise or how many you managed to do, in the appropriate column.

HOW FIT ARE YOU GETTING?

If you follow the exercise programme outlined in the following chapter together with some form of regular aerobic or stamina-promoting activity two or three times a week, you will become fitter. You will find that exercises you previously found demanding can now be achieved with relative ease and that you can now run or cycle or swim faster and further without becoming tired or breathless. As you get fitter, your resting pulse rate will drop by several beats. It will take much more vigorous exercise to raise it to the levels reached when you were less fit and it will recover more rapidly once exercise has ceased. Make use of these observations to fill out this progress sheet.

To fill out the progress sheet: pick one exercise day each week and note down the date together with details of the exercise taken. Before starting, sit down and take your pulse for 60 seconds to get your resting pulse rate – making sure that you feel comfortable and relaxed first. Take your pulse again immediately you stop exercising (i.e. at the point at which you feel tired and/or breathless), note it down, wait for five minutes and then take it once more. This should give an indication of how quickly your heart and lungs recover after exertion.

Week	Date	Exercise taken (type and duration)	Resting pulse rate	'After exercise' rate	'Recovery' rate
1					
2					
3					
4					
5					
6					
7					
8					
9					
10					
11					
12					

If you have been advised to exercise carefully, or if any of the points listed on page 36 apply to you, you can assess your 'safety' limit when exercising by taking your pulse. Here is a simplified version of a scientific method developed by the Cardiac Research Unit at London's City Gym. Take the constant figure 200, subtract your age and an additional 40, which acts as your 'handicap'. As soon as you begin to tire or to feel breathless when exercising, count your pulse for a minute. If it is racing above your safety figure, STOP. As soon as you feel comfortable exercising within these margins (one to two weeks if exercising regularly), subtract 10 from your figure. Continue until you have taken off the 40-point handicap. If you are over 45, subtract in groups of five and leave an additional 20 with your age.

N.B. If you have hypertension (high blood pressure) and are taking drugs, known as beta-blockers, for it, you should not use the pulse rate method as a gauge of how much exercise you can take or of how fit you are getting. These drugs work to lower blood pressure and may disguise a true pulse reading.

How well are you eating?

This profile is designed to give you an insight into how healthy your eating habits and your attitudes towards food are. First, to get as objective an assessment as possible, compile a food diary. Note down everything you eat and drink over a two-week period.

Use a small notebook and fill it in immediately after eating. Include everything, from the smallest snack upwards. Note down the time, when and where you eat or drink, and how you feel after doing so, using the rating system given here, together with any symptoms that you feel may be food related, such as constipation, indigestion, pronounced mood or energy swings, or migraine.

RATINGS

When and where was food eaten?
5 With others, sitting down, undistracted.
4 On your own, sitting down, undistracted.
3 With others, sitting down, distracted (e.g. watching TV).
2 On your own, sitting down, distracted.
1 On your own or with others, standing up, in a rush.

How satisfying was it?
5 You enjoyed it: it was just what you wanted.
4 It was good initially, but you ate too much.
3 It did not really satisfy your hunger but you ate it anyway.
2 You were not really hungry; felt bloated/guilty after.
1 You did not enjoy it and soon lost interest.

YOUR APPETITE AND OUTLOOK: how healthy are they?

Add up the total number of meals eaten (nourishing snacks are meals; crackers and potato chips are not) and divide by 14. Add up the ratings separately and divide each by the total number of entries, to give an average. Now add the three figures together. Between 12 and 16: you have a good appetite and a healthy outlook towards what you eat. Less than 10 points: you are unlikely to be eating in a balanced way. Less than 8 points: you are certainly not. Three areas might be responsible.

• <u>You are not balancing your food intake.</u> Do you tend to eat nothing at all for most of the day and then eat one large meal? Or do you tend not to eat meals at all and to subsist on unhealthy snacks? Or is your appetite generally poor? Eating in a regular, balanced way does not necessarily mean eating three conventional meals a day, but it does mean balancing your eating timetable carefully so that your energy is sustained throughout it.
• <u>You do not give yourself enough time to eat, or you eat amid so many distractions that you do not have the space in which to enjoy your food.</u> Make meals a more central feature of your life. Do not rush them.
• <u>You are not a good judge of what your body needs.</u> Listen to your appetite – and stop before you reach the point of satiation.

YOUR DIET: how nutritious is it?

Go through the notebook again and check your diet against the list of foods below.

Over the two-week period, did your diet include the following?
1. Eggs – at least three a week.
2. Milk – at least 275 ml (10 fl oz) whole or skimmed a day.
3. Cheese – at least 175 g (6 oz) a week.
4. Offal, such as liver or kidney – at least one serving a week.
5. Meat or poultry – at least four servings a week.
6. Fish – at least one serving a week.
7. Seafood – at least one serving in the two-week period.
8. Vegetables – at least two different types a day.
9. Starchy carbohydrates – wholemeal bread, cereal, potatoes, rice, pasta, pulses (at least two slices/helpings a day).
10. Fresh fruit – at least one or its juice a day.

There is a maximum score of 14 for each of the 10 food groups. For foods specified on a daily basis, score 1 point for each day on which these foods were eaten; for foods specified on a weekly basis, score 7 for <u>each</u> of the respective weeks; for seafood score 14. If you have an allergy to any of the foods, and therefore cannot eat them, skip the offending category and award yourself 14. (If you are vegetarian, few of these groups will apply, so miss this section altogether and turn to page 60.) Now add up your score.
<u>Maximum total score 133.</u> You should be able to gain top marks on this test very easily, but scores of over 115 still indicate that you are eating in a healthy, balanced and varied way. Scores below this and, particularly, scores of less than 95, indicate that you should make some immediate alterations in your eating habits. If you are omitting some, or even most, of these foods from your diet, the chances are that you are eating too much highly refined and processed food. Rebalance your diet around these 10 essentials and omit, or at least cut down on, the rest. Read the Nutrition chapter for further guidelines on healthy eating.

YOUR FOOD PSYCHOLOGY: are you a compulsive eater/dieter?

Compulsive eating, often accompanied by obsessive weight watching and stringent 'crash' dieting, is particularly miserable. This test is based on a recognized method of checking your attitudes towards what you eat and what you weigh, and is known as the Herman & Polivy Scale of Restrained vs Unrestrained Eating.

1. How often do you diet?
a) never b) rarely c) sometimes d) usually e) always

2. What is the maximum amount of weight that you have ever lost in one month?
a) 0-1.8 kg (0-4 lb) b) 1.9-4 kg (4.1-9 lb) c) 4.1-6.3 kg (9.1-14 lb) d) 6.4-8.9 kg (14.1-19.9 lb) e) 9 kg or more (20 lb or more)

3. What is the maximum amount of weight that you have ever gained in a week?
a) 0-0.5 kg (0-1 lb) b) 0.6-1 kg (1.1-2 lb) c) 1.1-1.3 kg (2.1-3 lb) d) 1.4-2.2 kg (3.1-5 lb) e) 2.3 kg or more (5.1 lb or more)

4. In a typical week, how much does your weight fluctuate?
a) 0-0.5 kg (0-1 lb) b) 0.6-1 kg (1.1-2 lb) c) 1.1-1.3 kg (2.1-3 lb) d) 1.4-2.2 kg (3.1-5 lb) e) 2.3 kg or more (5.1 lb or more)

5. Would a weight fluctuation of 2.2 kg (5 lb) affect the way you live your life?
a) not at all b) slightly c) moderately d) very much

6. Do you eat sensibly in front of others and binge alone?
a) never b) rarely c) often d) always

7. Do you give too much time and thought to food?
a) never b) rarely c) often d) always

8. Do you have feelings of guilt after over-eating?
a) never b) rarely c) often d) always

9. How conscious are you of what you are eating?
a) not at all b) slightly c) moderately d) extremely

10. How many pounds over your desired weight were you at your maximum weight?
a) 0-0.5 kg (0-1 lb) b) 0.6-2.2 kg (1.1-5 lb) c) 2.3-4.5 kg (5.1-10 lb) d) 4.6-9 kg (10.1-20 lb) e) 9.1 kg or more (20.1 lb or more)

Score 1 for each **a** answer, 2 for each **b**, 3 for each **c**, 4 for each **d** and 5 for each **e**. Add them up. Out of a maximum of 45, scores of 30 or more indicate very definite compulsive eating/dieting patterns (find guidelines on breaking the compulsive habit on page 76); scores of between 20 and 30 that, although you are conscious of what you eat, you have a healthy outlook to eating and dieting; scores of less than 20 that you are almost entirely unconcerned with what you eat and how much you weigh.

What are your beauty routines?

Do you think of your beauty care in terms of routine? You should do. The small details – what you do every day in terms of looking after your skin, hair, teeth and nails – have much more bearing on their health and appearance than occasional extravagances. The perfect routine is four things: regular, thorough, simple and, most important of all, suited to your own needs. It should be flexible enough to take account of changes – an increased oiliness in face and hair just before menstruation, a change in climate, a change in scalp condition... Do not let routine simply slip into habit. Habit, like a smooth groove in the brain, is a process so automatic that you no longer have to think to do it. You should think about your beauty routines. You should be awake to the possibility that they are no longer appropriate for you. You should, if necessary, change them. These four questionnaires ask some of the questions you should be asking yourself.

YOUR SKIN TYPE: how much note do you take of it?

Allow skin type to determine skincare routine and you will be giving your skin the best possible attention. But how much attention do you pay to your skin? Inspect your face closely in a magnifying mirror in the daylight. Then answer the following.

1. Is your skin tone
a) even in colour and texture **b)** blotchy in colour and bumpy to the touch **c)** shiny, fairly soft and supple to the touch?

2. Are the pores on your chin and around the base of your nose visible?
a) when you hold the mirror at about 15 cm (6 inches) distance. **b)** only when you peer into it **c)** when you hold the mirror at arm's length

3. Do you have a tendency to break out in spots?
a) sometimes **b)** never **c)** frequently

4. Which age group do you come into?
a) between 25 and 35 **b)** over 35 **c)** under 25

5. Do you have a 'break through' problem with make-up?
a) occasionally during the summer; never in the winter **b)** never **c)** frequently

6. Do you have any of the following and, if so, how many? Fair or red hair; blue, green or grey eyes; a very fair complexion; asthma or eczema; a tendency to burn easily in moderate sunlight; a tendency to blush easily when nervous or embarrassed and/or a tendency to flush after drinking moderate amounts of alcohol; a dry, tight feeling after washing your face with soap and water; a tendency to blotchiness after using certain types of skincare or make-up products; rashes on your face that seem to appear and disappear for no reason at all?
a) yes, three or more **b)** yes, less than three **c)** no

7. When you sunbathe do you
a) keep your face well out of the sun or use a special sunscreen with a high SPF factor or a total sunblock **b)** use the same tanning lotion that you use for the rest of your body **c)** put nothing on your face at all – sunlight seems to help your skin?

8. How would you describe your beauty routine?
a) simple and regular – you cleanse, tone and moisturize twice a day **b)** elaborate – you are always trying new products and new routines but you have never yet found one you have been able to keep to **c)** erratic, obsessive or non-existent

9. When were you last aware of any change in the behaviour of your skin?
a) within the last month **b)** within the last year **c)** you have never noticed any change

10. How often do you use an exfoliant (peel-off mask, washing grains, abrasive glove) on your face?
a) regularly – once or twice a week **b)** occasionally – whenever your skin is looking grey and dull **c)** never

Questions 1 to 6 are designed to give you an idea of your basic skin type: **a** answers for questions 1 to 5 indicate that you have a fairly normal skin type; **b** that you have a tendency towards dryness and **c** that you have a tendency towards oiliness. A combination of answers? A combination skin type. If you answered 'yes' to **6a** you have a more than normally sensitive skin; **6b** may also indicate this. Find guidelines on caring for each skin type in the skin section and, if you have a sensitive skin, read pages 138-9 too.

Questions 7 to 10 are designed to give you an idea of how well you look after your skin: **b** and **c** answers indicate that you may not be giving your skin the chance to look its best. This may not be having immediate effects on the appearance of your skin now but it might well do in 10 or 20 years' time.

YOUR HAIR AND SCALP CONDITION: are they inflicted or inherited?

Your hair condition owes much more to what you do to it than to what nature, in terms of genetic inheritance, does to you.

1. Which best describes the texture of your hair?
a) fine and straight **b)** neither fine nor coarse and slightly wavy **c)** coarse and wavy or curly **d)** none of the above

2. Which best describes the colour of your hair?
a) fair or mouse **b)** dark **c)** red, auburn or grey

3. Which best describes the condition of your hair?
a) shiny but lank **b)** glossy **c)** dull and frizzy

4. Three days after washing, how does (would) your hair look?
a) oily and limp **b)** just about ready for a wash **c)** shinier and more manageable than it was immediately after washing **d)** it would look OK, but the scalp would feel oily and itchy

5. Do you use heated rollers, curling tongs or a hair drier hot enough to make your head feel very warm when drying your hair?
a) yes, frequently **b)** yes, occasionally **c)** never

6. Have you had any of the following done to your hair within the last year?
a) highlights, temporary or semi-permanent tints **b)** bleaching at the salon or in the sunlight, perming or straightening, permanent tint (does not include 'natural' dyes such as henna) **c)** none of these

7. Does your hair lose its texture when wet?
a) no **b)** yes, it becomes very matted and limp like wet cotton wool.

8. Scrape the scalp gently with a comb. Is there any scaling?
a) yes, small white flakes **b)** yes, larger scales **c)** no

9. If you answered yes to 8a or b, do any of the following apply? You have a generally dry skin; you have been away to a hot climate recently; you tend to rinse your hair once only after shampooing; you use hair sprays and/or setting lotions; you eat a lot of hot spicy or salted foods and/or drink a lot of alcohol; you suffer from psoriasis or eczema?
a) yes **b)** no

Questions 1-4 are designed to give you an idea of your current hair type. Predominantly **a** answers indicate that your hair is oily; predominantly **b** answers that it is normal or mixed condition (dry at the ends, oily on the scalp – particularly likely if you answered yes to **4d**); predominantly **c** answers that your hair has a tendency to dryness which you may have either acquired through lack of proper care (**5a**) or through chemical processing (**6b**). This is particularly likely if your hair is porous (**7b**).

Questions 8 and 9 are designed to help assess the condition of your scalp. If you answered **8a** or **b**, you could have a flaking scalp condition – not necessarily dandruff. Positive answers to anything listed under **9** indicate other culprits. Consider these first and take the appropriate action, before switching to an anti-dandruff shampoo which may be unnecessarily harsh on your hair.

YOUR TEETH AND GUMS: how well do you look after them?

If your teeth cleaning routine is thorough, your mouth will be healthy. If dental hygiene is lax, your gums will be infected and your teeth may be in jeopardy.

1. When did you last see your dentist?
a) within the last six months **b)** within the last year **c)** you cannot remember

2. Have you ever been shown how to brush your teeth properly and how to look after your mouth?
a) yes **b)** no

3. When did you last have your teeth professionally cleaned and polished?
a) in the last six months **b)** in the last year **c)** more than a year ago

4. Do you use plaque disclosing tablets?
a) regularly **b)** rarely **c)** never

5. What happens when you use dental floss?
a) it slides easily up and down between the teeth once past the point where they meet **b)** it gets caught and snagged **c)** you never use it

6. With regular (twice daily) brushing, how long does a toothbrush last before the bristles splay out?
a) about three months **b)** one to three months **c)** less than a month

7. Look carefully at your gums in a mirror. Note how they look. Then clean them thoroughly and inspect them carefully again. Are they
a) the same colour as they were before and lying fairly flat against the teeth **b)** reddish in colour, slightly inflamed and/or bleeding a little especially at the gum/tooth margin **c)** very sore, inflamed and/or bleeding profusely?

8. How often do you clean your teeth?
a) twice a day **b)** once a day **c)** erratically, whenever you remember

All these questions are designed to help you test the relative health of your teeth and gums – in themselves a reflection of how well you are looking after them. If you scored all **a** answers, congratulations – you are one of two per cent of the population with no signs of gum disease, a healthy mouth and an efficient teeth cleaning method. If you scored any **b** and **c** answers, turn to pages 111-12 to see how your current teeth cleaning routine might be improved. If you answered **1b**, **c**, **2b** and **3c**, make an appointment to see your dentist or dental hygienist.

YOUR NAILS: how sound is your health, how good is your manicure routine?

Nails, rewardingly, will repay every minute spent looking after them – provided that you manicure them properly and protect your hands from damaging influences. Look at them carefully, then answer the following.

1. Are your nails the same colour as the skin beneath them (or the palm of your hand if you are dark skinned)?
a) yes **b)** no, they are significantly lighter or darker

2. Is the nail surface
a) smooth and even **b)** ridged?

3. Are your nails brittle and inclined to crack or to break easily?
a) no **b)** yes

4. Do you wear rubber gloves for wet domestic chores?
a) yes **b)** no

5. Do you do a lot of housework, gardening and/or decorating?
a) no **b)** yes

6. Are your cuticles damaged – cut, puffy or sore?
a) no **b)** yes

7. Do you ever use anything made from steel, including scissors, when manicuring your nails?
a) no **b)** yes

8. When you manicure your nails, do you cut or trim the cuticle?
a) no **b)** yes

Questions 1-3 are designed to give you an insight into your general health, as it is reflected in the condition of your nails. **b** answers indicate that it is not – or recently has not been – as good as it might.

Questions 4-8 are designed to check on how carefully you look after your nails. If you answered **b** to any of these, your less-than-perfect nails are probably owing to careless manicuring (turn to pages 115-17 to see where you are going wrong) or to exposure to damaging chemicals, such as detergents, paint stripper and nail varnish remover.

Do you make the most of your face?

Make-up is highly individual. Faces are different, preferences vary, fashions change. Personality makes a difference too. But even with so many variables, there are still basic principles that can make all the difference between a make-up which works and one which does not.

YOUR FACE AND FEATURES: how close to 'perfect' are they?

Measure your face to see how it compares with the perfect proportions given below. This will help you towards a better appreciation both of its general shape and of the relation of your features to each other – how close together your eyes are set, for example. Find further details on page 142.

Feature	Measurement/ comments	'Perfect'
Length of face		1 ½ x width
Width of face		⅔ of length
Width of jaw		slightly less than face
Eye spacing		1 eye length
Width of mouth		between inner edges of iris

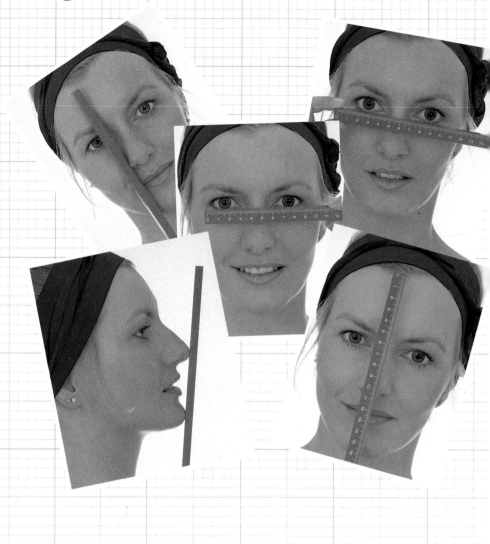

YOUR COLOUR QUIZ: how compatible are your make-up and your natural colouring?

There are no absolute rules about make-up colours. Unusual combinations of colour, even obvious contradictions, can be very effective – but you must know what you are doing. This quiz aims to guide, not to dictate. If you already have a colour scheme that works well for you, fine. If not, complete the questionnaire to see where you might be going wrong and to get some fresh ideas.

1. Is your natural colouring
a) very pale, with no pink or orange in the skin b) fair with a pinkish colour c) reddish d) sallow e) olive f) brown or black?

2. Is your foundation
a) the same colour as your skin b) lighter than your skin c) darker than your skin?

3. Where do you test for colour when buying foundation?
a) on the back of your hand b) on your face

4. Is the predominant colour tone in your foundation
a) ivory b) light with a hint of pink c) light to mid beige d) cream with a tinge of bronze e) mid beige f) tan brown or dark brown?

5. Which best describes your blusher colour?
a) light shimmery pink or mid pink b) bright pink, peach or coral c) tawny brown or chestnut d) bronze e) tawny red f) strong deep pink, such as fuchsia or raspberry

6. Are your lip colour and blusher
a) about the same general colour family b) completely different in colour?

7. Are your eyes
a) blue or grey b) green or hazel c) brown?

8. Which of these eye colours/colour combinations do you like?
a) silver/lilac shading with grey to emphasize b) pink/gold shading with brown to emphasize c) soft beige/pink/apricot shading with charcoal to emphasize d) soft neutral colours – pinks, beiges, browns e) pastel colours – powder blue or pink and green f) strong, solid colours – bright blue, deep pinks and purples?

9. How much note do you take of what you are wearing when choosing eye colours?
a) a great deal. Depending on the look you want to achieve, you choose subtle tones of the same colour or complementary neutral shades or a deliberate contrast for a dramatic effect. b) little, if any

Mistakes are almost inevitable when making up if skin tone is misjudged or overlooked. Here, as in real life, blusher and foundation tones should match up with natural colouring. Hence, if you answered **a** for question 1, you should have also answered **a** for questions 4 and 5. Foundation should always match skin (2) – the skin of your face not your hand (3). If the skin is naturally dark (**1d,** perhaps, **1e** and **1f**), the foundation can be a tone or two darker. But going lighter makes any face masklike. Lip colours and blushers should also coordinate (6); very fair skin tends to look stagey with strong lip colour and blusher, darker coloured skins look good with deeper, more vibrant shades. Almost any colour can look good on almost any colour eye. Particularly effective combinations: **8a** for **7a**; **8b** for **7b**; **8c** for **7c**. **8d** is good for anyone and makes a marvellous, natural daytime look. Clothes should always be taken into account when choosing eye colours as should skin tones: **8e**, for example, will look good on **1b** (not so good for darker coloured skins) while **8f** will look marvellous on **1e** or **1f**.

Do you pass your stress test?

YOUR HAZARD POTENTIAL: how much change is there in your life?

Variety and change are the spice of life. Too much of it and you increase your susceptibility to stress and stress-related illness and your chances of having an accident. In 1972, US Navy Doctors Thomas Holmes and Richard Rahe devised an 'early warning' system to enable you to estimate your 'hazard' potential. The system involves adding up a number of units relative to the degree of change in your life over a period of six months. A high score does not necessarily mean that you are bound to become ill or have an accident, but it does place you significantly more 'at risk'.

1. Death of husband or lover	100
2. Divorce	73
*3. Giving up 'hard' drugs, including alcohol if dependent	71
4. Marital separation or end of a long-standing relationship	65
5. Prison sentence	63
6. Death of close family member	63
7. Personal accident or illness	53
8. Marriage	50
9. Being dismissed or made redundant from work	47
10. Reconciliation with husband or lover	45
11. Retirement	45
12. Change in the state of health of one of the family – for better or for worse	44
13. Pregnancy	40
*14. Giving up cigarettes (40 or more a day)	39
15. Sexual difficulties	39
16. Birth of a baby in the immediate family	39
17. Changes at work (moving offices, having a new boss, etc)	39
18. Change in your financial state – for better or for worse	38
19. Death of a close friend	37
20. Change to a different type of work (promotion, new job)	36
21. Change in number of arguments with lover or husband	35
*22. Premenstrual tension	33
23. Taking out a mortgage or loan over £20,000 ($40,000)	30
24. Change in the amount of responsibility at work	29
*25. Jet lag	29
26. Children leaving home or going to school	29
27. Difficulties with in-laws	29
28. Outstanding personal achievement	28
29. Changing personal habits	24
30. Difficulties with superiors at work	23
*31. Giving up cigarettes (less than 40 a day)	21
32. Moving house	20
33. Taking up a new interest or giving up an old one	19
34. Change in social activity	18
35. Taking out a large mortgage or loan	17
36. Change in sleeping habits	16
37. Change in eating habits	15
38. Seeing your family more or less often than previously	15
39. Holidays	13
40. Christmas	12
41. Minor violations of law, such as driving offences, etc	11

150 or under. You are living in a safe and stable way and are less likely than average to have an accident or to become ill.

150-200. Your likelihood of having an accident or of becoming ill is 37 per cent greater than usual.

200-300. Your chances of having an accident or of becoming ill are now 51 per cent greater than usual. You should attempt to limit the degree of change to those areas of your life that are within your control.

300 or over. Your chances of having an accident or of becoming ill are now very high – 79 per cent greater than usual. (US Airforce pilots with this score are forbidden to fly because their chances of having an accident or making a miscalculation are so high.) You should be careful, too, and lead as quiet and unstressful a life as you possibly can, until your score drops.

*Do not appear in Holmes' and Rahe's original list of Life Change Units.

YOUR PHYSICAL RESILIENCE: how fit are you for managing stress?

The body and the mind were once thought to be two quite separate entities. But now scientific research into psycho-somatic (literally 'mind-body') disease is showing that the body and the mind interact on a number of complex and very subtle levels. Negative emotions, such as fear and anxiety, can increase susceptibility to physical stress of all kinds, from indigestion to infection, and can certainly aggravate, if not produce, tangible symptoms. Positive emotions, on the other hand, seem to be able to protect. To find out how fit you are for managing stress, answer the following.

1. Do you walk less than 3 km (2 miles) a day (see fitness test)?

2. Do you smoke?

3. Do you drink more than five cups of tea or coffee a day?

4. Do you rely on sweet, sugary things, such as soft drinks and chocolate, to keep you going?

5. Are you 3 kg (7 lb) over or under the weight range given for your height (see page 31)?

6. Do you sleep badly?

7. On balance, do you work for more than nine hours a day?

8. Were you unable to take at least one complete day off last week?

9. Did you fail to take some type of exercise last week?

10. Did you find you had no time in which to pursue an interest last week, such as painting or photography, quite apart from your work at home or in the office?

11. Do you find that you are more sensitive to the comments and criticisms of others than you used to be?

12. Do you find that you are more irritable than you used to be and that it takes smaller and smaller things to upset you?

13. Do you have consistently low physical, though not necessarily nervous, energy?

14. Do you have difficulty in 'letting go' and laughing?

15. Do you suffer from any of the following: persistent mouth ulcers; digestive problems, such as frequent indigestion or loss of appetite or a diagnosed peptic ulcer; outbreaks of dry, scaly skin on your face; frequent headaches that get worse as the day wears on; nagging pains in the neck and lower back and general stiffness in the muscles and joints?

Count up the number of 'yes' and 'no' answers. A score composed entirely or very largely of 'no' answers (13 or more) indicates that you are living in a way that will not add additional and unnecessary stresses to your life and, just as important, that will tend to minimize the potentially negative effects of other, unrelated stresses that you do encounter. Three or more 'yes' answers indicate that a sedentary inactive lifestyle and/or too little time to relax and enjoy life outside the pressures exerted at home or at work (questions 7 to 10), may be undermining your ability to manage stress. More than seven 'yes' answers indicate that you are over-working, over-worrying and definitely increasing your chances of succumbing to stress-related ill health. Perhaps you already have (question 15). Analyze your answers carefully, try to lower your score and read the Lifestyle chapter for guidelines on managing stress.

YOUR PSYCHOLOGICAL RESILIENCE: do you have an 'at risk' personality type?

Some personality traits have been shown to be more likely to lead to stress-related ill health than others. Of two 'at risk' personality types, the first predisposes to excessive stress by inviting it, and the second by allowing it to become too important. Do you recognize yourself in either profile?

1. Are achievement and personal success extremely important to you?

2. Do you thrive on competitions, sports and games where you are pitting your wits or your physical strength against others?

3. Do you find other people's failings (inefficiency, incompetence, unpunctuality) infuriating?

4. Are you time conscious and do you expect others to be so too?

5. Do you tend to do everything in a rush, including walking, talking and eating?

6. Are you easily bored?

7. If your life is relatively quiet, do you tend to crave excitement?

8. Do you feel most stimulated when under pressure, such as trying for a deadline, starting a new job or undertaking something that you feel may be beyond your capabilities?

9. Do you consider sleep a waste of time?

10. Do you always wake to an alarm and/or do you feel guilty if you 'oversleep'?

11. Do you find it difficult to relax and 'switch off'?

12. When you have finished an important task or project, do you plunge into the next without savouring a sense of achievement?

13. If you have a problem at work or at home, do you tend to rehearse the scene endlessly in your head?

14. If 'yes' to the above, do you find yourself unable to act it out without becoming angry, tearful or self-effacing?

15. Do you find it difficult to express your feelings for others?

16. Would you find it difficult to ask for a raise in salary at work?

17. If something you do is criticized, do you accept the criticism, even if you feel it was unjustified?

18. Do you find it difficult to turn down invitations that you are being pressed to accept when there is something that is more urgent or that you would prefer to do?

19. Do you find it difficult to express an opinion with which others might not agree and/or to speak up when someone else is expressing an opinion with which you strongly disagree?

20. Do you find it difficult to ask for money that is owed you?

21. Would you find it difficult to take a new and faulty item back to the shop and to ask for a repair or your money back?

22. Do you feel that you have achieved nothing in life and have very little to be proud of?

Questions 1 to 12. Six or more 'yes' answers indicate very definite type 'A' personality traits. While type A women tend to be 'achievers', they also tend to be more prone to the negative effects of stress than the more easy-going type 'B' (see page 172). So, learn how to relax and find creative rather than competitive activities outside your immediate sphere of work. You will then be extending your potential and substantially reducing your chances of succumbing to stress-related ill health.

Questions 13-22. Four or more 'yes' answers indicate that your self-confidence is low and that you find it difficult to assert yourself. In addition, the difficulty you find in expressing what you feel may result in prolonged psychological stresses. Try to assert yourself, to build up more self-esteem, by finding things in yourself and in what you do that you like and feel are worthwhile. You may well find that your relationships – at home, at work and socially – improve as a result.

What do you lean on?

Props, physical and psychological, are integral parts of many twentieth-century lifestyles – particularly lifestyles that are either very high or very low in the level of stimulation they provide. In this respect, pressure and boredom seem to be equally stressful.

Smoking and drinking, two of the most common and socially acceptable props, are examined separately in the questionnaires on the following pages. But almost anything can act as a prop – people, food, music, television, sleeping pills, addictive and non-addictive drugs… anything used to buffer you from the harsher realities of life or to step up the degree of excitement it provides.

Do you know what your outlets are? What you turn to in moments of crisis? What you take refuge in when angry, anxious, frustrated or depressed? Here is a short list of questions to ask yourself. Read each through carefully; trying where possible to visualize specific events that have happened to you. You might find it illuminating.

1. Think back to the last major upheaval or set-back in your life. Replay it in your mind, detail by detail. What was the first thing you did, and the second…? How did you respond? What, if anything, did you reach out for?

2. How do you respond to smaller dramas, disappointments and frustrations, such as spending hours on a project at work to be told it is not right and will have to be done again? Do you burst into tears or lose your temper? Do you keep your cool? Do you talk it 'out of your system'? Do you attempt to put as much space as possible geographically between you and the situation? Do you seek consolation in something or from someone?

3. If you keep your cool, how long do you keep it? Indefinitely?

4. If you seek consolation, do you seek it in people or in things? If you seek it in things, what sort of things are they?

5. Do they make you feel better?

6. How were you consoled as a child? Can you see any connection between the way you were treated then and the way you respond now?

7. When you achieve something (a tight deadline, a difficult weekend with your relatives), do you reward yourself in some way? If so, is it the same way you consoled yourself when upset or is it different?

8. How were you rewarded for the things you did as a child? Can you see any connection between the way you were rewarded then and the way you are rewarding yourself now?

9. Think back to the last time you were bored. How long ago was it? What did you do to amuse yourself?

SMOKING: when and why do you smoke?

This questionnaire has been designed to help you to discover the cues, conscious and unconscious, that prompt you to reach out for a cigarette and to help you to reflect on your own habit more deeply. Once you can recognize which your particular cues or weak moments are, you can then take steps to deal with them.

If you smoke at all, answer the following.

1. Do certain things feel 'wrong' if you do not have a cigarette in your hand?
Examples: having a drink; after a meal; telephoning a friend; chopping the vegetables for dinner; watching TV; talking to someone else who is smoking. Analyze each cigarette you smoke as you smoke it, try not having one in similar circumstances next time round, and write down those circumstances in which you would feel uncomfortable without one.

2. Do you find that you sometimes absent-mindedly light a cigarette without being aware of it or that you ever have more than one cigarette alight at once?
a) yes **b)** no

3. Here are five occasions in which you might feel the desire to smoke. Rate them in order of priority.
a) You have been in a meeting or at the theatre and have not had a cigarette for two hours.
b) You have just had a furious row at work.
c) You are sitting in front of the television watching a programme that only vaguely interests you.
d) You are sitting in a bar having a drink with a friend; there is a bowl of peanuts on the table.
e) Someone else is smoking and offers you a cigarette.

Here are four occasions in which your desire to smoke may vary with the particular circumstances. Which most sums up yours?

4. When driving
a) You smoke at fairly regular intervals regardless of what is going on inside or outside the car.
b) You smoke more if you are infuriated by the traffic (there is a traffic jam, for example) or if arguing with your passenger.
c) You smoke more if there are few distractions – you are on your own, or cruising down the motorway.
d) You smoke more if someone next to you is eating chocolates.
e) You only smoke if someone else is, if then.

5. When telephoning
a) You smoke as soon as the telephone rings or you start to dial the number.
b) You smoke only if it is a call that you feel particularly nervous or excited about.
c) You smoke only if you 'settle down' to a long conversation.
d) You smoke very rarely or not at all.

6. When eating
a) You smoke in much the same way, regardless of the occasion and of who else may or may not be smoking.
b) You smoke when stimulated by the conversation – a cigarette helps to focus your mind.
c) You smoke when the coffee arrives.
d) You smoke instead of dessert; sometimes you smoke instead of eating altogether.
e) You would smoke if others were.

7. When at a party
a) You smoke as much as you normally would, perhaps a little more.
b) You smoke considerably more, particularly if you feel nervous or do not know many people.
c) You smoke less and then, usually, only if conversation is lagging.
d) You smoke to prevent yourself from tucking into the canapés and dips.
e) You smoke only if you are offered a cigarette.

8. If you were asked to give your reasons for continuing to smoke, what would they be?
a) You have never even thought about why you do it, you just do.
b) It keeps you calm and helps you to relax.
c) It gives you something to do; you enjoy it.
d) It helps you to control your appetite and hence your weight.
e) You smoke so rarely and erratically, you do not really think of yourself as a smoker.

9. Have you ever tried giving up? What was the main withdrawal effect that you noticed?
a) Craving.
b) Irritability (either noticed by yourself or commented on by others).
c) Listlessness and fidgeting.
d) Increased appetite.
e) You were not aware of any ill effects at all.

10. If 'yes' to 9, why did you start smoking again?
a) You were 'overcome' by the desire for a cigarette.
b) You were undergoing a major crisis.
c) You were curious to try it again.
d) You put on a lot of weight.
e) You were offered one and, in a moment of weakness, accepted it.

To find out which your general smoking 'type' is, count up your **a, b, c, d,** and **e** answers to questions 3 to 10. While a clear majority of one over the others indicates a definite smoking type, it is quite possible to combine the characteristics of two, or even three, of the five groups.

● The Habitual Smoker (predominantly **a** answers). You are addicted physically and psychologically to your smoking habit. You may smoke so much that you are unaware that you associate certain activities with lighting up a cigarette (1) or, even, that you have lit one at all (2).
Best time to give up: when there is going to be a change in routine – moving house, changing jobs, going away on holiday – that will temporarily remove some of the cues that fuel your desire to smoke.
Main pitfall when giving up: straightforward craving. Nicotine gum or lozenges may help by weaning you first off the habit, then off the drug.

● The Nervous Smoker (predominantly **b** answers). You smoke to counteract anxiety, to focus your mind and to sedate yourself from pressure and frustration. You smoke more if going through a particularly anxious period; less if happy and relaxed. (You are also probably a type 'A' personality, see opposite.) Try alternative ways of negotiating potentially frustrating or aggravating situations, such as practising the relaxation methods outlined in the Lifestyle chapter.
Best time to give up: when things are relatively quiet and peaceful – if you are the sort of person to make room for quiet spaces in your life.
Main pitfall to giving up: any crisis.

● The Listless Smoker (predominantly **c** answers). You smoke to relieve boredom and monotony and to give yourself something to do. Make yourself busier, seek out new interests and you should find that your desire for a cigarette fades as your involvement grows.
Best time to give up: when there is some excitement in your life – a challenge, such as a job promotion, a party or big occasion to organize.
Main pitfall when giving up: boredom; having a cigarette out of curiosity to see whether you still like it. You will, so don't.

● The Weight-watching Smoker (two or more **d**s). You smoke out of a desire to curb your appetite and so control your weight. In fact, the prospect of gaining weight is probably your biggest 'reason' for not giving up. But weight need not be a necessary corollary to giving up smoking, and even if you do put on a few pounds in the first three months, research studies show that you are unlikely to be permanently the heavier for it (see page 184).
Best time to give up: when you are happy with yourself (including with what you weigh) and are unlikely to seek emotional refuge in food.
Main pitfall when giving up: being discouraged by initial weight gain in first three months.

● The Social Smoker (predominantly **e** answers). You are an occasional' smoker who persists in smoking cigarettes (usually other people's) because the health risks do not seem to apply. They do.
Best time to give up: when you are going through a relatively quiet time socially; when spending your time with someone who does not smoke.
Major pitfall when giving up: not taking your resolution to stop seriously enough.

DRINKING: how large a part does alcohol play in your life?

Because alcohol is so easily available and drinking so socially acceptable, it is important to be awake to the perils as well as the pleasures. Answer the following.

1. Do you ever drink on your own?

2. Can you remember the last day when you did not have a drink?

3. Do you sometimes find that you 'need' a drink before going out in the evening in order to relax?

4. When you feel disappointed, angry, frustrated or tense, do you tend to drink more heavily than usual?

5. If you went out for the evening and alcohol was not available, would you feel uncomfortable?

6. Do you tend to drink more or faster than your friends?

7. Do you minimize the amount you drink – to others or yourself?

8. Do you sometimes find that you cannot remember part of the previous evening after you have been drinking?

9. Are you drinking more or a stronger type of drink than you were six months ago?

10. Do you sometimes feel guilty or anxious about the amount you drink?

11. Do you say or do things after drinking that you would not have said or done while sober?

12. Have you tried to limit or to control your drinking or to cut it out entirely and found it impossible to do so?

13. Have other people commented on the amount you drink?

14. Do you ever find that you resolve to do something and fail to do it because of your drinking?

15. Do you 'plan' your drinking so that your family and close friends are unaware of how much you are drinking?

16. Are you having an increasing number of problems at home, at work and financially?

17. Do your hands ever shake in the morning?

18. Do you ever drink in the morning?

19. After periods of drinking, do you sometimes hear or see things that are not there?

Count up the number of 'yes' answers. These all indicate that you may be drinking abnormally. If your 'yes' answers are to the first 10 questions, try to analyze your reasons for drinking in the manner that you do and try, too, to find alternative methods of dealing with disappointments, setbacks or challenges without resorting to alcohol. And read pages 186-7. If your 'yes' answers are to questions 11-19, you are not just drinking abnormally but dangerously so. Resolve to give up alcohol entirely for at least three months. If you find it difficult or impossible, you should see your doctor.

How health-conscious are you?

Health consciousness encompasses three things – none of them faddish or obsessional or unnecessarily time-consuming. First, it involves accepting the responsibility for your own good health – not handing it over wholesale to your doctor. Second, it involves being conscious about the details that really matter – eating healthily, exercising, not smoking. Third, it involves having regular check-ups to ensure that there are no early signs of conditions that may require medical attention. If such conditions are detected, they will be treated a stage before you feel unwell, so securing the best possible outlook.

YOUR CHECK LIST: how up-to-date is your preventative health prescription?

1. Have you ever had a complete physical check-up?
2. When did you last feel your breasts?
3. When were your breasts last checked by a nurse or doctor?
4. If you are over 35, have you had a mammogram – and, if so, how recently?
5. When did you last have a cervical smear ('Pap' test)?
6. Have you ever had herpes (sexually transmitted cold sores)?
7. Do you know what your blood pressure is?
8. When did you last have your blood pressure checked?
9. If you are over 35, have you ever had your blood/cholesterol levels checked?
10. If you are over 45, have you had your eyes checked for glaucoma?

Now turn to page 208 and consult the health calendar to see which aspect of your preventative health prescription needs updating.

How well do you know yourself?

YOUR DAILY AND MONTHLY RHYTHMS: is there a pattern?

This section is for you to note down specific details and observations that will help you to understand how your body works, both over the course of the 24-hour day when your state of vitality and alertness changes with the clock, and over the course of your menstrual cycle, when fluctuating hormone levels may also affect your mood, energy levels and general susceptibility to physical and psychological stresses.

These biological rhythms should not be confused with the 'biorhythms' of a 23-day physical cycle, 28-day emotional cycle and 33-day intellectual cycle, which have given rise to special 'calculators' claiming to be able to pinpoint propitious or unpropitious days according to your date of birth. Events such as Sebastian Coe's triumphant win in the 1500 metre final at the Moscow Olympic Games in 1980, on a day when his biorhythm readings were all registering critical, have combined to discredit this theory.

This method is purely observational. It should also be illuminating. Do you know how long your menstrual cycle is or whether your weight rises or remains stable prior to menstruation, or exactly when you are ovulating? It may prove helpful by enabling you to reserve your energies for those days when you are likely to be feeling at your most capable and resilient and to safeguard yourself against those times when you feel 'lower' than usual. While the set of symptoms known collectively as the premenstrual syndrome are fairly well recognized (see below), not so well recognized is the fact that these 'lows' are balanced by 'highs' elsewhere, usually over ovulation, when your strength and general capacity for coping are many times greater than average. Capitalize on this by filling in the chart and making use of your observations where appropriate. The principle is not to be ruled by your body rhythms, but to have a rough guide that enables you to work with, rather than against, them. Copy the chart and record relevant details over three, or preferably six, cycles.

Your monthly rhythm chart

Day of month																														
Weight																														
Menstruation																														
Ovulation																														
Temperature																														
Energy highs and lows	morning																													
	noon																													
	evening																													
Symptoms																														

Key to Filling in the Chart

● The day of the month on which this chart begins is deliberately left blank so that you can start it immediately, whatever the date. Simply fill in today's date against day 1, continue until you reach the last day of the month and then start again at 1 for the new month.

● Menstruation and ovulation. This is to enable you to see at a glance when your period is/was and to enter in the day when you think you have ovulated (see below). If you skip the temperature section, you can still get a rough indication of when you ovulated (though only in retrospect) by subtracting 14 days from the beginning of your period. Once you have filled in a complete cycle, look back over the chart to see how you felt.

● Temperature. There is no need to go through the rigmarole of taking your temperature every day unless you are interested in knowing when you have ovulated, are using 'natural' methods of contraception (in which case you will also need skilled instruction, see page 199), or you are trying to conceive and have been having some difficulty (see page 206). Taking your temperature is one of two observational ways of knowing when ovulation has occurred. To do so, take your temperature first thing in the morning, while still in bed and before you have had anything to eat or to drink. Leave the thermometer in your mouth for five minutes and use a clearly marked clinical thermometer. Look for a slight dip in temperature (this does not always occur), followed by a rise of about 0.5°C (0.9°F). The dip indicates ovulation has just occurred; the rise that you are anywhere from a few hours to a few days past it – the rise continues for the rest of the cycle.

● Energy highs and lows. Simply place an H, M or L (high, medium or low)

in the appropriate place, according to the time of day and how energetic you feel. We all have circadian rhythms – energy levels that rise and fall over the stages of a 24-hour day. While some of these peaks and troughs are so common as to apply generally (an example is the 1 pm lunch energy slump which occurs even when a midday meal is not eaten), others are more idiosyncratic. When the month is over and you have finished charting your various ups and downs, look to see whether any clearly decipherable pattern appears. If it does – your energy is high in the early morning, say, slumps at lunchtime and picks up in the early evening – you can help yourself by arranging your day around this, capitalizing on high-energy times to get things done and protecting those times when your energy reserves are lowest.

● Symptoms. The symptoms involved here are mainly connected with the premenstrual syndrome (see also pages 194-5). But the chart can be just as flexible as you want it to be. If you feel you have other symptoms that may or may not be cycle-related, such as acne or compulsive eating, simply award them a code letter and enter them up. There is now a certain amount of evidence that blood sugar levels rise before menstruation and drop immediately afterwards. This may affect your appetite and your general 'susceptibility' to food. So if eating habits turn out to follow a definite and discernible pattern, one way round the problem might be to take appropriate evasive action in advance.

● Suggested codes for symptoms:
PHYSICAL: AB swollen, bloated abdomen (or ankles, wrists, fingers – specify with appropriate initial); B breast tenderness; H headache; M migraine; S stomach pains.
PSYCHOLOGICAL: C clumsy; D depressed; I irritable; L lethargic.

shape

'Vogue knows that chic begins with a good figure...'   *Vogue*, **1938**

Your shape is a mixture of things, a reflection of your genes and your lifestyle — the way you eat, the way you exercise, the way you hold and use your body. This chapter begins on the premise that most of us would like to be in better shape than we are.

Being in good shape is where health and beauty start. The dividends of being lithe and fit are enormous and they are reflected in every area of your life: you look good; you feel confident, alert and involved; you give an impression of unbounded vitality and perfect physical fitness; you feel vibrantly well. If such a positive sense of wellbeing has always seemed beyond your reach, take heart. It is not as elusive as it seems, but it does require motivation and discipline. Learn discipline by practising it and you will change both your shape and your outlook for the better.

Although shape can be improved, often dramatically, by holding and using your body correctly (the most immediate body shaper), by toning your muscles to give a sleeker, tauter line and by shedding excess weight with a well-balanced diet, there are certain elements of your shape that you cannot change. So be realistic. Recognize that you have a basic body type (frame). Work with what you have. If you are out of condition, unfit, over or under weight, then what you have is probably considerably more promising than you think it is. All bodies obey their own laws of proportion and such laws are usually naturally harmonious. The less-than-perfect aspects of your shape are much more likely to be owing to a less-than-perfect lifestyle than to anything intrinsically 'wrong' with your body. Inactivity, unhealthy eating patterns, a lack of attention to small but important details, such as posture... Improve on these and you may well find that imperfections you have become resigned to are ones that you can do something about after all.

What would you like to change? Appraise your shape honestly, considering your good points as well as your bad ones. Stand in front of a full-length mirror in a good light and take a good long look. Fill in the appropriate charts and questionnaires in the Personal Profile and complete the fitness tests on the following pages. Record your starting point, work out your aims and objectives and go for them. Give yourself three months in which to get into really good physical shape and then work steadily towards your deadline, plotting your progress as you go and gradually increasing the effort you put into your exercising week by week.

THE UNCHANGEABLE ASPECT
Body type

The critical changing elements in any shape strategy are posture, exercise and diet. The constant is your body type, known as your somatotype. Because this is determined by your genes, no amount of dieting and exercising can change it. The basis of body wisdom lies in learning how to identify and how to accept your body type — learning how to like yourself the way you fundamentally are. This is healthy realism, not complacency. Excess weight, out-of-condition muscles and an unfit, unexercised body do not belong to any body type. They detract from it. So start by distinguishing between the imperfections that you can do something about and the inherited characteristics that you cannot.

Then take yourself to task and see how specific body contours — determined both by the tone of your muscles and by the distribution of fat on your frame — can be improved through diet, exercise and small, but important, adjustments in the way you hold and use your body.

There are three criteria for assessing body type, each based on the relative predominance of one type of body tissue over another. The first is nerves and skin (ectomorphy), the second is muscle and bone (mesomorphy) and the third is fat (endomorphy). While no-one is 'pure' ectomorph, mesomorph or endomorph, one type is usually predominant. Recognizing which general category you come into can be useful because it gives you an idea of your basic frame and of the sports and activities likely to suit you best.

THE CHANGEABLE ASPECTS
Weight

As your correct weight depends first on your height and second on your frame, or body type, the weight graph, opposite, allows for a wide variation for each height. So use it as a rough guide only, bearing in mind that, if you are lightly built, you may come within this range and still be overweight, while, if you are big-boned and large-framed and weigh in at the lower end of the scale, you may be up to 12 kg (26 lb) under your ideal weight. For this reason, signs of overweight and underweight are also given, together with guidelines on measurement and a technique to help you to assess your degree of fat. Put these together, and you can determine fairly accurately how much you should weigh.

The chart gives no 'allowance' for age. It is now generally recognized that there is no need to grow any wider as you grow older. The weight you reach at 25, provided that it is within the limits given here and appropriate to your build, is the weight that you should maintain throughout your adult life except, of course, when pregnant. At any other time, fluctuations in weight may disrupt your menstrual cycle, lead to stretch marks and varicose veins and cause your skin to age prematurely. Maintaining a reasonable and consistent weight should be a priority whatever your age.

In the years between puberty and the menopause, your weight will fluctuate quite naturally within a range of about 1-2 kg (2-5 lb) and sometimes more as your hormonal levels change over the stages of the menstrual cycle. If you are conscious of a large fluctuation or have been puzzled by the fact that your weight seems to go up and down almost daily despite the fact that your diet is quite constant, you may find it helpful to assess your 'real' weight as opposed to your 'random' weight. Weigh yourself every day over a complete cycle and fill in the amount for each day on the chart provided in the Personal Profile. At the end of the cycle (the onset of menstruation), add these amounts together and then divide by the total number of days. See which stage of the cycle correlates most closely with the final figure — your 'real' weight — then weigh yourself once a month at this point of the cycle to see whether you are losing or gaining.

If you are trying to lose or to gain, weigh yourself weekly (making allowance, if necessary, for hormonal disruption) and plot the amount lost or gained on the graph given in the Personal Profile.

Ectomorphy. Lean and angular, with long limbs, narrow joints, low body fat and muscle and few curves, ectomorphic types are often likened to greyhounds and racehorses. Unlike endomorphs or mesomorphs, ectomorphs tend to be able to eat quite substantially without putting on weight. At least one study has suggested that this is because they have a shorter intestine and thus less space in which to digest their food. Because ectomorphs have low weight-to-height and bone-to-muscle ratios, they are not suited for sports that require bursts of speed or strength. They often excel at distance sports, however, such as marathon or steeplechase, because their low body fat (male ectomorphic athletes have as little as five per cent) speeds up heat loss and prevents the build-up of internal body heat that leads to exhaustion. Ectomorphs will also tend to do well at sports where height and length of limb is important, such as high or long jump.

Mesomorphy. Mesomorphic types are constitutionally strong with no special concentrations of weight anywhere on the body. They are reasonably compact, with broad shoulders and pelvic girdle and well-developed muscles, particularly at the calf and forearm. Mesomorphy has been linked with a direct and naturally aggressive, even pugnacious, temperament and a greater physiological need for exercise. Men, who have a greater ratio of muscle to body fat, have higher mesomorphy ratings than women, who tend to combine this characteristic with one of the other two. Hence the terms 'ectomorphic' or 'endomorphic' mesomorphs. Such women have the capacity for great stamina and power and, with training, will do well at some of the more demanding sports that require explosive bursts of speed and/or strength. Examples are sprinting, cycling, hurdling and gymnastics.

Endomorphy. Endomorphic types are shorter limbed than either of the other two groups, have a lower centre of gravity, wider hips, larger joints, a higher proportion of body fat to muscle and a tendency to put on weight easily. They must concentrate on keeping their weight down to reasonable limits, if they are to pursue more vigorous types of exercise. With training, endomorphs can be good at sports and activities that require a good sense of judgement, agility and the ability to twist and turn easily. Some champion women tennis players have tended towards endomorphy, as have some long distance swimmers – where the higher degree of body fat can act strongly in their favour, adding buoyancy and generating heat.

typetypetype

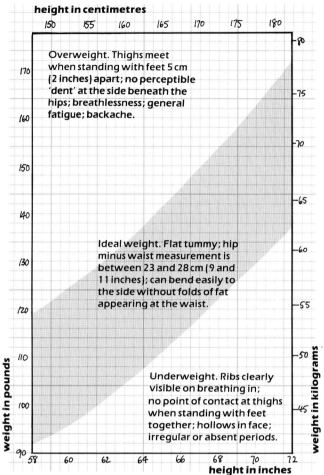

height in centimetres

150 155 160 165 170 175 180

Overweight. Thighs meet when standing with feet 5 cm (2 inches) apart; no perceptible 'dent' at the side beneath the hips; breathlessness; general fatigue; backache.

Ideal weight. Flat tummy; hip minus waist measurement is between 23 and 28 cm (9 and 11 inches); can bend easily to the side without folds of fat appearing at the waist.

Underweight. Ribs clearly visible on breathing in; no point of contact at thighs when standing with feet together; hollows in face; irregular or absent periods.

weight in pounds / **weight in kilograms**

58 60 62 64 66 68 70 72

height in inches

The weight graph, above, is based on national insurance figures and shows very broadly the weight range appropriate for your height. Check you come within it. Then look at the notes on under, over and ideal weight. These should help you to be more precise.

Measurements

The contours, or general shape, of your body are determined, first, by your body type, second, by how well-toned your muscles are and, third, by specific concentrations of flesh and distributions of fat. To find out how well-proportioned you are, measure yourself around the bust (when breathing in), around the waist (at its narrowest part, about an inch above the navel) and around the hips, thighs and calves (all at their widest parts).

Fill in your measurements in the table provided in the Personal Profile, leaving a space for assessment in three months' time when you will have followed the exercise programme outlined on the following pages and, if necessary, the diet too.

An ideal example of how you 'should' measure up is given here. Taking your bust and hip measurements as the baseline (the same), your waist, thighs and calves should be about 25, 41 and 56 cm (10, 16 and 22 inches) respectively, less than this. These are the dimensions you should work towards. But remember that they are approximations only — not an absolute set of statistics.

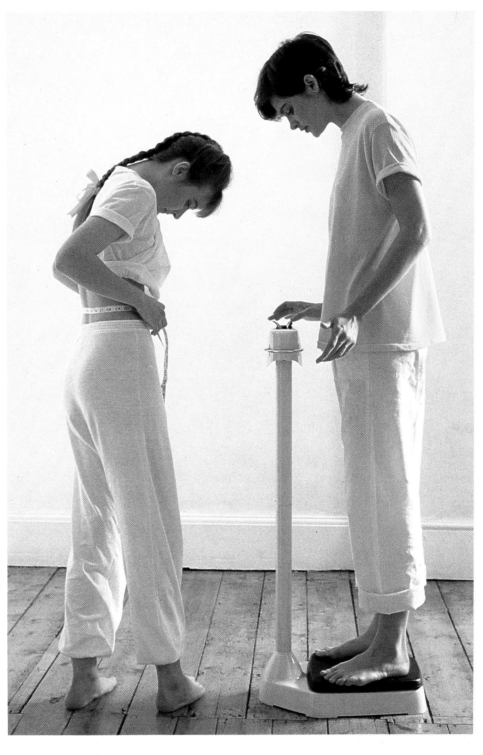

However, while small variations (2.5-5 cm/1-2 inches either way) are in order, notably smaller differences are not, and indicate that you are almost certainly overweight or under-exercised. It is up to you to determine which.

BUST	WAIST	HIPS	THIGH	CALF	
89	64	89	48	33	Measurement in cm
35	25	35	19	13	Measurement in inches
—	25	—	41	56	Differences comparable
—	10	—	16	22	to hip measurement

Aim to keep your weight within reasonable limits – a range of 3.2 kg (7 lb) at the outside – by keeping a regular check on yourself.
Best type of scales: the traditional type, as above. Place modern scales on a hard floor, not a carpet, for a reliable reading and check them for accuracy against another pair every six months.
Best time to weigh yourself: in the morning, before dressing and breakfast, and after going to the lavatory.

Body fat

Women have a higher ratio of fat to muscle than men — about 22-28 and 15-22 per cent respectively. If you are in good physical shape, about 1 kg (2 lb) in every 4 kg (9 lb) that you weigh will be fat. Of this kilogram of fat, half is situated just beneath the skin where it provides essential insulation and support, helping to keep the skin smooth and supple and giving firm contours. Nothing is more prematurely ageing to the skin than a rapid or excessive loss of weight. With too little fat, the body loses its shape and the skin sags as its underlying support shrinks away. With too much fat, the skin dimples and stretches as the surplus layers of fat accumulate beneath it. Either way the body loses its shape.

Not only do women have more fat than men, but it also tends to be distributed differently — accumulating around abdomen, buttocks and thighs — and seems to be more sensitive to hormonal influences. This would explain why bloating caused by sodium and water retention within the cells can be a problem in the few days preceding a period.

With the exception of a fairly drastic medical procedure (see page 169), fat cells cannot be broken down or 'dispersed'. Their number appears to be determined by heredity and early conditioning factors and to remain unalterable from the first year of life. Although diet cannot reduce fat cells numerically it can reduce them in size. Estimate your degree of body fat with the pinch test below.

Pinch test graph

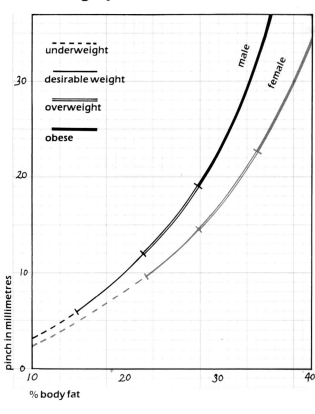

Because fat situated directly beneath the skin constitutes a predictable proportion of your total body fat (about 50 per cent), you can estimate how 'fat' you are by pinching the flesh on the underside of your upper arm. Pinch firmly but not painfully, making sure that you are pinching fat, not muscle which feels much firmer to the touch, and ask a friend to measure it for you. The width of the pinch constitutes the distance between the inner edges of your thumb and forefinger.
The pink line on the graph, right, should enable you to identify your approximate percentage of body fat. (Use the black line if carrying out the test on a man.)
A pinch of between 10 and 15 mm falls into the desirable weight range. Any more indicates that you are overweight. A pinch of 23 mm or more? Your body fat is over 34 per cent of your total weight. Definitely too much.

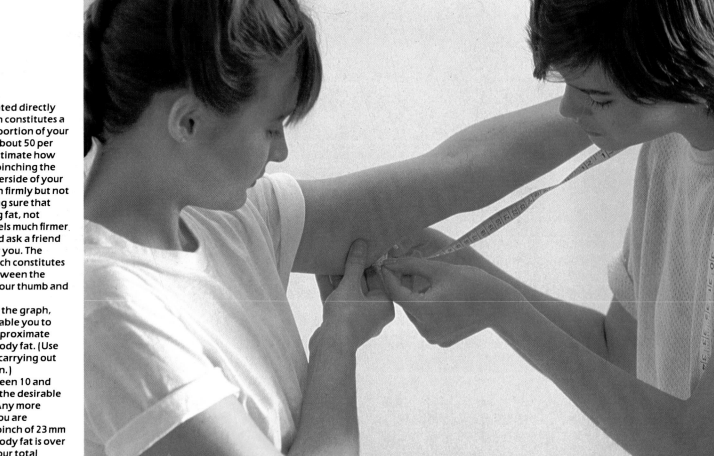

posture

'It has taken me years of struggle, hard work and research to learn how to make one simple gesture ...' Isadora Duncan

How are you sitting as you read this? Are your shoulders in line with each other, your back straight, your weight evenly distributed on both buttocks, your knees relaxed and parallel and any forward movement coming from your hips and not your upper back? Or are you slumping forwards, with your neck curved and your spine rounded, one shoulder marginally higher than the other, your legs crossed and your weight supported through your elbows? If so, you may be in perfect physical shape but you certainly will not look it.

Of all the shape determinants, the most immediate is posture. Diet and exercise may give you the figure you want, but if you do not hold it correctly, it will never be seen to advantage. Most people, once into their teens and often much before it, stand, sit, even rest incorrectly. Teachers of the Alexander Principle, an impressive method which concentrates first on asking you to unlearn bad habits and then on setting them to rights, maintain that virtually everyone misuses their bodies to some degree, often severely so. Such misuse undermines your natural shape, robs you of the ability to move easily and freely, predisposes you to aches, pains and muscular tension and many of the more specific symptoms of 'dis-ease'—lower back pain, headaches, poor circulation, digestive troubles... If you concentrate on improving your posture, you may well find that the general quality of your life also improves enormously.

BALANCE

Your posture can only be as good as your sense of balance—no better—and you should therefore work at improving both simultaneously. Most people do not even begin to become aware of their sense of balance until it starts deserting them. But balance is much more than the difference between remaining upright and falling over. It is, or should be, a finely tuned mechanism working via a number of reflex centres in the brain.

Perfect balance is not perfect stillness. Balance is never static. It is achieved by allowing your body to move and to make the numerous fractional adjustments that enable it to remain poised and upright. Try the 'tree' exercise (right) and feel how much you oscillate as soon as you close your eyes. This is the result of the body finding, not losing, its balance as it re-establishes its links with gravity.

Three factors influence your sense of balance. The first are the eyes. You learn from an early age that walls are vertical and the floor is flat and you use your eyes to maintain these reference points when standing, sitting or running. The second factor derives from three semi-circular canals in the inner ear and is known as vestibular balance. Whenever your body moves, the fluid in one or more of these canals is also set in motion and sends messages to the brain of 'up', 'down', 'left', 'right', 'stop' and 'start'. If these messages become confused, as can happen when spinning round very fast or when rocking up and down in a boat, your sense of balance will be affected and you will feel nauseous and

dizzy. Giddiness and seasickness may be felt in the stomach but they do not originate there. The third factor that affects your sense of balance is more general. It is called proprioception and it refers to sensations of pressure gleaned from different parts of the body — the soles of the feet, the knees, the buttocks, the neck — and fed back to the brain via the central nervous system. In theory, once your brain has learned to distinguish a symmetrical norm — how it <u>feels</u> when the weight is evenly balanced on both feet — it can then make the fractional adjustments in your posture that enable you to keep your sense of balance and to remain upright. Although proprioception <u>should</u> enable you to achieve a constant state of perfect balance, it rarely does. The brain soon becomes attuned to uneven distributions of weight and adapts its messages accordingly. This is why it is quite possible to stand in a lopsided way and still to be under the impression that you are standing perfectly straight. In fact, as you may have already found out, it can take a photograph to show you just how lopsided you are.

While years of incorrect sitting and standing can give a misleading feeling of 'rightness', and any change for the better is almost bound to feel 'wrong', persevere. With time, your brain will learn what it feels like to be truly balanced and will adapt its messages accordingly.

PRINCIPLES OF GOOD POSTURE

Learning the principles of good posture and putting them into practice is one of the best investments you can make. The principles themselves are not difficult. *Vogue* summed them up more than 60 years ago as 'an utter lack of rigidity, an appearance of having been dropped into one's clothes and remaining there by accident...' This delightfully carefree image conveys the feeling exactly. Good posture looks and is effortless. It makes for the least effort, or strain, because it enables you to perform any movement from the simplest to the most complicated with freedom and absolute economy of action. If the posture is right, only the relevant muscles and joints will be used to perform the movement, whether it is reaching out to turn out a light or walking along a tightrope.

Most people do not move economically. They over-react. They walk along a tightrope when they only need to turn out a light. The consequence is considerable strain on the body, both while the movement is being performed and after it has been completed. Residual tensions can remain in the muscle for days, if not months, at a time. Multiply such strains by a lifetime, and you will soon see how using the body incorrectly may restrict your ability to move freely and easily. Good posture, on the other hand, will do much to preserve your muscles and joints from the wear and tear of the advancing years.

While the principles of good posture are not difficult to grasp, putting them into practice will take a determined and committed effort. Start by identifying your weak points. Complete the tests and exercises in the Personal Profile and study the various guidelines listed over the page. Commit them to memory and, to begin with, maintain a state of fairly constant vigilance over the way you stand and sit and move. Only when the adjustments begin to feel right can you afford to let your vigilance relax.

A finely tuned sense of balance is essential for posture. Test yours by taking up the 'tree' position, above: one foot on the floor, the other resting as far up the inner thigh as possible, the arms extended upwards, the eyes open. You should feel comfortable enough to stay there for minutes rather than seconds. Now close your eyes. If you feel yourself beginning to topple over, your sense of balance needs attention. Practise this exercise daily until you can stand quite comfortably for at least a minute with your eyes closed. The ultimate goal? To be able to stand with the foot resting slightly lower down the leg (knee not thigh) and to change legs, transferring your weight to the opposite foot, without opening your eyes once.

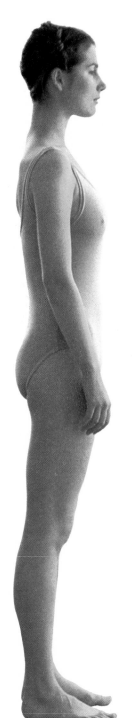

Your **HEAD** weighs up to 5 kg (12 lb). How you hold it influences the position of the vertebrae, not only at the neck, but also the whole way down the spine.

Place your hand along the middle of your back and tip your head first forwards towards your chest and then backwards as far as it will go. You will feel the vertebrae moving quite distinctly beneath your hand as the position of your head changes. Much smaller movements, such as holding your head slightly to one side, will also cause your spine to adjust its shape. To hold your head centrally balanced, imagine a string attached to the crown of your head gradually becoming taut and pulling it upwards, so that the back of your neck lengthens. At the same time, let your shoulders drop slightly, keep your eyes facing forwards and your chin at right-angles to your neck.

Holding the **NECK** in a set and rigid manner can lead to shortened and strained neck muscles, tension headaches and even migraine.

Free it by holding the head as directed and by feeling the sensation of lift as the vertebrae extend away from each other and the neck lengthens.

Aches and pains in the upper back are usually caused by holding the **SHOULDERS** incorrectly. Most of us tend to stand or to sit with one shoulder fractionally higher or further round than the other. Bring them level by standing with your weight evenly balanced on both feet and holding your head centrally so that the length between the ears and base of the collar bone is the same on both sides. Now rotate the shoulders, as above, to bring them comfortably back and down. If you do this correctly, your shoulder blades at the back and clavicles (collar bones) at the front will both lie quite flat.

Look upon your **ARMS** as an extension of the shoulders and upper back. Hold them loosely and easily by your sides, with the elbows turned slightly out away from the body in order to maintain the wideness in the chest and shoulder girdle, and the wrist and fingers loose and supple, not clenched.

Think in terms of making as much space between your **RIBS** and **HIPS** as possible. Keep your shoulders down and your back lengthened and extended, so that your respiratory and digestive systems have the room in which to work properly and your spine is extended right from its base at the coccyx to its tip at the back of the skull. To help get the sensation of lift, span your hands so that the middle finger is resting lightly on the hip bone and the thumb on the lowest rib. Adjust your posture as directed and see the distance growing between your thumb and finger as your body lengthens upwards from the back.

Your **SPINE** is one of the most susceptible areas of the body to the strains exerted by standing, sitting, moving, even lying down incorrectly. To meet the stresses of standing on two feet – a fairly recent event in our evolutionary history – the spine curves naturally in at the neck, to enable you to move your head freely, and at the small of your back, to relieve the pressure on your lower back. This receives the equivalent of a 45-kg (100-lb) jolt every time your foot touches the ground – considerably more when running or jumping. Poor posture may cause these curves to flatten or, more commonly, to become too pronounced. Keep your spine lengthened and supple and neither unnaturally straight nor unnaturally curved. Think in terms of 'growing' upwards so that each vertebra is extending away from the next.

When held correctly, your **PELVIS** supports your spine, takes the pressure off your lower back, keeps your buttocks firmly in the right place and enables your tummy to be held in naturally. When standing, your pelvis should be held forwards, facing the front.

Practise the wall exercise and the pelvic tilt, given here, to help you position your pelvis correctly.

When standing, walking or running, your **KNEES** should be slightly flexed to take the weight of your body and to act as shock absorbers, thus preventing jarring. If knees are held straight and rigid, the pelvis will be 'frozen', movement restricted and too much pressure exerted on the spine.

Your **FEET** take the weight of your body and provide its base for balance. The further apart they are, the more stable and balanced you will be. Stand with feet slightly apart, weight evenly balanced between them and supported mid-way between the ball and heel of your foot. Rock gently back and forth until you find this point.

EXERCISES TO BEWARE OF

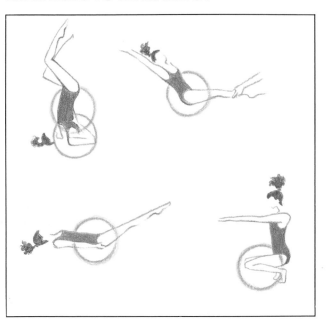

Unless you are really strong and fit, and your posture is good, some exercises may place unacceptable strains on the body. Bicycling while balancing on your shoulders will encourage shoulders to round and exaggerate an arch in the upper back. Practising sit-ups with feet anchored, legs straight, encourages your lower spine to curve. Bend legs instead. Raising and lowering both legs from the floor is equally bad for the lower back. Knees are vulnerable joints. Protect them by doing deep knee bends with heels flat on the floor (see page 38). In addition, try to keep buttocks above standing position knee level and avoid full squats and 'Cossack' dancing – kicking out with the legs while crossing the arms in front. All these may stretch ligaments on either side of the knee, so weakening the joint.

USE AND MOVEMENT

Now that you know how you should hold your body, extend these principles into the way you use it. The most perfect standing position is unlikely to do much for you, if you slump or move awkwardly for the rest of the time. The main principle is to safeguard the health of your spine. Keep it lengthened and extended, straight but not stiff, and when bending down to pick something up, however light or heavy, always bend your knees, never your back.

Walking

Step forwards lightly on to the ball of your foot and land on the heel. Landing on the ball of the foot will exaggerate an arch in the lower back. High-heeled shoes pitch your body forward on to your toes and cause your hips to rotate inwards to compensate for the unnatural angle of the feet, so wear flat or low-heeled shoes for everyday use — a maximum of 5 cm (2 inches).

Sitting

Although sitting down is a position that most of us associate with great comfort, the strain on your back is actually greatest when sitting — about twice that when standing upright. Because prolonged periods of sitting, especially sitting in the wrong type of chair, can weaken the intricate network of muscles and ligaments that supports the spine, help yourself by choosing a chair that makes good posture easier, not more difficult, for you. 'Easy' chairs are not easy on the spine. Bucket-type chairs also cause your spine to curve and offer little or no support at the lower back, where you need it most. Go, instead, for chairs that are fairly straight-backed and that offer some support in the lower back. If your chair does not (car seats are common examples), place a folded towel or a small cushion in the small of your back so that your spine is supported.

When working or reading, try not to lean forwards over your work. Bring whatever you are doing towards you — the typewriter to the edge of your desk or the newspaper up to eye-level, for example — so that you do not have to bend your neck, drop your shoulders forward and curve your spine in order to be able to type or to read. When driving, make sure that your seat is close enough to the steering wheel so that you do not have to reach forwards to hold it.

Lying

The next time that you feel like relaxing do not collapse into the nearest chair. Instead, lie flat on your back on the floor, with your head supported by a book or a small cushion. This extends rather than bends the spine and reduces the strain exerted upon it to just about zero. Lying down is the best way of 'resting' your back and your body. Squatting and kneeling come next, sitting a very poor fourth.

Sleeping enables you to recover from the stresses and strains of the day, but an ill-designed mattress may rob you of the chance to do just that by placing additional stresses on your spine. While beds should be firm, they should not be hard-as-a-board firm as too much rigidity forces the body into an unnaturally straight line. Go for a bed that supports your spine and body well, however. A mattress that allows your body to sag, so that your buttocks are lower than the rest of you, is too soft. So are most waterbeds. Test a mattress by lying down on it — never buy it blind.

Bending

When you lean or bend over, whether to pick something off the floor, to wash your hair, or to make a bed, the bend should come either from your knees or from a natural rotation at the hips, so that the spine is still as straight as it would be when upright — it just changes its plane. Bending from the lower back is a major cause of backache and sore strained muscles.

Think laterally when doing or attempting to do anything that might affect the position of your spine. Kneel down when making the bed, bend your knees when lifting heavy weights, including young children, sit on a stool when washing your hair if the basin is too low, use a long-handled hoe when gardening, place heavier and more frequently used casserole dishes and pans in cupboards that will not entail bending or stooping to retrieve them. Standing or sitting, your work height should be such that you do not have to bend your lower back at all or your neck too much — small details, perhaps, but they may save you any amount of trouble, particularly back trouble, in later years.

When sitting, keep the spine lengthened and extended, the bottom well to the back of the chair and your weight evenly distributed on both buttocks. Do not cross your knees. It cuts down circulation to and from the legs, may aggravate, if not actually cause, varicose veins and will multiply the strains on your spine by throwing the body out of line. Instead, let your thighs lie parallel, and only cross your legs at the ankle, if at all.

exercise

'For the past fifteen years, I have made fitness a priority because I have experienced its very real rewards. I simply schedule it into my life as if my life depended on it, which in a way it does...'

Jane Fonda

Exercise tones the body, alerts the mind, increases resilience to physical and psychological stresses, firms muscles, loosens joints, banishes stiffness and general aches and pains, builds up the efficiency of heart and lungs, lowers blood/cholesterol, helps overcome insomnia, regulates appetite and generates a vigorous and vibrant sense of wellbeing. Of all the beauty routines you could adopt, exercise is undoubtedly the most worthwhile.

Energy generates energy. The more you move, run, stretch, jump and bend, the more vigorous and energetic you will feel. The next time lethargy descends, try overcoming apathy with activity. Take a brisk walk, jog up and down on the spot for a few minutes and see how much more alert and refreshed you feel. Now plan to increase the amount of activity you take during the day, first carrying out the general fitness test outlined in the Personal Profile to find out how active, or inactive, you are.

In addition, you should also aim to exercise fairly vigorously for at least 20 minutes three times a week. Exercise is one of the easiest things in life to find excuses not to do. Cold weather, alternative arrangements, indolence...all undermine the best of intentions. So make it as easy as possible for yourself. Choose a sport or activity you enjoy, and set out gently. Sudden enthusiasms and frenetic bursts of activity can lead to fatigue, exhaustion, sore aching muscles, strains, sprains, even fractures — all signs that you have pushed your body too far and have asked it to do something for which it was insufficiently prepared. Incorporate more than one exercise or activity into your fitness programme for maximum benefit. Start gently, build up gradually and progress more vigorously as you become fitter. The more unfit and the older you are, the more gradually you should go.

You should be especially careful if you are over 35; have not had a recent medical check-up; have not exercised for a long period of time; drink or smoke heavily; are more than 9 kg (20 lb) overweight; have a specific medical problem or a family history of heart disease. Check with your doctor first. However old you are and whatever the shape you are in, always observe certain cautions when you begin exercising. Never rush it, never pace yourself against someone who is younger or fitter than you are, never push yourself beyond your limits or force yourself into positions that feel painful and learn to listen to your body. Stop when you feel fatigued or breathless, or when your pulse rate is approaching its maximum safety figure (see page 18). Never attempt to 'run' off a sprain or a strain. If you do sustain an injury, rest instead and start more cautiously the next time round.

Lastly, try to make sure that all three basic essentials of exercise are incorporated into your programme. (A tailor-made exercise sequence that does this for you can be found on the following pages.) These three essentials are strength, suppleness and stamina. While other aspects, such as coordination, timing, balance, agility, judgement and skill, are also important, these are the three major benefits. Choose activities that are complementary in this respect. If you are a keen jogger or runner, practise yoga or go dancing once or twice a week. Running and jogging are long on stamina and short on suppleness. Yoga and dance, on the other hand, are two of the best suppleness exercises that there are.

STRENGTH

Your physical strength and athletic ability are largely determined by the strength of your muscles. Strong muscles are firm, give a sleek contour to the body and enable you to perform most types of movements with ease. The two exercises here are designed to test the relative strength of the upper and lower 'halves' of your body. Poor ratings indicate that you need to work at toning and firming the major muscle groups. This is achieved through exercise.

While the number of muscle fibres per muscle is determined genetically and cannot be increased or altered, exercise will enlarge the diameter of the individual muscle fibres and increase the blood supply within the muscle, thereby increasing its overall strength. One of the major advantages of a regular, well-integrated fitness programme is that, over a period of time, it will enable you to build up both muscular strength (the ability of your muscles to exert maximum force at a given moment) and muscular endurance (their ability to perform repeatedly without fatigue). Inactivity will cause muscles to diminish in size and to atrophy, or waste away. Diminished muscle fibres not only weaken the muscle, but also make it much more susceptible to injury by sudden and unfamiliar stresses. As the joints are supported and moved by the groups of muscles on either side, weak muscles will also tend to make for weak joints that are more susceptible to dislocation or injury to some or all of the supporting ligaments.

The strength of the large muscle groups is increased by working them, either through specific types of sports or activities or by using an exercise routine that combines certain movements to persuade the muscles to contract and then to extend. The second is the more reliable method, provided, of course, that the routine is sound, because it works systematically through each of the large muscle groups in turn. The most effective way of increasing the strength of the muscles is by long-term resistant exercise that makes muscles work harder by providing a counter force. Examples are swimming against the tide or using buoys to add 'drag', bicycling into the wind or incorporating the use of weights into your exercise programme.

To test lower body strength. Start by standing with your back to the wall. Now gradually bend your knees and bring your feet away from the wall until you are 'sitting' with your thighs parallel to the floor. How long can you stay there? Over 90 seconds (60 if over 50) is good; 60 to 90 seconds (40 and 60 if over 50) is fair; less than 60 seconds (40 if over 50) is poor.

To test upper body strength. Place a table against a wall so that it is quite steady. Now, do a series of modified press-ups, with hands shoulder width apart and back as straight as possible, trying not to arch or to hollow your spine. Bend both arms and bring your chest to the table, then straighten them. Do as many as you can without straining and then stop. How many did you do? More than 15 (10 if over 50) is good; between 10 and 15 (seven and 10 if over 50) is fair; less than 10 (seven if over 50) is poor. A poor score in this area indicates that you should work at increasing the strength of your chest, arm and shoulder muscles, often weak in women.

SUPPLENESS

Suppleness is both an inherited and an acquired characteristic and is determined by the relative ease with which you can move your joints through their full, or potentially full, range of movements — to reach, stretch, bend, twist and turn with ease and grace. On the whole, women tend to be more supple than men and we all grow gradually less supple as we get older.

Touching your toes is not a good indicator of suppleness because the ability to reach the floor with your fingers is determined as much by the length of your upper body relative to the length of your legs and by the length of your hamstring muscles, as it is by your ability to 'bend in half' from the hip. Try the four tests, given here and over the page, instead.

If the tests indicate that you are naturally supple, or loose-jointed, you will excel, when fit, in those sports, such as gymnastics and yoga, that demand a high degree of suppleness. If, on the other hand, the tests indicate that you are naturally tight-jointed, you will have to work hard to acquire flexible, mobile joints.

While suppleness is certainly desirable, both extremes can have their disadvantages. The greater range of movement of the loose-jointed carries a risk of dislocation or injury through moving the joints too far. If you are very supple, concentrate

To test for suppleness at shoulders. Stand or kneel, place your left arm along your back and take your right arm over your shoulder to meet it. If you can clasp your fingers together you have good rotation at the shoulder joint; if your fingers meet, fair; if they fail to touch, poor. (Try this test on both sides, as one shoulder is frequently stiffer than the other.)

To test for spinal mobility. Kneel down on all fours. Keeping hands in line with shoulders, drop your forehead down and bring your knee up to meet it, as shown. If you can touch your head with your knee without straining, you have good spinal mobility; if they almost meet, fair; if they are some way (10 cm/4 inches or more) apart, poor.

A sensible use of weights will not over-develop your muscles. Instead, it will firm and strengthen them, thereby protecting the joints. It will also greatly improve the general line and contour of your body, particularly those areas, such as thighs, buttocks and upper arms, that tend to be most resistant to weight-reducing diets. By working muscles not commonly used in everyday activities, these exercises can help you to 'sculpt' a better body shape. Dumb-bells and weights held in the hand will strengthen chest, arm, shoulder and upper back muscles — commonly weak in women. Strap-on weights, that can be attached to ankles as well as to wrists, will strengthen the muscles in the calf, thigh and abdomen as well as in the upper body. Both types are available from most sports shops and department stores or you can improvise with cans of food or bags of sugar from your store cupboard. If you are using weights, first make sure that you are relatively fit and able to carry out your basic exercise programme without any straining of the muscles or joints, or stiffness or soreness afterwards, then increase the amount of effort you put into your exercising by incorporating weights of between 1 and 3 kg (2 and 6 lb) each. You can exceed this amount if taking part in a carefully supervised weight training programme, such as the Nautilus system which was first developed about 10 years ago and is now widely available at gymnasiums and health centres throughout the USA and in London. The system uses a series of machines to work specific isolated muscle groups — arms, chest, back, thighs, etc — and is safer than using free weights because the amount of strain is very carefully controlled. Twice weekly workouts at 30 minutes a time will have an impressive toning and conditioning effect on the body when combined with stretching and aerobic exercises, but you must use it regularly — not more than every 48 hours (the muscles need time to recuperate) and not less than every 90 hours (the muscles soon slack off if under-used).

strength of your muscles, it depends first on the strength (efficiency) of your heart and lungs. Muscles run on oxygen which arrives from the lungs via the heart — the more oxygen the muscles require, the harder the lungs and heart must work. When exercising really hard, muscles account for about 90 per cent of the body's total energy requirement. To meet this demand, the lungs must work harder to supply the oxygen the muscles need and the heart must beat faster to deliver it. Unaccustomed exertion can cause the unfit heart to double its rate. This may place unreasonable stresses upon it. Steady, regular exercise, meanwhile, will increase the capacity of the heart to pump blood through the system. Repeated studies have shown that, with regular fairly vigorous exercise, the heart muscle actually becomes stronger and may increase its output by as much as 20 per cent. By doing so, it will also lower the heart beat because, with each stroke, a greater volume of blood is being sent around the body. Athletes in training tend to have pulse rates that are as much as 20 beats lower than average.

There are several ways of building up stamina, while protecting your heart and lungs from the potential dangers of over-exertion. When you start running, jogging, swimming or cycling, intersperse periods of activity with periods of rest. Start by running for 100 metres, walking for the next 100, running again over the same distance and then walking home. Alternatively, if you are swimming, take breathers every third or fourth length rather than swimming 12 or 14 flat-out and feeling exhausted and nauseous at the end of them. As you get fitter and can manage more, prolong the distances you swim, run or jog and reduce the periods spent walking or resting.

A more scientific method of assessing your exercising capacity and keeping it within healthy limits has been developed by the Cardiac Research Unit at London's City Gym. This safe and practical method is called pulse rate control and is particularly recommended for men over the age of 35 (between 11 to 17 per cent of whom are judged to be at risk from sudden cardiac arrest without knowing it) and for women over the age of 45, particularly if they also drink or smoke heavily and are 6 kg (14 lb) or more overweight. Find instructions on using the method and a progress chart in the Personal Profile.

To test for mobility at knee and hip. Stand upright with feet apart. Keeping your back straight and your buttocks tucked well under, do a deep knee bend, keeping your heels on the floor, and return to the starting position. Do not strain the movement, just go as far as you feel is comfortable. Ability to do a deep bend with the knees well turned out to the side, to hold it for a few moments and then to return comfortably and easily to the upright position, indicates that you have good mobility at the knee and hip. Inability to bend more than a little way, with your knees tending to 'lock' after moving through an angle of 45 degrees or less, indicates that you have little rotation at the hip and knee joints – especially if you are aware of any creaking in the joints or find you cannot return easily and comfortably to the starting position. In between the two? Fair.
N.B. This test is quite demanding on the knee and should not be attempted if you have any history of knee trouble.

on building up the strength of the muscles that stabilize and support the joints, particularly the quadriceps at the front of the thigh, which protect the vulnerable knee joint. Find an excellent exercise for this on page 51. The restricted range of the tight-jointed tends to make for general stiffness and also renders the muscles more prone to strains and pulls. Concentrate on the simple lengthening and suppleness exercises, outlined in the following pages, to increase the mobility of the joints without in any way forcing them to move in an unfamiliar and potentially harmful direction. Do these regularly for at least a month before attempting any of the more demanding activities (i.e. those with high suppleness ratings, such as gymnastics or yoga).

A general loss of mobility that comes with age imposes certain, sometimes severe, limitations on the ability to move freely and easily. In order to keep joints moving freely and easily, everyone needs to build up and to maintain their suppleness, even those lucky enough to be born supple. To do this, each of the major body joints should be exercised through its complete range of movement at least three times a week and, preferably, once a day.

STAMINA

Stamina is staying power and it is the factor by which fitness is most commonly judged. Stamina enables you to go faster and further without becoming exhausted or breathless. See how good your stamina is by carrying out the test, opposite. If you did not achieve the highest rating, aim to improve it. Any type of 'aerobic', or oxygen-using, exercise will increase your stamina, if carried out for a sustained period of time over a number of weeks or months (see examples right).

While stamina depends, to a certain extent, on the

Ten examples of exercises and activities that will push your pulse rate up and so help to increase your stamina – rated here in order of effectiveness.

1. Running two miles in maximum of 16 minutes.
2. Skipping for six minutes with 30-second breathers after each minute.
3. An energetic 30-minute game of squash or racquet ball.
4. Running up and down stairs for three minutes.
5. Cycling at a moderate to fast pace for 15 minutes.
6. Swimming for ten minutes continuously.
7. A vigorous game of tennis, badminton or any other team game, such as baseball.
8. Walking briskly up a steep hill for 10 minutes.
9. Jogging for a mile in a maximum of 12 minutes.
10. Brisk walking for two miles.

To test for stamina: see how long you can skip or jog on the spot (lifting your feet well off the ground) before becoming breathless. This test is demanding, so do not attempt it unless you are fairly fit and healthy, and do not become discouraged if, even then, your rating is poor: regular, fairly vigorous exercise will help to improve it.

Skipping 1½ minutes or more (1 minute or more if over 50) is good; between 1 to 1½ minutes (½ minute if over 50) is fair; less than a minute (less than ½ minute if over 50) is poor. Double these times if you chose to jog.

To test for suppleness at ankles: sit on chair, knees together and brush big toes as far off the floor as possible. Measure the distance from the top of your toe to the floor. Was it between 12.5 and 15 cm/5 and 6 inches (good); between 10 and 12.5 cm/4 and 5 inches (fair); less than 10 cm/4 inches (poor). If rating was poor, aim to improve it with the ankle exercise on page 51.

Strong mobile ankles help to keep feet in good shape, are important for most types of activity, crucial for athletic ones.

daily exercise programme

These exercises are divided into two sections: a daily programme which combines stretching and loosening exercises (blue leotard) with strengthening and firming ones (red leotard) and a sequence at the end designed to give you a really good general workout (yellow leotard). Between them, they should exercise every muscle and joint in the body.

● The secret of success with any exercise programme is to keep at it. The most effective exercises will do little to tone muscles and firm contours if abandoned after only a week or two. Set aside five or 10 minutes each day whenever you like but never after a heavy meal. Start by working systematically through the first section and, once you have mastered the programme, repeat it twice a day rather than adding further repetitions indefinitely.

● Start gently. The blue exercises are less demanding than the red, so concentrate on these to begin with if you are very unfit. When you get more proficient, many of the exercises can be made stronger by holding the positions. Once you become acquainted with the exercises, you can concentrate on particular weak points. If you find that you are stiff at the shoulders, or have little flexibility at the feet and ankle, put more work in there. If you are slimming, be particularly conscientious with exercises for abdomen, buttocks and thighs. Take as much as you need from the programme.

Wear whatever you like to exercise in, with two provisos: you should be comfortable and you should be able to move freely. Leotard, track suit, vest and pants, a loose baggy T-shirt over tights are all good. If your knees are weak, leg warmers can be very helpful.

● These exercises are designed for relatively fit, healthy people. If you are not, ask for your doctor's approval before starting. If you have a knee condition, avoid vigorous kicking exercises. If you have a chronic back condition, consult your doctor or specialist first and stick to the first exercise only in the back section and do all leg lifting exercises with a bent, not a straight, leg. If you are pregnant, the exercises on your front are not for you. Turn to pages 202-3 for specially designed postures and exercises.

● The exercises call on two basic principles. The first is posture. Check the way you are standing, sitting, or lying before each exercise. If you are not holding yourself properly, you may not be working the appropriate muscles and joints. It is particularly important that you master the pelvic tilt (see page 34). This is integral to many of the exercises as it helps to centre the pelvis and take the strain off the lower back. The second principle is breathing. Always breathe out as you exercise — as you kick out or curl up or lean back — and in as you rest the movement. You may find that this requires some concentration to begin with, but persevere and you will find that it soon becomes a spontaneous part of the routine.

● Finally, always finish exercising with 10 minutes of total relaxation, following the progressive relaxation technique outlined on page 176.

facefaceface

Tiny muscles, not bones, shape the expression of your **FACE**. You use them to frown, to smile, to raise your eyebrows, to flare your nostrils — to produce the range of expression that adds up to your unique way of responding to people and to situations. These muscles are important for another reason too: by providing the underlying support structure for the skin, they help to keep it firm and youthful. But no muscle remains firm without use, and you must therefore exercise your face muscles just as purposefully and as systematically as those elsewhere in the body.

These exercises will also help to remove any visible signs of tension. Anxiety always registers most tellingly on the face by freezing the expression and setting the jaw. So thaw out with these exercises. If you are anxious or tense, you will find it difficult to remain so while pulling faces at yourself. If you can actually laugh, so much the better. Laughter is invigorating, stimulating, liberating — a wonderful exercise for the face and body and one of the best ways of getting the tummy muscles into shape...

Exercise the muscles of your face by running through this routine. Start by crunching your face up into your nose, as though you have smelled something unpleasant (1). Then open your mouth and eyes as wide as you can (2) and stick your tongue out to release your throat muscles so that you are doing a silent 'scream' (3). This should be marvellously stimulating and relaxing. Proceed by pulling pursed lips to left (4) and right (5), and follow with a wide Cheshire-cat grin (6). Open your eyes wide and see if you can make the grin stretch from ear to ear. Hold, release and repeat, this time tucking in your chin and pulling your lower lip down as you do it. This will help firm the muscles at the front of your neck. Now run through the whole routine again.

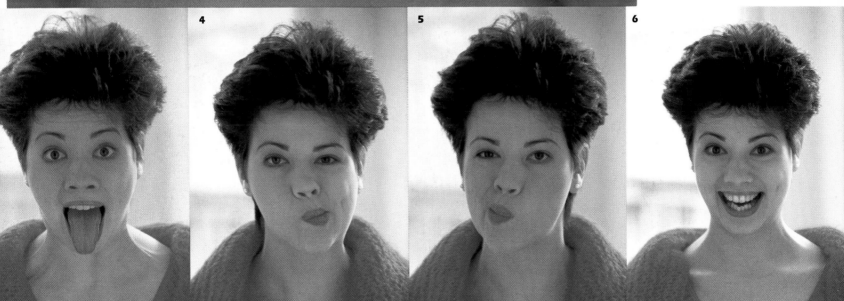

4

5

6

necknecneck

The **NECK** is remarkably delicate. It supports the weight of the head, acts as a pathway for blood vessels, central nervous system, digestive and respiratory systems, and transmits messages from the brain to all outlying parts of the body. It is also one of the most critical parts of the body when it comes to exercise, posture and relaxation.

External tensions produced by stress, anxiety or simply the habit of holding the head incorrectly (too far forward or back, too much to one side or the other) create internal tensions in the muscles that connect the neck to the shoulders, upper back and spine. Women seem to be particularly susceptible to tension and stiffness in the neck and shoulders. The purpose of the neck massage, below, and of the 'blue' stretching exercises is to persuade the tension to unlock. Commit these exercises to memory and run through them whenever you are aware of any tightness in the neck or shoulders or feel anxious and tense. You should find that it helps enormously. You can use the second exercise (2 and 3) as a barometer to see how tense you are. If you are extremely tense, the stretch you feel at the back of the neck will continue right down to the base of the spine. Either repeat the exercise gently until the tension eases or place an orange between your shoulder blades for an instant back massage (see page 176). A stretch that radiates from the neck down into the shoulder blade indicates tension in the diagonal trapezius muscle. Exercise 4 should help to release it.

Before you start these exercises, or graduate to the ones beyond them, check that you are sitting correctly. Use the picture here for reference, and bear these points in mind.

Sit squarely on the chair or stool, so your weight is evenly distributed on both buttocks (you should be able to feel the bones), your thighs apart and parallel with each other and your feet hip-width apart. Now lift your rib cage away from your hips to create as much length in front and behind as you can. But resist the temptation to pull your shoulders up too. Pull them down away from your ears and let your arms relax and hang downwards. Your shoulders should now be directly in line with your hip joints. Notice that, as you pull your shoulders down, the back of your neck lengthens freely. Hold your chin at about a right angle to your throat and enjoy the sense of lift flowing through you. Take a few good deep breaths. Now you are ready to start.

1 2 3

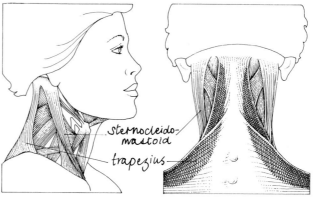

Above. Of the complex network of muscles at the neck, there are three critical ones: the narrow sternocleidomastoids at the side turn the head and tilt the chin upwards; the deep erector spinae muscles (hidden here) attach to the base of the skull and run all the way down the spine; and the trapezius muscle at the back – dark shaded areas, above right, are often tense.

sternocleido-mastoid
trapezius

Below. The neck is composed of seven vertebrae. These should follow the pattern of the first string of beads – each extending and lengthening away from the other. If the vertebrae are allowed to collapse, as in the second string, extra strain will be placed on the spine and supporting muscles.

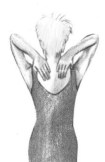

Give yourself a neck massage. Start at shoulder blades and, keeping fingers together, stroke firmly upwards.

Continue kneading around the base of neck, paying special attention to tense areas.

Finish by clasping one hand over the other and pressing heels of hands firmly on to the neck on either side. Press and release as you move hands up and down the neck.

Start with stretching exercises to free tension and spend as long as you need on them. There is little point in working the rest of the body if the neck is tense and stiff. As you do the stretches, remember that your hands are there only to add weight and so to help with the exercise, not to pull the head down. If you feel the stretch is too strong, do the exercises without using the hands.

Stretch up to ceiling (1). Reach as high as you can, relax, and repeat. Now clasp hands on back of head (2) tuck chin in and lower it towards your chest (3). Keep going until you feel a stretch in the back of your neck. Hold and then release further into it. Check breathing is free, front of neck is soft, and jaws are unclenched. Come up slowly, breathing in. Anchor one hand on to back leg of chair or stool. Place other hand on head and let head drop diagonally forwards towards your knee (4). You should feel a stretch radiating from the top of your shoulder blade diagonally upwards to the base of the skull. Hold and release further into it when you feel you can take more stretch. Repeat on the other side. To complete the neck stretches, anchor one hand as before, place your other hand over the opposite ear and lower head to side, bringing chin in and shoulders down (5). You will feel a stretch along the side of the neck. Repeat to the other side. To complete this section, a neck strengthener and anti-double-chin exercise combined. Think back to front on this one; the jawline is kept trim by muscles at the back, not the front, of the neck. Clasp hands at back of head, press the head back and pull forwards with hands at same time (6). Place two thumbs just below the base of the skull so you can feel the neck muscles tighten. Hold for a moment, release and repeat.

Counteract the effects of gravity and improve your posture permanently with these exercises. Start by resting the hands flat on the lower ribs in front (1). Now pull the arms strongly together behind you. Pull back sharply several times. This is good for firming 'bra-strap' flab at the upper back. Now clasp hands behind back (2) and squeeze shoulder blades tightly together. Repeat several times. Progress to the stronger version (3). Make loose fists and holding both arms out at shoulder level, pull the shoulder blades together. Hold, and press arms back

several times, pressing the chest forwards slightly at the same time. Repeat until you begin to tire, remembering to keep arms up at shoulder level throughout. Rest for a few moments. Arms up at shoulder level again. Pull shoulder blades tightly together and hold them there as you press arms upwards strongly several times (4). Drop arms and circle shoulders backwards.
Lying on your back, use weights of no more than 0.5kg/1lb (or improvise, as here, with two cans of food) to strengthen upper arms (5) and (6). Pull arms upwards to the vertical position and lower again. Repeat several times slowly and then more quickly. Finally, compensate with a stretch in the opposite direction (7). Clasp hands in front, drop chin forwards, round your back, and pull your hands away from you.
Repeat two or three times.

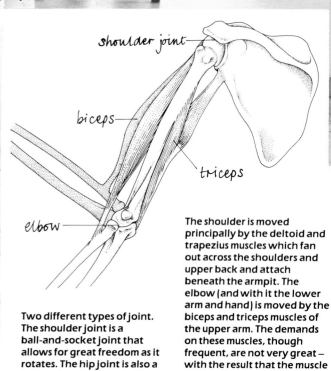

shoulder joint

biceps

triceps

elbow

Two different types of joint. The shoulder joint is a ball-and-socket joint that allows for great freedom as it rotates. The hip joint is also a ball-and-socket type but it is set much deeper in its socket and so tends to be more stable. The elbow joint, like the knee joint, is a hinge joint designed to work on one plane only.

The shoulder is moved principally by the deltoid and trapezius muscles which fan out across the shoulders and upper back and attach beneath the armpit. The elbow (and with it the lower arm and hand) is moved by the biceps and triceps muscles of the upper arm. The demands on these muscles, though frequent, are not very great – with the result that the muscle can lose its tone and become slack. But it is rewardingly responsive to exercise, particularly to exercise that incorporates the use of weights.

armsarmsarms

The **SHOULDERS** are the most mobile joints of the body. You only have to try the rotation exercise here (8 and 9) to see that you can move your shoulders through 360 degrees. This natural looseness at the shoulder has its disadvantages. It makes it much more prone to dislocation than either the knee or the hip because it has few ligaments to keep it firmly in place. Another major disadvantage is that it is possible to hold the shoulders in any number of ways that feel 'comfortable' and 'right' but that are, in reality, far from correct from the point of view of posture.

Look at yourself in a mirror, front on as well as side view. If you can see a dip between your clavicles (collar bones) and your neck or you can catch sight of your shoulder blades sticking out, all is not well. Both should lie flat. Round shoulders, which most of the population possesses, are aggravated by many factors from gravity to any occupation which encourages a slump forwards. These exercises are designed to reverse this tendency by encouraging the shoulders back and down.

UPPER ARMS are a problem area for many women. While no-one wants bulging muscles, the reverse — loose flesh caused by slack muscles on the underside of the arm — also leaves much to be desired. Happily, this is one area where exercise can count for a great deal. Carry out the upper arm strengthener exercise (10 and 11) at least twice a day and you will soon notice a difference.

The arms, like the face, are very expressive of tension, particularly the **HANDS** and the **FINGERS**. Tell-tale signs are shoulders lifted up towards the ears, arms held defensively into the body and clenched fisted hands. Next time you are anxious or upset, feel what happens to your body. Then unwind by releasing tension first in the hands (using exercise 12 and 13), then in arms, shoulders, neck, jaw. You will probably find that your mood improves as your muscles unlock. Although the hands and fingers are used constantly, they can become stiff. Counteract this by carrying out the stretching exercise daily, spacing your fingers wider apart as the joints become more flexible.

8

9

10

11

12

13

This is a good exercise for working shoulder, elbow and wrist joints simultaneously. Sit with elbows 'inside out' and palms facing the ceiling (8). Now turn the arms the right way round again, so that the palms are still facing the ceiling (9). Repeat several times. Continue with upper arm strengthener: make loose fists in front of you (10) and punch strongly back and upwards in firm movements, rotating the arms inwards so the backs of the hands face the front (11). Continue until tired and finish with a stretching exercise for the hands (12) and (13), making as much space between the fingers as possible.

frontfrontfront

There is a limit to how much exercise can do to help keep the **BREASTS** firm and well-toned, because the breast is not a muscle. As breast 'developing' exercises will not develop the breasts at all, but the pectoralis major muscle lying beneath and to the sides of them, you should avoid them if you do not want unsightly bulges at the armpit. Water therapy and massage treatments are similarly questionable 'aids' to beautiful breasts. Aim, instead, to keep the muscle toned, so providing a firm base of support for the breasts, and think in terms of preserving the shape of the ligaments known as the ligaments of Ashley Cooper, which provide the primary means of support for the breasts. Ligaments, unfortunately, do not have the elastic properties of muscle. Once they stretch, they do not spring back into shape; they remain stretched. The consequence? The breasts droop and sag. The culprit? Gravity. So, while braless is fine if the breasts are small enough and you do not move in ways that will jerk and stretch the ligaments (jogging is a major example of one that will), a good well-fitting bra should be worn at all other times.

You cannot separate the shape you are in at the front from the shape you are in at the back because each interacts with and affects the other. Think of your spine as the frame around which the rest of you is constructed and start adjusting your shape from there. Lower shoulders, lengthen spine, tuck buttocks under you and you should notice an immediate improvement at the front. Length at the spine opens the **CHEST** and makes space for the ribcage to work efficiently.

Achieve longer-term improvements through diet and exercise. Both are important. While exercising can firm the **WAIST** in a matter of weeks, it will take a good deal longer before you can expect to see similar results at the **HIPS**, where the underlying muscles are deeper.

It is important, too, to distinguish between fat at the waist and fat at the hips. Unlike the purely superfluous fold of fat at the waist, fat in the form of the natural curve at the hip is there for a good biological reason — to protect the reproductive organs. So firm up your abdomen (firming up your buttocks will do much to help, see next page), and lose weight there too if you like, but do not expect to lose it altogether.

2

To exercise muscles around the waist, sit on stool or chair, arms above head, fingers interlocked (2). Keeping shoulders down, bend first to the right (3), trying to bend further with small successive movements. Repeat to the left (4). Return to starting position (2), twist round to the side (5). Now lower right elbow towards right knee, imagining that you have a bar at your waist and have to lift your top half up and over it (6). You should feel the stretch along the left side of your back. Bend lower with small successive movements. Repeat to other side. Place hands on chest and twist from the waist so that you are looking as far around towards the back of the room as possible (7). Hold and continue in small successive movements.

Right. The breast, with the pectoralis major muscle underneath. This broad sheet of muscle should be exercised at three levels in order to keep it toned. The ligaments of Ashley Cooper, largely responsible for determining the lift and preserving the line of the breasts, attach to the fascia, or outer covering, of this muscle.

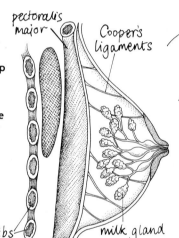

pectoralis major
Cooper's ligaments
ribs
milk gland

windpipe
lungs
diaphragm

Sit with arms crossed, as shown, and, holding the biceps firmly, press strongly inwards several times (1). You should feel a tightness beneath the breasts. Repeat at eye and waist level in order to work every part of the muscle.

1

Above. You take six litres of air into your lungs a minute while at rest, up to 180 during vigorous exercise, so you need plenty of room in which the diaphragm can contract downwards and the lungs fill with air, when necessary. Normally, breathing should be fairly slow, even and relatively deep. To see if yours is, try this exercise: place one hand on your chest, the second on your navel. While the second should rise and fall to the rhythm of your breathing, the first should hardly move at all. If it does, you are breathing from the top of your chest – a sign of anxiety and tension...

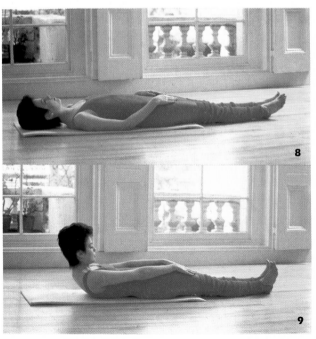

8

9

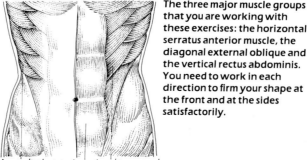

horizontal vertical diagonal

To exercise abdominal (tummy) muscles start lying on back with hands on thighs (8). Flex feet and slide hands down towards knees as you bring your head up to look at your toes (9). Hold for a few moments and release. Repeat several times. Now sit up with legs bent and feet hip-width apart. Breathe out as you bring your chin towards chest, round your back and lower your body backwards, pulling forwards with the elbows at the same time (10). Hold it at the point where you feel your abdominal muscles tightening to prevent you falling backwards. Repeat several times. Take up starting position (11), breathe out and curl up bringing arms in front (12). Start by holding for two seconds and try to build to slow count of five. Repeat several times. As you get fitter, start with hands by your sides, then fold them in front, then finally, interlock fingers behind your head. (But do not attempt to curl up beyond the head and shoulders.) Repeat this exercise to either side (13) to work diagonal abdominal muscles, pulling well across the body with the top arm each time. Starting with your hands on your ribs, let your knees roll from side to side (14), so that the twist comes from the waist and the shoulders remain quite still. Lying flat on your back, bring one hip towards the ribs so that you feel a pinching at the waist where you are working the side abdominal muscles (15). Repeat to each side several times. Finish by lifting both legs up together (16) and feel a tightening under your hand where side abdominal muscles are contracting. Repeat slowly three times on each side.

The three major muscle groups that you are working with these exercises: the horizontal serratus anterior muscle, the diagonal external oblique and the vertical rectus abdominis. You need to work in each direction to firm your shape at the front and at the sides satisfactorily.

backbackbackback

BACKS need careful looking after. The spine, susceptible to the strain of simply standing upright, is soon weakened by poor posture and a sedentary, inactive lifestyle.

Exercises can help to keep your back strong and healthy by working the intricate network of muscles that support the spine, but these must be bolstered by good posture all the time. 'Corrective' exercises for a bad or damaged back should only be attempted under the strict supervision of an orthopaedic specialist and for this reason are not given here. If you do have a weak back or a previous history of back trouble, take these exercises very gradually. Start with a bent leg (4) and graduate to the more advanced exercises only when you feel that you have mastered the first ones. See page 35 for exercises that all but the fittest and the strongest should beware of if they want to safeguard their spines.

Of these exercises, those that involve lifting the head and shoulders will mainly work the muscles of the upper back, while those that involve lifting the legs will mainly work the lower back muscles and the gluteus muscles of the buttocks and backs of the thighs (see illustration on page 50). ALWAYS stretch out the muscles of the back after working them strongly, with the spine stretching exercise shown here (13).

Think of the **BUTTOCKS** as part of the back. Firm strong buttocks, integral to a healthy back and to good posture, are also extremely important in determining the general line of the body. Slack buttock muscles creeping round the side can add considerably to a bulge below the hips and at the sides of the thighs. While any exercise routine will help to firm up the buttocks (they are worked simply by lifting the legs), a specific buttock strengthener (such as 12) is of especial benefit. If your buttocks are slack — and they certainly are if you cannot see a definite 'dent' at the side just beneath the hip — do this exercise several times a day. The results will be rewarding. The buttock muscles, being broad and relatively shallow, are particularly responsive to exercise. Differences can often be seen in weeks, rather than months.

Work shoulders and upper back by lying on floor with hands interlocked on bottom (1). Lift head and shoulders off mat as you pull hands downwards. Look up (2) and hold for a few moments. Lower head again and repeat several times. This is a marvellous corrective exercise for over-rounded upper back and shoulders.

The spine is composed of vertebrae placed like building bricks one on top of the other. Safeguard your spine by holding it so that each vertebra lengthens away from the next.

To strengthen the lower back and buttocks, work through each of the exercises, progressing to the next only once you have mastered the one before it. Start with forehead on the hands. Have legs hip-width apart. Bend your legs (3), and slowly lift them alternately, up to six times if you can (4). Progress to straight legs and lifting alternately (5). Now place a cushion under your pelvis (6) to take any strain off your lower back. Lift one leg, then the other, as (5), then lift both legs together (7) and, finally, take legs apart (8) and lift them several times. Then describe wide circles in clockwise and anti-clockwise directions with both legs. Discard cushion, stretch arms out (9), and perform a 'diagonal arabesque', lifting alternate arms and legs off floor, looking up as you do so (10). Try to get the upper arm and thigh as far off the floor as possible. Lying in starting position (9), tighten buttocks and lift arms and legs off the floor simultaneously (11). Look up, hold for a few moments and lower. ALWAYS finish back work by curling up into a ball (13). Exercise buttocks by sitting on a chair or stool, rounding the back and pressing thighs downwards so buttocks pull firmly together (12). Release and contract several times, slowly and quickly.

legslegslegs

Exercise, rather than diet, is responsible for improving the shape of the legs. Shedding extra weight may help to slim thighs by removing extra pounds, but it is unlikely to make a significant difference unless accompanied by exercise. Loose flesh, not fat, is the culprit and this is produced by insufficiently exercised muscles. Firm these up, and you could be amazed at the difference.

THIGHS can be slimmed down with a series of exercises that work all the major muscles of the upper leg. These comprise the group of hamstring muscles at the back of the thigh, the deeper underlying adductor (contracting) and abducter (extending) muscle of the inner and outer thigh and the large group of four muscles, known as the quadriceps, at the front (see below). This group is particularly important because it maintains strength and ensures stability at the **KNEE** — a vulnerable and unpredictable joint. Swimming is excellent for streamlining and toning the upper legs. Alternate a vigorous crawl kick with a backstroke one for best effect.

CALVES are common victims of high heels, poor posture and unwise exercising. Always loosen muscles at the back of the calves before and after any exercise that is at all demanding on legs or knees, such as jogging. Incorporate a few deep knee bends and/or stretching exercise 10 into your warming up routine.

Your feet are likely to carry you more than 70,000 miles during the course of your lifetime and so are worth looking after properly. This means keeping **ANKLE** joints mobile, **FEET** strong and supple. It means standing and moving properly too. Think of your feet as a tripod, with the weight of your body descending into the feet via the ankles and radiating out between the heels and the big and little toes. With the weight thus evenly distributed, the foot is freed from any incorrect pressures (provided, of course, that your footwear is good). If, however, the feet are at all weak, the ankle joints stiff or the shoes ill-fitting, you are asking for any number of problems from corns to backache, so beware.

Work outer thighs and hips by lying on side (1), with body and legs perfectly in line. Raise leg (2), keeping foot flexed and knee facing forwards. Do not aim for great height, as this will mean turning leg out from the hips, so defeating the object of the exercise. Lower leg to half-way position (3) and raise again slowly.

quadriceps

adductor

front

gluteus

hamstrings

back

The muscles at the front of the hip and thigh, far left, and on the back of the hip and thigh, left, which include the gluteus muscles of the buttock.

1

2

3

4

12

13

14

15

Continue for at least 10 lifts. Feel it all the way from hip to outside of knee. Repeat to other side. Exercise back of thighs and buttocks by lifting leg half-way up (3) and then pressing it back, letting shoulder and hip drop forwards (4). Raise and lower half way 10 times. Repeat on other side.

Strengthen the inner thighs by lying, as shown, with a large cushion between the knees (5). Press firmly. Hold for a slow count of five before releasing. Repeat three times. Then do 10 quick squeezes. Strengthen front of thighs by sitting with hands on hips and back rounded (6). Flex foot, bend knee and kick out vigorously (7). Go on until the leg feels tired and well used. If your knee is weak, bend and stretch without kicking and skip the next exercise. Stand, holding on to a wall, and bend the knees (8). Bounce lightly up and down. Continue until you tire. This is an excellent pre-skiing exercise.

Work the metatarsal arch along the base of the toes, by clenching toes inwards (12) and then spreading them apart as much as possible (13). Now work the instep (longitudinal arch) by placing feet firmly on the floor and lifting up from the middle, while keeping the toes and the heels on the floor (14). Exercise ankles: sit with knees together and heels apart. Bring big toes together (15), trying to lift them up as much as possible. Then brush outwards along the floor again, pulling little toes upwards and pressing big toes down (16). Repeat until ankles and calves tire.

Strengthen calf muscles by going up on to balls of feet, bringing heels half-way down to floor and going up again (9). Continue until you feel a pull in your calves. Stretch out the muscle by standing as shown (10) and, keeping knee in line with heel on forward foot, press your back heel down until you feel the stretch along the back of the calf. If cramp or soreness strikes in the calves, hold scarf or towel around balls of feet and pull towards you to stretch the muscle and so ease the tightness (11).

51

movemovemove

Start with a salute to the day: a really big stretch, arms straight, feet hip-width apart (1). Stretch one up further, then the other, several times. Next circle each arm backwards in wide circles to loosen shoulders, follow by circling both arms together and then bend forwards from hip and swish arms through legs (2). Bend your knees as you do this if you have a weak back. Repeat three or four times, before returning to starting position (3). Reach up to ceiling and bend to sides, keeping arms straight (4), so that you feel the stretch along your side, not in your back. Bend from side to side rhythmically several times. Now build a sequence, circling

the body in one continuous movement. Bend (4), then twist into a diagonal forward stretch (5), continue down to brush past ankles (6), repeat diagonal stretch and side bend to other side and return to starting position stretching up. Make four circles each way, stretching as much as you can. Drop into 6 and swing loosely from side to side. Now try this marvellous body loosener. Start with arms extended out to sides (7) and swing around, bending knee as you go (8) and focusing on something on a wall behind you. This will help prevent you from getting dizzy. Repeat to other side (9) and continue twisting from side to side until you feel really warmed up.

● These general body conditioners will exercise all major muscle groups and joints and give heart and lungs a good workout too. But you should be relatively fit before starting. If you have not taken any exercise for a long time, spend two weeks practising each of the basic exercises illustrated on the previous pages every day before you graduate.

● The sequence should be fun to do. Work, first, at getting to know the movements and establishing a good rhythm. Then go, using whatever music you like — jazz, pop, classical, blues — to help you. Once you have a rhythm to your routine, you can start to improvise. Add a few deep knee bends, twists, turns, jumps, leaps or leg swings…keeping each new movement controlled and precise and letting it flow expressively into the next. While the sequence is flexible, it is important to keep to the basic framework. Always warm up into the jogging and wind down properly afterwards, finishing with the progressive relaxation routine outlined on page 176.

3 4 5 6

0 11 12

Now you are ready for the jogging. Before you start, do at least four deep knee bends, keeping your heels on the floor, to stretch out calf muscles. Begin simply by transferring your weight from foot to foot, lifting the heels only (10). Continue by lifting and stretching each foot (11). Then start to jump lightly from foot to foot, gradually lifting legs higher. Finish with the ultimate test: place arms out in front (12), and bring thighs up to touch as you spring from foot to foot – avoiding temptation to bring hands down to meet them. Always emphasize the upward spring. Continue until comfortably out of breath.

13

14

15

16 **17** **18**

Whether inside in the gym or outside on the track, never stop exercising abruptly. Warm 'down' instead with this series of loosening and stretching exercises to keep joints supple and to prevent muscles from becoming stiff. Start with this 'rowing' sequence: sit on the floor with straight back, arms extended out to sides (13). Breathe in. Bend forwards towards feet and breathe out (the bend should come directly from the hip joint) (14). Breathe in and return to starting position (13). Breathe out as you round the back and curl backwards with arms crossed over in front (15). Breathe in as you return to starting position (13). Continue with a series of straight leg kicks, starting on back (16) and proceeding through the side (17) and front (18), before ending on the opposite side. Try to do 12 of each. Finish with this newer version of the traditional press-up. Start on all fours, back straight. Breathe in. Breathe out as you bend one leg and bring knee and forehead inwards to touch (19).

19 **20** **21**

(This is also a good test for spinal mobility, see page 37.) Breathe in and extend leg back, lifting head (20). Breathe out, lowering elbows and chin to floor (21). Breathe in as you come up, leg still extended behind, and prepare to start again. Repeat twice slowly and four times quickly on each leg. To finish, curl up in a ball, breathe well and relax.

55

sportsportsport

Jogging: one of the easiest and most flexible of all the aerobic alternatives. To get into shape: start by walking briskly for five to eight minutes, intersperse with brief stretches of jogging, and gradually build up by shortening periods of walking, extending periods of running, until after three or four months you are running 20 or 25 minutes non-stop three times a week.

Details of common sports and activities are given here, together with relative exercise value ratings, and basic cautions. Approximate calorific 'burn-off' values are also given – but they are approximate. The amount of energy you burn off depends, first, on the effort you put into it, and, second, on your size to begin with (the larger you are, the more you burn).

SPORT OR ACTIVITY	SUPPLENESS	STRENGTH	STAMIN...
WALKING (brisk) 300-350 calories an hour	*	*	**
JOGGING (steady) 360-420 calories an hour	*	**	***
RUNNING (moderate to fast) 500-600 calories an hour	**	***	****
CYCLING (brisk) 300-420 calories an hour	**	**	****
SKIPPING 150 calories for 15 minutes	*	**	***(*)
TENNIS AND BADMINTON (energetic) 300-400 calories an hour	***	**	**
SQUASH AND RACQUETBALL up to 650 calories an hour	***	**	***(*)
SWIMMING (fairly energetic) 540 calories an hour (800 crawl)	***	**	***
YOGA 180-300 calories an hour	****	**(*)	*
GYMNASTICS 380 calories an hour	***	***	**
SKATING (ice or roller skating) 500 calories an hour	**	**	**(*)
SKIING downhill (up to 600 calories an hour) cross-country (up to 1,200)	***	***(*)	**(**)
RIDING 200-400 calories an hour	*	**	**
FENCING 350 calories an hour	***	**	**
WATER SPORTS (water skiing, surfing, wind surfing) 400-700 calories an hour	*	**(**)	**(*)
WEIGHT & CIRCUIT TRAINING up to 800 calories an hour	***	****	**

OMMENTS	CAUTIONS
Walking has good toning effect on foot and calf muscles and is good gentle exercise for everyone. Aim to walk 5-6.5 km (3-4 miles) per day. Walking makes a valuable 'interval' pace when jogging or running – much better than stopping and starting again.	Remember to look where you're going.
Jogging will exercise heart and lungs and strengthen calves. It will do little to tone thighs or abdomen or to improve all-round mobility because it only exercises the hip, knee and ankle joints in a limited way, upper body not at all. To jog: stand up straight with arms hanging loosely by your sides, elbows bent, and push off from the ball of your foot and land on your heels. (You do not exercise your thigh muscles by running on the balls of your feet.) Build up as detailed, opposite.	Always warm up before jogging, warm down afterwards (see previous pages). If hip, knee or ankle joints are at all weak, use elasticated bandage for additional support, particularly if jogging on hard surfaces. Make sure that your shoes offer good support and are high-soled at the heel to protect the foot and absorb the shock (the heel takes five times the weight of the body each time it contacts the ground). Wear a bra to prevent breasts sagging. If you have heart, lung, back or joint problems consult your doctor before starting.
A wider running stride and swinging arms make for much more extensive and efficient movement of legs, arms and shoulders than jogging. Build up as jogging.	Ankle or knee joints unused to the demands of running may be sprained or injured, while sudden bursts of speed may result in sore, strained hamstrings (the muscles at the back of the thigh). Use a good pair of running shoes (see above) and elasticated bandages, too, if necessary. Always start slowly and cautiously. (See also jogging.)
Good, vigorous cycling over a period of 40 minutes or more will exercise heart and lungs, tone buttocks, front of thighs and calf muscles, and will increase flexibility at the knee and ankle. Start gradually if very unfit.	Go for conventional handlebars, not the curved racing ones which encourage a forward movement, and may put considerable strain on the lower back. Warm up first and stretch out calves afterwards (page 51) to prevent sore, stiff muscles.
Skipping can be a very useful part of any fitness programme, provided that it is built up gradually. Start by skipping in 30-second bursts, interspersed with short rest breaks of three to five minutes, and progress to skipping in one and a half minute bursts for 10 to 15 minutes.	Skipping is very demanding on the feet, ankle and knee joints and on the heart and lungs, so you should be reasonably fit and supple first. If you are tight-jointed or feel any jarring when you jump, use elasticated bandages for additional support.
An energetic game of tennis or badminton will exercise heart and lungs, promote flexibility in some, but not all, joints and strengthen shoulders, forearms (playing arm only), thighs and calves. Good players combine suppleness with strength for agility: the ability to turn and twist with speed. Skill, judgement, co-ordination and timing are also important.	The asymmetrical practice of serving and hitting the ball or shuttlecock with the same arm tends to make for uneven muscle tone and development. For best effect, combine with another more balanced sport, such as swimming. Sudden position changes may result in strains to muscles or twists and sprains to ankles, knees or elbows.
Squash and racquetball are more strenuous than tennis (hence higher stamina rating).	Both types exercise the heart and lungs quite vigorously, so make sure you are fairly fit first. Wear a protective visor: squash balls travel at speeds of up to 80 mph . . .
Water is the perfect exercise medium. Its buoyancy enables you to work muscle groups frequently missed out by other sports or activities; the resistance doubles the effectiveness of the exercise and the water supports your weight, so removing any risk of strain. Start slowly, resting every third or fourth length, building up until you are swimming 30 minutes without stopping. Different strokes have different exercise values; alternate them for best effect. The crawl is marvellous for improving the overall line of the body and the best for heart and lungs. Back butterfly exercises chest, thigh, arm and shoulder muscles. Backcrawl tightens abdominal muscles, slims inner thighs and upper arms. Sidestroke tones waist, legs and arms. Breaststroke is a great upper body strengthener (an area most women do not exercise enough).	Swimming is a marvellous exercise during pregnancy, but avoid breaststroke, as the wide leg action can put an additional strain on the sacro-iliac joints at the base of the spine. Try backcrawl and crawl instead.
Yoga is excellent for suppleness and, as you get better at it and able to hold the postures for longer, good for strengthening most of the large muscle groups. Start by using the postures on pages 178-9 and, if keen to pursue it further, seek instruction from a qualified teacher.	Build up general mobility first, particularly if generally stiff and tight-jointed. Remember that if you have to force your body into a position, you could be exerting unreasonable strains on it. In addition, observe all the more specific cautions on page 178.
Size and shape are important factors. On the whole, small, compact people tend to be better at gymnastics than longer, leaner types. This is probably because the centre of gravity is lower – giving additional stability and better balance.	Gymnastics are best suited to young and fit individuals who have the additional advantage of softer, more flexible bones should they fall or land awkwardly. Gymnastics are very physically demanding, so always increase your general level of fitness first.
Skill, balance and a degree of suppleness are very important – whether skating on four wheels or one thin blade. Also important: strength in the leg muscles and resilience.	Do not be too ambitious when starting out. When roller skating, protective clothing, including padding at the knees and elbows, will help to minimize the impact of falls.
Brackets apply to cross-country skiing – one of the most demanding forms of exercise.	Ankles, knees, and hip joints must be flexible for both forms of skiing and the leg and abdomen muscles strong. Get into shape well before you start – strong enough, ideally, to enable you to hold the wall sit (page 37) for three minutes or more.
First requirements are skill and a certain amount of courage. While ability counts for more than strength, riding is good for inner calf and thigh and will improve balance and posture.	Start by taking lessons and always wear a hard hat, however experienced or inexperienced you are.
Speed, agility and timing are important, not great strength. Fencing can be practised by anyone, provided that they are fairly flexible first. Fencing is very good for posture.	If tight-jointed, very unfit or stiff, increase your level of suppleness first. Proper protective clothing and qualified instruction are essential.
Water skiing strengthens leg muscles and increases flexibility at the knee; wind surfing strengthens upper body and is more generally demanding (hence the higher rating).	Instruction is essential for water skiing and wind surfing, helpful for surfing. You must be a competent swimmer before attempting any of these sports.
Weight training (not weight lifting) is one of the best ways of firming and toning areas that other types of exercise seem to leave untouched, such as upper arms and inner thighs. Provided that it is responsibly supervised, weight training will not over-develop muscles.	Weight training must be carried out under supervision, started gently and built up gradually to avoid placing unreasonable strains on any of the muscles or joints involved. You should also be relatively fit before starting (see also pages 36-7).

nutrition

'Tell me what you eat and I will tell you what you are.' **Anthelme Brillat-Savarin**

Eating well means eating in a balanced, moderate and unanxious way. If this does not describe the way you normally eat, then your eating habits and, probably, your attitudes towards food require a certain amount of revision. (Check both of these by completing the nutrition tests in the Personal Profile before you start.)

The basics of good, healthy eating are simple, need not be expensive or unnecessarily time-consuming, and can be summed up as follows:

1. Make sure that you are getting good quality protein, especially if you are vegetarian.

2. Regulate and balance the amount of fat you eat.

3. Eat plenty of fresh fruit and vegetables (preferably raw).

4. Cut out most refined flour from your diet and replace it with wholegrains.

5. Make sure that you are eating enough fibre.

6. Cut out as much refined sugar from your diet as possible.

7. Eat less salt.

8. Drink plenty of water. Watch your intake of coffee, tea, cola drinks, refined soft drinks and alcohol.

9. Balance your food intake over the day and enjoy your food.

Ways in which you can achieve these objectives are outlined in the following pages. If your eating habits are way off these, be realistic, do not expect to be able to change them overnight. Give yourself three months in which to relinquish your bad habits and to adopt better ones — and to lose some weight if you need to. You will be reassured to find that it is possible to diet while learning the principles of good nutritious eating, so establishing a healthy framework that can be carried into your normal, non-dieting way of life. Once you have overhauled your eating habits, return to the nutritional profile and check your progress by seeing how you score.

FIRST PRINCIPLE — PROTEIN

The ideal proportions of any diet are 55 to 65 per cent carbohydrate, 25 to 35 per cent fat and 10 to 15 per cent protein. Although the percentage of protein is the smallest, it is one of the most crucial components of the diet, necessary to growth and to the repair and replacement of different body tissues. The need for protein is highest when the body is growing, such as during childhood, puberty or pregnancy, and lowest in adulthood. Adults do not require great quantities of protein. In fact, as little as 45 g/1½ oz of protein a day is now thought to be enough, provided that the quality is right.

Although protein is often equated with a large, rare steak, it is found abundantly in other foods. Some plants, such as the soya bean, actually have more protein, weight for weight, than roast beef. But quantity is not the major consideration. Of the 22 amino acids necessary to body function, there are eight which the body cannot make. These are found exclusively in protein-containing foods although, confusingly, not all protein-containing foods contain all eight amino acids. Eggs provide a nearly perfect amino acid balance, although relatively 'low' in protein. Fish and meat come next, then cheeses, milk, grains and legumes (soya beans and sprouts, mung beans, lima beans, peas, kidney beans, etc). Nuts and seeds provide relatively low quality protein. The best way of ensuring that you are getting all the protein you need? Eat a varied and balanced diet — and it need not necessarily be a carnivorous one.

Vegetarianism

Studies have shown that vegetarians tend to be healthier and slimmer, to have lower blood cholesterol levels, and to live longer than their meat-eating peers. Although one reason for this may be that vegetarians, as a group, are more conscientious about their health than the general population (few smoke, for example), it convincingly puts paid to the myth that a diet lacking in meat is a depleted one.

There are two different types of vegetarians. The first group are the ovo-lacto vegetarians, who eat no animal flesh but eat animal produce. For this group, diet is no problem, as long as it is nutritious. Alternative protein sources, found in milk, cheese and eggs, are abundant. Supplementation of iron, vitamin B12 (only if very little milk is drunk) and vitamin D in winter, principally found in fish oils, may be necessary during pregnancy. The second group are the vegans, who eat no animal produce whatsoever. This diet will take more manoeuvring if it is not to be protein or mineral deficient. This is particularly crucial for children and pregnant women. All strict vegetarians should be aware of protein-rich vegetable sources and how best to balance them for healthy eating, combining grains (rice, wheat and corn) with legumes (peas, beans, etc), as these have a complementary amino acid make-up. Vegans should also be aware that they need foods high in iron (all dark green vegetables, watercress, cabbage, whole grains, cocoa) and calcium (sesame seeds, all green vegetables) and should take extra vitamin B12 (available in non-animal form) to guard against pernicious anaemia, extra vitamin D in the winter (during summer it is synthesized naturally by sunlight), and a zinc supplement if eating large amounts of soya.

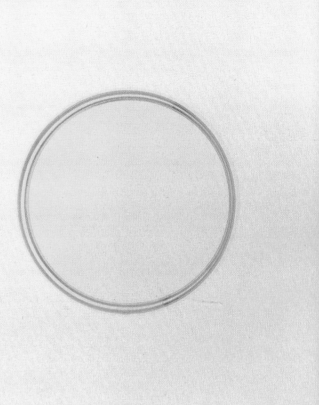

SECOND PRINCIPLE — FAT

Fat is important in the diet. It provides one of the most concentrated sources of energy; it is essential for healthy teeth and bones and for brain function; it is a vital natural source of the fat-soluble vitamins, A, D and E, and, lastly, it makes food palatable and pleasant. In general, as the standard of cooking rises, so does the proportion of fat used.

While we all need some fat in the diet, we do not need the excessively high amounts that many people consume daily. These may affect blood cholesterol levels, constituting one predisposing factor to coronary heart disease, and will certainly cause you to put on weight — a sizeable health risk on its own. Fat leads to fat — carbohydrates, despite their reputation, are much less likely to.

Aim to reduce the total amount of fat in the diet from the average 40 to 45 per cent to about 30 per cent. In addition, replace some saturated fat with polyunsaturated fat. Such adjustments need not entail any radical changes in your

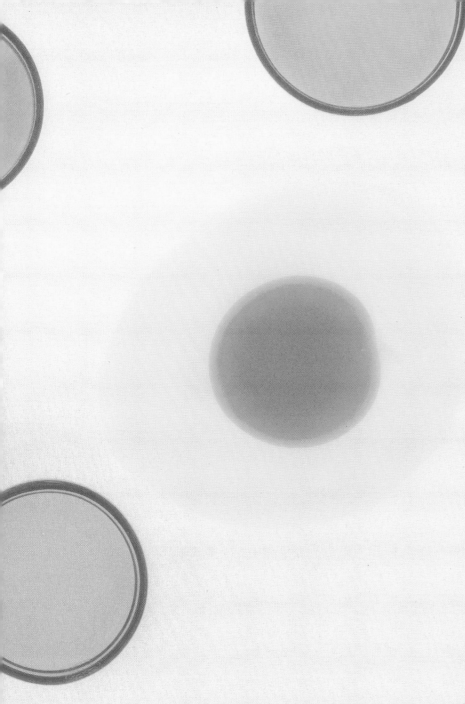

bread. Substitute polyunsaturated for saturated oils and lard when cooking or when making dressings.

● Take cream and top of the milk in moderation. If you are slimming, or have been advised to watch your intake of fats, avoid both and substitute skimmed for whole milk.

Which fats are which?

Saturated fatty acids are solid fats principally, though not exclusively, of animal origin. Milk, butter, meat and cheese are obvious examples. Because some plants and vegetables, notably coconut and cocoa, are high in saturated fat, an oil labelled simply 'vegetable oil' or a margarine containing 'edible oils' is not necessarily polyunsaturated and may, in fact, contain high amounts of saturated fat. Fats and oils that are normally unsaturated may become saturated when hardened through hydrogenation. These include hard margarines, lard, suet, etc. Saturated fatty acids have been shown to raise blood cholesterol levels.

Polyunsaturated fatty acids (PUFA) are found in some, but not all, vegetable oils. Rich sources are sunflower, safflower, corn (maize) and soya bean oils and some soft margarines. Chicken and fish oils are also rich sources and most nuts, except coconut, contain some. Interest in these fatty acids stems from the fact that they lower blood cholesterol levels.

Cholesterol is an essential precursor of cell metabolism and we all need it to function properly. Of all the cholesterol in the blood, only 25 per cent arrives via the diet. The rest is synthesized inside the liver, under the control of the stress-sensitive adrenal glands. Although cholesterol is not commonly found in foods — exceptions are egg yolks, offal, such as liver, kidney, brain and heart, and some types of shellfish — some foods, such as those containing saturated fats and sugar and alcohol in excessive quantities, can raise blood cholesterol levels. A number of other factors can also do this. These are obesity, smoking, excessive stress, physical inactivity, and the contraceptive pill.

These independent risk factors can add up to a sizeable one when combined, especially if you are male and middle-aged or female and have passed the menopause. In fact, it is becoming increasingly apparent that the much talked-about 'protective effect' conferred by the female sex hormones before the menopause is progressively whittled away by factors such as smoking. Heart disease and heart problems are not, as was once thought, an all-male preserve. As women's lifestyles become more highly pressured — and similar in many ways to those of men — these illnesses are showing a significant increase. So, whatever your sex, take steps now to eliminate risk factors within your control, such as smoking (now considered the major risk factor) overweight and inactivity. In addition, if you come within the age category given above, you should watch your intake of dietary cholesterol and saturated fat. Eat no more than one meat meal a day, restrict the number of eggs eaten to three a week, and substitute polyunsaturated margarine for butter and polyunsaturated oils for animal fats when cooking.

eating habits. Simply follow the guidelines given here. Do not become obsessive or fat 'phobic'. Saturated fats and cholesterol are not synonymous with heart attacks. Eggs, butter, milk and meat are all excellent sources of energy. In the wake of the great cholesterol controversy, it is worth remembering that the egg remains the best quality protein food there is.

● Eat less red meat and more poultry and fish. Choose lean meat and remove all visible fat before cooking. To find out which are the leaner and which the fattier types of meat and fish, turn to page 74. Grill rather than fry, bake or casserole rather than roast.

● Eat eggs in moderation, but do not feel that you have to exclude them from your diet. A sensible limit would probably be seven eggs a week. If you come within the 'at risk' category, or have been advised to watch your cholesterol intake, restrict yourself to three eggs a week.

● If you prefer the taste, by all means use butter on your

THIRD PRINCIPLE – FRUIT AND VEGETABLES

Fruit and vegetables tend to be high in carbohydrates (starch and natural sugar, or fructose), rich in vitamins and minerals and low in protein and fat. Together with grains and pulses (legumes), they should form the bulk of the diet and, to get maximum nutritional mileage, at least half should be raw. This will ensure that you are getting important vitamins and minerals —the elusive potassium, in particular —that tend to be destroyed or leached out during cooking. Fruit and vegetables should also be fresh: the closer they are to their natural state, the higher in vitamins and minerals and the more nutritious they will be. It is well worth looking around for shops that buy their produce fresh every day.

The way in which you prepare and cook your vegetables will also determine how nutritious they are. While overcooking is the greatest crime, there are other, less obvious ways in which goodness can be depleted. Follow these guidelines to get the best from your vegetables.

● Scrub rather than peel. Essential vitamins and minerals tend to be concentrated in the peel, rather than in the flesh, of the vegetable. The peel also provides more fibre and seals in flavour.

● Break vegetables into rough pieces or chop them into large slices. Dicing or shredding vegetables with a steel blade will deplete vitamin content.

● Only prepare as much as you need. Leave the rest whole (do not immerse in water) and keep in the refrigerator.

● Preferably, cook by boiling in a minimum of water in an ordinary saucepan or pressure cooker. This method is now thought preferable to steaming. Avoid roasting or frying.

● Add the vegetables to the water only once it is boiling and then cook as lightly and briefly as possible. Soft, soggy vegetables that do not need chewing are overcooked.

● Avoid adding baking soda to give 'colour' to green vegetables and do not use copper pans or utensils. Both dramatically reduce vitamin C levels.

● Do not throw away the cooking water, as some vitamins and minerals will always be leached out during boiling. Use it, instead, for making soups, sauces and gravies.

● Once the vegetable is ready, eat it immediately. Do not leave it for ages in a warming oven and try to avoid reheating.

FOURTH PRINCIPLE – GRAINS

A grain of corn in its natural state consists of three parts —the inner heart or germ, the starchy centre and the bran or outer husk. The first and the last of these are removed during the milling and refining processes, the germ because it contains a small amount of oil which shortens the shelf-life of the finished product, and the bran because it is coarse-textured and, therefore, considered undesirable. This is a pity because these are the two most nutritious parts of the grain, rich in B vitamins, essential trace minerals, protein and fibre.

If you want to benefit from the goodness in the original grain, you should buy wholegrain products — rice, bread, flour, pasta — and use them whenever you would use their refined equivalents (except when baking and making sauces, if you prefer a finer, lighter texture): At the very least,

you should incorporate two pieces of wholemeal bread into your diet each day. This is extremely nutritious in its stone-ground wholewheat form — a rich brown flour that contains every part of the grain. Combine these two slices with an imaginative filling (see suggestions on page 74), and you have a complete, satisfying meal that provides all the nutrition the body requires. Bread is more, not less, important when dieting as it provides essential carbohydrate and bulk and will help to guard against constipation, an occupational hazard to most dieters.

FIFTH PRINCIPLE – FIBRE

Fibre is the indigestible carbohydrate found on the outsides of foods — concentrated in the peels and rinds of fruits and vegetables and in the outer layers of grain. Although fibre contributes nothing in terms of nutrients to the diet, it is important because it controls and regulates the process of food absorption and enables the food to pass easily and smoothly through the gut, protecting against constipation, haemorrhoids (piles), appendicitis, diverticular disease and now, it is thought, certain types of cancer, obesity and coronary heart disease. Food that is high in fibre combines with water in the stomach and swells into a soft and spongy mass that can travel easily through the intestines, where it is gradually broken down and metabolized. Food that is lacking in fibre is much more rapidly broken down and has a difficult and constipated journey along the gut and out of the bowel. If this is the type of food you eat, you may be increasing your chances of succumbing to one or more of the diseases listed above and may well be suffering from constipation.

The list of foods, right, gives relative fibre contents. Although fresh fruit and vegetables provide relatively low sources of fibre when compared with pulses (legumes), nuts and dried fruit, recent research suggests that pectin, the type of fibre concentrated in the peel of some fruits, such as apples and plums, may be valuable because it appears to contain a cholesterol-lowering factor. Unprocessed bran is by far the highest natural source of dietary fibre.

If you do suffer from constipation, give the laxatives a rest. Try the fibre-rich muesli cereal given on page 71 and/or one tablespoon of unprocessed bran on your food, gradually increasing to two or three, if it does not have any effect.

SIXTH PRINCIPLE – SUGAR

On average, we eat 140g (5oz) of sugar a day, and some children and sweet-toothed adults eat three or four times as much. The consequences are overweight, tooth decay, maturity-onset (sugar-related) diabetes, kidney and even, perhaps, coronary heart disease. Resolve to cut out all or, at least most, refined sugar from your diet today, and you will be much slimmer and much healthier for it.

The metabolism of sugar in the body is regulated by the pancreas and the adrenal glands. The first lowers blood/sugar by releasing insulin which converts what sugar is needed into usable glucose for energy and stores the rest away in the form of glycogen (starch) in the liver. The second raises blood/sugar levels once they fall below a certain level by releasing hormones, principally cortisol, capable of un-

% Fibre in foods

Bread and flour	
Bread (white)	2.7
Bread (wholemeal)	8.5
Crispbread (rye)	11.7
Flour (plain white household)	3.4
Flour (100% wholemeal)	9.6
Oatmeal	7
Rice	2.4
Wheat bran	44
Cereal and pastries	
All Bran	26.7
Cornflakes	11
Doughnuts	0
Muesli	7.4
Pastry	2
Rich fruit cake	3.5
Vegetables	
Cabbage (raw)	3.4
(boiled)	2.8
Carrots	2.9
Celery	1.8
French beans	3.2
Haricot beans	7.4
Lettuce	1.5
Peas (frozen)	12
(fresh)	5.2
Potatoes (boiled)	1
(baked with skin)	2
Fruit and nuts	
Almonds	14.3
Apples	2
(apple peel)	3.7
Apricots (raw)	2.1
(dried)	24
Brazil nuts	9
Dates	8.7
Desiccated coconut	24
Figs (raw)	2.5
(dried)	18.5
Lemon juice	0
Lemons, whole	5.2
Orange juice	0
Oranges	2
Peanuts	8.1
Prunes	16.1
Raisins	6.8

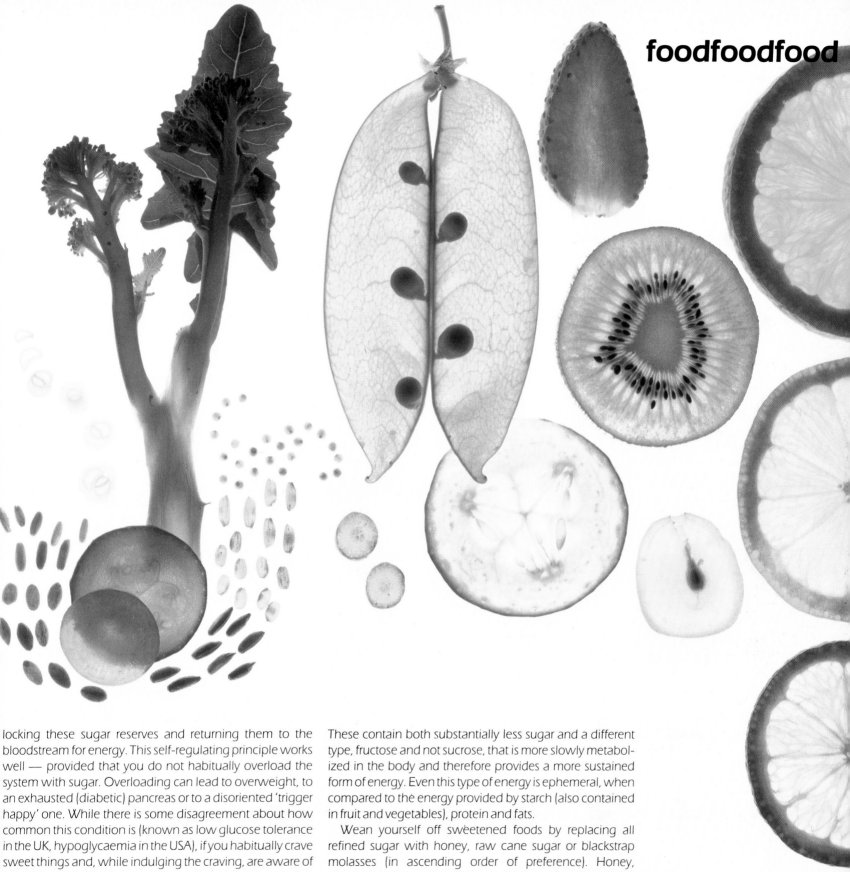

locking these sugar reserves and returning them to the bloodstream for energy. This self-regulating principle works well — provided that you do not habitually overload the system with sugar. Overloading can lead to overweight, to an exhausted (diabetic) pancreas or to a disoriented 'trigger happy' one. While there is some disagreement about how common this condition is (known as low glucose tolerance in the UK, hypoglycaemia in the USA), if you habitually crave sweet things and, while indulging the craving, are aware of mystifying mood swings and fluctuations of energy during the day, they may not be as mystifying as all that. Try cutting sugar out of your diet entirely for two weeks, eating little and often, substituting protein or fat for sugars and starches (cheese instead of biscuits, for example) and see how you feel.

Find alternative sugar sources in fruit and vegetables.

These contain both substantially less sugar and a different type, fructose and not sucrose, that is more slowly metabolized in the body and therefore provides a more sustained form of energy. Even this type of energy is ephemeral, when compared to the energy provided by starch (also contained in fruit and vegetables), protein and fats.

Wean yourself off sweetened foods by replacing all refined sugar with honey, raw cane sugar or blackstrap molasses (in ascending order of preference). Honey, although delicious, is nothing more than diluted sugar (25 per cent water, 75 per cent sugar and the merest trace of other nutrients) and has enjoyed a long, but quite undeserved, reputation as a 'health' food. Raw sugar and molasses are thought to be more nutritious, as they contain some vitamin B, together with other nutrients stripped out during the process of sugar refining.

SEVENTH PRINCIPLE – SALT

Most of us eat far too much salt — an average of between two and two and a half teaspoons a day, more than 20 times the body's needs. This quantity is exceeded only by the Japanese, who eat half as much again and have an unequalled record of hypertension (high blood pressure) and stroke to show for it. Both these conditions have now been strongly linked to an excessive amount of sodium in the diet.

Some sodium, probably as little as 1 g (0.04 oz) a day, is essential to the healthy functioning of the body because, together with another mineral, potassium, it regulates water balance. Too little salt and essential water is lost through sweat or in the urine and the body dehydrates.

Most of us, however, are much more likely to have too much salt in the body rather than too little. In addition to high blood pressure, high amounts of salt in the diet can lead to bloating and discomfort, particularly before a period, because it is so water-absorbent. A teaspoon of salt is said to be able to hold 70 times its weight in water.

In order to reduce salt consumption to a healthier 5 g (0.2 oz) a day, you will probably have to cut your intake by three-quarters. Here are some ways in which you can achieve this.
- Avoid processed foods —all hidden sources of salt—and avoid eating excessive amounts of seafood, smoked meat or fish and salted meats, such as bacon and corned beef.
- Avoid processed and smoked cheeses, which tend to be twice as high in salt as natural, hard, cheeses.
- Use unsalted butter.
- Add a minimum of salt to the cooking water when boiling vegetables and add it only in the last few minutes of cooking time.
- Reduce the amount of salt you use when making soups, stews, casseroles and other meat or vegetable dishes. Experiment with herbs and spices to add and enhance flavour.
- Taste, then season. If you habitually add salt to your food without tasting it first, you are certainly eating far too much. Taste it first, add a small amount of salt to the side of the plate and gradually wean yourself off it.
- Never add salt to the food of young children. It is an acquired taste not a natural preference. Adding salt to baby foods may actually be dangerous as a baby's kidneys are not strong enough to handle it.

EIGHTH PRINCIPLE – WATER AND DRINKS

Water is undoubtedly the healthiest way of quenching a thirst. It is also essential to the functioning of the body, because it maintains the fluid balance, both inside and outside the body cells. The 2 litres/3½ pints (USA 4½ pints) of water that is lost a day through perspiration and in the urine must be replaced. Drink at least eight glasses of water a day, straight from the tap or in its bottled mineral form.

Coffee and tea are fine in moderation, not in excess. This is because they contain caffeine, which acts as a stimulant by releasing the 'stress' hormone noradrenaline (norepinephrine) into the system. Although we tend to equate caffeine with coffee, a strong cup of tea contains the same amount of caffeine as a cup of coffee made from ground beans, and slightly more than a cup of instant coffee. Caffeine is also found in cola drinks. Too much tea, coffee or cola will make you nervous and jumpy, may interfere with the digestion and the absorption of vitamins and minerals, such as iron, can have a bad effect on the skin and may rob you of up to two hours sleep. Because caffeine is a drug, you can become 'addicted' to it. Withdrawal symptoms are irritability, agitation and headache. While this type of addiction is linked to relatively high coffee or tea intake (11 or 12 cups a day), smaller amounts may still have a significant effect. Restrict the number of cups you drink to three a day and drink them early in the day, so that they will not interfere with your sleep at night.

If you are a tea or coffee 'addict', try replacing tea with herbal infusions (tisanes) and coffee with the decaffeinated variety or one of the numerous coffee substitutes available from health food stores. Alternatively, try floating a wedge of lemon on a cup of hot, boiled water and drink it first thing in the morning. The freshness and slight acidity of the water may remove the desire for the muddier taste of tea and coffee.

Refined soft drinks, carbonated and still, contain large quantities of sugar and/or saccharin and high levels of phosphates. Too much phosphorus can interfere with the absorption of other minerals that the body needs for good health. Make your own soft drinks, instead, by blending fresh fruit with a little honey or liquid sweetener to taste, and topping with soda or mineral water. If you have a blender, these drinks can be made in minutes (see recipes on page 188).

Alcohol is pleasant and enhances the enjoyment of any meal. Taken in moderation, it will help to relax you and will give your digestion system the chance to work well and properly. Taken in excess, it will rob you of appetite and may seriously undermine your health . Women are particularly at risk to the physical ill effects of alcohol. Balance is the key. Find guidelines in the Lifestyle chapter.

NINTH PRINCIPLE – BALANCE

Most nutritionists recommend a large breakfast, an adequate lunch and a small dinner, so that protein and energy needs are met in the early part of the day and not concentrated in the last few hours when you are unlikely to be able to digest and absorb the food you eat before going to bed. There is more than a little wisdom in all this. Experiments have repeatedly shown that the body's ability to metabolize and digest protein and other nutrients deteriorates as the day wears on, that we make more efficient use of our food at breakfast time than we do at dinner.

The value of eating three 'good' meals a day, however, is not so clear cut. In most people, cues for eating derive from contractions, or 'hunger pangs', of the stomach muscle which are in turn prompted by lowered levels of sugar (glucose) in the blood. These hunger contractions occur at three-to-four-hourly intervals — though they can extend to six when fasting. This means that, if you sleep for eight hours, are up for 16 and act on your biological rather than your cultural food cues, you will probably eat four or five meals a day.

While some people manage to synchronize biological food cues happily with cultural ones, others do not. Such people will either suppress their natural hunger messages, probably over-eating at the next meal to 'compensate', or will indulge them guiltily on 'guilty' foods (sweet fattening snacks rather than nutritious 'mini' meals) because the indulgence is seen not as natural but as a weakness. An interesting British study looking at blood/sugar levels in both men and women after fasts of 24 hours or more has shown that women's blood/sugar levels tend to fall more rapidly after long periods of non-eating. If the same applies, albeit less dramatically, to day-to-day eating, it may do much to explain why women tend to feel hungry more frequently than men and why they are particularly prone to snacking between meals.

If you have never managed to adjust happily to a conventional three-meal-a-day framework, start by considering what your natural eating pattern is. Let your body 'free run' for a week or two, and allow it the space to adopt its own eating schedule. You should find that, with a bit of flexibility, you can adapt fairly easily to it. This need not be unnecessarily anti-social because you can always time your eating phases to coincide with at least one main meal a day.

Whether eating at conventional meal times or not, do try to balance your food intake over the day, so that you get your main source of nourishment and, particularly, protein before 2 pm, and taper off towards nightfall. You should also try to set aside at least 30 minutes for your meals when you can relax. Nervous energy and anxiety interfere both with appetite and with digestion and will affect your ability to get the most from your food.

Whatever you are eating, savour its taste and enjoy its flavour. Indulge your appetite for taste, smell and colour. Think of food as an adventure — experimenting with new ways of cooking and with unusual herbs and spices. Even familiar foods can be novel and exciting when cooked in a different and unfamiliar way. The recipes that follow should give a lead.

APPROXIMATE COMPONENTS OF WEEKLY DIET

eggs	between 3 and 7 times
liver	1-2 times
fish	3 times
meat	5 times
poultry	2-3 times
raw vegetables	7 times
cooked vegetables	12 times
fruit (raw and cooked)	18 times
cheese	4-5 times
yoghurt	almost daily

foodfoodfoodfoodfood

menusmenusmenus

	LUNCH	DINNER
Sunday	*Lunch with friends* * Aubergines (Eggplant) with Mozzarella * Braised Veal with Basil New Potatoes Mangetout (Snow Peas) * Prune Mousse	* Lentil Soup with Yoghurt * Watercress Omelette Tomato Salad Grilled Feta Cheese
Monday	* Cold Borsch (en Gelée) * Grilled Chicken Wings with Yoghurt or Garlic Sauce Green Salad Fresh Fruit Salad	* Spinach, Mushroom and Bacon Salad Gnocchi Baked Tomatoes Baked Apples with Cream/Yoghurt
Tuesday	* Vegetable Bouillon Grilled Liver and Onions Carrot Purée * Compote of Dried Fruit	* Caponata Grilled Mackerel Tomato Salad Pink Grapefruit and Kiwi Fruit
Wednesday	Leek Vinaigrette * Stuffed Peppers with Yoghurt or Garlic Sauce Fresh Fruit	*Dinner Party* * Seviche of Sole or Scallops Roast Beef with *Horseradish Sauce Purée Potatoes Steamed Marrow (Squash) * Floating Islands
Thursday	* Braised Fennel Cold Beef Salad Potato and Onion Cake *Cucumber with Yoghurt * Apple Snow	* Eggs with Watercress Sauce *Chicken with Herb Sauce (summer) or * Chicken Couscous (winter) Orange Salad and/or Sorbet
Friday	Chicken Noodle Soup or Chicken Couscous Soup Lentil Vinaigrette with Smoked Sausage, or Hard-boiled Eggs Cheese	* Fresh Tomato Soup *Steamed Prawns (Shrimp) with Vegetables or * Poached Rainbow Trout Yellow Sauce (2 versions) Melon with Limes
Saturday	* Salade Niçoise (summer) or *Chicken Liver Pilaff (winter) * Mango Fool	*Supper Party with Friends* Crudités with * Ricotta Sauce * Shabu-shabu Baked Apricots with Cream/Yoghurt

---

BREAKFASTS: three alternatives, to be varied.

1. ½ grapefruit
   1 slice wholemeal bread with butter and honey
   Tea
2. Yoghurt with a whole unpeeled apple grated into it
   2 oatcakes with butter and honey
   Tea
3. Homemade muesli (see recipes)
   1 crispbread with butter and honey
   Tea

ALTERNATIVE (PACKED) LUNCHES

Monday	Raw spinach and grilled bacon sandwich, on wholemeal bread Yoghurt, nuts and/or raisins
Tuesday	Chicken salad (chopped celery, carrot, apple, chicken and watercress in yoghurt dressing, with herbs) Brown bread and butter Fruit
Wednesday	Raw mushroom salad, or sandwich in wholemeal bread Water biscuits (crackers) with low-fat cream cheese and chopped herbs
Thursday	Cold roast beef sandwich, with horseradish sauce, in wholemeal or rye bread Cucumber and yoghurt salad Fruit
Friday	Hot chicken soup in flask Lentil vinaigrette with sliced smoked sausage or hard-boiled egg Yoghurt

*The Recipes

SUNDAY

Aubergines (Eggplant) with Mozzarella

Metric/Imperial/American
2 large aubergines (eggplant)
salt
1 Spanish onion
500 g/1 lb tomatoes
olive oil
freshly ground black pepper
sugar
125 g/¼ lb mozzarella, thinly sliced

Cut the aubergines (eggplant) in 1-cm (½-inch) slices, salt them and leave to drain in a colander. Cut the onion in half, then cut each half into 3-mm (¼-inch) slices. Divide the slices into rings. Peel the tomatoes, discard the seeds and juice and cut the flesh in strips like the onion.

Heat some olive oil in a broad, heavy frying pan and fry the aubergine (eggplant) slices until brown on both sides. Place the

slices on a flat dish and keep warm. Add more oil to the pan and cook the onion until soft, then add the tomatoes and cook the mixture a few minutes more. Season with salt, black pepper and a little sugar. Spoon the tomato and onion mixture over the aubergine (eggplant) slices and top with the sliced cheese. Bake in a moderate oven (180°C, 350°F or Gas Mark 4) for 30 minutes. *Serves 4.*

Right: Braised Veal with Basil

Braised Veal with Basil

Metric/Imperial/American
1.5 kg/3½ lb rolled shoulder of veal
40 g/1½ oz/3 tablespoons butter
1 large onion, thinly sliced
1 large carrot, thinly sliced
3 stalks celery, thinly sliced
150 ml/¼ pint/⅔ cup dry white wine
150 ml/¼ pint/⅔ cup chicken stock
sea salt and freshly ground black pepper
5-6 sprigs basil, when available, or
    watercress
2 tablespoons potato flour, or rice flour
75 ml/⅛ pint/⅓ cup single (light) cream

Brown the veal all over in the butter in a heavy casserole. Remove the veal and set aside. Put the sliced vegetables in the casserole and sweat them gently for 6 minutes, then lay the veal on top of them. Heat the wine and stock together and pour over the veal. Add sea salt and black pepper, and cover with foil and the lid. Simmer very gently, allowing 40 minutes per 500 g/1 lb, from the time the liquid starts to bubble. This can be done either on top of the stove, or in a moderate oven (160°C, 325°F or Gas Mark 3).

When done, remove the veal and stand, covered, for 5-10 minutes before carving, while you make the sauce. Strain the juices into a jug, reserving the vegetables. Make a bed of the vegetables on a shallow dish and keep warm. Remove the fat from the cooking juices, and pour half into another jug. Measure 150 ml/¼ pint/⅔ cup into a small bowl and cool, standing in a sink half full of cold water. Reheat the remainder with most of the basil (or watercress), reserving about 12 large leaves. When it simmers, cover and remove from the heat, leaving to infuse while you carve the veal. Cut the veal in medium thin slices and lay them over the bed of braised vegetables. Put the potato flour (or rice flour) in a bowl, and mix to a smooth paste with the cooled stock. Remove the branches of basil from the hot stock, and pour the thickened mixture into the same pan. Stir over gentle heat until it starts to bubble; cook very gently for 4 minutes, adding sea salt and black pepper to taste, also the cream. Pour enough of the sauce over the veal to almost cover it, and serve the rest separately in a sauceboat. Cut the reserved basil (or watercress) leaves in strips, using scissors, and scatter over the surface of the veal.

This can be served either hot or cold. If serving cold, do not carve the meat and assemble until all is cold, then serve at room temperature (do not chill). If the veal is to be served hot, accompany with new potatoes and mangetout (snow peas); if cold, with hot new potatoes and a green salad. Serves 5.

Prune Mousse

Metric/Imperial/American
250 g/½ lb prunes
cold tea, to cover
50 g/2 oz/¼ cup sugar
1 tablespoon lemon juice
3 egg whites, stiffly beaten

Soak the prunes overnight in the cold tea. Add the sugar and cook them slowly in the soaking liquid, until soft. Cut out the stones (pits) and put the flesh in a blender or food processor with enough juice to make a thick purée. Stir in the lemon juice and fold in the stiffly beaten egg whites. Pour into a buttered 900 ml/1½ pint/3¾ cup soufflé dish and bake for 25 minutes in a moderate oven (180°C, 350°F or Gas Mark 4). Serve at once. Serves 4-5.

Lentil Soup with Yoghurt

Metric/Imperial/American
125 g/¼ lb/½ cup brown lentils
125 g/¼ lb spinach
1 onion
1 clove garlic
2 tablespoons sunflower-seed oil
sea salt and freshly ground black pepper
300 ml/½ pint/1¼ cups yoghurt
juice of ½ lemon

Wash the lentils carefully and cover with cold water. Bring to the boil and cook gently until almost tender, about 45 minutes. Wash and slice the spinach. Add the spinach to the lentils and cook for another 15 minutes, or until both vegetables are tender.

Chop the onion and garlic and sauté in the oil. (Add the garlic about 5 minutes after the onion.) When golden, add with the oil to the rest of the soup. Put in a blender or food processor and process until smooth, then pour into a bowl and leave to cool. When cold, stir in the yoghurt. Add lemon juice to taste. Serve very cold. Serves 6.

Watercress Omelette

Metric/Imperial/American
1 bunch of watercress
50 g/2 oz/¼ cup butter
8 eggs
sea salt and freshly ground black pepper

Use only the tender sprigs of watercress, discarding the tougher ends. Wash and drain well, leaving them whole, then pat dry in a cloth. Divide in 2 equal parts.

Heat half the butter in an omelette pan and cook half the watercress until wilted, about 2 minutes. Pour on 4 lightly beaten eggs, seasoned with sea salt and black pepper, and cook gently until set. Do not attempt to fold, simply slide on to a hot dish. Repeat the process with the remaining ingredients. Each omelette will serve 2.

MONDAY

Spinach, Mushroom and Bacon Salad

Metric/Imperial/American
250 g/½ lb young (summer) spinach
175 g/6 oz/1½ cups mushrooms
125 g/¼ lb streaky bacon rashers
freshly ground black pepper
4-5 tablespoons sunflower-seed oil
1½ tablespoons white wine vinegar

Wash the spinach well, removing the stalks, and cut the leaves across in 1-cm (½-inch) strips. Pile in a salad bowl. Wipe the mushrooms, discard the stalks, and slice the caps. Lay over the spinach. Fry the bacon slowly until very crisp, drain well on soft paper, then crumble or chop in small bits. Scatter over the mushrooms. Add black pepper — salt will not be necessary — and dress with the mixed oil and vinegar. Serve immediately. Serves 4.

Spinach, Mushroom and Bacon Salad

Cold Borsch (en Gelée)

Metric/Imperial/American
1 kg/2 lb raw beetroot (beet)
sea salt
½ Spanish onion, thinly sliced
600 ml/1 pint/2½ cups good chicken stock
2-3 tablespoons lemon juice
25 g/1 oz powdered gelatine

Start 36 hours in advance. Scrub the beetroot and chop in a food processor, or by hand. Put it in a pressure cooker with roughly 900 ml/1½ pints/3¾ cups very lightly salted water. Bring to the boil and cook for 30 minutes under pressure. (Alternatively, cook for 1½ hours in an ordinary pan.) Strain the juice, throwing away the chopped beetroot. Measure the juice; you should have about 600-750 ml/1-1¼ pints/2½-3 cups.

Put the sliced onion in the beetroot stock when it has cooled, then leave overnight in the refrigerator. Strain again, and mix with the chicken stock, reserving 150 ml/¼ pint/⅔ cup. Dissolve the gelatine in the reserved stock, then mix with the rest of the soup. Strain once more, then chill in the refrigerator until set. This makes a firm jelly, which should be roughly chopped with the edge of a palette knife and served piled up in soup cups or glass bowls.

This recipe makes enough for 6-8 people. It is not worth making in small quantities, and it keeps well for a day or two in the refrigerator. Serves 6-8.

Grilled Chicken Wings

Metric/Imperial/American
1 kg/2 lb chicken wings
4 tablespoons olive oil
juice of 1 lemon
1-2 cloves garlic
sea salt and freshly ground black pepper
yoghurt, to serve

1-2 hours before cooking, line the grill (broiler) pan with foil and rub it with oil. Lay the chicken wings on this and pour over them the olive oil and lemon juice. Crush the garlic and spread over the chicken; sprinkle with sea salt and black pepper. Turn over once or twice while marinating, then grill (broil) slowly, allowing about 8-10 minutes on each side. They should be very well browned, almost slightly charred, on the outside, but not over-cooked within. Serve with a bowl of plain yoghurt and a green salad. Alternatively, omit the garlic in the marinade and serve with a garlic sauce (see below). Serves 4.

Garlic Sauce

Metric/Imperial/American
300 ml/½ pint/1¼ cups yoghurt
2 cloves garlic
½ teaspoon sea salt
1 tablespoon chopped fresh mint, or
    ½ teaspoon dried mint (optional)

Beat the yoghurt until smooth. Stir in the crushed or pounded garlic and the sea salt. Add mint, if desired. Chill before serving. Serve with grilled chicken wings, or stuffed peppers. Makes 300 ml/½ pint/1¼ cups.

TUESDAY

Caponata

Metric/Imperial/American
500 g/1 lb aubergines (eggplant)
salt
1 small onion, chopped
about 150 ml/¼ pint/⅔ cup olive oil
3 stalks celery, chopped
250 g/½ lb/1 cup tomatoes, skinned and chopped
12 green olives, stoned and chopped
1 tablespoon capers, drained
freshly ground black pepper
½ tablespoon sugar
2 tablespoons white wine vinegar

Cut the unpeeled aubergines (eggplant) in cubes about 1-cm (½-inch) square. Put them in a colander and sprinkle with salt; weigh down lightly and leave to drain for ½ hour. Cook the onion gently in 2 tablespoons oil in a sauté pan. When it starts to colour, add the celery. A few minutes later add the tomatoes; cook slowly until thickened, adding the olives, capers, pepper, sugar and vinegar.

Heat the remaining oil in a broad pan. Dry the aubergines (eggplant) cubes and fry until soft and golden brown. Lift out with a slotted spoon and add to the other vegetables. Mix well, pour into a shallow dish and leave to cool. Serve at room temperature. *Serves 4 as a first course.*

Vegetable Bouillon

Metric/Imperial/American
1 large leek, quartered
2 large carrots, halved
2 stalks celery, quartered, with leaves
2 large tomatoes, halved
2 stalks parsley
a few stalks watercress
a few lettuce leaves
900 ml/1½ pints/3¾ cups water
1 teaspoon sea salt

Put all the ingredients in a pressure cooker and bring to the boil. Cook for 30 minutes under pressure. Strain, adjust seasoning as necessary, and serve either hot or chilled. Two tablespoons freshly cooked rice may be added, if desired. (If you do not have a pressure cooker, add 1.2 litres/2 pints/5 cups water to allow for evaporation, and cook for 1½ hours in an ordinary saucepan.) *Makes 900 ml/1½ pints/3¾ cups. Serves 4.*

Compote of Dried Fruit

Metric/Imperial/American
250 g/½ lb mixed dried fruit: apples, pears, apricots, peaches, prunes, figs
2 tablespoons raisins
½ teaspoon grated orange rind
½ teaspoon grated lemon rind
1 tablespoon sugar
juice of 1 orange
2 tablespoons coarsely chopped almonds
whipped cream and yoghurt, to serve (optional)

Soak the fruit for an hour or two if necessary. Cover with cold water, or the water in which it has been soaking, and cook quite quickly, until soft but still whole. The timing varies widely according to the quality of the fruit; it should only take about 15 minutes.

At the end of the cooking, add the raisins, the grated rind and the sugar. Leave to cool, then stir in the orange juice and the chopped nuts. If there is too much juice, lift out the fruit and nuts with a slotted spoon, leaving the juice in the pan. Boil up the juice until it is reduced to the right amount. Only add the orange juice after cooling. Serve warm, or after cooling, but do not chill.

For special occasions, serve with a bowl of whipped cream and yoghurt folded together, in equal parts. *Serves 4.*

Above right: Floating Islands
Below: Caponata

WEDNESDAY

Stuffed Peppers

Metric/Imperial/American
1 medium onion, chopped
3 tablespoons sunflower-seed oil
1 clove garlic, crushed
2 tablespoons pine kernels (nuts)
125 g/¼ lb/1 cup rice
600 ml/1 pint/2½ cups chicken stock
2 tablespoons raisins
salt and freshly ground black pepper
a pinch of mace or grated nutmeg
a pinch of cinnamon
2 tablespoons chopped parsley
4 peppers
25 g/1 oz/2 tablespoons butter
yoghurt or garlic sauce, to serve

To make the filling, cook the onion in oil in a frying pan until slightly coloured. Add the garlic and the pine kernels, and cook for another 2 or 3 minutes. Add the washed rice and stir around until coated with oil. Pour on 300 ml/½ pint/1¼ cups heated stock, and add the raisins, salt, pepper and spices and simmer until the rice is almost tender, about 15 minutes, stirring now and then. Cool.

To prepare the peppers, cut a thin slice off the top and remove the interior membrane and all the seeds with a small sharp knife. Rinse with water to remove any remaining seeds. Spoon in the stuffing when it has cooled, and stand the peppers upright in a deep dish with a lid. Heat the remaining stock with the butter and pour on. Cover with the lid or a double layer of foil and cook in a moderate oven (180°C, 350°F or Gas Mark 4) for 45 minutes. Serve hot or cold with a bowl of yoghurt or garlic sauce. *Serves 4.*

Seviche of Sole or Scallops

Metric/Imperial/American
2 medium sole, skinned and filleted, or 8 large scallops
150 ml/¼ pint/⅔ cup fresh lime or lemon juice, or a mixture of both
1 tablespoon finely chopped shallot
1 tablespoon finely chopped parsley
1 tablespoon sunflower-seed oil

Cut the fillets of sole into diagonal strips about 1 cm (½ inch) wide. If using scallops, discard the orange tongues and cut the white part into 1-cm (½-inch) slices. Put the sole or scallops into a bowl and pour over the citrus fruit juice; there should be almost enough to cover them. Place in the refrigerator for anything from 12 to 24 hours, stirring occasionally.

Just before serving, drain off the juice and stir in the finely chopped shallot and parsley. Add a little oil, just enough to moisten them without leaving a pool in the bottom of the bowl, then divide the fish between 4 individual dishes. (Flat scallop shells are ideal; the curved ones are a little too big.) *Serves 4 as a first course.*

Horseradish Sauce

Metric/Imperial/American
4 tablespoons/¼ cup yoghurt
2 tablespoons sour cream
1 tablespoon freshly grated horseradish
2 teaspoons white wine vinegar
freshly ground black pepper

Mix the yoghurt and sour cream together, stir in the grated horseradish and vinegar, and add a little black pepper. Serve with hot or cold roast beef. *Serves 4.*
Note: for an extra low-fat version, use 6 tablespoons/⅓ cup yoghurt and omit the sour cream.

Floating Islands

Metric/Imperial/American
3 eggs, separated
4 tablespoons/¼ cup vanilla sugar
450 ml/¾ pint/2 cups milk

Beat 2 of the egg whites until stiff, and fold in half the sugar to make a meringue mixture. Have a large broad pan of water at simmering point. Drop in tablespoons of the meringue mixture, a few at a time, so that they do not touch each other. Poach gently, barely simmering, for about 3 minutes, then turn them over with a skimmer and poach for a further 2-3 minutes. Lift them out and drain on a cloth (paper will stick) while you poach the rest. When drained, lift off the cloth on to a plate and place in the refrigerator.

Beat the egg yolks with the remaining vanilla sugar. Heat the milk until almost boiling and pour on to the yolks. Place the bowl over a pan of boiling water and stir until slightly thickened, about 12 minutes. Cool quickly in a sink half full of water, stirring to prevent skin forming. Refrigerate for a few hours. To serve: pour the custard sauce into a shallow dish and lay the meringues on it. *Serves 4-5.*

THURSDAY

Braised Fennel

Metric/Imperial/American
3 heads fennel
25 g/1 oz/2 tablespoons butter
200 ml/⅓ pint/⅞ cup stock (chicken, game or vegetable)
1 tablespoon lemon juice
salt and freshly ground black pepper
extra 1 teaspoon butter
1 teaspoon flour

Trim the fennel, cutting off any discoloured leaves and scrubbing well under running water. Cut each root in half and lay them in one layer in a sauté pan. Cut the butter in small pieces and scatter over the fennel. Pour over the stock and add the lemon juice, salt and black pepper. Cover with the lid and cook very gently on top of the stove for 1½-2 hours, turning the fennel over from time to time, and adding more stock if necessary. When the fennel halves are soft (test by piercing them with a fine skewer) transfer them to a shallow dish then thicken the juice slightly by stirring in the butter and flour which you have mixed to a paste. Stir until smooth and pour over the fennel. *Serves 4-6.*

Cucumber with Yoghurt

Metric/Imperial/American
300 ml/½ pint/1¼ cups yoghurt
½ large cucumber
sea salt and freshly ground black pepper
a few drops of Tabasco

Beat the yoghurt until smooth.

Peel the cucumber and cut in small cubes. Stir into the yoghurt, adding sea salt and black pepper, and a dash of Tabasco. Serve with cold beef or barbecued or tandoori chicken. *Makes 450/¾ pint/2 cups.*

Apple Snow

Metric/Imperial/American
4 medium Bramleys (Greenings), peeled and cored
sugar
2 egg whites
whipped cream, to serve

Slice the apples and cook with a very little water and sugar to taste until soft. Push through the medium mesh of a vegetable mill. Cool, then fold in 2 stiffly beaten egg whites. Pile into glasses and serve with cream. *Serves 4.*

Eggs with Watercress Sauce

Metric/Imperial/American
2 bunches watercress
450 ml/¾ pint/2 cups chicken stock
2 tablespoons potato flour, or rice flour
sea salt and freshly ground black pepper
3 tablespoons single (light) cream
7 tablespoons yoghurt
6 hard-boiled eggs

Chop the watercress coarsely, stalks and all, and put in a saucepan with the chicken stock. Bring to the boil and simmer for 5 minutes, then cool slightly. Strain off 150 ml/¼ pint/⅔ cup of the stock, and put the rest of the mixture in a blender or food processor. Process until reduced to a purée, then return to the clean pan.

When the reserved stock has cooled, stir it gradually on to the potato flour (or rice flour) in a small bowl, beating with a small wooden spoon until a smooth paste is formed. Add this to the watercress purée in the pan, stirring until it is incorporated. Heat slowly until it simmers, stirring constantly, then cook very gently for 4 minutes. Add sea salt and black pepper to taste, and the thin cream. Remove from the heat and after a few moments, stir in the yoghurt.

Have the shelled eggs (hot) lying in a shallow dish, and pour the watercress sauce over and around them. Serve in shallow bowls. *Serves 4.*

Chicken with Herb Sauce

Metric/Imperial/American
1.5-1.75 kg/3½-4 lb chicken
8 thin leeks
3 long thin carrots
1 onion
4 stalks celery
1 bay leaf
sea salt
5 black peppercorns
2 tablespoons potato flour, or rice flour
4 tablespoons single (light) cream
4 branches chervil or dill

Put the chicken in a pressure cooker with the green ends of the leeks, 1 halved carrot, 1 halved onion and 1 stalk celery. Add the bay leaf, sea salt and black peppercorns, and enough hot water to cover the legs of the bird. Bring to the boil and cook under pressure for 20-25 minutes, depending on the size of the bird. (Alternatively cook in an ordinary pan for 1-1¼ hours.)

Lift out the chicken and boil up the contents of the pan for about 5 minutes, to reduce the quantity and strengthen the flavour. Cut the white parts of the leeks in long thin strips; cut the remaining 2 carrots and 3 stalks of celery likewise. Lay them in a steamer and cook over the boiling chicken stock for 3-4 minutes, until halfway between crisp and tender. Remove immediately and lay on a shallow serving dish; keep warm.

Carve the chicken in neat strips, free from all skin and bone, and lay crosswise over the vegetables. Strain the stock, and cool 150 ml/¼ pint/⅔ cup quickly by standing in a bowl of iced water. Pour this slowly on to the potato flour (or rice flour) in a small bowl, mixing to a paste with a wooden spoon. When smooth, pour it into 300 ml/½ pint/1¼ cups of the remaining stock, skimmed of fat, add the cream and heat slowly in a pan. Stir constantly while heating, and simmer for 4 minutes. Remove from the heat, and put in the branches of chervil or dill, after removing a heaped tablespoon of the best leaves. Cover and leave to infuse for 5 minutes. Meanwhile, chop the reserved leaves. Discard the branches of chervil or dill, and pour the sauce over and around the chicken. Scatter the chopped herb over all. Serve with steamed new potatoes and a green salad. *Serves 4-5.*

Chicken Couscous

Metric/Imperial/American
350 g/¾ lb couscous
1.5 kg/3½ lb chicken, jointed
6 small onions, peeled
4 leeks, thickly sliced
4 carrots, thickly sliced
2 stalks celery, thickly sliced
4 courgettes (zucchini) unpeeled and thickly sliced
6 tomatoes, peeled
1 packet (¼ teaspoon) saffron
sea salt and freshly ground black pepper
225 g/½ lb chick peas (garbanzos), pre-soaked and cooked (optional)

Put the couscous in a bowl and pour over it 450 ml/¾ pint/2 cups cold water. Leave for 10 minutes to absorb.

Put the chicken in a deep pan (or the bottom of a *couscoussière*) with the peeled onions left whole. Cover with 1.5 litres/2½ pints/6¼ cups hot water and bring slowly to the boil, skimming off any scum that rises. When boiling point is reached, and the surface is clear, add the leeks, carrots, and celery, all cut in thick slices. Tip the couscous into a colander or strainer lined with muslin (or the top of the *couscoussière*), and lay over the boiling stock. Cover with a lid and keep boiling steadily but gently for 30 minutes.

Lift off the couscous and add the courgettes (zucchini), also cut in thick slices. Stir the couscous, breaking up any lumps, and replace over the stock. Ten minutes later, add the whole peeled tomatoes to the bottom

Chicken with Herb Sauce

pot; after another 5 minutes, remove from the heat. Tip the couscous into a heated dish and break up any lumps with a fork. Lift off the fat from the surface of the stock, and stir in the saffron, and sea salt and pepper as needed. Lift out the pieces of chicken, discard the bony parts of the carcase, and lay the nice pieces over the couscous. Add the chick peas (if using) to the vegetables, reserving a few to scatter over the couscous. Reheat briefly, then tip into a large tureen and serve together with the couscous.

Serve in soup plates, with knife, fork and spoon. Any remains can be used to make a marvellous soup. *Serves 6.*

69

FRIDAY

Fresh Tomato Soup

Metric/Imperial/American
750 g/1 ½ lb ripe tomatoes
600 ml/1 pint chicken stock, free from all fat
sea salt and freshly ground black pepper
1 teaspoon sugar
1 tablespoon lemon juice, or to taste
2 tablespoons chopped basil, chervil, or dill (when available)

Skin the tomatoes and cut in quarters. Heat the chicken stock in a large pan and, when it is nearly boiling, drop in the tomatoes. Add sea salt, black pepper and sugar, bring back to the boil and simmer for 5 minutes only. Push through a medium mesh food mill (or wire strainer) to retain the seeds, then return to the pan to reheat. Add more salt and pepper if needed, plus a little lemon juice. Serve in cups, sprinkled with chopped basil, chervil, or dill. *Serves 4.*
Note: For a cold soup, serve chilled, with a lump of ice floating in each cup, and omit the herbs.

Below. Steamed Prawns (Shrimp) with Vegetables

Steamed Prawns (Shrimp) with Vegetables

Metric/Imperial/American
16 giant prawns (shrimp), or large scampi
3 long thin carrots, cut in long thin strips
3 straight courgettes (zucchini), cut in long thin strips
1 bunch large spring onions, cut in long thin strips
2 leeks, cut in long thin strips

Wash and drain the prawns (shrimp), or scampi, and chill them in the refrigerator until ready to cook. Keep all the vegetables separate. Lay them in a steamer, keeping them in clumps, and place over rapidly boiling water for 2 minutes only. Remove them from the heat, and transfer immediately to a hot flat serving dish, preferably round, arranging them like the spokes of a wheel. Keep warm while you cook the prawns (shrimp).

Lay the prawns (shrimp), unshelled, in the same steamer and cook over boiling water for 2 minutes if already cooked, 4 minutes if raw. Quickly remove the shells and heads, leaving the tails still attached to the bodies, and lay 4 prawns (shrimps) between each row of vegetables. Serve immediately, with a yellow sauce (see right). *Serves 4.*

Yellow Sauce I

Metric/Imperial/American
25 g/1 oz/2 tablespoons butter
1 tablespoon flour
150 ml/¼ pint/⅔ cup fish stock (use either liquid from steaming shellfish, or from poaching trout)
sea salt and freshly ground black pepper
150 ml/¼ pint/⅔ cup yoghurt

Melt the butter in a saucepan, stir in the flour, and cook for 1 minute. Reheat the stock and add to the pan; bring to the boil and simmer for 3 minutes. Cool slightly. If necessary, add salt and pepper to taste, then stir in the yoghurt, beating until smooth. Do not attempt to reheat after adding yoghurt or the sauce may curdle. Serve warm, with steamed prawns (shrimp) or poached trout. *Serves 4.*
Note: This is also good served cold, with cold shellfish, or fish pâtés. To serve cold, cool quickly by standing in a sink half full of icy cold water, stirring frequently to prevent a skin forming.

Yellow Sauce II (low-fat version)

Metric/Imperial/American
1 egg, separated
a pinch of sea salt
1 teaspoon Dijon mustard
150 ml/¼ pint/⅔ cup sunflower-seed oil
3 teaspoons white wine vinegar
2 tablespoons yoghurt

Put the egg yolk in a bowl and beat with a wooden spoon, adding the sea salt and mustard. Start adding the oil very gradually, literally drop by drop, beating constantly until an emulsion is formed. Then add it slightly more quickly; adding a teaspoon of vinegar if it gets too thick.

When all the oil is amalgamated, add the remaining vinegar, also slowly. Beat the egg white until stiff and fold 2 tablespoons of it into the sauce, together with the yoghurt. Serve with steamed prawns (shrimp), poached trout, or other fish dishes. *Serves 4.*

Poached Rainbow Trout

Metric/Imperial/American
4 smallish rainbow trout
court-bouillon:
1 medium onion, halved
1 carrot, halved
1 stalk celery
1 small bay leaf
6 black peppercorns
150 ml/¼ pint/⅔ cup dry white wine, or 2 tablespoons white wine vinegar
900 ml/1 ½ pints/3¾ cups water

To prepare the court-bouillon, put the vegetables, seasonings and liquids together in a saucepan and bring slowly to the boil. Simmer gently, covered, for 30 minutes, then strain and cool.

Pour the strained court-bouillon into a flameproof oval pan just large enough to hold the fish. When it is hot, but before it reaches boiling point, put in the trout. Reheat until the water starts to shake, then keep at that temperature, a very low simmer, for about 8 minutes, when the trout should be cooked. Lift them out carefully, lay them on a flat dish and serve with a yellow sauce (see above), or simply with lemon quarters. *Serves 4.*

SATURDAY

Salade Niçoise

Metric/Imperial/American
4-5 large lettuce leaves
3 tomatoes, cut in quarters
1 green pepper, cut in strips
½ Spanish onion, cut in half rings
175 g/6 oz string (green) beans, boiled and cooled
3 hard-boiled eggs, halved
500 g/1 lb canned tuna fish, drained
8 anchovy fillets (optional)
sea salt and freshly ground black pepper
¼ teaspoon Dijon mustard
6 tablespoons olive oil
4 large basil leaves, cut in strips

Line a large salad bowl with the lettuce leaves. Lay the quartered tomatoes and pepper strips in it, and cover with the semi-circular onion rings. Lay the whole string

(green) beans over this and surround with the halved eggs. Divide the tuna fish into chunks and arrange in the centre of the bowl. If using anchovies, cut them in half and scatter over the dish. Put the sea salt, black pepper and mustard in a small bowl and mix with the olive oil (I don't use any lemon juice or vinegar with this salad). Pour over the dish at the table and mix well, adding the basil. *Serves 5-6 as a first course, or 4 as a light main dish.*

Chicken Liver Pilaff

Metric/Imperial/American
1.75 litres/3¼ pints/8 cups water
sea salt and freshly ground black pepper
300 g/10 oz long-grain rice
1 Spanish onion, chopped (about
   350 g/¾ lb)
2 tablespoons sunflower-seed oil
75 g/3 oz/6 tablespoons butter
25 g/1 oz pine kernels (nuts)
250 g/½ lb chicken livers, coarsely
   chopped

Bring the water to the boil, adding salt, then shake in the rice. Boil for 10 minutes, then drain and rinse. Brown the chopped onion in 2 tablespoons oil and 25 g/1 oz/2 tablespoons butter. When it has coloured, add the pine kernels and cook gently, stirring, until they are straw-coloured. Then add the chopped livers and cook for 1 minute, till fairly coloured but still pink inside. Add sea salt and black pepper and set aside.

Melt the remaining 50 g/2 oz/4 tablespoons butter and pour half of it into a heavy pot. Lay half the rice over the butter, and the chicken livers over the rice. Cover with the remaining rice, and pour the rest of the melted butter over all. Cover the pot with a folded cloth and the lid, and cook very gently for 45 minutes. Turn off the heat and stand for 5-10 minutes before serving. *Serves 4.*

Mango Fool

Metric/Imperial/American
1 large ripe mango
1 lime (about 2 tablespoons juice)
300 ml/½ pint/1¼ cups yoghurt

Skin the mango and cut the flesh off the stone (seed). Put the flesh in a blender or food processor with the lime juice and yoghurt. Process until smooth, then pour into 4 small glasses and chill for 3-4 hours. This is a rather startling colour, but full of vitamin C and very good. *Serves 4.*

Ricotta Sauce (for Crudités)

Metric/Imperial/American
125 g/¼ lb ricotta cheese
150 ml/¼ pint/⅔ cup yoghurt
juice of ½ lemon
2 tablespoons grated Parmesan
2 tablespoons chopped parsley

Mix the ricotta and the yoghurt until smooth. Add lemon juice to taste, about 1½ tablespoons, then stir in the grated Parmesan and the chopped parsley. Serve with crudités: strips of carrot and celery, slices of turnip, sprigs of cauliflower, etc. The raw vegetables should be well chilled after preparing. *Serves 6.*

Shabu-shabu

This is a Japanese dish, based on the Chinese Mongolian Hotpot, perfectly suited to a small party of close friends. Ideally, it should be made in a fire-pot in the centre of the table, but can be done very well on the stove. It is a very healthy dish, consisting of lightly poached meat and vegetables in a clear broth.

Metric/Imperial/American
stock:
2.5 litres/4½ pints/5½ pints water
1 leek, halved
1 carrot, quartered
1 stalk celery, quartered
3 stalks parsley
1 chicken stock (bouillon) cube
main ingredients:
2 leeks, cut in thin diagonal slices
1 large carrot, cut in very thin sticks, like
   long matchsticks
250 g/½ lb Chinese cabbage, cut across in
   1-cm (½-inch) strips
1 bunch watercress, divided into sprigs
125 g/¼ lb bean sprouts (optional)
250 g/½ lb entrecôte (sirloin) steak, cut
   across the grain in thinnest possible
   slices (see below)
75 g/3 oz Japanese noodles, or vermicelli,
   freshly boiled and drained
sauces:
1) 4 tablespoons/¼ cup soy sauce
   4 tablespoons/¼ cup medium sweet
   vermouth, or dry sherry
   1 teaspoon sugar
2) 4 tablespoons/¼ cup tahini, or smooth
   peanut butter
   4 tablespoons/¼ cup sunflower-seed
   oil
   3 dashes Tabasco

Put all the ingredients for the stock into a deep pot and bring slowly to the boil, breaking up the stock (bouillon) cube. Simmer gently, half-covered, for 30 minutes, then discard the vegetables. Pour enough of the stock into a heavy round pot (failing a fire-pot) so that it is filled by not more than two-thirds. When ready to eat, bring to the boil, either on a table heater or on the stove. (Crudités are useful for eating in the meantime.)

Have the two sauces prepared beforehand by simply mixing the ingredients, then pouring some of each into tiny individual bowls — one of each for each guest. When ready to eat, put about half the sliced leeks, carrot and cabbage into the pot and simmer for about 3 minutes, then add half the watercress and the bean sprouts, if used. After another couple of minutes, start adding the slices of beef, dipping them up and down in the boiling stock just until they change colour all over, about 1 minute. (If cooked in the middle of the table, each guest can cook his own meat, using chopsticks.) Once the meat is ready, each guest lifts out the slices and dips them into one or other of the sauces for a second to cool, then pops them in his mouth. The broth must be skimmed regularly, and replenished as needed from the remainder which is keeping hot on the stove. When all the meat and extra vegetables are eaten, add the noodles or vermicelli to the broth; 2 minutes is long enough to reheat them. Serve in the same bowls, with some of the stock, flavoured with a little of sauce no 1 (the soy-based sauce). Finally, the remaining stock is ladled into the bowls and drunk as soup, again flavoured with sauce no 1, or simply with extra soy if the sauces are finished. *Serves 4.*
Note: the only difficult part of this dish is getting the meat cut thin enough. A useful tip is to half freeze it first, then cut it on a bacon slicer. Alternatively, keep a chunk of sirloin steak in the freezer, and thaw it for 30 minutes before slicing. Ready-sliced beef for shabu-shabu can be bought frozen from Japanese shops. This can then be kept until needed in the freezer.

FOR SLIMMERS

Yoghurt Salad Dressing

Metric/Imperial/American
150 ml/¼ pint/⅔ cup yoghurt
2 tablespoons sunflower-seed oil
½-1 tablespoon lemon juice
a dash of Tabasco (optional)

Mix the yoghurt and oil very thoroughly, then add lemon juice and Tabasco to taste. This is best done in a blender or food processor, as the oil and yoghurt tend to separate until properly emulsified. This makes a useful low-fat dressing for all types of salad. *Serves 4-5.*

FOR BREAKFAST

Muesli

This recipe is closely based on that of Dr. Bircher-Benner, the great Swiss dietician who invented muesli, the ideal grain dish to be eaten in conjunction with his regime, based largely on raw fruit and vegetables.

Metric/Imperial/American
1 tablespoon rolled oats, medium oatmeal,
   or oat flakes
3 tablespoons water
1 tablespoon lemon juice
1 tablespoon sweetened condensed milk
1 hard green apple, i.e. Granny Smith,
   unpeeled
1 tablespoon grated nuts, preferably
   hazelnuts or almonds

If using rolled oats or medium oatmeal, these must be soaked for 12 hours (or overnight) in 3 tablespoons water. If using oat flakes, simply mix them with the water when preparing. Mix the lemon juice and the condensed milk, and stir into the moistened oatmeal. Grate the apple and fold in lightly. Scatter the grated nuts over the top and serve immediately. *Serves 1.*

Below: Shabu-shabu

VITAMINS AND MINERALS

Vitamins are essential to nerve, muscle and brain function and are a vital part of the metabolic chain, whereby food taken in is broken down and used for energy. Vitamins are found in a wide range of foods and are provided in abundance by a good balanced diet.

Minerals, similarly, are essential to good health. These micronutrients are present in the soil, cannot be created by the body and must, therefore, come to us via the diet. As the land becomes more and more intensively farmed, ecologists are expressing concern at the rate at which the soil is becoming stripped of its minerals. In one British study, a sample group of lettuces grown on different types of soil showed dramatic differences in iron content — the richest at 516 parts per million and the poorest at only nine.

There is considerable disagreement among scientists about how much of a particular mineral or vitamin you need. The UK's recommended daily requirement for vitamin C (30 mg), for example, has been doubled by the USA and almost doubled again by the Soviet Union, who recognize that there is a large divide between getting enough of a vitamin or mineral to protect against the deficiency diseases and getting enough for good health. Early signs of depleted vitamin or mineral levels constitute the all-too-familiar signs of poor health — dandruff, rough dry, scaly skin, bleeding gums, weak decaying teeth, fatigue, irritability, bloodshot eyes, styes, brittle finger nails and a lowered resistance to viruses and other types of infection. If any of these apply to you, look first to your diet not to vitamin or to mineral supplements. You cannot transform a poor diet into a good one simply by sprinkling on a few vitamins or minerals.

'Raw' and 'fresh' are the watchwords of any mineral or vitamin-rich diet. Many vitamins and up to 80 per cent of the trace minerals are stripped out of foods during the refining process. The B and C vitamins, in particular, are extremely unstable and are easily destroyed by air, light, heat, water and storage. Just toasting a piece of wholemeal bread, for example, can take 30 per cent of the various B vitamins out of it, while an even greater proportion of vitamin C will be lost if vegetables are allowed to wilt and then over-cooked.

While a well-balanced diet, built around the mineral and vitamin rich food sources listed below, should always constitute your first line of defence against depleted vitamin or mineral levels, more specific supplementation may be necessary if you are a strict vegetarian, if you are pregnant or breastfeeding, if you suffer from premenstrual tension, if you are under considerable stress, or if you smoke heavily. If you do take a vitamin supplement, always keep within the limits specified on the label. Although huge 'mega' doses, sometimes hundreds of times the daily requirement, have been used experimentally in the treatment of diseases ranging from schizophrenia to rheumatoid arthritis, they should always be supervised by a doctor. Some vitamins, notably A and D, can be toxic when taken in excess and almost all can have unpleasant side-effects.

Vitamin and mineral-rich food sources

● 100 g (4 oz) of offal (liver, heart, kidney, brains) a week for iron. If you dislike these organ meats, make up your iron requirement with two good helpings of red meat, or one helping of seafood, and some dried fruit. In addition, eat a vitamin C-rich fruit or vegetable with your meal, which increases the uptake of iron from your food by at least four times, and avoid drinking tea while eating. Tannin reduces iron absorption to about zero.

Watching your iron and vitamin C intake is particularly important if you have very heavy periods or use an IUD, because the increased amount of blood lost over menstruation places you at an increased risk of iron-deficiency anaemia (see also page 215).

● 300 ml (½ pint) milk and two slices of wholemeal bread a day and three to four eggs a week will provide you with the complete range of B vitamins, necessary for metabolizing and making available the energy contained within food you eat. The B vitamins are also important mood vitamins. Deficiencies in vitamin B6 (pyridoxine) have been implicated in the premenstrual syndrome and in morning sickness, while deficiences in B12 (found exclusively in foods of animal origin) can lead to a form of anaemia, known as pernicious anaemia. Vegetarians are the obvious group at risk.

The need for the B vitamins rises under stress or when using high amounts of energy — whether nervous, mental or physical — and when drinking large amounts of alcohol or eating large amounts of sugar. Veterinary surgeons prescribe it for animals to improve the condition of their coats and it is also thought to be helpful for improving the condition of human hair. Bolster B vitamin levels with yeast extracts, wheatgerm, seafood and, if you like, six tablets of brewer's yeast daily — also a good source of most of the essential trace minerals.

● At least two helpings of fresh fruit and vegetables daily, one eaten with your main meal for vitamin C. Nearly all vegetables contain some of the vitamin, but blackcurrants, citrus fruits and green leafy vegetables are particularly good sources. Vitamin C is important for strengthening resistance to infection, for increasing the uptake of iron from your food, for maintaining the health of all body tissues and for neutralizing some of the damaging nitrates in meats and processed foods. It is particularly important if you smoke, because it helps to clear the lungs of traces of heavy metals such as cadmium which are present in the 'tar' of the smoke; if you are under considerable or prolonged stress (the adrenal glands use significant amounts of the vitamin in the manufacture of its stress hormones); or if you are taking drugs, such as aspirin, barbiturates or the tetracyclin group of antibiotics for a long period of time. You also need more vitamin C if you take the contraceptive pill, as the additional oestrogen seems to interfere with its absorption in certain cells.

● At least one dark green or deep yellow fruit or vegetable every second day for vitamin A (and C) and the minerals calcium and magnesium. These richly coloured vegetables contain beta carotene, a precursor of vitamin A which is necessary for healthy bones, a good clear skin, a keen sense of smell and good night-time vision. Vitamin A is now thought to have a value in protecting against certain forms of cancer. As too much can be toxic, these vegetable sources (carrots are particularly good) are preferable to supplements.

ABCDEFK

OVERWEIGHT

If you want to be fit and healthy, you must also be slim. While overweight predisposes you to almost any chronic complaint you can think of, obesity (that is, a weight 20 per cent or more above your desirable weight) triples your chances of succumbing to diseases such as stroke, coronary heart disease and diabetes. Remove the weight and you remove the risk.

It is as simple as that. Or is it? Diets have a conspicuously high failure rate. One New York study showed that, of 100 people embarking upon a calorie-controlled diet, only 12 will manage to lose substantial amounts of weight after a year and, of those 12, only two will have sustained that loss by the end of the following year. A dismal record. Yet there is no shortage of good advice, of well-balanced diets, of information on how to lose weight or, indeed, of people trying to lose it. At least half the women in the USA, for example, are thought to be anything from 1 to 12 kg (2 to 28 lb) overweight, and most of them will probably have lost (and put on) hundreds of pounds during the course of their dieting lives.

If your own dieting history is erratic, you may need to rethink your attitudes, before you revise your eating habits. Read the section on psychological eating problems on pages 76-7 before returning to this section.

Slimming

There is no reason why you should not follow any diet you wish as long as you take the following precautions.

● Check with your doctor before starting to make sure that he or she approves of the eating plan, considers that you do need to lose weight and confirms that you are healthy.

● Avoid diets, particularly long-term diets, which advocate a bizarre or highly restricted range of foods. The human instinct for variety is a healthy one because it helps to ensure that you get all the vitamins, minerals and essential nutrients you need. Balance is more, not less, important when you are slimming and eating considerably less than you normally would. The healthiest slimming regimen allows you to eat across the four main food groups: meat, fish and eggs; milk and milk products; wholegrains; fresh fruit and vegetables.

● Reserve a healthy scepticism when reading of the latest diet or wonder food. There is no truth in the suggestion that certain foods, such as hard-boiled eggs and apples, can be eaten with impunity because the energy it takes to eat them exceeds the energy (calories) they provide. Be wary, too, of claims such as that made in the famous Mayo ('Eat Fat and Grow Slim') diet which states that the acid contained in half a grapefruit, when taken before a meal, will 'dissolve' the fat in the food you eat. Untrue.

● Drink plenty of water, preferably eight or 10 glasses a day, and avoid diets suggesting that you should restrict your fluid intake. The body loses about 2 litres/3½ pints (USA 4½ pints) of water a day and it is essential that this fluid is replaced. As much of the water you need actually arrives via the food you eat —all foods, even the denser meats and cheeses, are at least 30 per cent water —the less you eat, the more you should drink.

● Avoid slimming 'aids' that may affect the normal function-ing and metabolism of your body, unless prescribed by your doctor for clearly defined medical reasons. Such aids include the following.

Slimming pills all have side-effects (agitation, irritability, insomnia, diarrhoea, raised heart beat). Most also succeed in depressing you while depressing your appetite. Their use is now generally limited to the excessively obese at some physical risk because of their weight or to those suffering from a weight-linked condition, such as hypertension (high blood pressure), diabetes or arthritis.

Thyroid extracts are ineffective in low doses and dangerous in high ones unless you have an established thyroid deficiency which is something only your doctor, certainly no slimming clinic, can decide.

Diuretics for water retention should not be taken unless prescribed medically because, by stepping up the rate of urination, they place an extra load on the kidneys. If you are taking diuretics, you should make a particular point of eating foods high in the water-soluble vitamins B and C (see opposite) and potassium (orange juice and bananas are the richest sources) as you are likely to be losing considerably more of these vitamins and minerals than usual.

Hormone treatments or injections claiming to 'mobilize' or 'redistribute' stubborn deposits of fat. The most popular use a hormone known as hCG (human chorionic gonadotrophin). Although sometimes promoted as a 'cure' for cellulite, these injections are highly dubious, ineffective and expensive.

Laxatives for weight loss are ineffective and potentially self-defeating because, taken on a regular basis, they lead to a condition known as the laxative habit whereby the bowel and gut become lazy and unable to function properly without them. They are also potentially dangerous when taken in excessive amounts (see page 77).

Can dieting make you fat?

While over-eating is by far the greatest cause of overweight, there are indications that over-frequent, and certainly over-stringent, dieting may affect the body's capacity to readjust to a normal food intake once the diet is over.

Bodies do not understand dieting. They understand survival. When underfed for considerable periods of time, the body adapts to a state of famine, gets used to subsisting on less and reorganizes its internal energy priorities so that the system becomes more efficient and more economical. Animal experiments have shown that, with continued food deprivation, the basal (resting) metabolic rate may drop by as much as 20 or 30 per cent as the animal conserves more energy and, even when fed very minute quantities, shunts more food to fat for essential reserves in case things get even worse. The same is probably true for people — in which case, continual bouts of crash dieting, bad for the figure and bad for the health, may also turn out to be entirely self-defeating.

Losing weight

People lose weight at different rates, even when following identical diets in very similar circumstances. The general pattern, however, is almost always the same. The reason for high weight loss in the early stages of a diet is that the body is losing water, not fat. Low-carbohydrate diets lead to a rapid initial weight loss because carbohydrate is water absorbent and, as stores in the body are reduced, this 'bound up' water can be freed and excreted in the urine. Follow-ups, however, show that, in the long-term, the weight loss is no greater.

The weight loss to aim for when dieting is about 1 kg (2 lb) a week. This is about one per cent of your total body fat and is a loss that you should be able to sustain when following a diet that allows 1,000-1,200 calories a day.

If you find that you are not losing weight at this rate and you are keeping strictly to the amounts of food in the stipulated diet, take more exercise. Research suggests that exercise, far from making you hungrier, exerts a powerful stabilizing effect on the appetite.

Weighing yourself

Weigh yourself regularly, but not obsessively — once a week, first thing in the morning before you get dressed and after you have been to the lavatory. Enter your weight on the graph given in the Personal Profile, and always weigh yourself on the same set of scales. The most accurate have a beam and sliding counterweights that you balance yourself. Modern bathroom scales, which work by means of a spring, are fairly accurate but may give different readings when placed on a carpet and on a hard floor. You should check these scales for accuracy against another pair every six months.

Slimming diet

This is a balanced slimming diet, which provides about 1,200 calories a day, for a weight loss of about 1 kg (2 lb) a week.
Breakfast 120 ml (4 fl oz) freshly squeezed fruit juice (see list) OR half a grapefruit OR slice fresh pineapple OR wedge of melon.
1 egg, boiled or poached OR 20 g (¾ oz) unsweetened breakfast cereal OR 120 g (4 oz) porridge made with rolled oatmeal and water or milk from allowance.
1 piece of bread or toast with butter from allowance.
1 cup of coffee or tea (no sugar) with milk from allowance.
Mid-morning 1 cup of coffee or tea (no sugar) with milk from allowance.
Lunch (can be exchanged with Dinner if you prefer to eat the larger of the two in the middle of the day).
One cup vegetable bouillon (see recipe) OR consommé OR fresh vegetable soup from the vegetables on list (boil, season, blend and add yoghurt from allowance or fresh or dried herbs for flavour).
Wholemeal sandwich made from two medium slices of bread, butter or margarine from allowance and 60 g (2 oz) chicken, lean ham, beef, turkey, salmon or tuna OR 30 g (1 oz) hard cheese. Add lettuce, watercress, tomato, endive, etc as required.
Small salad made from any of the vegetables on the list with one tablespoon of the yoghurt salad dressing (see recipe). One piece of fruit.
Mid-afternoon 1 cup of coffee or tea (no sugar) with milk from allowance.
Dinner can be exchanged with Lunch.
120 ml (4 fl oz) any fresh vegetable juice from the vegetables on the list.
90 g (3 oz) chicken or lean meat OR 120 g (4 oz) steamed, baked or grilled fish OR one two-egg omelette with chopped herbs (dill, parsley, basil etc).
Salad OR any vegetable (steamed or boiled) from the list.
One small baked potato OR one boiled potato (unpeeled) OR one tablespoon boiled rice.
One piece of fruit.
1 cup of coffee or tea (no sugar) with milk from allowance.
Allowances: 300 ml (10 fl oz) skimmed milk.
15 g (½ oz) butter or margarine.
1 carton plain, low-fat yoghurt.
Three cups of coffee or tea (without sugar).
As much water as you like (no alcohol).
7 eggs a week maximum.

Vegetables and fruit

EAT apples, asparagus, aubergine (eggplant), broccoli, French, runner or string beans, Brussels sprouts, cabbage, carrots, celery, chicory, all citrus fruits, courgette (zucchini), black, red and white currants, gooseberries, leeks, lettuce, melon, mushrooms, onion, peaches, pears, peppers, pineapple, plums, radishes, spinach, swede (rutabaga), tomatoes, turnips and turnip tops, watercress.

AVOID avocado pears, bananas, beetroot, broad beans, haricot and lima beans, canned or frozen fruit or vegetables (unless preserved without sugar), dried fruits (dates, figs, apricots, raisins etc), grapes, greengages, lentils, nuts, parsnips, peas and sweetcorn.

Meat and fish

EAT lean beef, chicken, game birds (such as partridge, pheasant or grouse), hare, lamb, offal (liver, kidney, heart, brains), rabbit, turkey, veal, venison, most white fish (bass, bluefish, catfish, cod, flounder, halibut, rockfish) salmon, shellfish (clams, cockles, crab, lobster, mussels, oysters, prawns, scallops and shrimps), sole.

AVOID bacon, canned meats and stews, corned beef, duck, frankfurters, goose, luncheon meats, minced meat (unless 100 per cent lean beef), mutton, rich pâtés, pork, processed meats, salami, sausages, spare ribs. Fish canned in oil (such as tuna or salmon) unless well drained and washed or canned in their own juices, fish roes, herring, mackerel, sardines.

Fasting and cleansing diets

Fasting has been called 'the ultimate diet'. It entails eating nothing at all. Cleansing diets usually entail eating a limited range of fruits and/or vegetables. It is claimed that these 'clear' the system, release accumulated toxins, regenerate the metabolism and take off weight at a magically rapid rate. While both can have their advantages, they can also be very dangerous when followed unwisely for extended periods.

dietsdietsdiets

The best way to approach any short-term fast or cleansing diet is to think of it, not as a means of losing weight, although you will probably lose a little, but as a means of giving your body and digestive system a refreshing rest from the excesses piled on by unbalanced eating patterns and an unhealthy lifestyle. Set aside one day a week, when you drink only water (tap or mineral) in plentiful quantity and eat simple fruit or vegetable salads, such as the one given below. This can be marvellously regenerating. It will clear and concentrate the mind, will generate, rather than deplete, energy, and will leave you feeling refreshed and relaxed. But you must set aside a time when you are unlikely to be doing very much and avoid all stimulants, such as coffee, tea or cigarettes and alcohol, if it is to have any value. Remember, too, that this is a one-day wonder only.

Try blending the juice of 4 oranges, 4 lemons, with 2 ripe bananas and 6 apricots, a teaspoonful of raw sugar or honey and drink a glass six times daily with as much mineral water as you like (at least eight glasses). This combination provides a good range of vitamins (A, C and some B) and minerals and the bulk added by the apricots and banana should offset any hunger pangs. The addition of 2 egg yolks will turn this into a highly nutritious drink and one that can be taken whenever energy reserves are low or you are feeling ill and cannot face the thought of food.

FOOD ALLERGIES AND ELIMINATION DIETS

It is not without justification that food allergy has been called the fashionable disease of the decade. In some circles, food allergy is little more than a fad, providing an instant and easy 'answer' to a whole range of unexplained disorders, from general aches and pains to respiratory illness, skin conditions and even emotional problems. While many of these may have little to do with the diet, however, some almost certainly will. A growing and reliable body of medical research is indicating that allergies and sensitivities to certain foods are not only much more common than have previously been recognized but also constitute a widespread cause of chronic ill health, giving rise to symptoms, ranging from a mild headache or skin rash to a raging migraine (see also page 219), intense nausea, vomiting and dizziness. While the reaction may be clearly apparent, isolating the cause can be difficult. All allergy testing is a time-consuming and confusing business and one that should be carried out under medical supervision. One problem involved in tracking down an offending nutrient is that anyone can be allergic to almost anything. Another significant complication is that an allergy to a food can also seem like an addiction. That is, if the food is eaten, you will feel better for it initially and the symptoms will only assert themselves as 'withdrawal' takes place.

If you suspect that you may have an allergy or sensitivity to a food or group of foods, a certain amount of lateral thinking may enable you to isolate the problem before seeking medical help. Before you even think of embarking upon the allergy-testing campaign detailed over the page, eliminate all sugar, refined and processed foods and stimulants (tea, coffee and alcohol) from your diet — all of which have been fairly conclusively linked with fluctuating mood swings, irritability, headache and a lumpy, blotchy complexion. Allergy-type reactions are often symptomatic of nothing more than an unbalanced diet or an unhealthy lifestyle. But do remember to replace the foods that you omit with plenty of raw fruit and vegetables, fresh meat and fish, milk and dairy products and wholegrains.

If your symptoms do not improve, start noting down everything you eat, together with your symptoms, if and when they occur. Code these on a sliding scale of zero to four — 0 being no symptoms, 1 mild, 2 moderate, 3 severe, 4 very severe. If you find that there is a connection between the familiar headache or hayfever-type symptoms and a certain food you are eating, try eliminating that food from the diet and see if your symptoms improve.

The next step is to eliminate the major food allergens, one by one, for at least a week. Then reintroduce them, eating them in normal but not excessive quantities. If you do have a sensitivity to a certain substance, such as the gluten in wheat flour, you will probably find that your symptoms appear fairly rapidly after a period of abstention, so making the job of detection easier. But you will need patience and perseverance. For groups that subdivide, you will have to test each type of fruit, fish or meat individually in the event of reacting positively to the group as a whole.

Major allergens
Grains containing gluten (found in wheat and wheat flour, not wheatstarch, also in barley, buckwheat, oats, rye — substitute soya, potato or rice flour, cornflour and sago)
Milk and milk products (including yoghurt but not cheese)
Eggs
Cheese
Fish
Meat
Fruit (especially bananas and the citrus group)
Alcohol (especially red wines and whisky)
Chocolate
Aspirin (use paracetamol/aminocetophen instead)
Refined and processed foods to which flavourings, preservatives and colourings have been added. This group includes the flavouring agent monosodium glutamate (found in particularly high concentrations in Chinese food) and the artificial colouring, tartrazine, found in a wide range of foods, from ice cream to orange juice.

EATING PROBLEMS
Stress-induced eating
People under stress display shortened oral cycles. That is, they eat more often, light cigarettes more often, drink more cups of tea or coffee and chew more gum. These cycles, which may shrink by about 20 per cent, are considered regressive because they mimic the shorter feeding cycles of small children.

While not everyone responds to pressure by eating more often, everyone does seem to respond by adjusting their eating patterns in some way — either up or down. In one experiment, the food intake of college students, led to believe they were taking part in a psychophysiology test,

was assessed first during their exams, when the pressure was considerable, and again three weeks later, when the pressure had subsided. On measuring the changing levels of small chocolate sweets in a bowl left on a side table during the tests, it was established that, while the students ate about the same amount when relaxed, one group ate significantly more (in fact double) over their exams, while the other ate significantly less (in fact half).

When questioned, many of the students were unaware of any change in their eating patterns. This suggests that stress-induced eating, unlike compulsive eating which may also be stress-induced (see below), is an unconscious activity — an accompaniment to and natural outlet for the pressure. For women, especially, it is a perfect outlet — socially acceptable in a way that drinking would not be and always available. It also makes an ideal 'displacement' activity because you can always find a pretext for eating, so excusing yourself from what you really should be doing.

Stress-induced eating is very common. Most women are thought to increase their food intake under pressure. To establish how stress-sensitive your appetite is, look back over recent crises. If you put on weight then or immediately afterwards, the key to your weight problem in the future might be simply to be aware of this potential pitfall and to seek a more appropriate outlet.

Compulsive eating
Compulsive eaters are compulsive dieters. They are not necessarily fat, but their weight fluctuates constantly. Unable to eat in moderation or for enjoyment, their lives revolve around food — either with eating it and hating it or with slimming and diets. Compulsive eating is so common that it probably explains why, for every successful dieter, there are at least 20 failures.

If this describes your eating habits, ask yourself what is causing you to eat so abnormally and why. Examine your notions of fatness and thinness. Ask yourself why all your previous attempts to lose weight have failed. Was there a pattern? Before you can break the vicious circle and, incidentally, successfully manage to lose weight, you must examine your attitudes — towards yourself, towards the food that you eat or do not eat, and towards the various pressures exerted upon you by society, employers, colleagues, friends, strangers, lovers, husbands, children and parents. In addition, some simple guidelines are given here. You may also find it helpful to join forces with a friend or to join a self-help group.

● Take two weeks out of your dieting life. Do not weigh yourself once. Instead, explore your hunger. Miss a meal or fast for a day and then re-examine your appetite. What do you feel like eating? Go through all the foods you can think of — not just the ones you happen to have in the cupboard — and then eat or buy the one that most appeals. Do not give a thought to how slimming or fattening it is. Think of how you feel as you eat it and whether or not it has relieved the hunger and satisfied the appetite. Go on in this way until you feel you are in touch with your hunger and can begin to trust your appetite.

● When the urge to eat descends on you, ask yourself what

else you are feeling. Is it anger, misery, boredom, pressure, professional, social or sexual frustration, rejection, anticipation, even excitement? Recognizing these underlying emotional clues, especially if they can be linked to a particular event, may help you to deal with them more appropriately the next time around. Food, at best, is a temporary anaesthetic.

● Be decisive about what you want to eat and give yourself time to enjoy it. Concentrate on the food in front of you — not the food you have just eaten or feel that you may be about to eat. If, after eating your meal, you still feel 'hungry' for more, try to let at least 20 minutes elapse before reaching for it. This is the time it takes for physiological sensations of satiation to convince the appetite it has had enough.

● Just as you should not rush your eating, so you should not rush your 'therapy'. Destructive eating habits can take some time to break. So do not be discouraged by setbacks. Try to learn from them, instead, by asking some of the questions given here and any others that seem appropriate to you. If you persevere, you may well find that your compulsive eating becomes a thing of the past and that you can lose weight without recourse to calorie or carbohydrate counting, willpower or weighing scales.

Bulimia nervosa

Although the compulsive starve/stuff routine can be confusing and deeply distressing, it is not fundamentally dangerous. It can become dangerous, however, if it is allowed to go one step further. Vomiting after bingeing or taking regular and excessively large amounts of laxatives, sometimes 20 times the dose stipulated on the label or more, describes an eating disorder known as *bulimia nervosa* (from the Latin, meaning 'appetite of an ox'). This condition is one of the most vicious of all vicious circles and one which women may be caught up in for years before seeking help. This is because it is often possible to maintain a normal, even slightly heavier than normal, body weight despite the illness.

The only way to avoid getting bulimia is not to start vomiting or becoming a regular laxative taker. If you have and you are in the early stages, stop at once. This habit has a terrifying tendency to snowball, however much you may think you are in control. If you find you cannot stop, you must seek medical help. Go and see your doctor. Bulimia is now a recognized illness and a treatable one. The sooner you realize that you have a problem and seek help for it, the greater the likelihood of a rapid and complete recovery.

Anorexia nervosa

Anorexia nervosa afflicts one to two per cent of all adolescent girls and is almost exclusively a female disease, affecting 99 women (usually in their teens and early twenties, but sometimes older) to every one man. Although anorexia is commonly known as the 'slimming or dieting disease', case histories reveal that relatively few anorectics begin by slimming their way down to an 'ideal' weight and then finding it impossible to stop. The psychology behind and the motives for the weight loss seem to be quite different from those of the dieter. Although both are deeply conscious of their own sexuality, the dieter seeks to express it by becoming slimmer

and so more desirable, while the anorectic seeks to repress it and, by starving, to return to the androgynous creature that she was before her breasts and hips began to develop. Anorexia is not so much a horror of being fat, but a phobia of being anywhere near a 'normal' body weight.

The topsy-turvy logic of the anorectic world is a deeply exclusive one, which cannot be shared or often even understood, by others. Family and friends remain on the outside, feeling guilty, frightened and helpless, as they watch the anorectic becoming more and more emaciated in front of their eyes. Strategies to get her to eat will almost always result in failure. The weight loss, meanwhile, will seem to follow an inexorable downward path of its own.

Anorexia must be treated medically, especially if the pattern of non-eating has continued for more than a year. People do not just become emaciated by the disease, they die of it. Research studies and clinical records are showing increasingly that success rates when treating anorexia depend very strongly both on the attitudes of the doctor or hospital and the follow-up they provide. Force feeding, together with the more punitive measures some hospitals take in order to get the anorectic to eat, such as withholding letters, visits from friends and family, newspapers, or television, are unlikely to be successful in the long term. Getting the anorectic to eat or, in advanced cases, to be fed, either by mouth or intravenously, is obviously important because her survival depends on it, but it must be bolstered by active and sympathetic counselling both while the weight is being regained and for some months afterwards.

skin, hair, teeth and nails

'...what with the creaming and splashing and putting on a mask and taking it off again and having her nails done and her feet ... as well as having her teeth completely rearranged and the hair zipped off her arms and legs — I truly don't think I could be bothered.'

Nancy Mitford

Lady Montdore's time-consuming and elaborate beauty rituals may have achieved their ends ('the whole thing,' Fanny had to admit, 'was stunning') but the price was high — no less than total dedication. Today, the pursuit of beauty is infinitely less demanding. Skincare and haircare routines take minutes rather than hours, manicures and conditioning treatments for the nails can be easily carried out at home, and 'complete' rearranging of the teeth should not be necessary at all if you look after them properly in the first place. Today's beauty routines are compatible with the busiest lifestyle and the fullest schedule: there is no longer any excuse for not being bothered.

Simplicity, regularity and commonsense are the watch-words of any successful beauty routine. If you are conscientious about using a sunscreen, if you keep your skin and hair well conditioned, if you floss your teeth each time you brush them and see your dentist regularly, if you protect your hands from damaging influences, such as washing-up water, and file your nails properly, the pay-offs will be enormous. The input in terms of time and effort and expense, meanwhile, will be virtually negligible.

A healthy lifestyle, balanced diet and positive outlook are important too. Your skincare and haircare programmes may be faultless, but if your lifestyle is frenetic, your diet poor, your emotions turbulent or your health one or two degrees under, you cannot expect to get the best from your skin or your hair. So think inside out. Recognize that attention from the outside may be important but it is not the whole answer. Look upon it as an integral part of a much more general beauty plan, reading each of these sections in the light of the chapters that precede and follow them.

Before you even do this, you may find it helpful to assess the present condition of your skin, hair, teeth and nails, using the questionnaires in the Personal Profile to help you. These have also been designed to test your current beauty regimes and to help you to assess, as far as possible, how appropriate they are for you. If you decide they need changing, you will find guidelines and suggestions in the following pages.

skin

'No beauty can be a beauty today without a good skin.' *Vogue*, **1935**

The type of skin you have is determined by two unalterables — your genes and your sex — governed by your age and affected by the environment. It can also be enormously improved by the way you look after it. Skincare today means thinking 10, 20 and even 50 years ahead, protecting yourself against the harmful effects of sunlight, pollution and stress and having the wisdom to take the best from science and the natural world.

One of the most versatile and remarkable organs of the body, your skin provides a most accurate key to its inner state of health — not only on a physical level but on emotional and psychological levels too. Nervous reactions, such as blushing, can have immediate and visible effects on the skin or a more complicated and intricate action on a wide number of skin conditions. Psoriasis, eczema, rosacea and some types of acne, for example, all tend to flare up under anxiety and stress. It is now widely recognized that removing the root of that anxiety can have a more positive effect on the condition than any of the medications currently on the market, although no-one knows exactly why.

What is known is that skin is a complex, dynamic structure, continually renewing itself and constantly changing in response to many external and internal stimuli. It regulates body temperature by adjusting the rate of water elimination — you can sweat as much as 2 litres/4-5 pints during the course of a good hour's workout, hardly at all when you are less active or the weather is cool. It insulates the body from the cold by means of a primitive response that causes the fine hairs to stand on end — goose pimples. It frees the system from accumulated toxins and metabolic waste and can be one of the first and most immediate aids to diagnosis in the event of illness, such as diabetes, anaemia and diseases of the liver, kidneys and bile duct. Finally, it acts in a protective capacity, keeping your insides in, protecting the system from harmful substances and particles in the atmosphere and screening it from the damaging effects of ultraviolet and other types of radiation. This is why only a few substances — some poisons, such as arsenic and lead, and some medically prescribed ointments — are actually absorbed through the skin. It is a powerful barrier to many of the potentially damaging substances with which you daily come into contact.

STRUCTURE AND REGENERATION

The skin comprises several layers. These divide into the outer, waterproof epidermis and the inner, sensitive dermis. The epidermis contains the sweat and sebaceous pores and the pigmentation cells, or melanocytes. (Both black and white skins contain the same number.) The dermis is supported by a layer of fat and contains the hair follicles, sweat and sebaceous glands, nerve cells, blood vessels and the tough network of protein fibres, collagen and elastin, which determines the suppleness and elasticity of the skin and gives it its characteristic ability to contract.

Key matrix cells, lying between the epidermis and the dermis at what is called the basal level, initiate a process of cell division and multiplication. The vital DNA or genetic 'blueprint' contained within the nuclei of the cells ensures that each successive generation of skin cells is a perfect replica of the previous one. The new generation then migrates upwards, gradually flattening out and losing moisture so that, by the time the cells reach the outer surface of the skin to comprise the *stratum corneum*, or 'horny layer', they are dead, and act purely in a protective capacity to shield the younger, more vulnerable cells below. The whole journey normally takes about 28 days, but age, sunlight, systemic or skin disease can all retard or accelerate it. With psoriasis, for example, the cycle can take as little as three days. This abnormally fast turnover produces the characteristic pink scaly patches over the affected area. When you sunbathe, the epidermis thickens, sometimes by as much as four times, protecting the skin beneath by absorbing and effectively diffusing the damaging radiation.

The skin's remarkable repair mechanism rapidly heals any type of superficial damage, such as grazes, cuts and mild burns. Within 28 days or less, the damaged tissue will have flaked away to reveal a new layer of healthy skin beneath. Any injury to cells at the basal layer, however, through deep wounds, severe burns or excessive exposure to sunlight, can have a permanent effect on the skin tissue (scarring) if it damages the DNA in the cell nucleus. The damaged cell will then go on to produce an abnormal 'daughter' cell — and the deeper and more extensive the damage, the greater the abnormality. This is why repeated or prolonged exposure to the sun will produce a gradual, rather than an immediate, deterioration in the quality of your skin.

GENETICS VERSUS THE ENVIRONMENT

Genes play as important a part in determining the texture and general look of your skin as they do in determining the height you will reach or the colour of your eyes. The number of your blood vessels, the relative concentration of your sebaceous glands, the size of your pores and the coarseness (diameter) and position of your hair within its follicles are all determined nine months before you arrive in the world and remain unalterable for the rest of your life. Nothing can change the overall genetic pattern which predisposes you to conditions as various as acne and vitiligo, and which determines your susceptibility to sunburn and the rate at which your skin will age, becoming thinner in texture and losing its

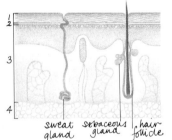

sweat gland   sebaceous gland   hair follicle

The skin comprises several layers. The uppermost layer of the epidermis (1) is known as the *stratum corneum*, or horny layer. It is composed entirely of dead skin cells and works to protect the young live cells beneath. These originate in the basal layer (2) and gradually travel upwards, losing moisture and flattening out as they go. Any damage to the skin at basal level may disrupt the genetic pattern of the cells and result in scarring. The dermis (3) contains sweat and sebaceous glands, is composed of tough connective tissue – elastin and collagen – and nourished by a network of tiny blood capillaries. A layer of subcutaneous fat beneath (4) gives the skin a springy, youthful texture.

bloom as the sebaceous glands become less active and the rate of cell division slows down.

However, the relative age or youth of your skin is also affected by a number of other factors that <u>are</u> within your control. You will never hold the ageing process entirely at bay, but a sensible skincare routine, started at an early age, may well retard it. 'Sensible' hinges not so much on choosing the right moisturizer or going for a monthly facial, though undoubtedly these can help, but on staying out of the sun, getting enough sleep, circumventing potentially stressful situations, cutting out or cutting down on the number of cigarettes you smoke and the amount of alcohol you consume and eating and exercising wisely. Anything, in short, that contributes to the health of your body will be reflected in the state of your skin.

SKIN DESTRUCTIVES
Sunlight

It has been estimated that, for every eight degrees you go south in America, there is a doubling of the skin cancer rate. So, if tanning as fast as possible without burning is your only consideration when choosing a sun cream, think again. You could be taking a short and sure route to a prematurely aged skin and significantly increasing the risk of getting two of the three types of skin cancer, developing a cataract or disrupting the body's immune system. Your strategy for maintaining a healthy skin and preserving its youthfulness should start with good sun protection and, preferably, a total sun block — at least on the face.

Sunlight damages the skin because, unless it is deflected by the upper layers of the epidermis, the ultraviolet radiation strikes at the nucleus of the basal cells, altering the DNA within them so that, instead of renewing themselves perfectly, the cells tend to divide defectively. A small change to the DNA will produce no visible signs of damage — we can all escape fairly lightly with a small amount of sun exposure. Intensive sunbathing repeated over the years, however, will cause the cells to divide more and more defectively and the damage to become more and more pronounced and, of course, visible. The effect is cumulative.

Any part of the ultraviolet spectrum carries the potential to damage the skin, although, up to now, the trend has been to single out the shorter wave, 'burning' UVB as the culprit and to exonerate the less energetic, 'tanning' UVA. UVB is therefore outlawed by most sunlamp manufacturers and is also the target for most of the sunscreens currently on the market. However, while sunburns are painful and suntans are not, both UVB and UVA can damage the skin and the only really effective sunscreens are those that protect you from both parts of the spectrum. Choose creams or lotions containing para-aminobenzoic acid (PABA), one of the B vitamins and a highly efficient UVB deflector, <u>and</u> benoxophenone, which screens out UVA as well as UVB.

While UVA is present in a fairly constant concentration from sunrise to sunset, UVB is partially absorbed by the atmosphere. This is why the overhead sun at midday is so hazardous: ultraviolet rays, travelling in a perpendicular line, have much less atmosphere to penetrate. So, if you want to tan safely, concentrate your sunbathing before 10 am or after

3 pm. If you do not have a watch with you, you can still assess your chances of burning by using your body as a sundial. Lie down on the sand and mark two lines where your head and feet reach. Stand at one of them so that your shadow slopes towards the other. If it falls short of the mark, there is a lot of UVB, the sun is burning and you should be especially careful.

The skin responds to sunlight in three ways. If the sunlight is very strong and the skin sensitive, it will burn. If the sun is milder or the skin more resilient, it will produce melanin, which 'spills' upwards into the epidermis to give a brown effect. As these cells gradually flake off, so will the tan — unless the stimulus is maintained, in which case the cells will continue to manufacture melanin and you will continue to look brown. Tanning confers only a moderate degree of protection against subsequent sun damage. A tanned body can stay out in the sun only twice as long as a white one before it begins to burn. What makes a sun-exposed skin more resilient to burning is the third factor — a natural thickening of the top layer of the skin cells which can multiply by as much as four times in depth. This layer absorbs the ultraviolet, translates it into heat and suffuses it into surrounding tissue before it hits the vulnerable cells deeper down. Nevertheless, brown bodies can still burn and none but the constitutionally dark skinned can afford to go out into the sun without first ensuring that they are well protected.

Up to two-thirds of UVB is scattered by the atmosphere before reaching sea level. This means that it reaches the skin via the sky rather than directly from the sun, which is why you can still burn when you are sitting under a parasol or are wearing a wide-brimmed hat. Ultraviolet light is also very strongly reflected by snow, sand, concrete surfaces and rippling water. If it hits the water head-on, it will penetrate up to a depth of about 1 metre (3 feet). Count swimming time as sunbathing time and remember that even waterproof or water-resistant sunscreens will eventually wash off. Reapply them frequently, especially along the backs of the legs, shoulders and neck, even if it means interrupting your swim. And do not forget tide marks around the bikini line.

Sunscreens and sun protection factors

The Sun Protection Factor (SPF) provides the only really reliable key to how much sun exposure you can take without risking a burn. The factors work from a base figure of one — the time a previously unexposed skin can lie in the sun without developing signs of redness — and are increased on a multiplication basis, according to the degree of protec-

SUN PROTECTION FACTORS: which should you be using?

Skin type	Very strong sun		Less strong sun		Skin's natural protection
	Untanned	Tanned	Untanned	Tanned	
Ultra-sensitive (always burns, never tans)	12	8	8	6	5/10 minutes
Very sensitive (often burns, rarely tans)	8	6	6	4	10/20 minutes
Averagely sensitive (burns then tans)	6	4	4	3/2	20/30 minutes
Less sensitive (rarely burns, tans easily and deeply)	4	3/2	3/2	3/2	40 minutes

Sunlight is important for the health of mind and body, potentially dangerous for the skin. Capitalize on the benefits and safeguard yourself against the dangers with a good broad spectrum, water-resistant sun cream for the body (see chart, above, to identify your skin type and the sun protection factor you should be using) and a total sunblock or high protection factor sunscreen (10 or above) for the face and neck.

When out sunbathing, assess your risk of burning by using your body as a sundial. Lie down on the sand or the ground and mark out two lines where your head and feet reach. Stand at one end so that your shadow slopes towards the other. If it falls short of the mark, the sun is especially burning and you should be extremely careful.

tion the cream or lotion provides. If you can normally stay out in the sun unprotected and without burning for 20 minutes, an SPF of three, for example, will enable you to increase that exposure time to one hour. Swimming, sweating and anything with which the skin comes into contact, such as towels and sand, all undermine the protective barrier. So apply the lotion frequently — every two hours at least and more often if you are swimming or perspiring a lot. Use the chart given on the previous page to identify your skin type and the protection factor you should be using.

Ideally you should use a total sunblock, or at the least a super-efficient sunscreen (SPF of 10 or more) on the face. The neck too. Often exposed and usually unprotected, it is hardly surprising that this is where the first real signs of ageing occur. So, start applications of your high-protection sunscreen at the collarbone, not the chin, and work upwards and reapply frequently.

If you do get too much sun, do not smother your body with creams and oils. These will only retain the heat and intensify the discomfort. Instead, soak in a tepid bath to which you have added 600 ml/1 pint of strong tea (tannin has remarkably soothing qualities). Stay there for 20 minutes, pat yourself dry and smooth on calamine ointment or a cream containing chamomile or allantoin — healing agents that help damaged skin recover. Alternatively, soak cotton wool in a milk and water mixture and use that as a soothing lotion.

Take severe burns to a doctor as soon as possible. An anti-inflammatory treatment, known as indomethacin (available only on prescription), can be effective if used within 48 hours of burning.

Sunlamps
As any ultraviolet has the potential to damage the skin, the current sunlamp boom may well bring a tide of skin cancers, dark liver spots and prematurely aged skin in its wake. No-one knows for sure as skin cancers can take up to 15 years to develop. So, while sunlamps give a good pre-holiday tan base or a healthy glow, you should not use them to maintain all-year-round brownness. This will damage the skin. Use them wisely and take the following factors into account:

● Do not go out sunbathing if you have had or intend to have sunlamp exposure that day. You are many times more likely to burn. Always use a high SPF when venturing into the real sun for the first time, however deep the tan. As the skin tans but does not thicken under UVA exposure, a sunlamp gives only minimal protection against burning in natural sunlight.

● Always shower before using a sunlamp. Cosmetics in general and perfumes in particular, present in deodorants as well as in scent, can produce excessive burning or tanning reactions and result in patchy pigmentation. Sun creams containing bergamot oil can have the same effect.

● If you are taking any form of medication, check with your doctor before using a sunlamp. Some drugs cause photosensitivity — that is, they increase the skin's sensitivity to sunlight and may produce a severe burning reaction.

● Do not use a sunlamp if you are one of the five per cent of the population with an intrinsic light-sensitive disorder which appears as a rash or as a series of raised lumps on the exposed area. This may last anything from a few hours to a few days after the exposure has ceased. This reaction or 'heat rash' is, of course, caused by direct sunlight too, but UVA will not reduce the problem.

● If you are pregnant or taking the contraceptive pill, there is a chance of developing chloasma (melasma) — dark pigmentation that usually appears above the upper lip, on the cheeks just below the eyes, on the forehead, on and around the nipples and under the armpits. This can suddenly appear for the first time after years of taking the pill or after previous trouble-free pregnancies. As the condition is aggravated and rendered more noticeable by exposure to sunlight, you should protect your skin from strong sunlight, including sunlamps, as much as possible.

● Always wear the special UVA goggles provided by the sunlamp manufacturer or buy your own. Although findings that ultraviolet causes cataracts in animals have not been substantiated in humans, it is known that pre-cataract conditions are more common in people who have had a lot of sun.

Smoking
Smoking seems to affect the skin in two ways. Firstly, the habitual inhalation will cause lines to develop around the mouth in much the same way as habitual squinting will cause lines to develop around the eyes. Secondly, carbon monoxide in cigarette smoke has a greater affinity for haemoglobin (the oxygen-carrying red pigment in the blood) than oxygen has itself, and displaces it, so substantially reducing the amount available to build up and replenish the skin tissue. Smoking 'suffocates' the skin.

An American study of crows' feet around the eyes of smokers, non-smokers and ex-smokers revealed some interesting results. It showed that smokers were much more likely to be wrinkled than non-smokers, even if they had abandoned the habit before the wrinkles first appeared. In addition, the degree of wrinkling could be surprisingly accurately linked to the number of cigarettes smoked per day. Finally, it was found that the most heavily wrinkled eyes belonged exclusively to smokers — a forceful aesthetic reason for giving up, even if the health risks seem remote.

Sleep and stress
With too little sleep the skin actually looks tired, becoming sallow, puffy, lifeless and grey. This is because while you are asleep your skin renews its texture. The hormones responsible for cell division and the renewal and replacement of skin tissue are at their most active during sleep, making this period of rest and regeneration as vital to the health of your skin as it is to the health of your mind and the rest of your body.

Most bodies adjust naturally to sleep deprivation by compensating over subsequent days, or even weeks, so do not become anxious if you feel that you are missing out on your sleep. Take a positive attitude, follow the guidelines on page 180 and you will probably find that your sleep returns (and your skin improves) as your anxiety diminishes.

skinskin

Confusingly, too much sleep can also affect the appearance of the skin. When you are lying down, body fluids tend to circulate less freely and to collect in the facial tissue, so that the skin often looks puffy on oversleeping. To avoid this, sleep with at least one pillow to keep the head slightly raised and resist the temptation to doze on for too long.

Living at fever pitch over a long period of time will almost certainly affect the appearance of your skin (you are unlikely to be sleeping well or eating properly for one thing), as will negative emotions, such as fear, grief, anger or excessive anxiety. But the mechanism that produces what often amounts to a dramatic loss of skin tone and suppleness is little understood.

Humidity

Ask any farmer, and he will tell you that it is not so much the drought that damages his crops, but the warm, drying wind that goes with it. The same is true for the skin. Dryness can be caused or accentuated by a low humidity atmosphere that literally lifts the moisture out of it. Central heating, ventilation and extractor fans all strip moisture from the atmosphere and bring your skin closer to its evaporation threshold (when the humidity is below 30 per cent). Central heating is the most drying of the three and can send humidity plunging as low as 20 per cent — a level on a par with that of the Sahara Desert.

Cut down moisture loss from your own skin by putting more moisture into the atmosphere. A number of steps can be taken to raise the humidity level, such as keeping house plants, putting a bowl of water on a table or work surface, or buying one of the more sophisticated humidifiers which can be attached to a radiator or simply placed in an unobtrusive corner of the room. You should also make a special point of putting a fine layer of oil on to your face to cut down the rate of evaporation when humidity is low.

SKIN TYPES

Skin types are confusing. Most of what we read encourages us to believe that the skin, like the hair, must either be oily OR dry OR normal. For most, however, some areas of the face will be dry while others are oily. Although it is difficult to be rigorously selective when caring for this type of 'combination' skin, a general guideline should be to use an astringent only where the face is oily and a moisturizer only where it is dry. A sunscreen, of course, should be used whenever the face is exposed to strong sunlight, whatever its skin condition.

Dry skin

Dry skin is dull, feels tight on washing — even with the mildest of soaps — flakes, scales and chaps easily. It is more likely to protest on coming into contact with harsh chemical substances and will tend to make wrinkles look more prominent, although it will not actually cause them. Most skins tend to get drier as they get older. The sebaceous glands become less active, produce less sebum and provide a less efficient barrier to prevent the loss of natural moisture into the atmosphere. As more moisture is lost from the skin when the weather is hot and humidity is low, dry skin should be especially well protected in summer. Use an oil-based sunscreen to protect the face and a good moisturizer to retain as much internal moisture as possible. A good moisturizer is also important in the winter when central heating can have much the same effect. Do not over-wash (one shower or bath a day is plenty), use a light exfoliant, such as washing grains, once a week, and always moisturize. As a general rule, the lower the humidity, the heavier (greasier) your moisturizer should be.

Oily skin

Oily skin feels relaxed and supple, but looks shiny and is much more prone to outbreaks of spots. This is because of a heightened production of sebum by the sebaceous glands. While we all need sebum on the surface of the skin in order to keep it lubricated and supple and to bind in moisture, too much sebum can cause a blockage in the duct, leading to inflammation and pimples. Children rarely have oily skins because their sebaceous glands remain small and dormant, only becoming enlarged at puberty when raised hormone levels provide a trigger for increased sebum production. Sebaceous glands are unevenly distributed, being more concentrated around the scalp, on the forehead, along the nose and on the chin, and scarcer on the cheeks and neck, and around the eyes. Consequently, most skins tend to be oily only in patches. Oily skin may or may not lead to acne, but it is important to distinguish between oil on the surface of the skin, which makes it look shiny, tends to break through make-up and gives the skin a slightly yellowish tinge, and oil trapped within the sebaceous duct. Oil on the surface is friend not foe. That is where it is meant to be — and any excess can be easily removed with careful and regular washing.

Normal skin

Normal skin is not at all normal. In fact, it is rarely seen on anyone other than very young children and a few adults — but you will know if you have got it. Normal skins are clear, soft and supple, uniformly textured and pigmented, neither too oily nor too dry and not over-sensitive to climate, cosmetics or your own internal environment. This type of skin may be an inherited blessing but it still needs careful looking after.

Sensitive skin

Sensitive skin is what we all have. However resilient it is (and it has to be), any skin will protest if it is assaulted by harsh sunlight or fierce chemicals. So remember that skin is delicate and treat it accordingly. Hypersensitive skins, on the other hand, are usually the preserve of the fair-skinned and the blonde- or red-haired. This is the sort of skin that never tans but only burns or freckles, that reacts to irritant substances by coming up in spots, rashes or blotches and that tends to belong to the allergy-prone, such as the hay fever or asthma sufferer. People with extra sensitive skins also tend to register their emotions more tellingly on the face. They flush and blush easily and pale visibly under stress, fear or nausea. They should be particularly careful of the products they use (find guidelines on pages 138-9).

washwashwash

Wash the face with a mild unperfumed soap, lather briefly and rinse thoroughly. Because soap is an alkaline substance, washing will temporarily raise the pH of the skin, which is normally slightly acid at about 5.5. Most skins have an in-built ability to readjust the balance within 20 minutes of washing, though sensitive skins may take longer. You can speed up the process by using a citrus-based toning lotion or astringent afterwards.
If the skin feels dry and tight after washing, try using a superfatted soap which incorporates emollients such as lanolin or mineral oil into the soap base. Other causes of dryness: over-washing, incomplete rinsing, hard water (calcium and magnesium salts in the water combine with the soap to form a drying 'scum' on the skin) or sensitivity. Try a cream cleanser instead.

TAKING CARE OF YOUR SKIN

The first principle of any skincare routine is not to disturb the skin's normal function any more than you have to. Left to itself, the skin is a remarkable, self-cleansing and self-nourishing organ — and both nourishing and cleansing come from the inside. The purpose of washing or cleansing is to take off surface grime, excess sebum and accumulated dirt regularly and efficiently, but never abrasively. The skin is a finely tuned and delicate structure; over-enthusiastic cleansing procedures and very rich creams can upset it.

Because the skin is constantly changing in response to different stimuli, what is right one week may not always be appropriate the next. Pay attention to your skin. If it feels dry and taut, you may be treating it too harshly, using over-strong products or exposing it to unreasonable amounts of sun and wind. If it is shiny and oily with a tendency to break out, ask yourself whether you are removing every trace of greasy make-up removers, whether you would be better off washing it with soap and water or whether, perhaps, you are over-washing it.

If your skin develops lumps, bumps, pimples or scaly patches, start by simplifying your cleansing and make-up routines. Wash or cleanse the skin once a day only, using mild, unscented soaps and lotions. Skip commercial toners and astringents and splash your face instead with plain cold water or distilled water to which you have added a squeeze of lemon juice. If the condition persists or becomes worse, consult a dermatologist.

Washing, cleansing and removing make-up

There is nothing wrong with soap and water. In fact, most skins are washed most effectively this way, but it may be unsuitable if you have a dry or very sensitive skin or if you are trying to remove make-up.

When washing your face, always wash your hands first, otherwise you will merely be working additional dirt into the skin. Use an unperfumed soap — try a 'superfatted' or glycerine-based soap if you have a dry skin, a medicated one if you have an oily skin. Lather it first in your hands and then on your face, massaging gently for a few moments and then rinsing thoroughly, as any residue can have a drying effect. Splash with cold water and pat dry.

Wash only twice a day (once a day if the skin is sensitive), as it is possible to traumatize the skin by over-washing. This not only removes the excess, but also the essential, oil that renders the skin watertight, by preventing too much of its natural moisture evaporating into the air, and waterproof, by preventing absorption of grease, dirt and even toxins from the outside. If using soap and water leaves the skin feeling dry and tight, it could be that you are not rinsing thoroughly, that you live in a hard water area (try adding a pinch of borax to the water to soften it) or that your face is better suited to a cleansing lotion.

Most face foundations, blushers, powders and make-up bases are water-soluble and can usually be efficiently removed with soap and water. If particles of make-up still cling to the face or come away on the cotton wool you are using for toning, you should use a cleanser. If you have an oily skin, choose a cleanser that flows easily from the bottle, is well absorbed by cotton wool and leaves no shiny residue on the skin surface. While a drier skin will benefit from a slightly heavier cream, both types should avoid the heavier, grease-paint type of make-up remover. Theatrical make-up belongs to the theatre, so if you do need a heavy cream to get your make-up off at night, it is probably time to rethink your make-up techniques (see Cosmetics chapter).

Use gentle sweeping movements to remove dirt and grease and continue with successive pieces of cotton wool until the last comes away clean. Do not use ordinary cleanser on the eyes. Choose a specially formulated eye make-up remover — a thinner, water-based lotion, which is more sympathetic to the delicate eye tissue. Combine the use of an efficient cleanser with the gentlest possible removing technique. Pat it on to the eyelids and over the brow and leave for a few seconds. This will give the make-up a chance to dissolve into the lotion, so that it comes away easily with a minimum of rubbing. Finally, remove eye make-up and cleanser with a piece of cotton wool, dampened to prevent fibres getting caught in the lashes or irritating the eye.

To take off mascara, skim some eye make-up remover lightly over the lashes, place a flat piece of tissue or dampened cotton wool underneath the lower eyelashes and, taking a dampened cotton wool bud, roll it over the lashes on to the tissue or cotton wool beneath. Wearers of contact lenses should take their lenses out before removing their make-up, to avoid smudging grease or particles of make-up on to the lens.

Sensitive skin, some types of face make-up and all types of eye make-up require either a cream or liquid cleanser.
If the skin is young and/or has a natural tendency to oiliness, choose a light cleansing milk that flows easily from the bottle. If the skin is more mature and/or has a natural tendency to dryness, choose a slightly richer cream.
Start cleansing from the neck upwards, using as many pieces of cotton wool or tissue as you need. Use firm upward strokes and follow with a toner. (See following page for details on removing make-up.)

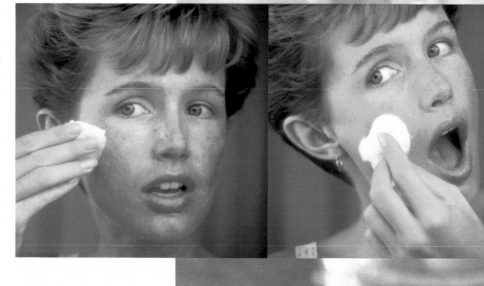

You should take as much care in removing your make-up as you do in putting it on. Particles of incompletely removed face make-up may block pores and contribute to skin problems while flaking mascara or eye make-up can irritate the eyes. Start by tying the hair well back from the face. If you wear contact lenses, remove these now.

Skim a light liquid make-up remover over face and lips, around the eyes and down the neck as far as you have taken the foundation.

Leave make-up and make-up remover on the face for a few moments, to help the make-up dissolve into the cleanser. This will enable you to remove your make-up with an absolute minimum of rubbing.

Take a folded tissue or a piece of cotton wool and wipe it over the face and neck in an upwards and outwards direction.

Toning

Skin toners have an evaporating and cooling action that causes muscles to contract and the pores to become temporarily (not permanently) smaller. Toning is pleasant and refreshing, can act as an additional cleanser on very oily or dirty skin and is valuable in removing any traces of grease the cleanser may have left behind.

Products are generally divided into fresheners, toners, clarifying lotions and astringents. Fresheners are the mildest and may contain lemon juice or citric acid to restore the acid balance of the skin after washing. Toners and clarifying lotions tend to be more abrasive, while astringents are the harshest of the lot. They contain a high proportion of alcohol, which has a drying effect on the skin, as it takes some of the skin's natural moisture with it on evaporation into the atmosphere. (Think how fast perfume — predominantly alcohol and water — evaporates when left in the open air.) Astringents may cause excessive dehydration and flaking on very dry or sensitive skins, so use them only on the oily areas of the face and on any oily patches across the chest and shoulder blades. You can make your own toner by mixing witch hazel, which has strong astringent properties, with gentler rosewater. Use equal quantities of rosewater and witch hazel for oily skins, two parts of rosewater to one of witch hazel for normal skins, and the same mixture diluted with distilled water if the skin is really dry. Bottle and keep in the refrigerator.

Straight witch hazel also makes an excellent 'emergency' treatment for spots and pimples. Apply it frequently to the area (at least four or five times a day) as soon as you feel a spot erupting. This will help to dry it out and, if applied early enough, may prevent it appearing at all.

Moisturizing

'Moisturizing' is a misleading concept. No moisturizer can or should put moisture into the skin. Everything works the other way round. 'Nourishing' is misleading too. Your food provides the nourishment, which is absorbed by the blood and carried to the skin cells along with essential protein, vitamins and trace minerals, all of which will have first been properly metabolized and minutely broken down by the action of enzymes, so that they can penetrate the cell walls. It is therefore improbable, if not impossible, for nutrition to reach the skin by any other means and, indeed, most cosmetics are only intended to act on the surface layers of the skin. So retain a degree of scepticism when you read the ingredients on product labels. Eggs, honey, assorted vitamins and minerals may all sound delicious but, if you really want to nourish your skin, do not plaster them on your face, eat them.

Moisturizers do have an important role to play in your beauty routine, but they must be used regularly and applied with care. They work by duplicating and strengthening the role of the body's own, naturally produced sebum and thus protect the skin against excessive moisture loss. Sebum emulsifies with sweat (99 per cent water) on the surface of skin, lubricating the upper layers of the epidermis by softening and plumping out the dry, dead skin cells, and produces a fine protective layer of oil to render the skin more water-

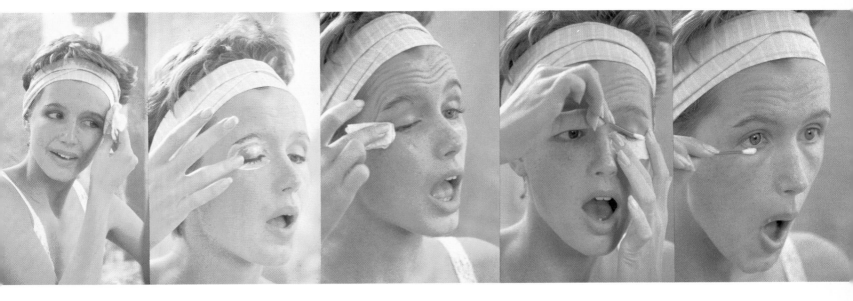

Continue with successive pieces of cotton wool or tissue until the last comes away clean.	Eyes need special attention. The skin is very delicate here and the eyes are susceptible to irritation, even infection, if make-up or make-up remover come too close. Use a specially formulated, water-soluble lotion so that, should any make-up enter the eye, it can be easily flushed out by the tear fluid.	Apply make-up remover lightly to browbone and lids. Leave for a few moments, to give the make-up time to dissolve, and wipe off with a piece of dampened cotton wool to prevent stray particles or fibres getting caught on the lashes or irritating the eye. Use a cotton wool bud around the immediate margins of the eye.	When removing mascara, attend to lower and upper lashes, underneath as well as on top. Place a moistened tissue underneath the lower lashes, then smooth a small amount of the cleanser on to a cotton wool bud and roll it over top and lower lashes together.	Finally, wipe any traces of eye make-up or mascara away from the eyes, use a toner to remove any traces of greasiness left by the cleanser and follow with a light moisturizer.

tight. Significantly, many moisturizers contain lanolin, which is derived from the natural oil (sebum) of the sheep. Like the oil on the skin's surface, moisturizers are water-and-oil emulsions. The richer day creams and most night creams have a greater oil-to-water ratio than the thinner, lighter ones, which are predominantly water based. If you have a very dry skin, you should use an oil-based emulsion, while younger combination skins will require only a lighter, water-based one. How can you tell the difference? Oil-based emulsions are thicker, cannot usually be poured and have to be scooped up with the fingers. They are not absorbed as well on to the superficial top layers of the skin and leave a fine, reflective sheen on it.

All moisturizers can be made to work more effectively by dampening the skin first, as the top, dead layer of skin will absorb a small amount of water. Body lotions are generally perfumed, and so should not be used on the face. But a good all-round moisturizer can be used everywhere, including on the forehead, neck and cheeks, gently around the eyes and anywhere else where the skin feels dry and tight.

Exfoliating

Cells that have been too long on the surface of the skin are greyish and dull in tone. They may flake and can clog the sebaceous pores, leading to superficial spots or blackheads and giving an uneven patchy look to the face and body. Cosmetic exfoliation helps to speed up the flaking and shedding process, by taking off the uppermost, dead layer of cells to expose the finer, more translucent tissue underneath.

it may also help preserve the youthful bloom of the skin. Some dermatologists now maintain that the reason why a man's skin tends to line less rapidly around the mouth and cheeks than a woman's is because the practice of shaving daily acts as a natural exfoliant.

The idea behind cosmetic exfoliation is controlled, not excessive, irritation and this can be accomplished in a number of ways. The ancient Egyptians used a recipe containing alabaster, honey and oatmeal and you can make up your own by combining roasted oatmeal with the zest of a citrus fruit and mixing to a paste with a little water. Alternatively, you can use one of the commercial brands. Other methods include a rough face glove or rotating facial 'scrubbing' brush, a peel-off mask or a chemical solution which usually contains a 'grease-stripping' solvent (salicylic acid, resorcinol or benzoyl peroxide) and is more likely to be marketed as a lotion for acne.

Whichever method you use, you should always exfoliate according to your skin's strength. The purpose is to leave the skin glowing, translucent and slightly pink, not red, inflamed and irritated. Exfoliants should be used with caution on dry and sensitive faces, but the tougher, body skin can well withstand a vigorous, twice-weekly sloughing session with an abrasive loofah to encourage the skin to flake off and to boost circulation through superficial skin vessels. Special attention areas: 'gooseflesh' on the upper arms, thighs and buttocks and rough scaly patches on the knees and elbows. Follow up with a body lotion to smooth new skin down and to leave it glowing and fresh.

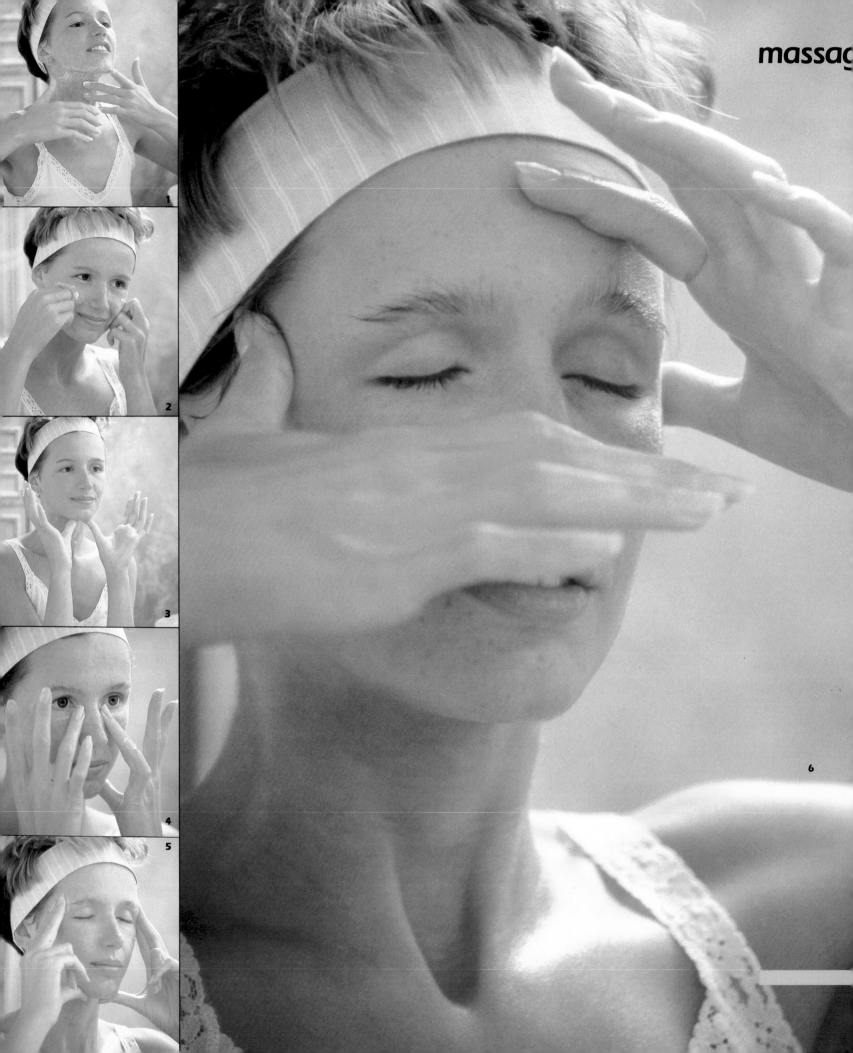

massag

1

2

3

4

5

6

assage

A good facial massage will relax you and invigorate your skin by boosting the circulation and dilating the blood vessels, so helping to bring more oxygen to the skin surface.
Use a light moisturizer if the skin is oily, a richer night cream if the skin is dry, and smooth it on to the face and neck.
Start at the collarbone. Brush fingers up the neck and out under the chin (1), turning them out slightly so that each hand finishes just underneath its opposite ear. Use the backs of the fingers, too, if you like. Tap fingertips all around the mouth and chin. Give a deeper massage on the cheeks. Hold the fingers as though grasping an invisible ball and let the knuckles of the fingers play over the cheeks (2). Roll the skin gently between the first and second fingers and continue until the skin begins to tingle.
'Anchor' your thumbs under your chin (3) to ensure the lightest touch when massaging the eyes. Starting at inner corners, smooth fourth finger up over browbone, down below the eyes and into the corners again (4). Leave a fairly wide margin around the eye. Relieve any underlying tension by placing first and second fingers firmly on the temples, rotating them without letting them move across the skin and pressing down as you go (5). Finish with a firm upward stroke along the bridge of the nose and forehead. Place thumbs on temples for stability and bring hands up alternately (6), concentrating the pressure on the outer edge of the first finger. Imagine all the creases and cares being smoothed out of the skin. Continue until you feel completely relaxed.

PROFESSIONAL TREATMENTS
Facial treatments

A good facial treatment has two main benefits. The first is that it leaves your skin tingling clean, fresh and glowing so that you look the better for it; the second is that it relaxes you and provides a psychological beauty boost, so that you feel the better for it. As almost anyone who has spent a week at a health farm or beauty spa will testify, being pampered is one of the best paths to feeling good in and about yourself.

There are many types of facial, ranging from the simpler mask, massage and herbal or oil treatments, which provide a more elaborate version of your own cleanse/tone/moisturize routine, to the speciality treatments, such as aromatherapy, which uses pure essential oils for specific therapeutic purposes, cathiodermie and ozone treatments, which use electrical currents to diffuse oxygen into the skin and lift impurities out, and 'freezing' facials, which use carbon dioxide because it evaporates on contact with the face and acts like a super-efficient astringent on oily and acne-prone skins. Faces react to facials in different ways. For some, the shock of such intensive attention seems to provoke a rash of spots and pimples. The face may actually look worse a few days after treatment — not necessarily a bad sign, according to some beauty therapists who maintain that it indicates that congested toxins and impurities in the skin have been freed and are coming to the surface. Other faces benefit more visibly and emerge after an hour or so in the beauty salon looking as though they have just spent two weeks in the country. The benefits, however, are temporary. Facials will not erase wrinkles or restore muscle tone, though they can do much for the tone and texture of the skin.

Laser therapy

A quite different and still relatively new type of facial treatment (widely available in Western Europe, less so in the USA) does claim to have long-lasting and far-reaching effects. This is the low-intensity helium/neon (class II) laser beam and it promises to soften and plump out lines and wrinkles, refine skin texture, tone up flagging facial muscles and generally take years off the age of the skin. The light, which penetrates the skin to a depth of only about one millimetre, is channelled through a fibre optic tube. The tip, which looks rather like the end of a ballpoint pen, is then traced along the lines and wrinkles of the face and applied to the acupuncture points to stimulate the muscle. While laser therapy is not, as has been claimed, a substitute for a face-lift, it does seem to have a 'youthifying' effect on some skins. But it is an expensive and time-consuming procedure — results usually only being perceived after 10 sessions or more and sometimes not even then, as not all faces respond to the therapy.

SKINCARE FOR EACH DECADE
What to do when

Your skin has its own chronological age which may or may not coincide with your real age. Determined first of all by the genes you inherit, it is also affected by your lifestyle, your state of health and, of course, how much sun-exposure you have had over the years. Too much sun combined with years

of hard living, for example, can add 10 or 12 'years' on to the life of your skin. Common sense and a careful skincare routine, on the other hand, can subtract them. But it means starting early, preferably in childhood.

Childhood

Children may have a good, clear, glowing skin, but they are not often born with it. A surprisingly high percentage of babies show signs of jaundice at birth. Although the yellowish discoloration of the skin, which can extend to the whites of the eyes and the inside of the mouth, looks alarming, the condition usually resolves itself and should give no cause for real concern. The same applies to any small spots or pimples on the face, which result from the continued presence of the mother's hormones in the baby's blood. Infantile acne, which usually appears at three to four months and can last for up to two years, is more serious, as it may be an indication of some hormonal disturbance.

Childhood or infantile eczema can be an enormous problem. These itchy, scaly patches on the skin can develop into deep, sore cracks which will continually itch and irritate. Cut fingernails short to help prevent scratching, keep the skin free from strong soaps and detergents and avoid putting wool or any coarse, irritant materials next to the skin. Consult your doctor about long-term treatment.

This is also the time for infectious diseases, such as chicken pox and measles, so be on the lookout for any untoward changes in the skin, which might be an indication that the child has one of them. Otherwise, the skin should be washed twice daily and then left to itself. Start a strong anti-sun campaign as early as possible, because young bodies are much more susceptible to sunburn and to deep tissue damage than older, tougher ones.

Teens

With the exception of the first four months in the womb, puberty is the time of greatest development and growth. Even the eyeballs expand under the onslaught of new and rising hormone levels in the blood. These levels can hardly fail to have an effect on the skin. Acne, accompanied by oily, shiny skin and greasy hair, is a major teenage problem, which affects boys and girls alike (see also A-Z). Fortunately, much can be done to improve acne. So if it does not respond to the use of lotions and scrupulous cleansing, do not wait for miracles, go to your doctor, who may either treat you himself or refer you to a dermatologist. Most cases of acne can now be treated with the tetracycline groups of antibiotics. But do not expect immediate results, for it can take three months and sometimes much more before you see an improvement. It is also essential to observe scrupulous hygiene. If you have acne or a tendency towards oiliness, wash the skin twice daily, apply a medium-strength astringent (strong astringents may stimulate rather than inhibit oil production) and use moisturizer over the dry areas only. You should wash your hair frequently, too. Use a mild shampoo and choose a hairstyle that keeps the hair off the face, as oil secreted on to the scalp can cause acne all around the hairline.

This is the best time to establish your priorities. Spare a thought for sunburn and sun-damaged skin. Tan sensibly

and use a sunscreen. The action you take now to protect your face from the harmful effects of sunlight will pay huge dividends in 15 or 20 years' time.

Avoid crash dieting for the sake of your skin, if for no other reason. A subcutaneous layer of fat beneath the dermis gives the skin its springy texture and literally moulds the softer contours of the face. If this is undermined, the skin will sag, lose its suppleness and may look prematurely old, even at 18.

This is also the time not to take up smoking. After sunlight, smoking is one of the principle causes of early wrinkles and lifeless skin.

Twenties

This is a time for experimentation and change and an age at which you have to make many crucial decisions about how you want to live. Career … marriage … children? It is also a time when your hormone levels are still high and when your oil and sweat glands may be even more active than they were in your teens. Acne and oily skin may continue into your twenties or they may disappear as your hormone levels settle and your skin becomes less sensitive to them. Alternatively, acne may appear for the first time. Unlike teenage acne, which is inflammatory and red and extends over cheeks, chin and forehead, 'twenties acne' tends to take the form of small, scaly, red spots around the mouth and on the chin. Use conventional acne treatments and avoid the use of steroid creams, which may only aggravate the problem.

Now, and in subsequent years, hormones are immediately affected by pregnancy and by the contraceptive pill. Both

can have a wide range of effects on the skin. While pregnancy is often a time of marvellous healthy skin and lustrous hair, it can also be a time when the skin and hair are quite unmanageable and the nails become very brittle and when, unless you are careful, varicose veins may appear for the first time (see page 221).

If you find you develop extensive, dry, scaly, flaking tissue on exposed areas and 'pressure points' of the body, such as the knees, elbows and scalp, you may have psoriasis, one of the most common and least understood of all the skin disorders. This completely harmless, but extremely distressing condition commonly appears for the first time between the ages of 15 and 30. (Find further details on page 220.)

Thirties

This is one of the most demanding phases of your life. You may be looking after a family and young children, managing a household, pursuing a career, or doing all three at once: responsibilities which may lead you to neglect your skin. Don't. What you do, or fail to do, now may seem insignificant but will certainly affect your skin's ability to weather the years later on. You may have already noticed some early signs of ageing. Fine lines around the corners of the eyes, caused by sun-exposure, squinting and the everyday movement of the muscles beneath the skin, are usually the first to appear, as the skin is thinner here, and sebaceous glands fewer, than anywhere else on the body. These are followed by 'smile' lines, running from the corners of the nose to the corners of the mouth, and 'frown' lines, running down the centre of the forehead. Dryness of the skin can accentuate wrinkles, although it will not actually cause them, so use a good moisturizer to keep the skin soft and supple and to encourage it to retain as much of its own moisture as possible. This will also seem to soften out any facial lines and wrinkles that you already have.

As the rate of cell division and replacement falls off by 50 per cent between the ages of 35 and 80, accompanied by an increasing tendency for the old cells on the surface of the skin to cling there for a bit longer, you should compensate for the slowdown by exfoliating regularly with a commercial lotion, washing 'grains' or abrasive brushes.

The oil glands also step down their production of sebum at this time. Where once your skin glistened because of the extra oil on your face, it may now be dry and dull. Be awake to this. The skin does change and your skincare routine should adapt likewise.

Forties

By now, your age will certainly be showing some effects on your skin, but how dramatically will depend on your own genetic make-up and on how much sun-exposure you have had. If your skin is showing the results of over-enthusiastic sunbathing in early life, remember that all damage caused by sunlight is cumulative and it is still not too late to protect it from further damage.

With the approaching menopause, the hormonally responsive sebaceous glands begin to shrink in size and to produce less oil, with the result that your skin may become dry and prone to flaking. Everything you put on to the skin now, whether cleanser, sunscreen or make-up, should put something back. Use a clear glycerine or 'superfatted' soap or switch to a cream cleanser and cotton wool. Choose sunscreens that will also moisturize the skin and use a 'hydrating' foundation. Counteract the drying effects of the atmosphere by using a good moisturizer and installing a humidifier in centrally heated rooms.

Although your skin is likely to be much drier, most unfairly, you can still get acne or, more precisely, acne-like spots known as rosacea. Accompanied by mild inflammation and redness, this is most common in middle-age among those who flush or blush easily and who may have had a quite pimple-free adolescence. Indeed, there is now evidence that the condition is rarer among earlier sufferers of acne. Avoid hot drinks, spirits and curries — all of which tend to aggravate the condition — and use creams and lotions sparingly and with caution because your skin is probably dry. So restrict application only to the affected area and, if it does not clear up, see a dermatologist.

As the skin ages, the collagen and elastin fibres, which give it its elasticity and tone, become fused into an inflexible mish-mash called elastone. The skin becomes thinner too — more rapidly in women than in men, who start with thicker skins in the first place — as does the subcutaneous layer of fat, even though you may be putting on weight everywhere else. All this adds up to sagging, wrinkling, loss of skin tone and uneven pigmentation. In addition, the skin on the neck, jaw, and around the nose and mouth may feel and look several sizes too big. There is no known way of counteracting this effectively once it has happened bar cosmetic surgery, which, if carried out well, can have remarkable results and may last for up to 10 years. (Laser therapy — see previous page — is <u>not</u> a substitute for a face lift.) The years between 45 and 50 are now considered the optimum period for a 'first lift' by many cosmetic surgeons (find further details on page 167).

Fifties and beyond

There is no reason why, at 50 or over, your skin should not be soft and supple and your hair shining and healthy. Nevertheless, the menopause does take its toll on the condition of the skin and hair, as production of oestrogen, the 'good skin' hormone, gradually decreases. One of the beneficial side-effects of hormone replacement therapy (see page 213) is that the skin improves immeasurably in texture and tone and may acquire a bloom it has not had since you were 30.

But you cannot go on taking the tablets indefinitely and so, sooner or later, you will have to come to terms with increased dryness on the face and body. To counteract it, use a good, rich moisturizer like a second skin — applying it first thing in the morning and again if you are exposed to a drying atmosphere, particularly wind, sun and central heating. Use a rich night cream, the greasier the better.

Exfoliation is more important than ever, in order to ensure the skin texture remains smooth and glowing. Because the skin is drier and more delicate, use only the mildest of lotions and bypass the more abrasive techniques. Finally bathe, like Cleopatra, in a warm bath to which you have added a glass of milk — a natural water-in-oil emulsion — mixed with a capful of oil. Follow with a good after bath oil. If your skin feels dry and itchy (a condition known as 'winter itch'), bathe less often and, when you do, try adding oatmeal to the bath water and use more oil. You should find that the itching disappears if the skin is protected and moisturized well.

If you have had a lot of sun-exposure over the years, you may develop dark, hyperpigmented patches known as liver spots. A commercial bleaching agent or a chemical peel, strong enough to take off the top layer of skin may make them less visible (see page 168), but some permanent marking is inevitable. These spots are completely harmless, but you should be on the lookout for any more suspicious skin changes, such as sores that do not heal, a small, pearly patch on the skin and brown or black, mole-like growths. If you find any of these, go to your doctor.

After the age of about 35, everything that you put on to the skin – sunscreens, soaps, cleansers, make-up – should put something back. Use a light moisturizer beneath a hydrating (moisturizing) foundation during the day and a richer cream at night. Choose a thick oil-based emulsion that leaves a fine reflective sheen when smoothed on to the skin.

hair

'Beauty draws us with a single hair...' Alexander Pope

Your hair should be your crowning glory. Not only is it the first thing that people notice about you (and that is something on which psychologists and hairdressers are in perfect accord) but it also offers you the most immediate prospect of change that you have. The way you wear your hair, its colour and condition all reflect a style, indicate an outlook and add up to a definitive statement about yourself. Change your cut and experiment with colour and you can spell out a whole new look.

Because there are few, if any, hard and fast rules about the way you should wear your hair and because fashions change, you will not find guidelines on cut below. This is a province for your hairdresser who will be able to match up a style compatible with your hair type, face shape and personality in a way that no book can do. Guidelines on colour are given, however, together with a chart for quick and easy reference so that you can check out each process against the present colour and condition of your hair and arrive at one that will work well for you. But first your hair and scalp must be in the best possible condition.

STRUCTURE AND GROWTH

Hair is made of a tough substance called keratin. It comprises the inner soft core (medulla), the central cortex, and the cuticle, an outer, transparent and protective layer. The cuticle is smoothed and flattened by natural secretions of sebum from the sebaceous glands situated at the upper end of the hair follicle. This fine layer of oil causes the cuticle to reflect light and gives healthy hair its characteristic lustre and shine. Under environmental or chemical influences, the position of the cells on the cuticle can be disrupted so that, instead of lying flat and smooth like tiles on a roof, they become raised and distorted, scattering the light and making the hair appear dull and lifeless. The hair also becomes dull if the cuticle is starved of sebum — a condition caused by inactive or clogged sebaceous glands or by dandruff, which soaks up the sebum as it arrives on the scalp and prevents it from travelling along the hair.

By the time the hair on your head emerges on the scalp it is completely dead. Living matrix cells, situated beneath the surface of the skin, divide every 12 hours and push the new cells towards the surface. Within a few millimetres of daylight, these are hardened and effectively 'fossilized' so that they emerge from the scalp impermeable, sealed and well able to withstand all normal environmental rigours, such as rain, moderate amounts of wind and sunlight and the action of milder shampoos and detergents. They are not always equipped to withstand the chemical onslaught of bleaching, perming, straightening or tinting, however.

We all lose hair at a rate of up to 150 strands a day, and we can all afford to lose hair at this rate, having between 100,000 and 150,000 strands on the head at any one time. Each of these observes a three- to five-year growth cycle. In some

exceptional cases, the cycle may take seven, but only one person in a million has such an abnormally regulated cycle and such tenacious follicles that fairy-tale, floor-length hair becomes a possibility.

The whole process of hair loss and replacement is a gradual and invisible one. It has been estimated that your hair needs to lose as much as 40 to 50 per cent of an area total before that area starts to look noticeably thinner. So if you find dramatic quantities of hair on your hairbrush or pillow, do not be alarmed; you will not go bald overnight. If the hair loss continues consult a trichologist or dermatologist and, in the meantime, reassure yourself that nearly all hair loss in women is completely reversible.

Hair grows at the rate of about 14 mm (½ inch) a month — one of the most prolific growth rates in the body. Any change in cell metabolism will affect the rate of growth, and fall, of the hair. Excessive hair fall, alopecia, can also be caused by stress, pulling, fluctuating hormone levels, ageing, anaemia and other metabolic disorders. While there is always a reason, isolating the cause can sometimes be difficult.

All hair gets finer as we grow older. After as few as three decades of constant renewal, the process of cell division can start to slow up. Some cells close down entirely. Others no longer have the muscle to push through the dense elastin fibres which form with age. Genetically induced hair loss is much more common among men than women, and it is always permanent. In the future, however, early hormonal control may prevent, or at least delay, its onset.

Temporary hair loss in women is commonly caused by hormonal fluctuation, such as while taking or coming off the contraceptive pill, during the menopause and, most commonly, after a pregnancy (see page 205). Patchy hair loss, *alopecia areata*, occurs when the hair falls out in small clumps, giving the head a moth-eaten appearance. It affects about one to two per cent of the population and should be treated by a trichologist or dermatologist. A condition most often seen among adolescent girls and thought to be a sign of sexual frustration, is caused by the sufferer actually pulling the hair out of the head herself. The family doctor, a psychiatrist or a sympathetic counsellor can often help with this psychological disorder. Patchy hair loss can also be caused by severe shock. If the shock is enormous, the loss may be permanent, but in most cases it will grow back.

Another type of hair loss, mechanical or 'traction' alopecia, is caused by over-rigorous brushing, any type of hair styling that pulls the hair back from the face and interferes with its natural direction of growth, and the action of chemicals used during processing (perming, straightening, etc), which undermine the strength of the hair. The answer to this type of hair loss is simple: leave it alone. The more naturally you style and treat your hair, the stronger and more resilient it will be and the less likely to fall out prematurely.

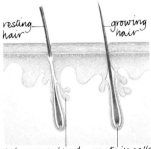

resting hair — growing hair

sebaceous gland   matrix cells

Hair grows from a cluster of matrix cells beneath the skin. These cells divide rapidly and push the new hair up towards the scalp. When the new hair emerges at the scalp it is effectively keratinized (dead). The sebaceous glands at the side of the hair follicle are largely responsible for the lustre of the hair: too much sebum will produce an oily hair condition; too little a dry one Each hair observes a growing phase (right), a resting phase of between two or three months (left) and a falling out phase. By the time the old hair is shed a new one will have already begun to form beneath it.

hairhairhair

To check the condition of your scalp, make a parting down the centre of your head and scrape it gently with a wide-toothed comb (right). If there is any scaling, your scalp needs attention – but consult the checklist of possible culprits here, before you assume it is dandruff.

If dandruff seems to be the problem, try a gentle home-based treatment – using a mild antiseptic lotion, parting the hair and applying it as shown, below – before tackling the problem with one of the harsher acting anti-dandruff shampoos.

Diet

Most hair responds very positively to a balanced, healthy diet — improving in condition and lustre as the diet improves. Wholegrains, yeast extracts, organ meats (liver, kidney, etc) and eggs are particularly beneficial because they are high in the B vitamins. This important complex is thought to play a crucial part in the health and growth of the hair at matrix level. Veterinary surgeons, interestingly, frequently prescribe extra vitamin B if the condition of an animal's coat is poor. If your hair is dull and out of condition, try doing likewise. Having first considered your diet and revised it where necessary, take extra wheatgerm on soups, cereals, stews or salads or up to six tablets (one tablespoon) of brewer's yeast a day to see if the condition improves.

TAKING CARE OF YOUR HAIR
Treating your scalp

You cannot get the best from your hair if you do not have a healthy scalp. But do not automatically assume a scaling scalp means dandruff. A dry, flaking scalp could indicate any of the following: a generalized dry skin and hair condition, which should be treated with a light almond oil massage (see below); too much exposure to bright sunlight causing the scalp to burn and peel, just as with any other part of the body; and, commonly, a residue left in the hair after shampooing or using a hair spray or setting lotion. Before you switch to a dandruff shampoo, give your regular shampoo a chance to work for you, by rinsing it out thoroughly after washing. Leave hair sprays and setting lotions off your hair for a week or two.

If your scalp does not respond to these simple steps, then you probably do have dandruff (see page 216). Treat it with a weak cetrimide solution, made by gently heating half a teaspoon of the powder (available from most chemists) in 1.2 litres/2 pints (5 cups) of distilled water until it is completely dissolved. Part the hair at 2 cm (½ inch) intervals, apply to the scalp with swabs of cotton wool, and work systematically all around the head, starting at the forehead and working backwards. If cetrimide is not available, use a straightforward commercial antiseptic diluted with four parts distilled water to one part antiseptic.

If the condition continues unabated, switch to one of the stronger anti-dandruff shampoos. Choose one containing tar or zinc pyrithione, which is thought to have a slowing effect on the rate of cell turnover.

Massaging the scalp can have several benefits for the health of the hair. It will also relax you generally. To massage your scalp, use the pads of the fingers on both hands arched into a dome shape. Start at the hairline on the forehead and move gradually back and sideways with a firm, circular movement, rather as though you were kneading dough, taking care not to move the fingers more than a few centimetres across the scalp at any one time. Keep the scalp damp, by dipping your fingers into one of the following: plain tapwater for normal hair and scalp; cetrimide or diluted antiseptic solution (given above) for dandruffed and scaly scalps; the juice of half a lemon in a cupful of water for oily and mixed condition hair; warm almond oil (left on for an hour and washed out thoroughly) for dry scalp and hair.

Brushing and combing

100 brush strokes a day are not the best way to healthy, glossy hair. They create friction, disrupt the cuticle and may even scratch the scalp. If possible, comb it instead with a wide-toothed, 'sawcut' vulcanized rubber comb with specially moulded teeth. This is much kinder to both the hair and the scalp than the cheaper, mass-produced plastic variety with sharp and scratchy edges.

Brushing or combing wet hair is especially hazardous, so always use a conditioner to help the comb glide through.

Washing

Wet hair loses up to 20 per cent of its natural elasticity, making it an easy and vulnerable target to over-vigorous shampooing and drying. Most people do more damage to their hair through insensitive washing and drying than through using the 'wrong' shampoos. Shampoos, however, are popular scapegoats.

Choosing the right shampoo is largely a matter of trial and error, unless you are already using a prescription treatment specially made up for you by a trichologist. When choosing shampoo, do not be blinded by protein, promises or pH numbers. Go by what suits you. A good shampoo should clean quickly and effectively, should be easy to apply and to rinse out and should never irritate the scalp. Do not judge the effectiveness of any given shampoo by the lather it produces. Some manufacturers add foaming agents to their shampoos for purely commercial reasons.

KNOWING YOUR HAIR TYPE

CONDITION	CAUSES	WASHING: how often, with what?	DRYING	PROCESSING
OILY	Overactive sebaceous glands in the scalp produce excess sebum, which coats the hair, causing it to glisten with oiliness and to become limp and lank in appearance. Oily hair tends to be more common among fair-haired people, who often have finer hair (coarser-haired redheads almost always tend towards dryness). All hair tends to become greasier at puberty when the sebaceous glands become much more active due to hormonal changes. In some cases it can also become noticeably oilier at times of smaller hormonal fluctuation, such as the week before menstruation. Oily hair usually improves during the last six months of pregnancy when there is a surge in several hormones.	Keep scrupulously clean and wash daily with a mild shampoo. This will not step up sebaceous gland activity, but harsh acting shampoos will. By stripping essential, as well as excess, oil from the scalp, they create a shortfall which then stimulates the glands to redress the balance. Avoid 'dry' shampoos: the powder can clog the hair follicles on the scalp and aggravate the problem. Use a conditioner before shampooing (see guidelines on page 102) or add the juice of half a lemon or one tablespoon of vinegar to a jugful of water and use it as a final rinse. The acid will remove any greasy residue left by the shampoo and smooth down the cuticle, making it easier to comb out.	Use lower heat settings on blow dryers. Hot air currents can activate the sweat glands and step up sebum production.	As processing tends to dry out cellular moisture within the hair shaft, mild colouring (not bleaching) can improve the appearance of oily or limp hair.
DRY	Four to 13 per cent of healthy hair is water. Dry hair is usually symptomatic of dehydration (loss of water content at cellular level), often caused by a lack of sebum on the hair. Dry hair not only looks dull and lifeless, but is also much more susceptible to breakage and splitting due to its reduced elasticity. While a normal strand of hair will stretch to an additional 30 per cent of its overall length before breaking, a dry strand of hair may only stretch about half as far, if that. In other words, far less stress is required to break a dehydrated hair. For this reason, you should take steps to protect it from any chemical or mechanical means of stress, such as brushing, pulling or harsh styling. As exposure to strong sunlight exerts a natural and damaging bleaching effect on the hair, anyone with a dry hair condition should take especial care to protect it from the sun by wearing a scarf or wide-brimmed hat in hot weather.	Shampoo once only with a mild shampoo. If you massage the scalp thoroughly, the hair will be cleaned effectively. Use a good cream conditioner, rinse thoroughly and keep any brushing or combing to an absolute minimum when wet. Dry hair is often accompanied by a dry and flaking scalp, but avoid using one of the harsher acting dandruff shampoos until you have tried the antiseptic scalp treatment opposite. This has the advantage of treating only the affected area, while leaving the rest of the hair alone. If the hair is very dry, massage two tablespoons of warmed olive or almond oil well into the hair, wrap in a plastic bag to increase moisture absorption and leave for at least 30 minutes. Finally, remove all traces of oil by pouring a cupful of shampoo directly onto the head, massaging well and then rinsing.	Finger dry or leave to dry in the open air, if possible. Hair dryers should be used with care. Stop drying while hair is still slightly damp to ensure against over-drying which can aggravate any tendency to dryness you may already have.	Most dry hair is inflicted not inherited – and colouring, perming or straightening and bleaching (in ascending order of severity) are the principal culprits. As the chemicals used have to penetrate beyond the cuticle, some loss of natural moisture is inevitable. Anyone with really dry hair should, therefore, avoid processing and wait for the condition to improve. Instead go for highlights or one of the milder, temporary colours that do not disturb the hair beyond cuticle level. Semi-permanent rinses are a good example.
NORMAL	Healthy-looking, shining hair is the result of well-balanced, internal chemistry (good genetic profile and well-regulated hormone levels), common sense and careful management. Most people can end up with normal hair if they look after it wisely.	Wash your hair as often as you think it needs it – every day if necessary. Because your hair is normal, it does not mean that it is more resilient or less susceptible to damage. Keep it clean and shining, by using a shampoo and a conditioner that suits you, and interfere with its natural function as little as possible.	Follow all guidelines given on pages 101-2.	Methods of colouring and/or perming the hair are now so sophisticated that there is no reason why you should not be able to achieve the cosmetic effect you desire, as long as you proceed with caution (follow guidelines on pages 102-3).
MIXED CONDITION	Active sebaceous glands produce a glut of sebum that is absorbed at the base line on the scalp and prevented from travelling along the hair shaft, robbing it of essential lubrication and gloss. With mixed condition hair, the scalp and hair at the roots are oily, while the ends are dry, frizzy and prone to breakage and splitting.	Discriminate between cleansing the scalp and cleansing the ends of the hair. Each qualifies for separate attention. Start by giving your scalp an astringent treatment before shampooing (see page 102), follow with a mild shampoo, used once only, and finish with a conditioner applied only to the ends of the hair.	As dry hair, using the lowest setting when blow drying.	As dry hair.

Hair carries a negative electrical charge and, because dirt clings to these negative ions, to cleanse it efficiently you must reverse the charge. You can do this by using any of the alkaline detergents (shampoos) on the market. Baby shampoos do not come into this category. They carry no charge at all in order to avoid irritating the eyes, and do not, therefore, cleanse as efficiently as an ordinary shampoo. While kinder to the eyes, they are not necessarily gentler to the hair. There is little evidence either to suggest that 'pH-balanced' shampoos are preferable to ordinary shampoos for natural unprocessed hair — but they can be helpful for hair that is damaged or porous (this is particularly likely if it has been permed, tinted or straightened). As all but the most permanent hair dyes will fade slightly with each wash, anti-dandruff shampoos which are harsher acting should be avoided if you are anxious to preserve the colour.

washwashwashwash

- Wash your hair as often as you need to. It cannot be worn out through over-washing and a mild-acting shampoo will <u>not</u> stimulate the sebaceous glands to produce more sebum. If you have dry hair, shampoo once only.
- Wash your hair by leaning over a bath or basin, preferably using a shower attachment to ensure that the hair is well and evenly dampened and that it is rinsed in absolutely clean water. Do not wash your hair in the bath. Soaps, bath oils and general body dirt are not a good washing or rinsing medium for your hair.
- Dampen the hair well, then apply a small amount of shampoo evenly over the head by pouring it on to your hands, rubbing them together and smoothing them through the hair.
- The purpose of washing the hair is as much to clean the scalp as to clean the hair itself, so work the shampoo well down on to the scalp and massage it for a few minutes.
- If you have longish hair, do not pile it on top of your head. This is asking for snarls and tangles. Let it fall down into the water and run your fingers through from front to back instead.
- Always use a conditioner.
- Always rinse thoroughly and, when you think you have rinsed enough, rinse again. A soapy residue will dry out the scalp and may lead to scaling.

Wet hair loses up to 20 per cent of its elasticity and, with it, much of its natural resilience. So treat it as gently as possible after washing.

● Squeeze out excess water, wrap hair loosely in a clean towel, turban-fashion, and press firmly against the head. Do not rub vigorously.

● Once hair is no longer soaking wet, the best thing you can do is to leave it to dry naturally.

● When using a blow dryer, capitalize on the control, minimize on the damage: do not start drying until the hair is three-quarters dry; do not hold the dryer over one area of the head for too long; do not allow the scalp to become hot; use a brush gently to persuade the hair into the style you want; and, most important, do not continue to blow hot air on to hair that is already dry.

Conditioning

All shampoos are detergent-based, alkaline and work by swelling the hair shaft and lifting the cuticle. They also carry an electrical charge which will cause the individual strands to react to each other, producing static. You can reduce this natural electricity by using a conditioner after shampooing. Conditioners tend to be acid and carry a positive electrical charge which encourages the hair to lie smoothly and flat on the head, enabling you to comb it through easily while wet. It is for this ease of combing out that conditioners are especially valuable and no hair, however fine and oily, should go without. If you do have oily hair use a simple acid solution as a final rinse (see oily hair, on chart) or condition before you shampoo: dampen the hair thoroughly, towel dry, apply the conditioner and leave for about 60 seconds before combing out, rinsing thoroughly and shampooing.

All conditioners are designed to work within 30 to 60 seconds. (Warm oil treatments for dry hair or scalp are an exception.) Apply the conditioner exactly as you would a shampoo, rubbing it first between the palms and then on to the hair away from the scalp, so that the cuticle is encouraged to lie flat. If you have mixed condition hair, which is oily at the roots and on the scalp but dry at the ends, apply the conditioner only to the ends. Then rinse thoroughly.

Drying

Hair swells on getting wet. It also loses it elasticity and so is easily damaged by over-enthusiastic drying. The first rule is always to treat the hair as gently as possible, preferably leaving your hair to dry on its own and using your fingers to persuade it into the shape you want. Unless you are fairly adept at this, however, it is unrealistic to expect the control or the style that you would get from using a blow dryer.

Blow dryers are fine, as long as you use them with care. They should not be too powerful (1000 watts maximum) nor should they be held too close or for too long over any one area of the head. Use them on damp, not soaking wet, hair and go for a dryer that has two or more drying speeds — start with the hotter and turn it down once most of the moisture has evaporated.

Heated rollers and curling tongs can both be damaging because they concentrate heat on hair that is already dry. While traditional rollers (buy them as smooth and even-surfaced as possible) are preferable, they are not as quick and convenient to use. In the interests of convenience, spare a thought for your hair and use heated rollers, which are less damaging than tongs. Putting your hand on a pair of hot curling tongs will cause you to burn the skin, so imagine what can happen when you use them on your hair.

Processing

No chemical process is 100 per cent harmless to the hair, because it is precisely by disrupting its internal structure that the desired effect, whether colour or wave, is achieved. Nevertheless, the potential to damage will depend on three main factors. The first is the severity of the process involved. Bleaching a whole head of hair, for example, is much more damaging than adding a few highlights. The second is the general health and texture of the hair before processing. If it is already weakened and damaged, it will not 'hold' a perm or colour as well and will also tend to be less resilient to the chemicals used than healthier, stronger hair. The third is the hands that apply the chemical. Use your own with caution, and always seek the advice and guidance of a good hairdresser if you are contemplating changing the colour or wave of your hair for the first time, because he or she will be able to give you a reliable indication of how well your hair is likely to withstand the chemicals used. Never declare war on your own natural colour. Work with it instead. Everyone has five or six distinct colour tones, or natural highlights, already present in the hair. The most natural effects are achieved by adding to, never subtracting from, these, either by creating new ones (see 'Highlights' overleaf) or by going one or two shades lighter than your natural colour and so 'lifting' it. Darkening has the reverse effect because it kills the highlights already present in the hair and flattens the colour to give an unnatural 'matt' look.

Finally, remember that, whether it is permanent dye or permanent wave, effects are irreversible and mistakes expensive. You may have to wait many months for the colour or the wave to grow out.

Perming or straightening

These processes use a chemical called ammonium thioglycollate, or one of its derivatives, to prise open the sulphur bonds — resilient interlocking cross linkages like the rungs on a ladder — which give the hair its natural stability and strength. When the hair is processed the 'rungs' are broken and realigned into the desired formation with rollers (waving) or by stretching (straightening). Once the chemical has taken effect, its action will be curtailed by the application of a neutralizer which will enable most (not all) of the bonds to reform in their new position.

Do go to a good hairdresser if you want a perm. Home perms are hazardous, both because it is extremely difficult to get the effect you require, and because the chemicals within the solution can leave you quite bald if you let them. The compound literally dissolves the hair away if left on for too long.

If you want to perm and colour your hair, never try to do both at the same time. The chemicals used react against each other and will weaken the hair. Always perm first and allow at least two weeks to elapse, preferably longer, before tinting. Never perm your hair more often than once every three months and avoid perming entirely if your hair is already damaged or weakened. Allow any dandruff or scaling scalp condition to clear up before processing.

Straightening the hair tends to be more hazardous than perming as the chemical has to be applied closer to the scalp.

Bleaching

Bleaching, whether in a salon or at home is one of the most damaging things you can do to your hair, and the hit-and-miss practice of applying lemon juice in order to obtain 'natural' streaks in bright sunlight is no better.

Bleach uses a combination of ammonia, to act as a colour stripper, and peroxide, to act as a catalyst. This has a highly abrasive action on the outer cuticle. Avoid it. If you want fine, light streaks, go to a good hair colorist and have the hair highlighted instead. The results will be much more effective, and the damage minimal, as the chemical (a lightener <u>not</u> a bleach) does not come into contact with the scalp and only a small amount of hair is being treated at one time.

Colouring

There are three main types of colour dye, of which the kindest and most temporary are the simple colour rinses, and the most dramatic and long-lasting are the permanent dyes and tints. These also offer the greatest control and versatility. The active ingredients are based on amine derivatives of which paraphenylenediamine is one of the more frequently used. These have had bad publicity in recent years, and controversy still surrounds the carcinogenic (cancer-producing) possibility of these compounds. While no conclusive evidence has yet been obtained, it is probably wise to forego colouring your hair during pregnancy, when chemicals can cross the placenta and reach the foetus. All hair dyes are now subjected to stringent tests and the amount of paraphenylenediamine has to be specified on the product label by law. As the percentage of active ingredient rises as the colour darkens (a blonde shade, for example, may contain only 0.002 per cent while a red or dark brown shade will have 15 to 20 times as much), a good general rule is always to go for a shade that is one or two shades lighter than your own. Not only is it safer from the chemical point of view, but it also looks much better.

It is always advisable to go to a good colorist for permanent tinting, but it can be expensive. If you do decide to do it at home, you must take the following precautions.

● <u>Test on a small area of skin before tinting the whole head of hair</u>, as it is possible, though unlikely, to develop a contact allergic reaction to the chemical. You should also do this if you are using a semi-permanent colour. Apply a small amount of the solution you want to use to an area on the inner forearm, cover it with a plaster, and leave for 24 hours. If there is any trace of irritation or inflammation, do not colour your hair. You should also do this if perming or straightening the hair for the first time or changing products.

● <u>You can also do a pre-colour test.</u> Take a few strands of hair, add the dye exactly in accordance with the maker's instructions and rinse it out after the specified time. This should give you some idea of the tone, but keep in mind that dyeing the hair en masse will intensify and darken the shade.

● <u>Always buy a well-known and reputable product.</u> Do not allow yourself to be unduly influenced by the picture on the front of the packet either. All colour photographs go through tone changes on printing and reproduction.

● <u>Never use permanent hair dyes for dying eyelashes, eyebrows or hair anywhere except on the head.</u> If you do want your eyelashes darker, go to a beauty salon and have them professionally done.

● <u>Always read the instructions at least twice,</u> however often you may have coloured your hair before. <u>Never trust them to memory.</u>

Black hair is usually coarse and often dry, but it can look marvellous when well-conditioned. Try a weekly oil treatment before shampooing. Use a warmed, pleasantly scented vegetable oil, such as almond, apricot or peach kernel. Massage it well on to the head (the ends and the scalp), cover with plastic and leave for 30 minutes. The oil will bond with the cuticle to give extra protection and gloss. To remove: add shampoo first, massage well into the hair, and then add water.

The three traditional ways of counteracting tight curls – straightening, tonging and cornrowing (tight plaiting/ braiding along the scalp) – are all potentially damaging, because they stretch the hair leading to breakage and increased hair fall. Try sewing artificial plaits (braids) on to the head instead, or putting the hair up with brightly coloured combs. For more shine and a larger, looser curl, use a setting lotion after shampooing and finger dry to shape.

CHEMICAL DYES

DYE	ACTION	BEST EFFECTS ON	LASTS	TO USE	COMMENTS
Temporary rinses	Water-soluble dye in a mildly acidic base coats, but does not penetrate, the hair shaft to give a nuance, or hint, of colour.	Light, mousy or greying hair. Effects may be imperceptible on very dark shades.	Until next wash	After shampooing, as directed on packet	Do not over-apply or the hair will become dull.
Metallic 'crazy' colour sprays	Colour molecules in the spray settle on the hair to give frosting of colour.	Lighter shades	Visibly until brushed or washed off – though an invisible deposit of the metallic substance may still remain in the hair; see comments.	As directed, but do protect your eyes when spraying	Never tint your hair if you have used any metallic preparation on it without first asking your hairdresser to do a strand test. If metallic traces remain, they could react chemically with the hair.
Semi-permanent rinses	Complex chemical formulae containing a thioglycollate, or similar sulphur derivative, together with tiny colour molecules, penetrate the outer transparent cuticle and are absorbed to give a darker, richer glint to colour already present in the hair.	Light to medium brown hair; lightish grey or white hair to give darker 'cover'	Four to six shampoos	After shampooing, leave for between 20 and 40 minutes, depending on intensity of tone required, and rinse out	Semi-permanent colours will not add or change colour; they will intensify the colour already present in the hair, giving marvellous chestnut or auburn tones to dark hair, for example; not recommended for fair hair. Always patch test (see previous page) before using it.
Permanent tints (also called 'shampoo-in tints' and 'oxidation colours')	'Para' dyes largely based on paraphenylenediamine (see previous page), work with an oxidizing agent, such as hydrogen peroxide, to penetrate the inner cortex of the hair where they strip the pigmentation molecules out and replace them with the new colour.	Any colour	Permanently; regrowth tint on the roots necessary at four to six weekly intervals	Strictly as directed on the packet. Never on eyelashes, eyebrows or hair elsewhere on the body. Preferably not when pregnant, when it is best to avoid any kind of chemical.	The most versatile of all the colouring options and the one which offers the professional colorist the greatest degree of control. Do observe all the cautions listed on the previous page, together with a patch test for allergies, if doing it yourself, however.
Highlights/ lowlights	Hydrogen peroxide/ammonia or colour solutions are mixed to lighten selective strands of hair and so to multiply colour tones already present in hair for added movement and depth.	Dark mousy blondes – though they can look good on almost any type of hair, including brown, red and grey. If you have brown or red hair, the addition of subtle chestnut or marmalade tone can look sensational.	Permanently; roots will need retouching after three to four months. A soapy residue after shampooing may dim highlights. Keep them bright with a rinse of baking soda and warm water (1 teaspoon per 8 fl oz/1 cup); pour on, comb through and rinse.	The oldest method uses a polythene cap and crochet hook. Preferably: section off hair with clips and brush fine strands with the lightening solution (back of head first, around hairline and crown last, where the colour develops more quickly). Wrap strands in silver foil to make neat parcels. Watch timing carefully and rinse thoroughly.	This is the most natural of all the colouring effects – though inexpertly done, it can make the hair look striped. So it is well worthwhile going to a professional colorist to have highlights put in. Always have your hair cut first if you are contemplating having highlights, as the cut largely determines the pattern they take.
Bleaching	DON'T!				

colourscolourscolours

NATURAL (VEGETABLE) DYES

DYE	ACTION	BEST EFFECTS ON	LASTS	TO USE	COMMENTS
Henna	Natural reddish dye derived from the leaves of the Lawsonia plant stains the outer cuticle of the hair. Of the many different types of henna (their strength and effectiveness vary with country of origin), the best are the pure red and neutral (i.e. non-dye) hennas.	All shades of brown and black. On the whole, the darker the tone, the more effective the result. The effects that you will achieve with henna will depend very much on your natural colour. It's not recommended for those with grey or fair hair as it can look very carroty. Neutral hennas can make fantastic conditioners and provide a beautiful sheen without producing a noticeable change in colour.	Permanently (henna is even more irremovable than a blue/black tint); roots will need retouching every six to eight weeks	Combine neutral henna with pure red Iranian henna, add hot water and stir to a paste (you can also add strong black coffee to add depth; hot red wine for chestnut tones on a light brown hair; a strong sage infusion for a warmer effect). Wearing rubber gloves, apply the paste first to the ends of the hair within an inch of the scalp and then to the roots where the colour develops much more quickly. Cover with plastic or foil and leave for about 35 minutes. Then check the colour by testing a strand of hair. DO NOT APPLY HEAT: this will affect the final colour. Shampoo and rinse out thoroughly.	Henna can either look marvellous or disastrous so, if you are doing it yourself, treat it with respect – going redder in stages until you get the effect you are after. Bear in mind that the theatrical red of too much henna is one of the most difficult colouring mistakes to correct. Never tint your hair if you have used a metallic (compound) henna as the chemical combination can cause the hair to disintegrate.
Rhubarb root	The strongest of all the herbal lighteners, this brightens and lifts colour on all types of hair and will give golden highlights to the hair even on first application.	Any colour from black (chestnut overtones) to light ash blonde (light gold overtones)	Permanently – once effects have been achieved	Boil 50g/2 oz rhubarb root in 1.2 litres/2 pints (5 cups) of water, cover, simmer for an hour, then cool and strain. Use as final rinse and run it through the hair again and again. To work most effectively, let your hair dry off naturally in the sun afterwards.	These pure herbal colours are all fun to use and entirely non-damaging to the hair. They do not, however, offer anything like the control that you can get with the chemical dyes and are also extremely time-consuming to use – taking many applications before an appreciable difference can be seen (rhubarb root is an exception). With patience and perseverance though, they can be quite effective. With the exception of the darkeners, they will all work most effectively if you let your hair dry off naturally in the sun after application. You can also combine the herbs: when marigold is added to the chamomile and quassia infusion, for example, it will produce a more intense effect; rhubarb root and chamomile are also effective together.
Chamomile	Very slight bleaching effect on blonde hair; combined with quassia chips (see right) and applied as a paste to hair, it will brighten darker hair; combined with red wine, it will give a warm glow to light/medium brown hair.	Naturally blonde hair	as above	Brew like tea, using 25 g/1 oz chamomile flower heads per 600 ml/1 pint (2½ cups) of boiling water; leave to infuse for 20 minutes and pour over the hair, as above. Alternatively boil 25 g/1 oz quassia chips in a little water for 30 minutes, pour over 25 g/1 oz ground chamomile and apply as a paste to the hair like henna (see above).	
Marigold	Rich honey tones to fair hair; soft yellow effect on white hair.	Blonde or white hair	as above	Make infusion, as above, using 75 g/3 oz crushed marigold flowers, and apply as final rinse.	
Sage; sage and tea/cloves; walnuts; dark tree barks, such as oak	All these combinations have a darkening effect – the sage combinations by dulling the hair, the walnuts and dark tree barks by staining it, provided that they are used in strong enough concentration.	Brown and, particularly, greying hair	Temporarily, unless applications are repeated frequently	Infuse 50-75 g/2-3 oz sage (preferably red) in plain water or in 600 ml/1 pint (2½ cups) of strong Indian tea or with a base of crushed cloves; infuse the ground bark and nuts in the same way. Apply as final rinses.	

While soft, downlike hair on legs, arms or face, as left, can be very attractive, a darker or heavier growth is not. The degree to which this occurs varies enormously. For some, a few coarse, dark hairs on the face, nipples, between the breasts or on the stomach present little more than an irritation that can be bleached or snipped away. For others, a thicker, more abundant growth can give rise to great embarrassment, considerable distress and may even require medical, rather than cosmetic, treatment

UNWANTED HAIR

With the exception of the lips, the palms of the hands and the soles of the feet, all of us, male and female, either have hair on the body or the ability to produce it in response to specific internal triggers. However, while women have as many hair follicles on their faces as men and an inherent capacity, therefore, for an equally abundant growth, most of these remain dormant throughout adult life. What hair we do have tends to be soft, downlike and invisible in all but the brightest of lights. It can become coarser and darker, however, under internal or external stimulation.

Many factors can be responsible for this. The first and most important one is undoubtedly hormonal and is caused primarily by a higher level of androgen (male hormone) circulating in the blood or by an increased sensitivity to existing hormone levels. One or both of these effects are

REMOVING UNWANTED HAIR

METHOD	DESCRIPTION	WHERE AND WHEN NOT TO USE
SHAVING	This is the most popular method of removing unwanted hair. It is quick, easy and efficient and does not cause the hair to grow back thicker or darker although the regrowth feels rougher because the hairs have been cut square. To shave: use soap and water, shaving cream, gel cleanser or anything that helps the razor glide over the skin. If you are using an electric razor the skin must be dry. Always shave in the direction of hair growth; down the legs from knee to ankle, for example. This will avoid getting an ingrown hair: tell-tale signs are a black dot or a thin line beneath the surface layer of the skin.	Shaving is the most temporary and least aesthetic of all hair removal options, as the hair grows back again within two to three days as a coarse stubble. Never shave hair on the face, around the nipples or the bikini line, where the angles are difficult to get right and there is a strong risk of cutting yourself.
TWEEZING/PLUCKING	This works best when there are only a few hairs to remove. Always pluck hair in a good light, with a magnifying mirror and in the direction of hair growth. Pluck hairs one at a time from the underneath of the eyebrow only. Clean skin and tweezers scrupulously before starting. If plucking is painful, place a warm damp towel or face flannel over the brows for a few moments to help open the pores.	Only pluck the eyebrows. Tweezing is the greatest stimulator of hair growth because it can activate a repair hormone which induces increased cell production within the hair follicle. It is impossible to tweeze a hair out by the root. The white bulb that you see at the end of the hair shaft is an indication of how strong and well nourished the hair is; it is not the root.
DEPILATORY CREAMS	These use an active chemical agent to dissolve the protein structure that gives the hair its strength and texture. The destructive action of the chemical is, therefore, limited by how far the cream can penetrate the skin tissue. Depilatory creams give a deeper removal than shaving and the regrowth will seem finer because the hair has been dissolved and not cut. But it is messy. When using a depilatory cream, always follow the maker's instructions and time yourself carefully. If you find that the cream does not work effectively within the time stated do not prolong it. Use another method instead.	You can use depilatories almost anywhere, except the eyebrows, where the tissue is too sensitive and the eyes too close, the breasts and the face, unless the label stipulates that it is safe for facial use. Always take especial care if removing hair around the bikini line. Wear bikini bottoms and use the margins as your guideline to prevent the cream getting too close to the vagina. Allergies or sensitive reactions to the chemical solvents in the cream are not unknown, so always do a patch test first, following the maker's instructions as though you were treating a larger area. If there is no reaction in 24 hours, you can then apply it where you wish. Repeat the patch test if changing brands.
WAXING (professionally)	Waxing is really 'mass tweezing' but, unlike tweezing, does not enable you to discriminate between the thicker and the finer hairs on the body or the face. Beauty salons use two methods of waxing: 1. HOT: the wax is heated, applied in patches, allowed to cool for a few seconds and stripped off the skin, taking the hairs with it. As hot wax dilates the hair follicle, the hair is almost always removed from its deepest possible point – just above the root. However, it also takes the uppermost layer of dead skin cells with it and can irritate a sensitive skin. 2. COLD: a fine film of sticky, honey-based, liquid wax is smoothed over the area to be treated and covered with a layer of gauze. The gauze is then stripped away taking the wax and the hairs with it. As cold wax is not as harsh on the top layer of skin, it is better for very sensitive skins. However, it is not as effective for removing very thick or coarse hair. You have to let your hair grow sufficiently long before waxing so that the wax has something to grip on to. Waxing breaks off the hair beneath the surface of the skin and is therefore more likely to lead to ingrown hair than any other depilatory method. Regrowth is slower than any of the other temporary methods and will seem finer.	Never wax painful, inflamed or sunburned skin. The method should not be used on the nipples or the delicate tissue of the face.

removeremoveremove

seen at the menopause. Hormone replacement therapy (HRT) often works to counteract this tendency.

Stimulation of the hair follicle can also be drug-induced, although the offenders are so well known that doctors only prescribe them with the greatest of caution. It is much more often self-induced. Plucking can stimulate the follicle via a response from a repair hormone and thereby create a more vigorous growth. Consequently, stray hairs on the nipples, stomach or above the lip should never be tweezed. Bleach them, snip them with scissors or go to an electrolysist.

Electrolysis is the only widely available way of removing excess hair permanently although some salons in the USA are now experimenting with radio waves. If you suffer from thick, pronounced coarse hair growth on your face or body you should see your doctor. If he or she suspects that you may be suffering from a hormonal disorder, you will be referred to an endocrinologist (hormone specialist) for treatment. With the exception of electrolysis, all the methods detailed here have only the most temporary effect on hair growth and they all have their advantages and drawbacks. Hair grows like grass — while some is being removed, more lurks just beneath the surface — so you are always going to have some regrowth after two to three days whatever depilatory method you use. Although waxing or using a depilatory cream may give the impression of producing a finer, sparser regrowth, because the ends are tapered, not stubbly, they actually leave the growth cycle unchanged. Plucking can even accelerate it.

If, after consulting the chart, you are still in a quandary, seek the advice of a beauty therapist. Advice never costs anything and most beauticians will only be concerned in helping you to decide which method will work best for you.

METHOD	DESCRIPTION	WHERE AND WHEN NOT TO USE
WAXING (at home)	More hit-and-miss than going to a professional beautician but, with practice, you can become quite proficient. It is also available in hot and cold forms: 1. HOT waxes are much trickier to use but the technique, once mastered, will give better results. If you are using hot wax, do make sure that you buy a kit which includes an in-built thermostat control. Apply the wax with a spatula, according to the instructions, and wait for it to set like toffee. On no account let it become brittle. It should be both applied and removed against the direction of hair growth. When taking it off, hold the skin down at the end you are starting with and rip it off at a backwards angle close to the skin. Apply a soothing lotion. If you are using a hot wax treatment for the first time, you may find that it hardens and becomes brittle before you have realized it. If this happens, do not panic, simply apply another layer of wax over the top and pull them both off together. 2. COLD pre-waxed strips have the advantage of being much more manageable and considerably quicker. They are not as effective, however. In cold weather, place them on a radiator for a few minutes to soften.	As for professional waxing. Do not be over-ambitious with the areas you attempt to treat yourself. It is always advisable to seek the services of the professional if you want to remove hair under the arms or around the bikini line and it is a good idea to go at least once to a salon to get an idea of the processes involved.
BLEACHING	Bleaching is an excellent way of dealing with dark hair on the face (and on the legs if you are going out into the sun, because the chemical bleach lightens them before the natural bleaching effect of the sun takes over). Although bleaching can be professionally done, the home kits are so good that, providing instructions are carefully followed, the results are equally impressive. As hair grows back at different rates, the interval left between each bleaching varies. The effect on facial hair can often last up to four weeks before the darker regrowth becomes visible.	Always use a bleach that has been specially formulated for the face and avoid commercial hair bleaches which have a tendency to turn the hair yellow. All facial hair bleaches are extremely mild (10 vol peroxide) and cannot bleach the skin underneath. If left on for too long, however, they may cause redness and irritation. If you find that the hair does not respond effectively to the bleach solution within the time allowed, it is probably worth considering electrolysis.
ELECTROLYSIS (professionally)	Electrolysis is the only widely used way of removing hair permanently. It uses an electric current (shortwave diathermy) to generate a heat reaction within the hair follicle producing a cauterizing effect on the tiny blood capillaries that nourish the hair root. It takes a fraction of a second to kill the hair and only the most sensitive of skins will find it painful. It is uncomfortable, however, and most skins tend to react quickly to the current, becoming pink and producing raised lumps over the follicles. These should subside within an hour or so. A newer method uses tweezers to pass the current through the hair shaft. Although it is completely painless, it is not as effective as diathermy. Not all the hairs will be killed the first time but, while some do grow back, the hair will be finer and the shaft weaker and less resilient with each regrowth. With patience and perseverance, electrolysis will work better than any other method, but it does take a long time before any improvement becomes really apparent. It can take as long as 18 months to clear a lipline, for example. For this reason, electrolysis is not a practical method for removing large areas of unwanted hair, but it is extremely good for stray dark hairs on the face, breasts or stomach.	Never use electrolysis in the inner ear and nostrils – these hairs should be snipped with scissors or left to themselves – on the eyelashes, in moles or warts, on or around the nipple if pregnant or breastfeeding and anywhere where the skin is infected, inflamed or unevenly pigmented – if you have chloasma (melasma), for example (see page 215). Avoid electrolysis if you are a diabetic and your doctor advises against it, if you have an allergy to metals or an underlying hormonal disorder. Go to a reputable and properly qualified electrolysist. Incorrectly done, treatment can lead to local infection or, more commonly, to scarring caused by the needle rupturing the wall of the hair follicle. If the skin is registering any signs of damage, such as red marks above the follicle, a day or so after treatment, cancel your next appointment. You can do much to help the skin heal quickly by keeping the treated area scrupulously clean and leaving it free from creams, lotions and camouflaging make-up for at least a day or two. Never squeeze a spot on the treated area as there is a risk of scarring.
ELECTROLYSIS (home kits)	At the time of writing, the use of do-it-yourself electrolysis kits is strongly advised against. The current is usually too low to guarantee a good result and there is a high risk of scarring if the needle is inserted incorrectly.	Not at all.

teeth

'Such a pearly row of teeth, that Sovereignty would have pawned her jewels for them.'
Laurence Sterne

We are not all born with the potential for perfect teeth, but heredity is a popular scapegoat for bad teeth and an unhealthy mouth. Conversely, good teeth and a healthy mouth can be acquired by almost anyone, provided that the battle against tooth decay and gum disease is started as early as possible, that the teeth are straightened or rearranged, if necessary, by a good orthodontist and that they are looked after with common sense and dedication. Teeth fall out or weaken for specific and preventable reasons. They do not fall out or weaken with age. In fact, it has been estimated that a healthy tooth will outlast its owner by some 200 years.

Human beings develop two sets of teeth during their lives. The first set of baby, or deciduous, teeth starts to form well before birth and erupts in the mouth during the first two years of life. The second set of 32 adult, or permanent, teeth starts to develop at birth. These lie buried in the jaw bone beneath the baby teeth until they are fully formed at about the age of six, when they begin to push through the gum and the baby teeth fall out. An orthodontic evaluation should always be carried out at about this age, so that the dentist can determine whether the adult teeth have enough room to come through and will not be knocked off-course by the baby teeth above them. If this looks likely, then the removal of one or more of the baby teeth may be all that is needed to ensure that the adult teeth come through correctly.

STRUCTURE

Each tooth comprises the crown, which is the part we can see, the neck and the root or roots. It is composed of the outer enamel, which is about 98.7 per cent mineral and the hardest substance in the body, the inner dentine, which is softer and more sensitive, and the pulp chamber right at the centre, containing blood vessels and the nerve which supplies sensation to the tooth. This chamber extends all the way down the root canal which anchors the tooth to the bone of the jaw. While the front teeth have only single roots, the molars right at the back of the mouth may have as many as four. The tooth is cushioned against the bone by an elastic membrane — soft sensitive tissue that acts as a shock absorber, gives additional support to the tooth and folds over to form the gum, creating a slight gap or crevice, before attaching on to the tooth.

The bite

The mouth is built like an extremely efficient food processor, with jaws that work both horizontally and vertically. When they come together, they cause the teeth to overlap, the upper jaw over the lower, rather like a closed pair of scissors. If they collide or miss each other entirely, then the bite will be

affected. An orthodontist (tooth-straightening specialist) will be able to correct this by means of removable or fixed appliances, which persuade the teeth to move into the required position. Sometimes, they are also used to restrain the growth of the upper jaw so that the lower one can catch up. The aim of orthodontic treatment is to get the bite right, so that the relationship between the jaws and the teeth is harmonious, with the teeth coming together correctly and pressure evenly distributed throughout the mouth. Happily, appearance always improves as a result.

LOOKING AFTER YOUR TEETH

Care of the teeth starts with regular and thorough cleaning of the mouth and, equally important, regular dental check-ups. Fluoride, too, is an essential part of any early preventative campaign. Taken from birth, or even, as some dentists recommend, from before birth, it will strengthen the teeth as they form in the mouth, making the enamel harder and much less susceptible to the acid attack that initiates decay. Fluoride is invaluable taken up to the age of about eight or nine, after which most adult teeth are fully formed in the mouth and can no longer be strengthened from the inside. Start by telephoning the appropriate local authority to find out whether the water is either artificially or naturally fluoridated. If it is not, use a supplement in the form of drops or tablets. Your dentist will advise you when to start administering it and how much to give.

The acid responsible for producing decay is a by-product of the sucrose in refined carbohydrates and certain bacteria in the plaque growing on the teeth. Painless in the early stages, decay attacks the outer edges of the enamel before spreading into the soft, sensitive dentine beneath. As all sticky, sugary things are candidates for causing decay, they should be avoided as much as possible. You will feel much better for eliminating sugar from your diet too. If you must eat it, however, always brush your teeth well afterwards. By substituting the natural sugar (fructose) found in fruit and vegetables, for refined sugar (sucrose), you will be safeguarding the health of your teeth. For, although all sugar is potentially corrosive, the sugar found in apples and carrots will not cling to the teeth in the same way as the sugar in a doughnut.

Tenacious and transparent plaque film forms from substances in food and saliva. This contains up to 300 different organisms. Some of these are benign and protect the mouth from viral and fungal infections, such as thrush. Others are toxic, capable of eating into the gum tissue and initiating the slow, insidious process of gum disease. If you have managed to keep all your teeth by the age of 16, the chances are that any subsequent loss will be caused, not by decay, but by

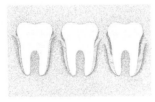

The tooth is composed of hard outer enamel, softer inner dentine and a sensitive pulp chamber right at the centre, which contains blood vessels and the nerve. The crown of the tooth (1) is the only visible part. The neck (2) extends down below the gum and the roots (3) anchor the tooth into the jawbone. Teeth have between one and four roots, depending on their position in the mouth.

After the age of 16, more teeth are lost through gum disease than decay. The insidious process is shown above. First, bacteria accumulate on the side of the tooth. If not removed in 24 hours, the bacteria harden and work their way down, forming a pocket beneath the gum which is inaccessible to the toothbrush. The bacteria then begin to attack the surrounding bone. If not checked in time, the tooth will become loose in the mouth.

teethteethteeth

infected gums. As plaque becomes damaging within 24 hours of formation, the teeth must be thoroughly and correctly brushed at least once, preferably twice, a day, so that the bacteria within it will not have a chance to infiltrate the gum tissue. Remember, it is not just the frequency that counts, it is how well you do it.

Protecting your gums

Gum disease is almost universal. Tell-tale signs are puffy, inflamed gums, which bleed on brushing, and soreness or irritation. Although the process can be halted and, to some extent, reversed, as long as the tooth is still in the mouth and has some bone around it, the measures necessary become increasingly more radical, time-consuming and expensive as the disease progresses. In its early stages, you can brush and floss your way out of it. However, if the bacteria are allowed to work their way down into the space between the tooth and the gum, a small pocket will form, inaccessible to the toothbrush, from which the bacteria will begin to attack and corrode the surrounding bone. At this stage, the disease can be treated by a minor surgical procedure, which involves cutting the gum away from the tooth and eliminating the pocket, so that the bacteria can be flushed out, the gums returned to health and good oral hygiene can be maintained. But, if the bacteria are allowed to remain in their pockets and continue to corrode the bone, the teeth will eventually become loose in the mouth and much more radical surgery will be needed to save them. Vigilance is all — both on the part of your dentist, who should make a gum evaluation an integral part of every visit, and on your own part, as professional attention will do little to safeguard your gums if you do not look after them properly in the meantime.

Orthodontics

Orthodontics is the science of straightening and rearranging the teeth. It is not cosmetic dentistry. If the teeth are out of line, if there are large gaps or overcrowding, or if the relation between the lower and upper jaws is unharmonious and the teeth do not come together as they should, then all is unlikely to be well in the mouth.

Overcrowding is by far the most common problem seen by orthodontists. If the mouth is too crowded, the teeth are pushed out sideways, the line becomes irregular, the bite is affected and the mouth becomes much more susceptible to gum disease, because plaque builds up on the overlapping edges between the teeth. It is also, of course, a problem from a cosmetic point of view. Fortunately, both this and many other irregularities with the teeth can be put to rights at any age, providing that the sufferer is prepared to put up with a certain amount of temporary inconvenience and minor discomfort.

In the long term, fixed appliances, usually consisting of brackets directly attached to the teeth by means of a strong bonding agent, are preferable to the removable kind. They offer the orthodontist greater control and enable the roots of the teeth to be moved into their correct position in the jaw. Removable appliances tend to be only about 50 per cent effective, because they do not offer the same control, nor do they move the roots into place. As a general rule, no discrepancy between the teeth or the jaws should be overlooked. So, if you feel distressed for yourself or your child, ask to be referred to an orthodontist.

Seeing your dentist

Do not wait until you find a hole in your tooth or are struck down with toothache before seeing your dentist. You should have regular dental check-ups at six monthly intervals, unless your dentist specifies otherwise. These check-ups will enable your dentist to establish that there is no decay, that your gums are sound and healthy and that there is no untoward change in the mouth, such as the eruption of wisdom teeth, that might alter the position of your teeth and affect your bite.

You should also make a point of seeing a dental hygienist at least once a year, so that you can have any tartar, a hard calcium deposit in the plaque, removed (scaled) and your

To brush your teeth:
Start right at the back on the outer side of the lower jaw. Hold the brush at an angle of 45 degrees to the gum, so that it is lying lengthwise across the teeth and the bristles can nudge just under the fold of skin tissue where the gum meets the tooth. Now, gently flex the bristles back and forth in about 20 or 30 small vibratory movements, so that they, but not the brush, are travelling over the teeth, rather like running on the spot. Once you have cleaned this area, move on to the next and so on, all the way around the jaw. You will probably complete it in five to seven stages. Now repeat the procedure on the inner tooth surface of the lower jaw. Next, scrub the top of the teeth, the biting surfaces, before turning your attention to the upper jaw. It is essential that you treat the upper and lower teeth independently. Finally, brush the tongue gently to remove any bacteria and food particles that may contribute to bad breath and rinse the mouth well.
Once you have finished, or think you have, use a plaque discloser. To begin with, continue to use the discloser every two to three days after brushing, as a useful check on yourself. Once all the plaque is off the teeth, stop brushing. Obsessive cleaning and scrubbing can be as bad for the teeth and gums as failing to clean them adequately in the first place.

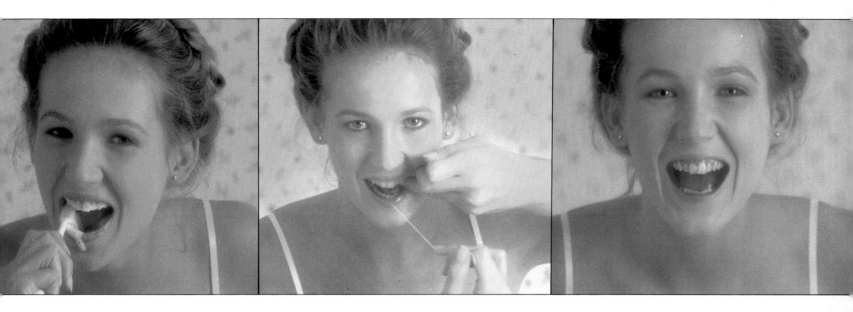

mouth professionally cleaned. Many dental practices now have a hygienist on the premises. If yours does not, ask your dentist to refer you to one. A really good teaching programme on cleaning and caring for your teeth will also stand you in good stead.

Unfortunately, finding a good dentist is not always easy. There are good and bad dentists, just as there are good and bad doctors, teachers or lawyers. Use the following guidelines as a safeguard.

● Never go to a dentist who does not give a local anaesthetic. He may leave decay in the tooth in order to save his patient pain. The infection will then continue to spread and the tooth will decay beneath the filling.

● Never go to a dentist who makes a routine practice of giving a general anaesthetic or one who gives his own anaesthetic without another practitioner present. Although general anaesthesia has its advantages in some areas of dentistry, the health risks do not justify its use for simpler procedures.

● Never go to a dentist who does not look for obvious or incipient signs of gum disease, by gently probing the areas between the gum and the tooth to test for bleeding, redness, inflammation and loss of tissue around the tooth. After the age of 16, your teeth are much more likely to be threatened by gum disease than by decay.

● Do go to a dentist who uses X-rays as an integral part of any dental evaluation. X-rays enable the dentist to check on decay, particularly decay that may have crept in behind the fillings (these tend to shrink over the years and can thus provide pockets for bacteria). They will also help him to see if there is any infection around the nerve and roots of the tooth and to spot any loss of bone caused by advanced gum disease.

● Do go to a dentist who, in the event of finding anything wrong in your mouth, will take the time and the trouble to explain what is wrong, why it happened in the first place and how you can prevent something similar happening, elsewhere in the mouth, in the future.

● Do go to a dentist who finishes off the work carried out in your mouth with care. If you do have your teeth filled, or crown or bridge work carried out or dental veneers fitted, there should be no rough edges and you should be able to clean around the treated area without difficulty.

Brushing

Your toothbrush should have bristles which are flat along the top and multi-tufted (i.e. densely packed). Nylon is better than 'natural' bristle, because, unlike hog's hair, it can be made to a precise specification. The bristles should be soft enough to flex over the tooth surfaces, reach into the gum crevices and flow into the irregularities between the teeth. Many dental practices keep a wide stock of toothbrushes for their patients together with interspace brushes, which look like miniature toothbrushes with a single densely packed tuft. These can reach into the corners that ordinary toothbrushes cannot.

Replace your toothbrush as soon as the bristles start to splay out and are no longer parallel. Used intelligently, a toothbrush should last about three months. If you find your toothbrush is wearing out after just a few weeks or, even worse, a few days, you are scrubbing too hard and your brushing technique is almost certainly wrong. So revise it, following the guidelines given here.

Toothpaste will help you to clean your teeth more efficiently. Always use a fluoride toothpaste. With regular daily use, a certain amount of the mineral will become absorbed into the enamel and will strengthen the teeth against decay. Toothpastes contain detergent, to help clean the teeth and remove the greasy plaque, sorbitol and saccharin, to make it palatable, and tiny abrasives, to remove surface staining. Tooth powders and commercial 'whiteners' have larger abrasive particles and should be avoided, as they will grind into the enamel and may gradually erode it. Avoid liquid 'stain removers', too, as they contain acid, which will remove some of the enamel as it removes the stain. If your teeth are badly stained, go to see your dentist or dental hygienist and

No tooth brushing routine, however efficient, can clean more than three of the five sides of the tooth, so the use of dental floss is essential. To use the floss: wrap it around the tooth in a wide V-shape. Slide it down just a little way into the gum crevice and up again. Repeat this about a dozen times, less if you are using the floss daily, before changing the direction of the V so that you are flossing the surface of the neighbouring tooth. Repeat all the way around the mouth.

To test a toothbrush: run the bristles backwards and forwards over the back of your hand. They should feel comfortable, even soothing – not scratchy – and should flow evenly over the contours of your knuckles. If they don't, don't use it.

111

have them professionally cleaned and polished. Enamel is not completely impermeable. Substances that cause the teeth to discolour on the outside might stain them internally, if adequate steps are not taken to remove them.

Dentists can treat bad staining or discoloration by bleaching the teeth, using a hydrogen peroxide solution. Often, the effect is only temporary and may last for as little as one year. In any case, it can do little to improve the condition if the discoloration has infiltrated the enamel and stained the tooth from the inside. Your first line of defence should be to prevent the teeth becoming stained in the first place by careful, regular brushing.

The primary purpose of brushing is to remove plaque. To do this, you need to combine a good brushing method with persistence. To see how effective your current method is, clean your teeth as usual and then use a disclosing agent. This is available from any good chemist in liquid or tablet form. Swill it round your mouth, so that the colour coats your teeth and gums, and then rinse out, once only, in clear water. This will wash away any loose colour on the enamel, but will leave traces of colour where the spongy and porous plaque has absorbed it. If you have any patches of staining around the teeth and, particularly, around the margin of the tooth and gum, then you have not cleaned your teeth properly and you should revise your brushing technique. Aim to clean your teeth thoroughly at least once, preferably twice, a day, as plaque matures and produces its corrosive acids within 24 hours of formation. The whole routine (see previous page) should take about five minutes.

If, while you are brushing this way, your gums bleed and your mouth feels rather sore afterwards, then you have the early stages of gum disease (gingivitis). Although your first impulse may be to slack off on your brushing, you should do the opposite. The only 'cure' for gingivitis is good, regular brushing, so carry on regardless. Although the gums may bleed quite profusely for the first few days and the mouth may feel sore, the condition should have righted itself after about 10 days. If it has not, make an appointment to see your dental hygienist as you probably have a build-up of tartar on the tooth which is irritating the gum.

Flossing

Once you have taken off the visible plaque, you must remove the plaque lurking between the tooth surfaces. These areas are inaccessible to any toothbrush, however good your technique. It is here that flossing is important, but take care — used wrongly, it can do more harm than good. A notorious jail break-out in the USA was achieved purely through toothpaste and dental floss which the prisoners used to 'saw' through the bars. Your gums are infinitely more vulnerable, so be careful.

Dental floss comes in two varieties — waxed and unwaxed. Unwaxed is better for perfect teeth or teeth that have completely smooth fillings with no sharp, hanging edges to catch and break the thread. If you find that unwaxed thread catches on your teeth, either have your fillings smoothed down by a good dentist, or use the waxed floss, which has the necessary lubrication to glide over the rough surfaces.

Flossing does require a certain amount of dexterity. This

comes with practice, so persevere. Alternatively, go for one of the ingenious dental floss 'holders' now available which hold the floss tightly across two prongs, making the job much easier for you. If you are confused about the technique you should be using, consult your dentist or dental hygienist. If you find that you cannot slip the floss between the teeth, that you cannot move it up and down once it is there or that you cannot get it out again, you have overhanging filling edges and/or tartar and you should see your dentist. If you find using dental floss impossibly fiddly, at least use the wooden interspace cleaners (they look like pared-down toothpicks) to remove debris caught between your teeth.

Mouthwashes

Most mouthwashes tend to be cosmetic rather than therapeutic and have little real value, as they will only disguise a bad smelling mouth for a few minutes.

Fluoride mouthwashes can be valuable, however, both because they give some additional protection to the teeth and because they tend to desensitize the mouth, reducing soreness when brushing sensitive teeth and gums. In fact, if your teeth are very sensitive, you may well find that a fluoride mouthwash is more helpful than some of the specially formulated toothpaste brands now on the market.

Ulcers and abscesses

Mouth ulcers are caused by complex, hereditary factors and tend to flare up under stress. Although they will disappear with time, little can be done to accelerate the natural healing process, beyond keeping the mouth as healthy as possible and trying to avoid any unnecessary stress.

While ulcers generally affect the upper and lower gums, roof or insides of the mouth, an abscess is a swelling just below or on the margin of the gum and tooth caused by infection inside the tooth. It should be treated by a dentist.

Tooth cleaning kit (right): toothbrush and fluoride toothpaste; small mirror to help you check teeth and gums at the back of the mouth; a dental floss holder, here shaped rather like a tuning fork, to make flossing easier; dental floss, which comes in two varieties, waxed and unwaxed to remove plaque and food debris from inner surfaces of the teeth; a neat interdental brush to help clean larger spaces between the teeth; wooden interdental sticks to reach into awkward corners and to massage the gum (if gums are sensitive, soak the stick in warm water first to soften it); plaque disclosing tablets to test your brushing routine and to see if you are using each of the above as it was designed to be used...

COSMETIC AND RESTORATIVE DENTISTRY

'Cosmetic dentistry' is an unfortunate and misleading term. While crowns, bridges, veneers and all the paraphernalia of dental repair work can do much to improve the appearance of the teeth, nothing is more attractive than a perfectly healthy and uncluttered mouth, with no tell-tale flashes of gold, nickel or even porcelain. On the whole, the less you do to a tooth, with the exception of orthodontics and the removal of decay, the better and stronger it will be. For this reason, the principle behind any form of cosmetic intervention must be to achieve the desired result with the minimum possible trauma to the surrounding teeth and gum tissue.

Cosmetic dentistry is always expensive, but the results can be extremely good and many satisfied customers consider that these justify the expense. While it is essential that any dentistry is carried out by a good and competent dentist, it is especially important in the field of crown and bridge work, where mistakes are invariably expensive and often extremely difficult to put right.

TYPE	DESCRIPTION AND MATERIALS USED	ADVANTAGES	DRAWBACKS
CROWNS	An artificial 'cap' is cemented on to a tooth, already fined down to about half of its original diameter, so that the crown slips easily and unobtrusively over the top. Material used depends on the position of the tooth in the mouth. Porcelain is the most natural looking but does not have the strength to withstand constant pressure, and is therefore used only on the front teeth. Even then, dentists usually prefer to fuse it on to a gold or metal alloy substructure. Crowns are often made entirely of 9-carat gold at the back of the mouth, where strength counts most and appearance matters least. Some of the new metal alloys on the market can now be substituted for up to 40 per cent of the gold, saving modestly on cost while losing little in the way of strength. A greater percentage of alloy to gold, however, will make the crown weaker and more susceptible to damage or splitting: they may be slightly cheaper but it is a false economy and should be avoided.	Unless badly fitted and barring unforeseen accidents, crowns are permanent and tend to 'age' well, staining and discolouring at much the same rate as natural teeth. The cosmetic result is usually very good, especially if the surfaces have been carefully matched to the surrounding teeth.	The cement fills a space between the crown and the tooth and, if infection is allowed to creep in and dissolve it, a space is created for decay to seep in behind the crown. This can result in loss of bone, infected nerves, abscesses or gum disease. The success of any crown or crown and bridge work also depends considerably on the dedication of the patient. Scrupulous cleaning is absolutely vital as the cement used is less resilient to the acid and bacteria in plaque than ordinary tooth enamel. Problems can also arise if the crown is fitted too ambitiously and the join buried beneath the gum line. The edge, however finely graduated, can rub against the soft tissue and may lead to gum disease.
BRIDGES	These are used to attach one or more 'dummy' teeth to the surrounding teeth, using crowns on either side to anchor the new tooth into position. Bridges are usually made from gold or a gold and metal alloy and covered with porcelain to give a natural effect. A new type of bridge, known as a Rochette bridge, is cheaper than the conventional bridge, kinder to the anchor teeth (which do not require crowning) and, if fitted well, will last for up to 15 years. However, it can only be used for small spaces with adequate clearance.	A bridge is an excellent solution in the event of a missing front tooth, as the new dummy tooth stays firmly and permanently in place and cuts out the need for dentures.	Badly done, the bridge may be ill-fitting and the dummy tooth, if insensitively matched, may look unnatural and false. As conventional bridge work involves crowning the supporting teeth, drawbacks for crowns will also apply.
VENEERS	Veneers are pre-moulded covers, rather like artificial fingernails in appearance. They are bonded on to the tooth with a special adhesive, or are painted on to the tooth in layers and left to 'set' in the mouth.	Veneers are cheap, require very little preparation and are easy to fit. They can be used to disguise a badly stained or blackened tooth but are most useful on children who have a chipped or broken front tooth that needs attention only until the adult teeth are fully grown.	Because the plastics used are more absorbent than enamel or porcelain, they tend to stain and discolour easily. Tea, coffee or red wine and cigarette smoke will all accelerate the staining process. If badly fitted, veneers may irritate the gum and lead to infection.
IMPLANTS	Implants are metal stumps which are fixed into the jaw bone and then crowned. The idea, though not often the reality, is that, if large gaps between the teeth can be 'crowned' in this way, there will be no need for false teeth.	There are very few advantages. For some, but by no means all, people who are able to tolerate them, implants may be preferable to false teeth, in a cosmetic sense. They are rarely preferable in a medical sense, however (see Drawbacks).	Implants have a high failure rate and rarely last for more than five years before the body rejects the artificial material. As any implant may undermine the strength and health of the jaw bone, there is also a high risk of infection. Gum disease may start to develop around the artificial 'roots'.
PARTIAL FALSE TEETH	False teeth are not so much cosmetic as essential, if you are unfortunate enough to lose some or all of your teeth. They maintain the shape of the face and enable you to chew and eat your food. Partial false teeth are most commonly made out of plastic materials bonded on to metal alloys and fixed into the mouth by means of clasps and brackets in order to maintain stability.	Partial false teeth are cheaper than extensive crown and bridge work or elaborate attempts to save weakened, existing teeth. Because they sit on, rather than underneath, the gum line, they carry little risk of irritation or infection. In the event of infection, they can be easily removed and the affected area treated.	The obvious disadvantages are aesthetic, together with the necessity of taking them out at night and using special cleaning materials. A band or plate across the roof of the mouth to hold the teeth in place may also be off-putting, as you need time to adjust to it and speech may be slurred at first.
COMPLETE FALSE TEETH	A full set of dentures is generally made entirely of plastic and is retained in the mouth by close fitting to the gum.	There are few advantages, but false teeth are better than no teeth at all, both from an aesthetic and practical point of view.	As feeling in the teeth comes from ligaments holding the teeth into the jaw, it can be difficult to adapt to the lack of sensation in the mouth when biting or chewing.

nails

Nails are useful. They protect your fingers, enable you to pick small things up, untie knots and shoe laces and pluck guitar strings. Over-long nails, though, will do few of these things without breaking or splitting, however strong they are. This is because most of the nail — the part you see — is made from layers of dead protein, held together by oil and moisture to keep it supple and resilient, and anchored to the nail bed beneath. The further the nail grows from its anchorage, the weaker and more susceptible to breakage it becomes. The first rule for healthy nails, then, is to keep them relatively short, with the tips shaped to a gentle curve, not to a point, in order to distribute any pressure as evenly as possible.

The nail grows out over the nail bed and is sealed to the skin by the cuticle. This protects it and the skin underneath by preventing bacteria and other substances working their way into the space between them. Never attempt to cut or clip away the cuticle. If you have a large fold of skin over the nail (hangnail), seek out the services of a professional manicurist. If you try to deal with it yourself, you may damage the new, living, nail at the lanula — the small, white half-moon at the base of the nail.

Fingernails grow at a rate of up to one millimetre (0.04 inches) a week, about twice as fast as toenails. On average, it takes about five months for a fingernail to grow out completely from base to tip, but it can take as little as three months or as long as eight months. Nails grow faster during pregnancy, during the spring and autumn and in youth, especially during the twenties and thirties. Trauma, illness, infection and crash dieting can slow and, in some cases, temporarily arrest the growth of the nail. When growth returns, a line or furrow often forms at the lanula and grows out with the new nail. Other signs of ill-health reflected in the nail are heavy ridging, flaking, splitting, white bands, and a yellowish discoloration on the surface. Brittleness, in particular, is symptomatic of certain types of illness and specific mineral or vitamin deficiencies, such as anaemia. This condition is often diagnosed by looking at the nail (see page 215) and usually corrects itself once the proper iron levels have been restored in the body.

While a well-balanced diet is vital to the health of the nails, as it is to the rest of the body, there is little evidence that particular foods, such as calcium or gelatin, have a specifically beneficial effect. Zinc may be an exception. As a lack of this mineral has recently been linked to leukonychia (white spots or bands in the nail), you should ensure that you are getting enough zinc in your diet. Try taking brewer's yeast tablets or eating a helping of seafood once a fortnight — oysters are a particularly rich source. Do not expect the spots or bands to disappear overnight, though they should grow out with the nail. Other possible causes for white spots: straightforward wear and tear (they are rarely seen on the toenails which are better protected) and over-vigorous manicuring.

Dry, brittle nails are more commonly caused by abuse than by any specific deficiency in the diet. Detergents, glues, film developers, paint strippers and many other chemicals will all dry out and weaken them. So, too, will excessive and repeated use of polishes, hardeners and removers, however carefully applied. Varnish removers contain acetone, a highly flammable and extremely powerful solvent capable of dissolving many materials — plastics and rubber included — in addition to nail varnish. It is also extremely drying for the nails, whether or not conditioning agents are added. So, keep varnishing to a minimum and protect your hands and nails from detergents and other chemical substances by wearing rubber gloves. Remember, too, that even the sturdiest and most resilient of nails will break if used to prise off lids. Use a mechanical lever, instead. It is stronger and, unlike your nails, specially designed for the job.

If you develop separated or ingrown nails, a fungus infection, or a stripy, uneven, discoloration on the nail surface, consult your doctor.

Artificial nails

Artificial nails were first developed in Hollywood in the 1930s using crude plastics which just about passed muster for photographic purposes. Today's false nails are much more sophisticated, the materials tougher and the methods used less likely to damage the nail underneath.

A single, artificial nail can be superimposed on to a chipped or broken one, using a strong adhesive and paring down the surfaces so that the join is virtually imperceptible. Alternatively, a complete set can be made, using a chemical formula painted on to the existing nail (pre-roughened with a file to hold the new surface) and shaped or 'sculpted' to the required length. Because the material has a clear base and a white tip, the new nail does not need disguising with varnish and can be left alone. It grows out with the ordinary nail, leaving a thin divide at the base after about 10 days, which then needs 'filling'. Although not recommended for normal nails, because the constant filing can weaken them, artificial nails can be a boon if you have resolved to give up biting your own.

Go to a reputable and competent manicurist. Do-it-yourself sets are not ideal, as the nails are pre-cast and tend to look unnatural, while the glue is often too weak to ensure reliable adhesion. Avoid techniques using machine filing, too, as these tend to take off the top layer of the nail, weakening it considerably. If you develop a reaction to the chemicals used, have the nails removed immediately, and, if the reaction does not improve, consult your doctor.

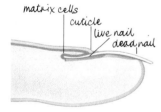

Nails start growing from matrix cells situated about 3-4 mm from the base of the nail. By the time they become visible they are often completely dead, though a patch of live nail can sometimes be seen at the white half moon (lanula). Any damage to the nail at this point may cause it to grow out unevenly.

MANICURE STEP BY STEP

Excessive or over-enthusiastic manicuring can injure the nail and damage the cuticle, particularly if sharp-ended, metal instruments are used. Signs of bad manicuring are ridges, dents or nicks along the nails and a pink inflamed cuticle. Consistent use of heavy lacquers, together with the chemical solvents needed to remove them, particularly acetone, will dry out the nail. So while your first impulse might be to disguise out-of-condition nails with a coating of colour, you would be wiser to leave them to themselves, giving regular manicures and warm olive oil treatments: soak the fingertips in a bowl of the oil for a few minutes each week and see the difference. Seek the advice of a good manicurist for any more specific problems. If your nails are in good condition and you want to use nail colour, use it with restraint and apply it carefully (see next page), but do try to give your nails an occasional rest. Fragile nails may benefit from a relatively new technique, known as 'wrapping', which uses strong tissue fibres to bolster the strength of the nail from the underside. It must be carried out by a competent manicurist.

If you can, file rather than cut, because cutting can weaken the nail and cause it to flake. File in one direction only, from sides to centre, using the softer (lighter) side of an emery board, _not_ a metal file. Aim for a rounded tip: the shape at the tip should reflect the shape at the base of the nail to make a perfect oval, as left.

PEDICURE STEP BY STEP

You should take as much care of your feet as you do of your hands. For, although the sole of the foot is admirably and necessarily tough, it is more prone to viral, fungal and other infections than almost anywhere else on the body. Many of the more common foot afflictions are caused by ill-fitting, restrictive footwear, so choose your shoes carefully. Make sure that they have their widest point at the base of the toes, that your toes can move freely inside them and that the uppers are soft and flexible and will not cause undue friction when you walk. Above all, never believe that a new pair of shoes must be 'broken in'. This is an almost certain guarantee of future trouble. Get into the habit of alternating shoes and, more important, heel heights, to give your calf muscles plenty of exercise and your heels and soles a rest.

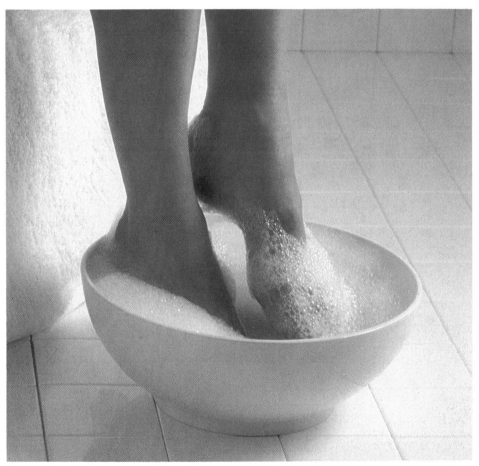

Start by soaking the feet in a warm footbath. Although many commercial products smell delicious, it is the temperature of the water that really counts – about 40°C (104°F). To make a traditional footbath: add a teacupful of Epsom salts or ordinary sea salt to every 4½ litres/1 gallon (10 US pints) hot water. Alternatively, use your favourite bubble bath and add two tablespoons of baking soda, to soften rough dry patches of skin if necessary.

115

1. Soak the fingers briefly in a bowl of warm, soapy water, or water to which you have added a slice of lemon, to loosen dirt beneath the tips and to soften the cuticle. (If nails are very dry, soak them in warmed olive or almond oil instead.) Dry the fingers and scrape any loosened dirt from the underside of the nail with an orange stick. Do not poke or prod. If dirt has become embedded in the pink part of the nail, let it grow out.

2. Flick a little cuticle cream on to the base of each nail in turn. The cream should be thick and firm in consistency, like lard. Massage it well into the cuticle and surrounding nail using the ball of the thumb in a firm rotating movement. This will also help to stimulate the circulation, so promoting a healthy pink glow beneath the nail.

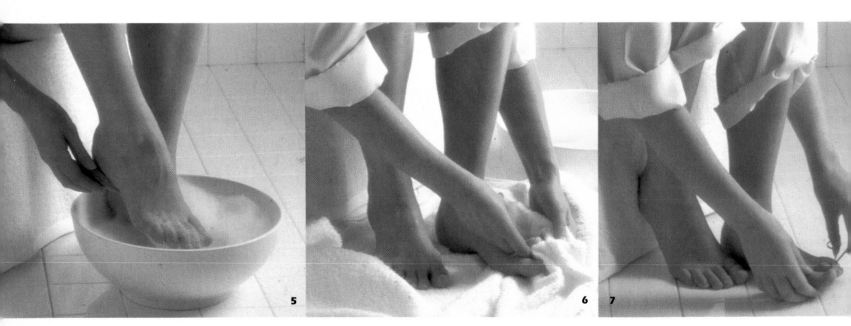

5. Once the feet are soaked, and the skin soft, take a pumice stone, rough skin remover or chiropody sponge. Remove any hard dead skin from the heels, sides and soles of the feet, but leave the toes well alone.

6. Dry your feet scrupulously, particularly between the toes where fungi and bacteria can breed easily. Once your feet are clean and soft, inspect them. Take any obvious incipient

problems to a registered chiropodist. (See also Athlete's Foot, Corns and calluses, Enlarged toe joints in the A-Z.)

7. Cut the nails square along the top, following the shape of the toe and taking care not to cut them too short. Do not cut the corners of the nails back into the nail grooves as this may lead to an ingrowing nail (see page 218). Smooth sharp corners with the coarse (darker) side of an emery board.

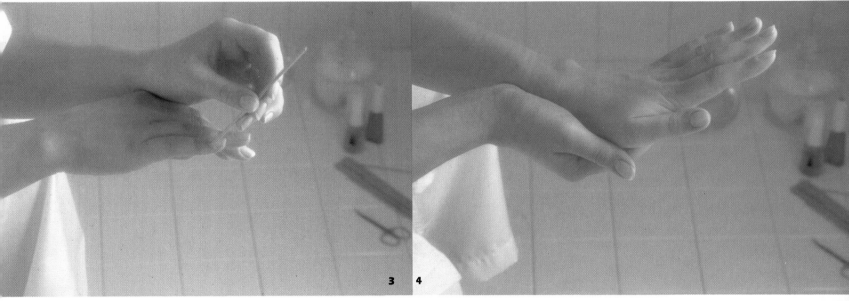

3. File down the sharp end of an orange stick so that it is smooth and rounded and then gently slide it a little way under the cuticle at the base and sides of the nail, lifting the cuticle slightly as you do so. Be gentle: persuade don't push; never use an orange stick with a pointed end or a metal instrument; never clip the cuticle and avoid cuticle 'removers', as they may open up the space between the skin and the nail, inviting dirt, detergents, even nail enamel into the matrix.

4. Rub a generous amount of hand cream on to the hand, first pulling the finger joints upwards, then using the first and second fingers to pull the skin tissue down towards the knuckles, as though putting on a pair of gloves. Finish by massaging the palm. See below if applying varnish.

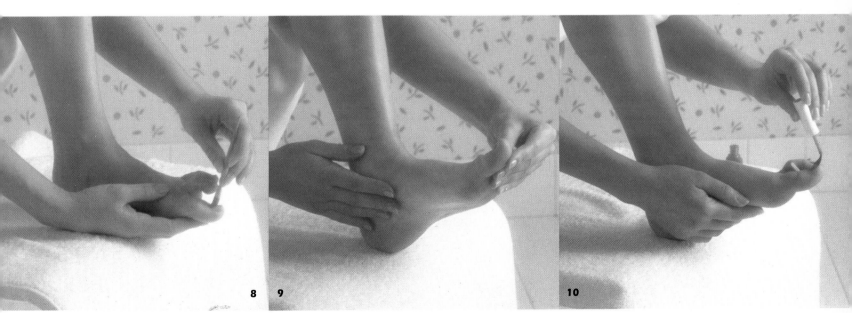

8. Repeat the cuticle cream/orange stick routine, massaging the cream well into the cuticle first. A rubber-ended implement, known as a 'hoofer', is particularly good for this.

9. Apply hand cream or petroleum jelly to the feet, rubbing in well and avoiding the spaces between the toes. (If the skin feels moist there, wipe with surgical spirit.) Knead and massage every inch of the sole, heel and top side of the foot.

10. When applying varnish, first ensure that any traces of the old colour are removed (to remove varnish around the cuticle, wrap cotton wool around an orange stick and dip in the remover). Begin with a clear base coat to prevent pigments being absorbed, follow with two coats of colour (three if frosted). Allow each coat to dry. Finish with a top-coat of clear polish to seal in colour and add gloss.

nailsnailsnails

the senses

'All our knowledge has its origins in our perceptions...'   Leonardo da Vinci

To the ancient Greeks, sensitivity constituted the essential difference between plants and animals, and between animals and humans. It was not that any one specific sense was better developed in humans — just one glance at the animal kingdom will give examples of more acute vision (birds of prey), hearing (dogs and bats) or smell (insects). Rather, it was that, between them, they provided a range of information that the intelligent brain could sift through and use for the purposes of communicating, socializing, improvizing and inventing.

Every moment of our waking lives, millions of sense signals from the eyes, nose, mouth, ears and skin are sent to the brain — most of which are never perceived on a conscious level. All these signals are constantly being adjusted, analyzed, edited, eliminated, even completed by the brain. It is, for example, hard to find the blind spot in the eye not because it is not there but because the brain 'fills in' the missing part of the visual jigsaw. The world of perception is very different from and much more selective than the world of sensation.

In adulthood, the senses have a strict hierarchy, ruled first by the eyes and then by the ears — the 'distance' senses of sight and hearing — and only later by the skin, the mouth and the nose — the 'proximity' senses of touch, taste and smell. You can see how this sensual hierarchy organizes itself simply by closing your eyes... What happens? Your subjective, inner world becomes filled with sound — you can pick up the rhythm of your own breathing, and background noise, which you may not have been aware of before, seems amplified. You do not need absolute quiet to hear a pin drop when your eyes are shut. If you carry this experiment one stage further and place your hands over your ears, you will now find that sensation arrives predominantly from your sense of touch. You will suddenly become aware of the comparative softness or hardness of the chair on which you are sitting, of the texture of the clothes you are wearing and of sensations arriving from different parts of your body — your neck, your back, your shoulders, even your scalp. These are not new sensations — they are continually being communicated to the brain via the skin. The difference is that you have only just begun to perceive them.

We are all much more receptive to the messages arriving from our senses than we, perhaps, realize — although most of the time we make use of just a fraction of their full potential. Think of the virtuosity displayed by the piano tuner, who carries all the notes of the scale in his head and can detect and adjust the slightest variation in pitch, or the discernment of the master of wine, who has educated his senses of smell and taste to such a point of refinement that he can identify, not only the vintage of a certain wine, but the locality and even the vineyard that produced it.

sight

'Each day as I look, I wonder where my eyes were yesterday.' Bernard Berenson

Sight is the most highly developed of all the senses. The eye forms from two of the three layers of embryonic tissue — ectoderm and mesoderm — and communicates with the brain via the optic nerve, which is not a nerve in the sense of all the other nerves found in the body, but is actually an extension of the brain.

How do we see?

In construction and function, the eye works in much the same way as a simple, pinhole camera. Light from an object within your field of vision — about 200° — strikes the cornea, is partly focused and passes through the pupil which cuts down the beam, thus improving depth of field and perspective. A crystalline lens inside the eye performs the last five per cent of the fine focusing. A clear image is then thrown on to the back of the eye, or retina, as an inverted or upside-down picture of the original object, translated into electrical charges and relayed to the brain, which reverses and makes sense of the image it receives. The point at which the smaller nerve fibres converge to make up the optic nerve is known as the 'blind spot', but this does not interfere with the visual picture we receive because the brain fills in the missing part to provide perfectly focused, binocular vision in most people.

Perfectly focused, however, is only partially focused. Only the few central degrees of vision are, in fact, in focus at any one time. All the rest, about 90 per cent, is out of focus.

Having your sight tested

Taking care of your eyes, or those of your children, starts with an eye test during which each eye will be checked to ensure that it is focusing normally, quite independently of the other, and that the muscles controlling the movement of the eyes are working properly as a well-matched pair. Babies' eyes should always be checked for possible signs of squint. If the eyes are not working in unison, this should be corrected as soon as possible. Left to itself, a 'wandering' eye can eventually go 'blind' because the brain ignores conflicting images and only accepts the image from the good eye.

Eyesight should first be tested at nursery school age. Children do not need to be able to recognize the alphabet in order to have their sight tested. If all is well, sight does not need to be tested again for some years, unless symptoms lead you to suspect that the quality of your child's vision may be slipping.

If you manage to weather your teens and early twenties without wearing glasses, you should find that your vision remains stable until the age of about 40 or 45. Everyone, whether they suspect their vision to have deteriorated or not, should have an eye test at about the age of 45. This will check

for early signs of cataract or glaucoma (see pages 215 and 217) which, if not detected and controlled soon enough, may lead to impairment or even loss of sight. It is particularly important that you have your eyes checked if there is a history of either or both of these conditions in your family.

A second reason for having your eyes checked in your forties is that everyone gets more long-sighted with age. This is caused by a gradual deterioration of the crystalline lens inside the eye. To 'accommodate' for objects seen at close range, usually 1 metre (1 yard) or less, the lens has to bulge outwards, but with age, it becomes less elastic. Where a child can see an object sharply at a distance of only 8 cm (3 inches) from the eye, the adult of 45 may not be able to focus clearly on objects less than about 45 cm (18 inches) away. By the age of 60, the lens is usually completely inelastic and reading glasses will have to be worn.

Standard of sight is given as a ratio of an individual's ability to see what a hypothetically 'normal' eye can at a given distance — 6 metres in the UK, 20 feet in the USA. So, if you have to stand at 2 metres to see what the normal eye can see at 6, you are said to have 2/6 vision — the US equivalent would be 6/20. It is also possible to have better than average vision: 6/5 vision, for example, means that you can distinguish letters at 6 metres that the normal eye can only pick up at 5.

Avoiding eye 'strain'

Although you cannot actually 'strain' the eyes they can feel strained, particularly if concentrating for long periods of time. Concentration is wearing for the eyes because the muscles controlling them are held in a fixed position and do not allow the eyes to swivel as they would normally and because you literally forget to blink. The normal blink rate of every two to four seconds falls to every ten seconds or so when reading or driving. Hardly surprising, therefore, that after an hour's solid concentration, your eyes feel sore and tired. The best way to avoid eye strain is simply to remember to blink when driving, and to break up periods of reading or close studying about every half an hour, to give your eye muscles a chance to unlock and your tear film an opportunity to replenish itself. You should also avoid reading in insufficient light or under glaring strip lighting, both of which generate tension in the muscles.

If your eyes do feel strained and tired, try bathing them gently in a weak salt water solution. Dissolve one teaspoon of salt in 600 ml/1 pint (2½ cups) of cold, boiled water. You can also place cotton wool pads soaked in milk, or slices of fresh cucumber, over the eyelids to cool, soothe and rest the eyes and thereby to relax the eye muscles. Even better — go to sleep.

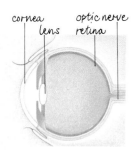

cornea optic nerve
lens retina

A vertical section through the eyeball showing the pupil, the small crystalline lens inside the eye, which is responsible for 'close up' focusing, and the optic nerve, which carries all information received by the eyes to the brain. The point at which the nerve fibres converge to form this nerve is the 'blind' spot.

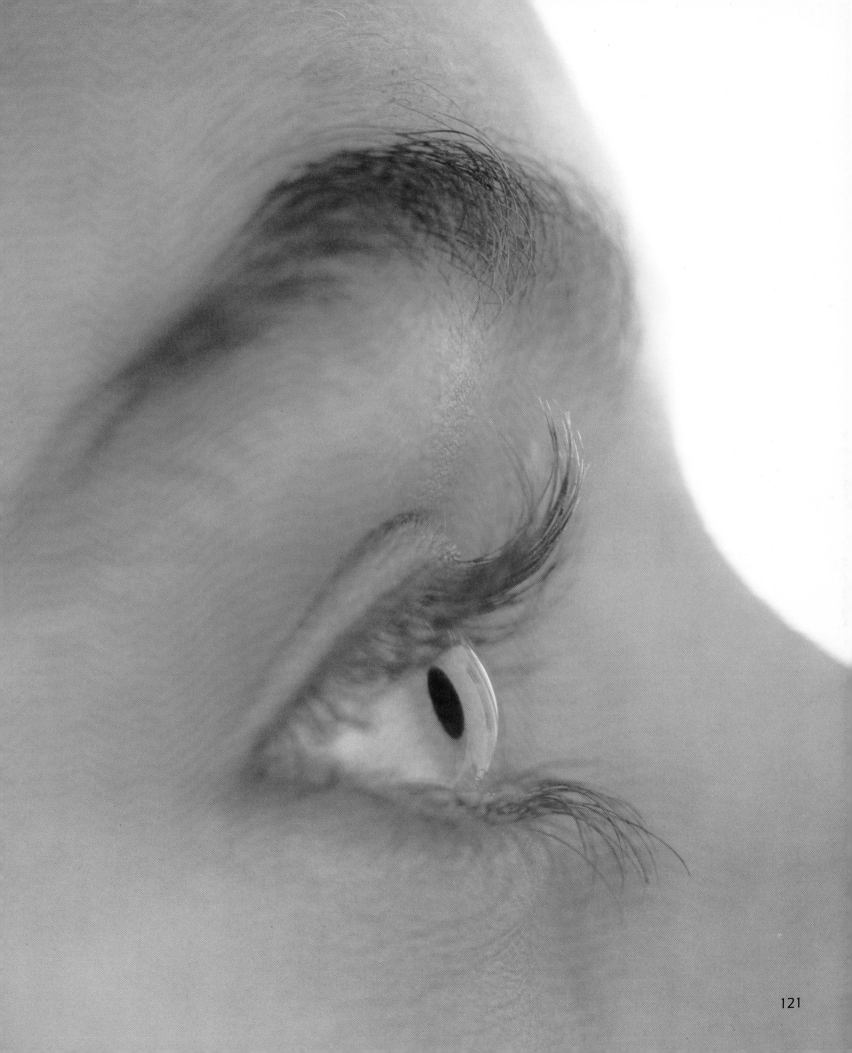

Most problems with vision arise from difficulties in focusing.
Long-sightedness (hypermetropia) and short-sightedness (myopia) are the most common of these and are usually caused by a slight defect in the proportions of the eyeball.

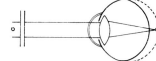

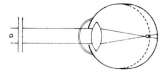

The long-sighted eyeball, above, is functionally too short, so that light arriving from a distant object converges behind the retina. A convex lens in front of the eye will shorten the focal point of the light.

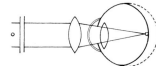

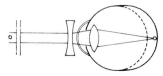

The short-sighted eyeball is functionally too long, so that light arriving from a distant object converges in front of the retina. A concave lens in front of the eye will lengthen the focal point of the light.

TAKING CARE OF YOUR EYES

On the whole, the eyes protect themselves remarkably well. The eyelids close instinctively whenever dust particles, smoke or irritants in the atmosphere come into contact with them; the pupil contracts in bright light or glare, in order to reduce the amount of light coming through; the gentle windscreen-wiper action of blinking circulates the tears, bringing fresh oxygen to the surface of the eye and keeps the white of the eye clean and clear; the tiny lipid pores along the inner eyelid secrete the fine layer of oil that maintains the integrity of the tear film, by preventing over-fast evaporation. Heavy creams, eye liners, some mascaras and even make-up remover can all block these pores, if carelessly applied, and will cause irritation if allowed to come into contact with the eye itself. Caution is the watchword.

● If you habitually wake up with swollen, puffy eyes in the morning, bathe them gently with cool water or witch hazel and leave them alone. Any puffiness should subside within half an hour or so. Puffy eyes later in the day can be treated in much the same way or soothed by specially formulated eye pads.

● When moisturizing the face, never put cream on to the area directly around the eye. Concentrate instead on the skin to the side and beneath the eye and, even then, leave a fairly wide margin. You will find that the cream migrates naturally upwards.

● When putting eye creams or shadows on to the lid, always use the lightest possible touch. A sable brush or cotton wool bud is ideal for this. If possible, avoid using kohl or an inner lid liner (or at least make sure the point of the pencil is soft enough for the eye, see right), keeping outside the eyelashes when defining the shape of the eye, so that the tiny lipid pores on the lid are not interfered with.

● False eyelashes, if very long and thick, can upset the natural balance of the eyelid. If you do use them, be especially careful when sticking them on as the glues may cause irritation if carelessly applied.

● Lash-building mascaras are fine for the lashes but not for the eyelids, so apply them carefully. Keep well clear of the lid and do not put too much on: an overload may cause small pieces to flake off, causing redness and irritation if they fall into the eye.

● Although 'artificial tear' solutions for uncomfortable itchy eyes are quite safe, you should avoid commercial eye 'whiteners'. These contain a blue pigment to give 'washing-powder' whiteness and a substance which causes the blood capillaries in the white of the eye to contract and temporarily to disappear. As they will reappear, and probably more conspicuously than before, you are altogether better off without them.

● If you wear contact lenses, you should be especially careful when applying or removing make-up. Always put your lenses in before applying it (you will be able to see what you are doing for one thing), and take them out before removing it, in order to avoid smudging grease or dirt on to the lens. Contact lens wearers should also avoid all cosmetics that might shed particles into the eye or stick to the surface of the lens, such as powder eye shadows, heavily 'pearlized' products and filamented ('lash building') mascaras. Try

to use water-soluble eye make-up instead.

● If your eyes do become sensitive, infected, red or puffy, do leave your make-up off for a few days. It could be that you have developed a sensitivity to one of the products you are using (see pages 138-9).

Sunglasses

Eyes are naturally sun-sensitive. The pupil regulates the amount of light entering the eye by contracting in bright light and dilating when the light is dim — when, like the shutter in a camera, it needs a greater exposure to make sense of what it sees. This is why it takes a few moments to 'acclimatize' to shade after bright sunlight and why eyes, habitually protected by sunglasses, can feel lost without them. Because the eyes have their own in-built protective mechanism, you do not damage them simply by being in bright sunlight, but you can place additional stresses on them. We strain to see well in bright light, forcing the eyes open and squinting through the glare. Over a long period of time, squinting tires the eyes and can even hasten the appearance of premature lines and wrinkles. Most sunglasses are designed primarily to protect the eye from visible light, not from ultraviolet. They do this by using a variety of tints to cut down as much as 65 to 85 per cent of transmitted light from various, and often extremely specific, parts of the colour spectrum — blue, for example, is colour specific for yellow (its opposite number in the spectrum) and therefore recommended for a desert environment.

Although your choice of tint, like your choice of frames, depends very much on your own personal preference, some colours, particularly those at the centre of the spectrum, offer greater protection than those at either end. The wisest choices are brown, sage green (which probably gives best all-round protection) and neutral, smoky grey. All these reduce the intensity but do not affect the values of the colours. Avoid the rosier tinted reds, pinks and oranges.

Sunglasses are extremely important in high glare conditions such as skiing, where the light is intensified by reflection off the snow or ice, or driving, where the dazzle may blind you to oncoming traffic. But you should not wear them superfluously, when the light is not bright and you need all the visual information you can get. Never wear sunglasses when driving at night, in fog, rain or any other conditions that already restrict visibility.

Choosing sunglasses

If made from a poor quality material, sunglasses can hinder, rather than help, your vision, so always test both for general and for optical quality before you buy. Check first that the two lenses are matched for colour and tone, that there are no surface defects or scratches, that the frame has strong enough hinges to withstand normal use and that the side pieces are narrow enough not to obstruct vision any more than necessary. Then, put them on to see how they suit you and look carefully in a mirror. With the exception of gradient and photochromic lenses, which will not darken in sunless shops, you should not be able to see your eyes, without having to peer very closely into them. If you can see them, the lenses are too light to afford effective glare protection.

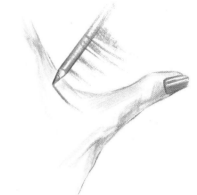

Sharp eye liner pencils will irritate skin around the eyes. Make sure that your pencil is soft enough by testing it between thumb and forefinger. This spot is closest in texture to the skin on your eyelids. If the pencil scratches or drags along the skin, do not use it.

To check for optical quality, hold sunglasses so that a patch of overhead lighting is reflected off the inside lens and move them slightly, so that the reflection moves across it. If the line waves or dips, the edges bulge anywhere but at the corners, where the glass is curved, or the colour seems streaky, the glasses will not give top optical quality. (Prescription sunglasses are intentionally distorted and cannot be tested in this way.)

SUNGLASSES

TYPE	DESCRIPTION	ADVANTAGES	DRAWBACKS
PLASTIC	Different types of plastic have different optical qualities. The degree of protection derives both from the depth and the type of the tint. The newer, gradient lenses give the cosmetic advantage of allowing your eyes to be seen, while screening out the more intense overhead light.	They are extremely light, often weighing less than 28 g (1 oz).	They are prone to scratching, so never place them lens side down. Poorer quality, cheaper plastics may cause distortion and interfere with vision. Always check optical quality before buying (see previous page). They give little protection against infrared. Gradient lenses are not suitable for reflected glare, such as when sailing or skiing.
GLASS	Glass lenses are individually ground and polished to the required surface finish and shape.	For optimum quality, glass lenses are preferable to plastic because they contain no distortion, unless they are prescription glasses (see previous page).	They tend to be fairly heavy.
POLARIZED	These lenses are made by sandwiching a sheet of polarized material between two pieces of plastic or glass.	Polarized materials have the unique property of cutting down reflected glare and will cut it out entirely, if reflected at a certain angle (53° on water for example). Extremely useful for high-glare conditions such as fishing, boating, skiing.	As laminated windscreen glass is already polarized, car windscreens can appear blotchy when driving.
PHOTOCHROMIC	Sun-sensitive or photochromic lenses darken in bright light and vice versa. The effect is caused by crystals in the glass which respond to ultraviolet. The brighter the light, the darker they go, cutting out about 80 per cent of all transmitted light in really high-glare conditions.	Ideal for most activities and light conditions, particularly if the light is ambient, as they give optimum protection when there is a lot of glare and optimum vision when it is less bright – the field of vision being assisted by the degree to which they lighten.	They can take several light/dark cycles before reaching peak performance. Photochromic sunglasses darken to 75 per cent in about 30 seconds in cold bright conditions, but take longer to adjust if the temperature is higher. As ultraviolet is deflected by a car windscreen, and as it takes time for the lenses to adjust from light to dark, photochromic lenses are less effective and potentially dangerous when driving (e.g. when entering a dark tunnel).
MIRRORED	A thin coating of a steel alloy over the lens cuts down light transmission by as much as 85 per cent by bouncing the light off the surface of the lens. Traditional sunglasses absorb it.	They protect against ultraviolet and infrared and are extremely good when there is a high degree of reflected light and/or overhead glare. They are especially good for sports activities, such as boating, bicycling, fishing and skiing.	They may restrict vision and affect perception when the light is only moderate.

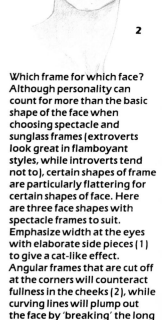

Which frame for which face? Although personality can count for more than the basic shape of the face when choosing spectacle and sunglass frames (extroverts look great in flamboyant styles, while introverts tend not to), certain shapes of frame are particularly flattering for certain shapes of face. Here are three face shapes with spectacle frames to suit. Emphasize width at the eyes with elaborate side pieces (1) to give a cat-like effect. Angular frames that are cut off at the corners will counteract fullness in the cheeks (2), while curving lines will plump out the face by 'breaking' the long vertical at the sides (3).

Contact lenses

The idea of wearing a convex lens on the eyeball to improve or correct vision was first mooted by Leonardo da Vinci in the fifteenth century, but it did not receive serious consideration for a further 400 years, when injuries to pilots in the First World War revealed that the acrylic material used in aircraft windscreens was inert, or chemically 'non-damaging', to the eye. After this came the first all-plastic contact lens which was worn over the entire eye surface. This cumbersome lens was gradually refined into a much smaller one that covered only part of the cornea. The first soft lens was produced in the 1950s. Since then, contact lenses have become so refined that today very few individuals are unable to wear them.

Contact lenses have many advantages over traditional glasses. Beyond their obvious cosmetic appeal, they tend to provide a more constant quality of vision than glasses do because they sit right on the eyeball and do not mist or fog up. They also eliminate the need for special prescription sunglasses. Some eye afflictions can only be optically remedied by the wearing of contact lenses.

It is essential to have contact lenses fitted well. To find a good contact lens specialist, go by local reputation or the recommendation of your doctor, never by the shop front. Once the prescription has been made up for you, your practitioner will show you how to put them in and take them out, how to look after them, what sort of cleaning agent to use and how long to wear them — in short, how to give your eyes the best chance to become quickly and easily accustomed to the presence of the lenses.

Always expect some initial discomfort. Although the edges of most lenses are so finely graduated that only the most sensitive eyes will be irritated, they are bound to

lenseslenseslenses

register a change of touch, rather in the same way as a finger with a new ring would do. This sensation should disappear within two or three weeks with hard lenses and within minutes with soft ones.

Once you have had the lenses fitted, your practitioner will arrange a future appointment to check how well your eyes are adapting to them and whether you are putting them in and taking them out correctly. Never exceed the wearing time specified. Some types of damage only become apparent hours, or even days, afterwards.

All contact lens wearers should go for regular check-ups. You may be unaware that the quality of your vision has deteriorated slightly, but your practitioner can check this and, if it has, will alter the prescription of the lenses.

CONTACT LENSES

TYPE	DESCRIPTION	ADVANTAGES	DRAWBACKS
HARD	The most traditional type of lens, made of polymethylmethacrylate. A hard lens is rather like having a miniature spectacle lens on your eye – with the advantage that it gives back the 15-20 per cent of range of vision that spectacle frames cut out.	Hard lenses give crisper, clearer vision than soft lenses, can be repolished if surfaces are scratched or damaged and day-to-day cleaning regimes are simple. With care, hard lenses will last for between 10 and 12 years, sometimes considerably longer.	Initially uncomfortable, hard lenses take between three weeks and a month to 'wear in'. They are unsuitable for occasional use and extremely sensitive eyes. Hard lenses distort the cornea very slightly, and so can cause vision to become blurred when lenses are taken out. The problem, known as spectacle blur, is not helped by glasses. Although the cornea will adjust back to normal in time, it can occasionally take some months. Dust can get underneath the edge of the lens and irritate the eye.
SOFT	Soft lenses look like drops of rainwater and contain 40 to 60 per cent fluid, depending upon the material used.	Soft lenses are much more comfortable initially than hard lenses. Most eyes adjust to them within four to five minutes. They are also suitable for occasional use, are less inclined to slip than hard lenses, and are preferable in dusty environments (see hard lenses).	Soft lenses react to external temperature and, in some cases, to altitude and lowered atmospheric pressure. Maintenance costs are high. They require special cleansing chemicals to remove accumulated calcium and protein, by-products of natural tear deposit, and wear out much more quickly than hard lenses. Eighteen months is a good span and, if you live in an urban environment or are a heavy smoker, you may need them replaced after as little as three or six months. Some individuals may develop a reaction to the chemicals in the cleansing solutions.
'GAS PERMEABLE' HARD LENSES	These combine the good qualities of both hard and soft lenses, while minimizing the drawbacks. They maintain the integrity of the cornea, by allowing it to absorb its oxygen from the atmosphere, rather than via the tear film.	They give crisper vision than soft lenses, will improve the quality of vision for those with astigmatism and do not lead to 'spectacle blur' when the lenses are taken out.	Gas permeable lenses are more like hard than soft lenses in structure and are therefore not as comfortable as soft.
EXTENDED WEAR	First developed in the UK about 10 years ago, these lenses can be worn for extended periods (usually between one and three months) without taking them out at night. After this time, the lenses should be professionally cleaned.	Excellent for the very young or the very old for whom the business of taking the lenses in and out every night presents obvious problems. (They are often fitted on babies, for example.) Extended wear lenses are also particularly good for post-cataract patients.	An accumulation of protein on the surface of a soft lens produces discomfort, but you may be unaware of any such build-up on extended wear lenses. It is essential therefore to observe follow-up visits. If you do not, it can lead to eye infection and may even affect your vision. Watch out for redness, reduction of vision or discomfort.
COLOURED LENS FILTERS 'COCKTAIL' LENSES	These lenses can be worn for medical reasons in the event of one or both eyes being damaged or for purely cosmetic reasons, to enhance or to change the colour of the eyes. They can be either hard or soft (the cosmetic type is usually soft) and can be made up to whatever prescription is required. As a general rule, the paler the eye the wider the choice of colours. People with grey, light blue or green eyes, for example, can choose any colour from violet or hazel to brown, while those with dark green eyes will have little choice other than brown. Very dark brown eyes can be made to look lighter with an orange filter.	They do not affect the quality of vision, are versatile, fun and useful for theatrical or cinematic special effects. They are also a marvellous boon for people whose eyes have been damaged, as the colour of the lens can be so carefully matched to the good eye that it is impossible to tell which is which.	As hard and soft lenses. If you are wearing coloured lenses for purely cosmetic reasons, remember that these are still lenses and the same care must therefore be taken when taking them in and out, putting on or removing eye make-up and generally looking after them.

hearing

'A lover's ear will hear the lowest sound...' **William Shakespeare**

The sense of hearing develops early, probably well before birth. The developing baby is surrounded by sound. In fact, the natural synchrony of the two heartbeats (the baby's is twice that of the mother's) is now thought to constitute our earliest appreciation of rhythm. Experiments, showing that babies can be soothed to sleep by recreating sounds left behind in the womb, have borne this out. New babies do not learn to recognize or to locate sound for some months. Like all information received by the senses, it must first be 'translated' and made sense of by the brain, before it becomes meaningful. Association is all, whether it is the rattle of a spoon against a cup, meaning food, or the soothing words of the mother, meaning closeness, security and pleasure. If a baby is not brought up in a world of sounds and, more specifically, words, he or she will fail to associate sound with meaning and may appear 'deafer' at the age of two or three than the child whose hearing is actually impaired.

How do we hear?

Sound originates as a movement or vibration of air, which then sets up smaller vibrations which get fainter and fainter as they move through the atmosphere. The function of the ear is to receive and transmit sound to the brain first by amplifying the pressure of the vibrations as they travel through the ear (see below right) and second by translating the vibrations into electrical nerve impulses, intelligible to the brain, which then decodes them. As with sight, we hear not with the ears, but with the brain.

Pitch and loudness

Frequency of sound, or pitch, is measured in Hertz. One Hertz is one cycle, or vibration, per second. Middle C on the piano, for example, is 256 Hertz, or cycles per second. We all respond to certain frequencies at a very subtle level, particularly at the lower end of the scale, because they set up and generate internal rhythms in the brain — hence the powerful effect of meditative mantras, chanting and rock music. The human ear starts to pick up low frequency notes at about 20 Hertz and goes on hearing successively higher notes to a level of about 20,000 Hertz, after which sounds become too high to be heard. Some animals, however, can still detect them. 'Silent' dog whistles, for example, are pitched at about 22,000 Hertz, and bats actually navigate by ultrasonics, emitting high-pitched squeaks and finding their way by means of the echoes bouncing off obstacles. The same principle is used for radar, depth sounders in submarines, burglar alarms and for medical scanning when X-rays are unsuitable, such as during pregnancy.

Intensity of sound, or loudness, is measured in decibels (dB). Nought decibels, or 0dB, indicates the threshold at which sound becomes perceptible to most people. Some people, with an extremely acute sense of hearing, will be able to perceive sound at minus 10 decibels, but this is rare. Hearing tests work by measuring the quietest perceived sound (decibels) for different frequencies (Hertz).

Hearing tests

One out of every 1,000 children is born with some degree of hearing impairment. If there is reason to suspect that the hearing might be damaged, a rudimentary test can be given at birth. All children should have a hearing test at seven months.

Hearing deteriorates appreciably with age. By the age of 80, one in two people will have a moderate to severe degree of hearing loss. This type of hearing loss is very similar in pattern to noise-induced hearing loss. In fact, one study carried out in the Sudan among a people who live in a world unassailed by urban and traffic noise and who show a much sharper sense of hearing in old age, suggests that the hearing deterioration we normally attribute to advancing age might, in part at least, be noise-induced. If you suspect that your hearing is not as sharp as it was, have a hearing test. The earlier any impairment is detected, the greater the chances of compensating successfully for it. Using a hearing aid takes practice and concentration, as it does not just amplify speech, but all foreground and background noise as well.

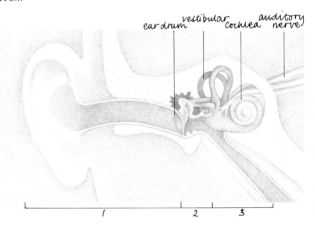

The ear is a highly intricate and complex organ containing, among other things, the vestibular mechanism of balance (see page 33) and dividing into three parts. The outer ear (1) receives sound at varying frequencies and intensities and transmits it, via vibration on the ear drum, to the middle ear (2). This sends it along progressively narrower corridors of bone (the hammer, anvil and stirrup), forcing up the pressure of the vibration and preparing it for detection in the cochlea. This snail-shaped organ in the inner ear (3) is filled with fluid and contains thousands of tiny, highly sensitive fibres, coded for pitch and loudness and capable of transforming vibrations into electrical nerve impulses that are intelligible to the brain.

126

Noise

Because noise is invisible and, often, intermittent, it is very difficult to assess — both in terms of what the population as a whole finds tolerable and of what constitutes a potentially damaging source of sound. Even so, it is now well recognized that exposure to excessive noise can cause irreversible loss of hearing — particularly of the lower pitched sounds. How loud is too loud? If you have to raise your voice to carry on a conversation with someone three to five feet away, the noise level is potentially damaging.

For most people, noise is most significant in terms of sleep disturbance. The relatively low decibel rumble of passing traffic not only extends the time it takes you to get off to sleep, even if you claim to be unaware of it, but may also rob you of your normal level of 'dreaming' sleep (see page 181). If you spend most of your day feeling tired, irritable and depressed, consider the possibility that your sleep is being disturbed by noise. Lack of sleep — and, it is now thought, lack of the right type of sleep — is both an important contributor to and result of excessive stress. A Dutch study revealed that all stress-related conditions, such as hypertension, headaches, ulcers and cardiovascular disease, were more common among those living near an airport and exposed to aircraft noise than among the rest of the population.

LOOKING AFTER YOUR EARS

The less you interfere with your ears, the healthier they will be. The ear is an efficient self-cleansing organ. The wax inside it picks up dirt and potential irritants as they enter the ear and prevents them from travelling further down. The warmth generated at body temperature melts the wax as it accumulates so that both it and the dirt can run out of the ear quite freely. The most you should do is to wipe the outer ear with the corner of a face cloth. Poking around with a finger or any type of instrument will tend to push the wax further down towards the eardrum where it is less accessible and more likely to harden and affect your hearing.

● If you suspect that an excessive accumulation of wax is affecting your hearing, go to see your doctor who will arrange to syringe your ears. This is done by directing a jet of water at the eardrum (not at the wax) so that the wax is pushed out from the inside. If you have any history of trouble with your eardrum, you should not have your ears syringed. Your doctor will use an alternative method.

● Earache is usually 'referred' pain and often accompanies dental problems. These should be your first grounds for suspicion when or if it strikes. If taking a painkiller every few hours does not help the problem, do not resort to home-spun remedies, go to see your doctor or dentist.

● Having your ears pierced is a perfectly safe procedure as long as it is carried out under sterile conditions. Stud sleepers are initially preferable to ring sleepers, as the dirt on your fingers may cling to the ring and infect the ear as you turn the ring round. Choose gold in preference to other metals, as this is the least likely to lead to infection. If your ears do flare up, consult your doctor.

● Keep your ears protected from the cold and use a good sunscreen while sunbathing. The cartilage at the top and back of the ear is particularly susceptible.

SOUNDS	LOUDNESS (DECIBELS)
Whispering	30-40
Conversation	60-70
Loudest recorded snore	69
Pneumatic drill	71-90
Inside small car	78
Crowded bar	79
Passing lorry	85-91
Pop music	87
Peaks of sound at rock concerts	105

touch

'Sight has to do with the understanding; hearing with reason; smell with memory. Touch is realistic and depends on contact; it has no ideal side...'

Arthur Schopenhauer

Our world evolves out of touch. Of all the senses, this is the first to develop and the last to desert us. At six weeks, the developing foetus apprehends sensation through the skin — long before the eyes or the ears have started to form. After birth, it is largely through contact with his mother's body, as she holds, cuddles, bathes, soothes and feeds him, that the child learns whether the world is to be feared or trusted. Touch gives a child his most fundamental ideas of the world: he is, for example, able to grasp an object long before he can focus on it and will acquire a better sense of roundness from holding and touching a ball than he will by looking at it.

Innumerable studies and experiments have shown that the child brought up and nurtured on a sense of touch and physical intimacy with his parents is more sociable, alert and curious, is better able to ward off pain and infection, has a healthier appetite, will sleep more soundly and will laugh and smile more often. We need to touch and to be touched to develop as normal, happy, healthy beings.

For most of us, ruled by our eyes and ears, the immediacy of the sensation of touch subsides as we grow older. Often, it is only reawakened in moments of doubt to make sense of what we see or hear and to verify the reality of a thing, such as a work of art in a museum or, more perversely, a 'wet paint' notice on a park bench. For people deprived of their senses of sight and hearing, however, touch becomes immensely important. Braille, an alphabetical and numerical 'reading' system, is perhaps the greatest celebration of the skin's ability to 'perceive'. Devised by a blind French boy of 17, it can be read by an accomplished reader at a speed equal to, if not greater than, a sighted person reading the text out loud.

How do we feel?

Touch keeps us informed of both our external and internal environments — we 'feel' aches and pains in our joints and muscles in much the same way as we feel and register changes of temperature in the outside world. There are over 50 sense receptors in a piece of skin the size of a small coin. Each of these is responsible for picking up and transmitting a separate impulse — warmth, cold, pressure or pain — to the brain.

The sense of touch is the most diffuse of all the senses and the threshold of sensation shifts, depending on the area being touched, the medium through which the sensation is being transmitted (bone, muscle or fat), the distribution of the various sense receptors, the individual's state of mind and even the time of day. We are also most sensitive to temperature and touch on the first encounter, becoming gradually less aware of the sensation as it continues.

Pain

Pain is the body's oldest warning system and its threshold, like those of warmth, cold and pressure, varies from person to person. The lower the threshold, the more sensitive to pain a person is. Sufferers of alagia, an extremely rare condition, are born without a sense of pain and can actually set fire to their limbs without being aware of it.

The pain threshold tends to be fractionally higher in men than in women and to increase with age, regardless of race or sex. Extroverts tend to be less sensitive to pain than introverts and we are all more sensitive to pain when anxious or upset, but considerably less so when the emotions or muscles are engaged. There is a strong, psychological component to pain — which is not to say that all pain is imaginary but that, on certain physical or mental cues, the brain releases its own morphia-like painkillers, called enkephalins and endorphins. These recently discovered hormones (10 years ago no-one knew they existed) are now thought to play an important role in childbirth. They may also explain why some of the ancient Chinese therapies, such as acupuncture, work.

The earliest and most instinctive way of dealing with pain is to 'rub' it away. Pressure, it seems, works whether it is in the most immediate or the 'long distance' sense. In acupuncture, one or more of the 657 *tsubos*, or energy points, of the body is stimulated in order to 'anaesthetize' or stimulate a quite different part of the body. The same can be done with finger pressure, instead of needles, and is known as *Shiatsu* or acupressure. Try pressing on the underside of the big toe or on the crown of the head to relieve headaches, or on either side of the ankle to relieve period pains.

MASSAGE

One of the most pleasurable and practical ways of reawakening, and communicating through, your sense of touch is massage. It is not difficult and, with practice, imagination and sensitivity, you can become quite accomplished, provided you remain within the 'safe', basic framework given on the following pages.

Before you start, it is essential to realize what massage can and cannot do for you. It will reduce aches and pains, relieve tension, promote a feeling of warmth and relaxation and have a demonstrable, though temporary, effect on the circulation. It will not 'break up' fat deposits or reshape the body and, although it is sometimes called passive exercise, it is not and should not be looked upon as a substitute for the real thing. Amateurs should start by using the four basic strokes on the following pages and extend and improvize their repertoires as they become more proficient.

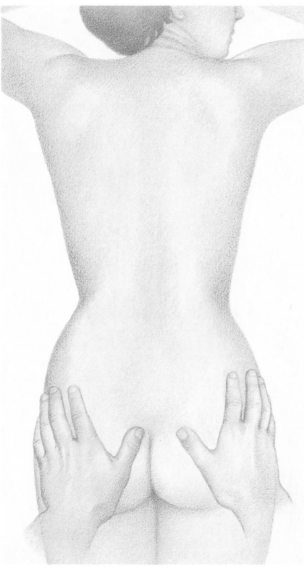

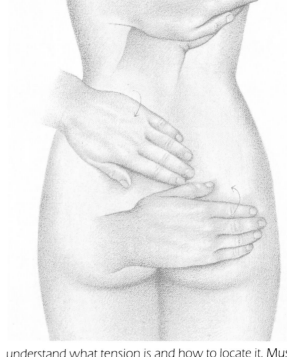

Basic rules

● <u>Practice, not theory, makes perfect.</u> The more you practise massage, developing and improvizing these four basic strokes the more sensitive your hands and sense of touch will become.

● <u>Your hands should be supple and relaxed</u>, so that they can shape themselves into and around the contours of the body on which you are working. Use the hands to communicate, the body to apply pressure and firmness, and let the movement come from deep within the centre of the body, rather than just from your wrists or elbows. You will then give a deeper, more even massage and you will also find that your arms become much less tired.

Massage only with the palms of the hands, fingers and thumbs. Applying pressure with elbows, knuckles or fists should be left to the expert.

● <u>Establish a smooth working rhythm</u> before you begin to experiment with more ambitious strokes or changes in pressure. Breathing evenly will help you to achieve this. Breathe in as you move the hands over the body and out as you apply the pressure. Start with an uncomplicated, shallow stroke that allows you to establish a basic rhythm.

● <u>To give an effective and relaxing massage, you must first</u> <u>understand what tension is and how to locate it.</u> Muscle is composed of a series of fibres which shortens as it contracts and lengthens as it relaxes. If it is held in a contracted state over a long period of time it will give rise to residual tension, aches, pains, even muscular spasm. To feel muscular tension, run your thumb along the muscle. It should feel soft and spongy. If you can feel a hard lump or knot along the muscle, you have found tension. Persuade tension to undo itself, either by massaging the entire length of the muscle or, if it is too tight and painful, by working around the area. You should find that the muscle unlocks as you release all the surrounding tension. Do not expect to eliminate all the tensions that you find in the course of a single massage, however. Massage is a progressive therapy, not a one-off cure-all.

● <u>Massage should always be lighter over those parts of the</u> <u>body where the bone is near the surface.</u> Bony areas include the face, the breast bone, the lower rib cage (back and front), the spine (the hands move alongside not on top of it), the hands, knees, calves and feet.

● <u>The more relaxed the body you are working on, the greater</u> <u>the benefits of the massage.</u> Ask your subject to have a warm bath before starting. Heat, whether the dry heat of a sauna or

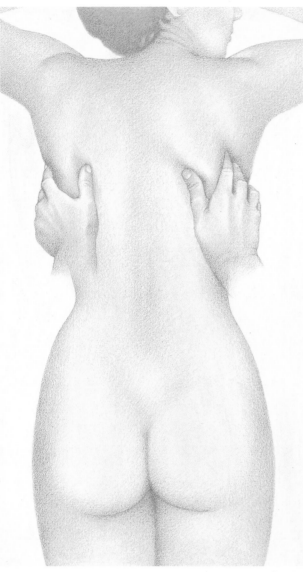

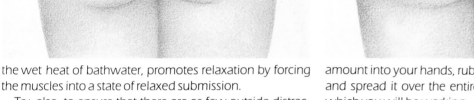

1. Light stroking (effleurage)
Start and end your massage with this stroke. It is a simple, long stroke of light to moderate pressure which can be used on arms, legs, abdomen, chest, back and shoulders. The hands should be relaxed and flexible and the fingers slightly apart, with the thumbs innermost. Proceed in a continuous gliding movement up or down the length of the area you are massaging. Massage in the direction of the heart, keeping the stroke very light to begin with and gradually increasing in depth as you progress.

2. Deeper circular stroking (petrissage)
This is a more difficult stroke. It takes time and perseverance to achieve the necessary co-ordination and manual dexterity, but it is worth persevering. To start with, keep the pressure fairly light and concentrate on using the two hands together in differing, circular directions. This is the difficult part: if the right hand is moving in a clockwise direction, the left hand should be working in an anti-clockwise one and vice versa. The hands should be about 10 cm (4 inches) apart, and the fingers soft and pliant. Add pressure by clasping one hand on top of the other and travelling clockwise up one side of the spine or body area and anti-clockwise up the other.

3. Kneading
Kneading is excellent for relieving tension on the muscular and fleshy areas of the body, such as the thighs, buttocks, upper arms, shoulders and base of the neck. It is relatively deep and, as with kneading bread dough, is performed with the pads of the fingers and thumbs. Do not knead the skin over the bony areas of the body.

4. Friction
This variation on kneading is performed only with the thumbs, which describe small circles. Friction is excellent for releasing areas of muscular spasm and can be used along the entire length of the spine, including the neck, the backs of the calves, the sides of the ankles, the heels and the lower inside arms.

the wet heat of bathwater, promotes relaxation by forcing the muscles into a state of relaxed submission.

Try, also, to ensure that there are as few outside distractions as possible, so that you can both concentrate on what the massage is aiming to achieve. Successful massage always asks and receives a measure of participation. Ask your subject to release his body into the surface he is lying on and to concentrate on the sensations generated through your hands. Always tell him to let you know when or if the massage becomes uncomfortable.

● If the massage is to work, you must both be comfortable. A bed is not ideal, as it is too soft to support the body correctly. Best of all is a table or bench at hip height, but a floor is fairly good, although more tiring for you — remember to stand up and stretch from time to time. When lying on the front, a pillow should be placed under the stomach in order to support the lower back, and a small cushion or folded towel placed underneath the forehead to support the head and neck. When lying on the back, a pillow should be placed under the knees.

● Use a light oil to enable your hands to glide easily over the skin. The essential or 'pure' oils are ideal for this, when diluted with a neutral oil, such as wheatgerm. Pour a small amount into your hands, rub them together to warm the oil and spread it over the entire area of the body surface on which you will be working.

● If you have never given a massage before, it is a good idea to concentrate on the back, which presents an ideal, large, flat, even surface and often contains most of the residual muscular tensions — particularly on the upper back, around the neck and shoulders. As you get more proficient, extend and adapt the strokes to the outlying parts of the body, with their more awkward angles and differing distributions of flesh, fat, bone and muscle.

● Do not massage anyone who is in ill health or suffering from infection, arthritis, rheumatism or any swelling in the joints. Avoid areas with warts, moles and varicose veins, too. As a rule, if in doubt, do not give a full body massage. Give a foot massage instead. This is one massage that you can also give yourself. Start by oiling the foot well. Then, supporting the foot in one hand, grasp the toes in the other hand and bend them as far as possible towards and away from the ankle. Stroke, rub and knead every centimetre of the sole of the foot, using a circular movement around the ankle bone. Finally, 'wring' the foot out rather as you would a dishcloth. You should feel deliciously relaxed.

131

smell and taste

Evolution has blunted some senses and sharpened others and there is every reason to suppose that our sense of smell is not what it once was. Animals live, communicate, struggle and perish in a world of smell which marks territory, asserts dominance, deters rivals, attracts mates and distinguishes species from species, male from female and friend from foe. By comparison, our sense of smell is obtuse indeed.

How do we smell?

The human mechanism for picking up and differentiating smells is, nevertheless, still remarkably delicate. Some 10 to 20 million olfactory receptor cells are situated in an area the size of a small coin in the roof of the nasal cavity just beneath the eye sockets. Not only can these cells detect as many as 4,000 separate and clearly identifiable odours, but they also only require the tiniest fraction of the essence to do this. The smell of garlic, for example, becomes perceptible at a concentration of less than one-millionth of a milligram in a litre of air and will also contribute very strongly to your appreciation of its taste.

Odours are created by moisture molecules evaporating into the air. All living and many inert things give off their separate, invisible and highly volatile essences — whether it is the balmy fragrance of roses or the acrid fumes of car exhaust — and, as long as the air temperature is just above freezing, will go on releasing them indefinitely. This is why leaving the stopper off a bottle of perfume or the petrol cap off a car will eventually cause perfume and petrol to evaporate entirely away.

Most smells have very distinct properties. We can say that they are spicy, fragrant, fruity, woody, aromatic, pungent or tarry, but our appreciation of them will be highly individual. Association, memory and even anticipation play an enormously important role in determining whether we respond positively or negatively to a certain smell. Smells, subconsciously catalogued away in the vast olfactory library of the brain, evoke strong associations of events, people or places, once they are reawakened. 'That unforgettable, unforgotten river smell' was Grantchester to the poet Rupert Brooke, but the same smell might have carried someone else back to somewhere quite different. Some psychiatrists are now exploiting these strong associative qualities by using the smell of vanillin in breast milk to unlock early painful associations or memories when treating patients with certain types of psychological disorder.

There is no doubt that scents and essences do exert a powerful psychological effect on the brain, influencing mood to calm and soothe, invigorate or even stupefy, if arriving in large enough doses. They also play an important role in human communication and sexuality, but just how

important no-one quite knows. It does seem likely tha human smell is a part of the highly complex body chemistry that sends out its signals of like and dislike, attraction and repulsion, excitement and fear. The ingredients thought to be responsible, known as pheromones, have now been isolated in the laboratory.

Receptivity to smell depends on several factors, such as the time of day (sensitivity increases as the day wears on), the stage of the menstrual cycle (women become between 100 and 5,000 times more receptive to smell over ovulation), and the length of exposure. Whether it is the smell of cabbage water or the exotic scent you have dabbed on your wrist, the nose soon tires of it. This is what makes people so impervious to their own body 'odour'.

HUMAN SMELL

All body odour — both the subtle odour that attracts and the stale odour that repels — derives from sweat. Sweating is an integral and essential part of the body's internal temperature control mechanism. If exertion, fever or emotional tension cause the body temperature to rise above 37.4°C (99.3°F) over 3,000,000 tiny sweat glands come into play. Known as eccrine glands, they release a substance (99 per cent water and one per cent sodium chloride) which exerts a cooling effect as it evaporates into the atmosphere. It is completely odourless. Emotional arousal, such as fear, embarrassment or sexual anticipation, steps up sweat production in the armpit, groin, hands and feet and brings a second set of glands, known as the apocrine glands, into action. Both types of sweat, however, are colourless, odourless and totally inoffensive and it is only when they combine with bacteria living on the skin and body hair that odour is produced.

Controlling and counteracting odour

● Stay clean. A daily bath or shower is the best way of guarding against odour, as it washes off the organic substances present in apocrine sweat. There is no need to become obsessive about cleanliness. Not all bacteria are harmful and many serve to protect the body against infection. An over-enthusiastic use of anti-bacterial soap, together with more elaborate types of germ warfare, may contribute to rather than eliminate problems by washing away the essential bacteria that live on the skin and body hair and destroying the natural layer of fatty acids that acts as a barrier to invading germs.

● Change your clothes frequently. Sweat clings to clothing, preventing it from escaping into the atmosphere so that it becomes 'stale'. Some synthetic fibres are particularly absorbent and you will probably find that it helps to wear natural

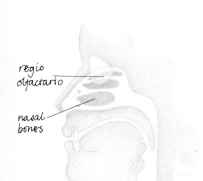

regio
olfactario

nasal
bones

The nasal cavity and *regio olfactorio*, a small area just below the eye socket which contains thousands of smell receptors each responsible for identifying specific smells and transmitting them to the brain.
The nasal cavity communicates not only with the nostrils but also with the back of the mouth. The appreciation of flavour derives from the joint action of the separate senses of smell and taste. Only a very few foods, such as salt and sugar, are identified by taste alone.

'One of the scourges that the woman of today has completely eliminated from her path is that of the trying outcome of perspiration in any form...' said *Vogue* in 1916. Had such a drastic measure been possible (which, thankfully, it was not), it would have had dire consequences for the body. Perspiration is a natural, healthy and important part of the body's temperature control mechanism. It is also essentially odourless. Perspiration is only trying when it is excessive or stale. Staying clean and bathing daily should guard against both of these. If not, the use of an anti-perspirant or deodorant certainly will.

fibres, such as cotton or silk, next to the skin. To remove sweat stains from clothing, rub on full-strength, liquid detergent and leave for about one hour before washing.

● Use a deodorant or anti-perspirant regularly, as protection builds up over a period of days, even with regular bathing, and tapers off if use is discontinued. Roll-ons tend to be more efficient than aerosols, and both are considerably more effective if applied to clean, cool, dry skin.

Deodorants contain perfume that masks odour by over-powering it. They are made more effective by the addition of an anti-bacterial agent. Anti-perspirants contain metal salts, usually aluminium compounds, which restrict the secretion of sweat from the eccrine and apocrine glands by as much as 50 per cent. They will not actually stop you perspiring altogether, nor will they adversely affect the body's thermostat as there are more than enough sweat glands in the rest of the body to compensate. Although you cannot become 'immune' to a brand of roll-on or aerosol, it does take a

smellsmellsmell

certain amount of trial and error to find the best for you.

● If you are already using a strong anti-perspirant and you continue to sweat copiously, see a doctor or dermatologist, who will be able to make up a special prescription for you. The same can be done for sweaty palms and soles, if your regular anti-perspirant does not work.

● Avoid using the so-called 'feminine' deodorant sprays. The healthy vagina keeps itself clean and does not need deodorizing. Straightforward washing with soap and water should constitute your first line of defence and, should you smell something abnormal, do not disguise it with a deodorant — go to see your doctor.

It is a myth, too, that menstrual blood smells. Like any other type of blood, it only begins to smell when it decomposes and that can only happen when it comes into contact with the air. Use an ordinary unscented, cotton or natural fibre tampon while menstruating and change it regularly — at least every six hours and preferably more often.

● Cut down foot odour by washing socks and stockings frequently. Wear wool and cotton, rather than synthetics, and shoes that enable your feet to 'breathe', by allowing air to circulate freely around them.

A liberal application of surgical spirit or a foot spray can be helpful in counteracting odour when applied to clean dry skin. While foot sprays do not entirely prevent perspiration, they do contain alcohol, which exerts a cooling and drying effect, and an anti-bacterial agent which inhibits the action of the naturally occurring bacteria that mingle with the sweat to produce the odour. A second line of defence is to buy medicated insoles which combat odour through absorption or through the slow release of a deodorant.

● Eliminate bad breath at source — not necessarily the mouth. The most common sources of bad breath are the throat (particularly if you have a throat infection), the stomach (particularly if you have not eaten for some hours) and the lungs (particularly if you smoke or drink). Because bad breath emanates largely from the digestive and respiratory systems, and not from the mouth, the usefulness of mouthwashes is limited. They may give the impression of fresh-smelling breath but it is only a temporary one.

Overcome or guard against bad breath by having regular dental check-ups, stopping smoking, cutting down the amount of coffee you drink and eating frequently. If you are fasting or crash dieting, you will become aware of an unpleasant taste in the mouth. Crunching an apple or a carrot should make it disappear.

Garlic, one of the strongest known smells, which has an unpleasant way of lingering on the breath for hours, and sometimes even for days, has no really effective 'antidote'. Of the many old folk remedies, the only one that really appears to work is that of eating large amounts of parsley with the garlic. Alternatively, make sure that those you live with have eaten it too — so you are all oblivious of the smell.

● Use scent judiciously to enhance your own natural smell, not to kill it. Using a cloying, heavy scent or excessive amounts of a lighter one will actually make you smell worse than if you had left it off entirely. (See pages 162-4 for guidelines on wearing scent and for ways of ensuring that it works with, not against, your own body chemistry.)

TASTE

If you blindfold people and offer alternate glasses of red and white wine, both at room temperature, you will find that they have the greatest difficulty in distinguishing between them. An appreciation of the differences in flavour depends first on colour, second on temperature, third on smell or 'bouquet' and only fourth on the sensation of taste. The same thing can be repeated with a large number of foods. Even onion, which most of us think of as having a very distinctive flavour, will taste exactly like a strawberry if you are not allowed to see or smell it first. This is because all these foods have considerably more smell than taste and your preference for one over the other originates, not from the sensations they produce in the mouth, but from the sensations they produce in the nose.

Unlike the appreciation of colour, sound, touch or smell, the appreciation of flavour arrives from a combination of senses, particularly the sense of smell, which is why nothing impairs your taste like a heavy cold. Even when certain types of food have arrived in the mouth, your appreciation of them may have more to do with sense receptors other than the taste buds. Mustard, peppers and spices are irritants that trigger the pain and touch receptors in the mouth, while smooth and crisp foods are more likely to be distinguished by virtue of their textures, rather than their tastes.

How do we taste?

Taste buds do not have anything like the extensive repertoire of smell receptor cells. They are capable of distinguishing four qualities. These are sweet (sugar), salt, sour (acidic juices, such as lemon) and bitter (coffee). It is the balance between these qualities that determines exactly how a food will taste. Although no food can stimulate all four types of taste buds at once, most foods stimulate at least two, and often three, of them.

Your taste 'threshold' or ability to taste certain foods, depends on three factors. The first of these is how acute your other senses are. Smoking, contrary to popular opinion, does not affect the transmission of taste impulses, but probably does undermine the sense of smell. The second factor is age. The number of taste buds in the mouth decreases as you grow older and, with them, your sensitivity to the tastes of various foods. The third factor is the intensity and duration of the taste stimulus. Taste buds tire very quickly. It is not flavour that makes you reach for a second helping, but unsatisfied appetite.

The appetite, a still little understood control mechanism situated in the hypothalmus in the brain, is influenced by a number of factors of which conditioning is probably greatest, and taste probably least. Appetite may be stimulated by taste sensations but it seems to 'free run' after that. In fact, experiments have shown that there is a lag of about 20 minutes between the stomach feeling full and sending its messages of satiation to the brain and the appetite responding to them and switching off. Put this observation to practical use. A failsafe way of regulating what you eat is to concentrate on sensations of taste rather than appetite, and to stop when they do.

bitter • salt
sour • sweet

The taste buds are responsible for transmitting one of four basic taste 'sensations' to the brain. Sweet is detected at the tip of the tongue, sour and salt along the edges and bitter right at the back of the mouth, which is why some foods are said to have a bitter 'aftertaste'. There are no taste buds in the centre of the tongue.

cosmetics

'One cannot use enough lip rouge.' Tallulah Bankhead

Before paint was ever splashed on to canvas or cave wall, it was splashed on to faces and bodies, where it was used not only for symbolic purposes but also for purely decorative ones.

The ladies of ancient Rome used the pulverized paste of crocodile intestine and dung to remove freckles and promote 'fairness' to the complexion, red *fucus* derived from moss to colour the cheeks and lips, saffron and charcoal for the eyes and, more painfully, a soot-filled needle to make the eyebrows more luxuriant by puncturing small holes into the skin. 'She who is blushing with no real blood is blushing with the aid of art,' wrote Ovid in his *Ars Amatoria* and counselled his female readers to do likewise, adding, ''Tis no harm, too, to mark the eyes slightly with ashes or with saffron.' But it had to look <u>real</u>: 'Let not your lover discover the boxes exposed upon the table; art by its concealment only gives aid to beauty.' It would be hard to find a better prescription for the 1980s.

What had been a fashionable diversion for the ladies of imperial Rome, became a positive rage in Elizabethan England. The range of ingredients incorporated into the cosmetics of the day reads more like a modern-day list of poisons than something which could be bought over the counter from the local apothecary: lead oxide, antimony and mercury compounds were all used to contribute to the unearthly pallor which was the prized possession of every Elizabethan lady. Although some women were fatally poisoned by the cosmetics they wore, the fashion persisted right through to the Victorian era, when make-up was firmly relegated to the stage and lower castes of society. No self-respecting Victorian woman would have allowed her appearance to suggest that it owed anything, even remotely, to artifice.

When cosmetics made their cautious come-back at the end of the last century, they were marketed as medical rather than beauty aids. One cold cream was even described as being good for constipation. By the 1920s cosmetics were firmly back in favour, but this time with a different emphasis — that of giving, not of robbing, expressiveness. A Cupid's bow hinted at sensuality, a touch of colour at coyness, a dark shadow at decadence. Expressiveness was pre-packed, promises abounded and the aim was always to achieve <u>the</u> look. Nothing else qualified.

Only in the last 20 years or so have attitudes towards cosmetics finally relaxed. There are no longer any rules. Instead, there are suggestions that will enable you to create your look — a look that is as individual as the clothes you wear or the attitudes you adopt. And one which, like your clothes and your attitudes, will change with your mood. Experiment with your make-up, define and enhance your features, add and subtract colour as you like. Find guidelines to help you on the following pages.

GETTING THE BEST FROM YOUR COSMETICS

Used sensibly and with reasonable regularity, most cosmetics will last just as long as you want them to. If used carelessly or applied only infrequently, you run the risk of irritation and/or infection from bacteria which will eventually form in even the most stable of products. Homemade cosmetics have about the same shelf-life as foods, must always be kept in the refrigerator and should not be used after a week. The shelf-life of commercial products is much longer and far beyond most people's 'usage' time once opened. Products most susceptible to contamination by the air, house dust or dirty fingers are those using cream formulae, such as moisturizers, eye colours and lipsticks. Powder- and alcohol-based cosmetics, on the other hand, will last infinitely longer. But remember to balance medical and aesthetic considerations. When your product starts to separate or discolour, lose its fragrance, flake, cake or harden, it has probably outlived its usefulness and the time has come to replace it. Use the following guidelines to get the best from your cosmetics.

● Heat, light, air and moisture all have a damaging effect on cosmetics in general and perfumes in particular (see page 164). Keep them in a cool, dark place and try to ensure that all containers are absolutely air- and water-tight.

● All cosmetics are subject to oxidization (contamination from oxygen in the air), although those with anti-oxidant preservatives are less so. Cosmetics in open top jars are much more susceptible to contamination than those in tubes. Stoppers or tops should always be replaced after use to prevent air circulating inside and to discourage the introduction of bacteria from dirt and dust.

● Keep your cosmetics to yourself. One study of over 1,000 eye cosmetics showed that, although they were all absolutely free from germs on purchase, nearly half had developed some degree of bacterial activity when examined after six months. Most of them had been used on more than one set of eyes. False sensitivities to products may develop after using a cosmetic that has come into contact with other people's skin or fingers. If you do have a sensitive skin, avoid free-for-all make-up displays on cosmetic counters — that is asking for trouble.

● Clean fingers are the safest cosmetic applicators of all, particularly if you are using cream-based cosmetic products, as bacteria and germs can cling to the greasy residue left on sponges and brushes. If you do develop a sensitivity, it may not be on account of the cosmetic at all, but of the applicators or brushes you have been using, particularly if you have been using them for years.

Replace brushes every year or 18 months and cream eye shadow applicators and sponges every six months. Be particularly careful with mascara wands, or applicators, because these pick up germs very readily and can infect the eye if carelessly applied. Return the wand to the tube immediately after application and limit yourself to, say, two refills of mascara before throwing the whole thing away and buying afresh.

ALLERGIES AND SENSITIVITIES

When you consider that there are over 100,000 differently formulated cosmetics, using several thousand ingredients, it is surprising not that some people develop allergies or sensitivities to one or more of them, but that so few of us do. The processes by which cosmetics are made are so carefully controlled and the ingredients so scrupulously screened, that most of us can put anything we choose on to our skins with absolute confidence and in perfect safety. Even so, there is always a chance of reacting adversely to a product at some time in our lives and it may quite possibly be one which we have been using happily for months or even years. The odds of this happening were put as high as one in two in one study, as low as one in 12 in another. The reaction itself may either be a 'true', demonstrable allergy or — more commonly — a sensitivity which may be slight or severe, temporary or prolonged, may arrive for no clear reason at all and may even disappear on reusing the product that produced it.

Allergic reactions

True allergic reactions to cosmetics are very rare and probably afflict no more than one per cent of users. They are the result of a highly complex immunological response to a substance to which you have already been exposed (see page 214). They can often be successfully isolated and are extremely specific. A similar, but not identical, substance will often produce no effect whatsoever. With very few exceptions, once you have an allergy you will always have it. The only way of avoiding a reaction is to take appropriate evasive action, either by avoiding the type or types of cosmetics likely to contain the allergen or by going for a cosmetic range that you know excludes the offending ingredient.

Sensitivities

Sensitivities to cosmetics are much more common and often more puzzling than allergies, as they tend to be produced in response to a group of substances rather than to one particular component. You may, for example, develop a sensitivity to perfumes in general rather than to geranium in particular. Because of this, sensitivities tend to be much harder to isolate and you may, therefore, find it more useful to adopt the general strategy detailed below than to try to detect the precise culprit.

If you frequently have dry, red, itchy patches on your face, neck and body, you are likely to be what is known as generally sensitivity-prone. This category tends to include those who are pale-skinned, red- or fair-haired, suffer from asthma, hay fever or eczema, burn easily in moderate sunlight and have naturally dry skins. These are all indications that you should use the gentlest skincare and cleansing routines. Choose simple, unscented products and stick with the ones that seem to suit your skin. Read labels before buying products. These have to state any ingredients used from a 'short list' of potential sensitizers and are currently being phased into the UK under EEC regulations; they have been statutory in the USA for some years.

Finally, remember that it is not only possible to grow out of but into a sensitivity and that all skin tends to become more sensitive as it gets older.

carecarecare

Common allergens and sensitizers

Lanolin, vegetable and mineral oils. Lanolin is an oil taken from the sebum of the sheep and used in a wide range of cosmetics — baby oils, moisturizers, night creams, nail varnish removers and some soaps and shampoos. 'Superfatted' or 'moisturizing' are the words to watch out for. Look for creams containing petrolatum instead. An allergy to lanolin can produce a dramatic reaction — a dry, scaly rash, often accompanied by severe inflammation.

Vegetable oils and mineral oils (linseed oil, olive oil, sesame oil, cocoa butter, petrolatum, oleic acid and butyl stearate in particular) are less likely to cause an allergic reaction but have been implicated in intermittent break-outs of small pimples known as acne cosmetica.

Paraphenylenediamine. This ingredient, used in the formulation of permanent hair dyes, is now well recognized as a common sensitizer. Always ask for a patch test, if having your hair coloured and, if colouring your own hair, carry it out yourself (see page 103 for instructions). An allergy or sensitivity to this chemical can be extremely unpleasant and may not necessarily be restricted to the scalp and the hands, appearing as scaling on the face or inflammation around the eyes.

Parabens. This group of preservatives has extremely effective anti-bacterial properties and is used in most cosmetic and medical preparations. Because of their effectiveness, the concentration is so low that it is often well tolerated, but reactions are not unknown. Other allergenic preservatives: quaternium-15 and imidazolidinyl urea.

Formaldehyde. This anti-bacterial agent, used as a preservative in some cosmetics and in much higher concentration in nail 'hardeners', can produce sensitivity reactions on the skin and discoloration or separation on the nails.

Perfumes. These are the most common sensitizers in cosmetics and, even though they are incorporated into cosmetics at a fraction of the concentration used in pure perfumes, may produce irritant reactions. Almost all cosmetic products contain perfume unless labels specifically state otherwise.

Aluminium salts. These highly acidic salts are used in the formulation of all anti-perspirants. While allergic reactions are rare, sensitivities and irritations are common, particularly if the skin is already sore, sunburned or newly shaved.

Allergy and sensitivity check list

If you develop a rash or a patch of sore, scaly skin and suspect that it is product linked, check the following.

● Have you started using a new product or a new version of an old product lately? Check bath oils, body lotions, shampoos, soaps, nail varnishes, moisturizers, cleansers and deodorants, as well as make-up and products that may have been used on your skin or your hair in a beauty salon or by a hairdresser. Check new formulae of old favourites, too, as they may contain new chemical compounds.

If you have a naturally sensitive skin, use one new product at a time to see how your skin reacts to it and patch test it first. Put a coin-sized amount of the product on to the skin every day for a week and discard it if there is any untoward reaction. Remember, too, that reactions may occur after years of contact with the 'offending' substance.

● Is the rash confined to one specific area of the skin or is it more generalized? The response may not be caused by the cosmetics you are using. Allergies to metal, such as nickel, may manifest themselves on the face where rings, bracelets or long drop earrings have come into contact with the skin. A body rash may be caused by a detergent used for washing clothes or bed linen. Confusingly, too, sensitivities to products do not always appear on the area to which they have been applied. An allergy caused by nail varnish, for example, is rarely seen on the hands and appears more commonly on the cheeks or chin where they have rested on the fingers.

● Is the reaction worse at some times and better at others? Does it coincide with times when you wear a different or heavier make-up — the more you put on, the greater the chance of irritation — or a different type of perfume? Or does it become noticeable after washing your hair or painting your nails? If there does seem to be a link with a specific product, stop using it. If the picture is less clear, start a gradual process of elimination, leaving one product aside at a time, until you manage to identify the culprit.

● Is the reaction severe enough to require medical attention? While amateur detection is fine if the response is mild, any severe reaction, such as pronounced inflammation, should be taken to your doctor and, if necessary, referred to a dermatological clinic for diagnostic patch testing. This should determine the ingredient responsible and the products to avoid using in the future.

● Is your skin damaged, sunburned or excessively dry? If so, do not be surprised if it reacts unfavourably to products previously tolerated quite well. This sensitivity is temporary and there is no reason why you should not return to these products, once your skin has regained its natural resilience.

THE LANGUAGE ON THE LABEL
What it's really saying

Hypoallergenic. The 'hypo' in hypoallergenic means 'less' not 'non'. Everyone is sensitive to something and some people will even react to distilled water sprayed on to the face. If you do have a sensitive skin, however, a hypoallergenic range can be very helpful. Products are usually unscented, exclude known sensitizers, such as lanolin, and keep to formulae that are as simple as possible.

pH balanced is a popular selling line used to indicate the relative acidity or alkalinity of a product — relative, that is, to the acidity of your skin and hair (5.5 and 6.8 respectively). The acidity/alkalinity scale is measured in numbers from one to 14. Seven is neutral; numbers below this are acid and above it are alkaline. PH 'balanced' soaps and shampoos are of questionable value for normal skins and hair, which have an in-built ability to adjust their pHs back to normal within about 20 minutes of washing. The process can be speeded up by the use of a toner or hair conditioner, both of which are slightly acid in nature. While pH shampoos can be helpful for processed or damaged hair, because they avoid the swelling caused by the alkalinity of detergents, people with sensitive skins that feel dry and taut after washing should forget their pHs and use a cream cleanser instead.

Organic (as in organic soaps, shampoos, etc) is pseudo scientific for owing its origins to the garden and not the laboratory. As the real meaning of organic is 'belonging to or having the characteristics of a living thing', no product can be organic per se. That is the province of plants, animals and humans. The fact that all cosmetics contain organic derivatives in varying degrees and concentrations probably accounts for the confusion. Although organic (i.e. 'natural and good') is usually considered preferable to synthetic (i.e. 'man-made and bad'), synthetic substances can make valuable and extremely effective cosmetic ingredients.

Natural, anyway, is not always good. There are more known plant or plant-derivative allergens than chemical ones — chamomile is one example. In addition, the possibility of developing a sensitivity or untoward reaction is compounded if preservatives are left out of the preparation. Be wary, therefore, of homemade recipes for creams and cosmetics. They may sound delicious, but it is difficult to ensure that the utensils and containers you use are scrupulously clean and sterile. The lack of preservative makes home preparations an ideal breeding ground for bacteria. Herbal enthusiasm is fine and can make for marvellous looking and smelling products, as long as it is tempered with a little scientific resource. The products to go for are those combining natural ingredients with synthetic preservatives.

Bio (as in bio-energetic and bio-active) is derived from the Greek word, *bios*, meaning 'life'. Whatever its implied sense, the only thing that can be said about a product that is 'bio'-something is that it is designed to be used, and to have an effect, on living tissue. But what product isn't?

Medicated soaps, lotions, deodorants and shampoos are those which have a specific action on the skin or hair beyond their normal cleansing, toning or deodorizing properties. Additives like benzoyl peroxide or salicylic acid have grease-stripping properties and are added to some soaps and certain types of make-up for excessively oily, acne-prone skin. Zinc pyrithione and selenium sulphide are used in anti-dandruff shampoos, aluminium salts are added to anti-perspirant roll-ons and sprays, and bactericides, such as triclocarbon, to anti-bacterial 'deodorant' soaps. These additives tend to make the products harsher and increase the chances of sensitivity or allergic-type reactions. Use them sparingly on sensitive skin and very dry or damaged hair.

Soapless shampoos and cleansing products have not been saponified (made into soap by mixing natural animal or vegetable oils with an alkali, such as potassium). Instead they use a combination of lanolin, oils, colouring, perfume and protein. Soapless preparations are particularly good for washing the face or hair in hard water, as ordinary soap tends to combine with traces of magnesium and calcium salts in the water, leaving tiny deposits on the skin and hair which may contribute to dryness and can even produce a dandruff-like scaling on the scalp.

Superfatted soaps are made by leaving unsaponified fat in the soap during the processing or by adding lanolin, glycerine, beeswax or mineral oils to the soap base. They are particularly good for dry skins.

Emulsions are products containing ingredients that would normally separate rather than combine. Creams and body lotions are emulsions of oil and water mixed freely together during processing but sometimes liable to separate, particularly if they have been kept for some time. Stirring the cream or shaking the bottle should remedy this.

Unscented products have no perfume added during preparation. Unless a label states that the product is unscented, it will probably contain a scent or group of scents — whether it is an innocuously bland-looking foundation or a richly coloured eye-shadow. Scents are usually present in cosmetics at a concentration of around 0.5 per cent (pure perfume 'concentrate' may contain up to 20 per cent). Although the concentration used in cosmetics is relatively low, perfumes are common sensitizers and people whose skins are easily irritated would probably do well to seek out unscented products.

Preservatives are essential to any product not destined for immediate use because they prevent oils and creams from going rancid. Preservatives used may include anti-oxidants to preserve the product from contamination from the air; anti-bacterial compounds (such as phenols and formalin-releasers) to prevent or, at least, discourage the growth of bacteria and moulds; and stabilizers with anti-bacterial properties (parabens) which combine the qualities of the first two and tend to make the best preservatives. They are widely used in cosmetic formulae. Alcohol and alcohol compounds also work as stabilizers and inhibit, but do not entirely prevent, the growth of bacteria. Toners, astringents and perfumes, which are often predominantly alcohol, may not require the addition of further preservatives.

wordswordswords

measuringmeasuringmeasuring

'There is no excellent beauty which hath not some strangeness in the proportion' said Sir Francis Bacon 300 years ago, recognizing that interest and beauty in a face derive much more from how the features work together than on how symmetrically 'perfect' they are.

Beginning your self-analysis with a similar appreciation of harmony, make the most of your face by working with it — accentuate the good, minimize the not-so-good and rebalance the shape where necessary. Make-up can help you to do this, but first consider your features not in isolation but in relation to each other — length of face in terms of width, shape of nose in terms of shape of chin, line of eyebrow in terms of line of eye. Assess your face shape too. If, as is probable, your face is so familiar to you that you cannot pinpoint exactly what is good or not so good about it or what its general shape is, try some objective arithmetic.

Take off your make-up and pull your hair well away from your face. Taking a ruler and holding it absolutely straight, measure the length of your face from the top of the forehead to the tip of your chin (left). Be as precise as possible and measure in centimetres, not in inches. Continue by measuring the widest part of the face (usually along the top of the cheekbone, as right). The perfect oval-shaped face has a length that is one and half times the width. If the width is two-thirds or more of the length, the face is wide (usually round). If the length is more than one and three-quarter's of the width, the face is long. Now measure your face across the jawbone. If it is significantly less than the width measurement and the chin is pointed, the face is heart shaped. If it is the same and the chin is blunt, the face is probably square.

Assess the width of the mouth by placing the ruler at the outside corner of the mouth so that it lies parallel with the bridge of your nose, as above right. Look straight ahead. The outside edge of the ruler should line up with the inner edge of the iris.

To see how well spaced your eyes are, measure them for length and then measure the distance between the eyes (below right). It should be one eye's length. If it is less than three-quarters of the length, the eyes are definitely close set; if more than one and a quarter times the length, they are wide spaced.

Test your profile by placing the ruler against your nose and chin (below left). Your lips should come well within it. If they touch the ruler, the chin is weak.

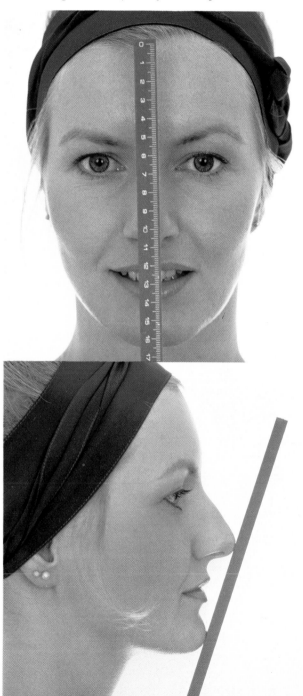

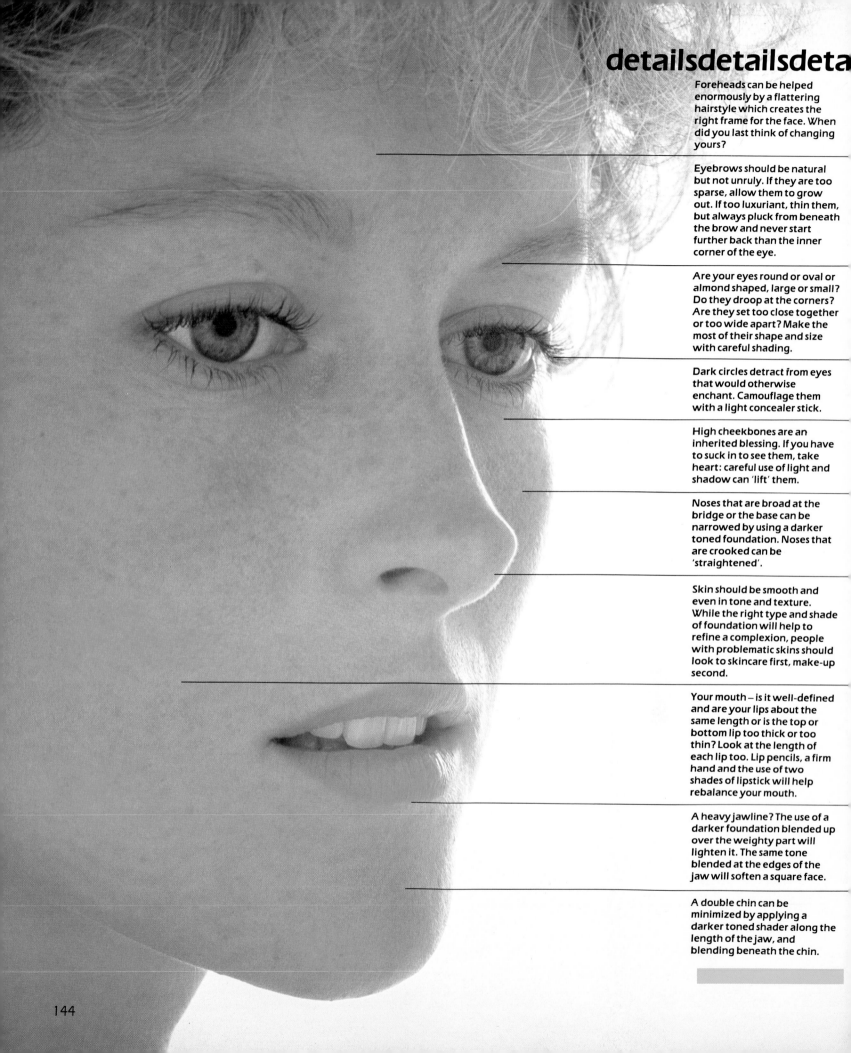

Foreheads can be helped enormously by a flattering hairstyle which creates the right frame for the face. When did you last think of changing yours?

Eyebrows should be natural but not unruly. If they are too sparse, allow them to grow out. If too luxuriant, thin them, but always pluck from beneath the brow and never start further back than the inner corner of the eye.

Are your eyes round or oval or almond shaped, large or small? Do they droop at the corners? Are they set too close together or too wide apart? Make the most of their shape and size with careful shading.

Dark circles detract from eyes that would otherwise enchant. Camouflage them with a light concealer stick.

High cheekbones are an inherited blessing. If you have to suck in to see them, take heart: careful use of light and shadow can 'lift' them.

Noses that are broad at the bridge or the base can be narrowed by using a darker toned foundation. Noses that are crooked can be 'straightened'.

Skin should be smooth and even in tone and texture. While the right type and shade of foundation will help to refine a complexion, people with problematic skins should look to skincare first, make-up second.

Your mouth – is it well-defined and are your lips about the same length or is the top or bottom lip too thick or too thin? Look at the length of each lip too. Lip pencils, a firm hand and the use of two shades of lipstick will help rebalance your mouth.

A heavy jawline? The use of a darker foundation blended up over the weighty part will lighten it. The same tone blended at the edges of the jaw will soften a square face.

A double chin can be minimized by applying a darker toned shader along the length of the jaw, and blending beneath the chin.

Begin your make-up with a good, even base. If you are fortunate enough to possess one naturally, a plain or tinted gel moisturizer with a light dusting of blusher over the cheekbones is probably the best daytime look. If the skin is blotchy in colour, or uneven in texture, a foundation will help to even out skin colour, making the complexion appear smooth and refined.

If the skin is dry, moisturize first, allow your skin five or 10 minutes to 'settle' and then use a hydrating foundation. There should be no sign of greasiness, certainly no shine, when you start. If the skin is oily, use a good astringent first to remove any immediate oil on the skin and cover with a medicated or matt foundation. Transparent gels and tinted moisturizers can look marvellous on a good, healthy skin.

Aim for a foundation that is as close as possible to your natural skin tone. Try to avoid shades that have a lot of pink in them (not good for any colour type) and go instead for a colour base that complements your natural colouring. Always test a foundation on your face, not on the back of your hand. You only have to put your hand up to your face, to see the difference in colour between them. Be sure to continue the colour as far down your neck as will be showing.

Once you have applied the foundation, conceal or contour where necessary (see right). For the purposes of shading or contouring you will need a foundation two shades or so darker than your natural skin tone and — most important — a light hand. Blushers and shaders that are clumsily applied or incompletely blended can make the face look bruised or striped.

Special covering creams camouflage surface scars admirably — and they are equally effective for birth marks, broken veins and dark circles around the eyes. These dark circles are caused not so much by late nights and lack of sleep as by a natural thinness of the skin, making blood vessels more visible because they are closer to the surface. In addition, the brow and cheekbones cast their own shadows. While concealing creams can be useful for taking the colour out of a pimple, they will not conceal it entirely. A bump in the skin will always show in certain lights. As the head is always turning and the face moving, the light is bound to strike it unflatteringly from time to time. It is therefore worth giving more thought to prevention than to concealment. Spots will disappear more rapidly if not smothered with make-up.

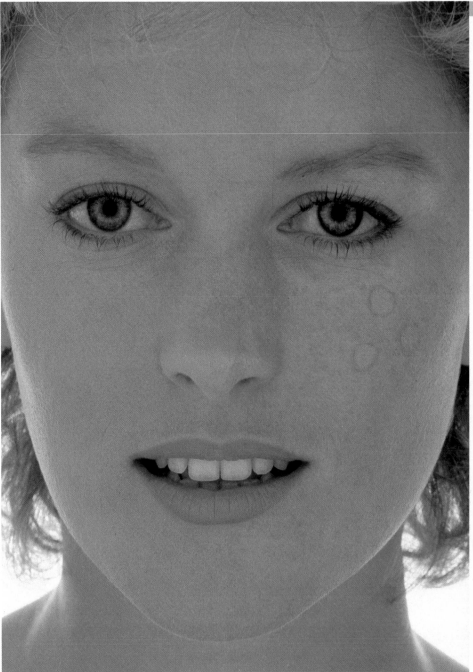

The right light is crucial when making up. First rule: it should be as close as possible to the light you will be seen in. This means making up in daylight during daylight hours and under an electric light after dark. Second rule: whatever your light source, it should be shining directly on to your face. A cross-light that leaves half your face in shadow will not produce an even make-up. Recommended lighting arrangement: a mirror with bulbs, as left, is ideal because it casts a flat even light; alternatively, place one lamp to either side of your mirror so that they are on a level with your face.

For an even foundation blend outwards, following arrows.

basebasebase

The smoothest way to apply foundation: dot it on forehead, nose, cheeks and chin, keeping to the centre of face and away from hairline. Then, using a slightly damp sponge, or fingers, blend outwards following arrows on diagram, below. Smooth some gently on and around the eyelids and lips too. Take foundation as far down the neck as will be showing. Finally, check that foundation is evenly blended around jaw, just under nose, and around the hairline.

Conceal dark circles under eyes and any other darker patches on face with a concealer stick just a shade or two lighter than your natural skintone. Press in with clean fingers over the foundation.

To take the colour out of a pimple, use a small make-up brush, dab it on to a concealer that is the same shade as your natural skin tone and stroke the spot gently. This will help to cover all the contours of the spot.

Narrow a nose that is too broad at the bridge or base by drawing triangles of foundation about three shades deeper than your skin tone on either side of the wide area (1). Then blend into surrounding make-up. Intensify the effect by adding blusher.

Straighten a nose that is slightly crooked by applying a darker toned foundation along the crooked side (2), a lighter one on the other.

Lift a heavy jaw by applying a darker foundation in a long triangle just above the weighty part (3) and blending it into the lighter more natural shade on the face and neck.

Lift cheekbones with clever use of shadow and light. But do not forget to blend. The shader should look like a shadow cast quite naturally by the bone, not a diagonal stripe. Suck in your cheeks to find your cheekbones. Place a triangle of the darker foundation colour in this hollow – the widest part extending towards the ears (4). Blend and add highlight across the bone above (5).

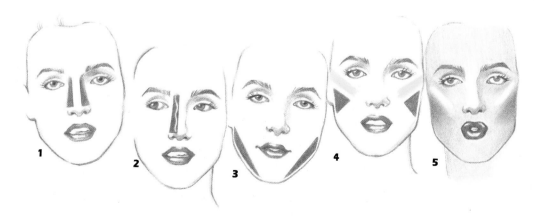

1   2   3   4   5

blushblushblushblush

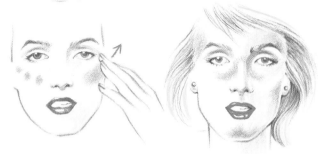

To find your starting point: look straight at yourself in a mirror and place blusher directly below each eyeball.

For evenings and an exotic look, apply iridescent blusher to temples, earlobes, chin and across the nose . . .

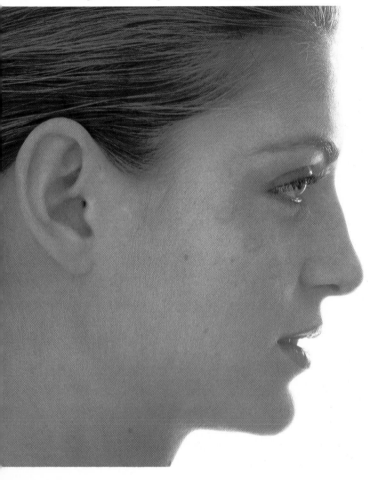

Blusher enlivens the face, adds colour and polish and, when whisked over eyelid and browbone, gives a natural no-make-up look for daytime. The art in using it lies in three things. The first is picking the right colour — go back to your basic skin and foundation colour and make sure your blusher tones well with it (see colour quiz, page 22). The second is knowing where to apply it (see above) and the third is knowing how much to use. It is much easier to add than to subtract colour. Start with just the lightest touch and build up until you get the depth you want. For evenings, intensify your make-up by moving one or two shades brighter with blusher and lip colours.

Of the three basic types of blusher, gels with their transparent effect are best applied over a moisturizer, or a light

148

Unless aiming for a dramatic effect, blushers and lip colours should complement each other. In fact, you can improvise very effectively by using your regular lip colour on your cheeks in place of blusher. As a general rule: the lighter the skin tone, the lighter the blusher.

Apply blusher along the cheekbones (opposite). Add iridescent highlights above the bone for shine, darker shading beneath for more emphasis. For daytime and a natural look, whisk blusher around the hairline at the forehead and temples, over the browbone, and centre it on the 'apples' of the cheeks to give a healthy glow. If the face is round, use shader, not blusher (pink has a plumping effect), and emphasize the diagonal slant of the cheekbones. If the face is long, apply blusher horizontally to give an impression of width. Set make-up with a fine covering of a translucent powder, as detailed below.

foundation, but with no powder; cream blushers should be blended over the cheekbones on top of foundation but under powder; powder blushers should be applied over the powder.

Loose face powder is the best way to set a make-up. Choose a fine translucent powder and apply it liberally on a young face, sparingly on an older one. If the skin is dry, the powder should be whisked on lightly with a powder puff or broad soft brush (paint brushes are ideal provided that they do not moult). Remove any excess with a brush. If the skin is oily, powder will help to counteract 'shine'. But it must be applied firmly. Take it across forehead, down centre panel of face and across the chin, pressing in well and releasing as you go.

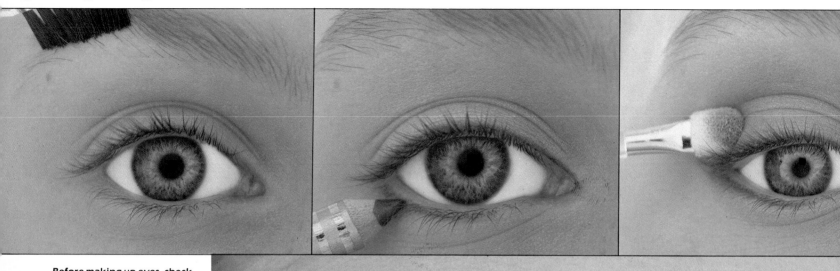

Before making up eyes, check that foundation is smooth, dark rings are camouflaged and all powder has settled. Attend to the eyebrows. Check them first for length, thin if necessary and brush upwards for an instant wide-awake look. If brows are sparse, fill in with light feathery strokes, using an appropriately coloured eyebrow pencil.

Now take an eye pencil. Check first that it is soft enough (page 123), then line the lids, top and bottom, preferably outside the lashes, keeping hand steady and pencil at a flattish angle to the eye. Neutral, smoky colours – charcoal, browns and greys – are the most natural. Stop the line short of the inner corners of the eye to avoid a narrowing effect. If eyes are close set, keep to the outer halves of the lids only. Use the same pencil to emphasize the natural contour of the eye at the crease.

Next the shadow. Choose one that tones well with your eye pencil, smudge it over the upper lids, blending it down into the line and up into the crease. You can continue building with the colour here in order to intensify the effect. Continue colour out to the sides of the eyes.

For a more elaborate make-up, add highlighter to brow bone. Use clean fingers or applicator and blend outwards.

Finish with mascara. Apply in several thin coats to underneath as well as to top side of lashes. Then remove any excess with a brush, separating lashes as you do so.

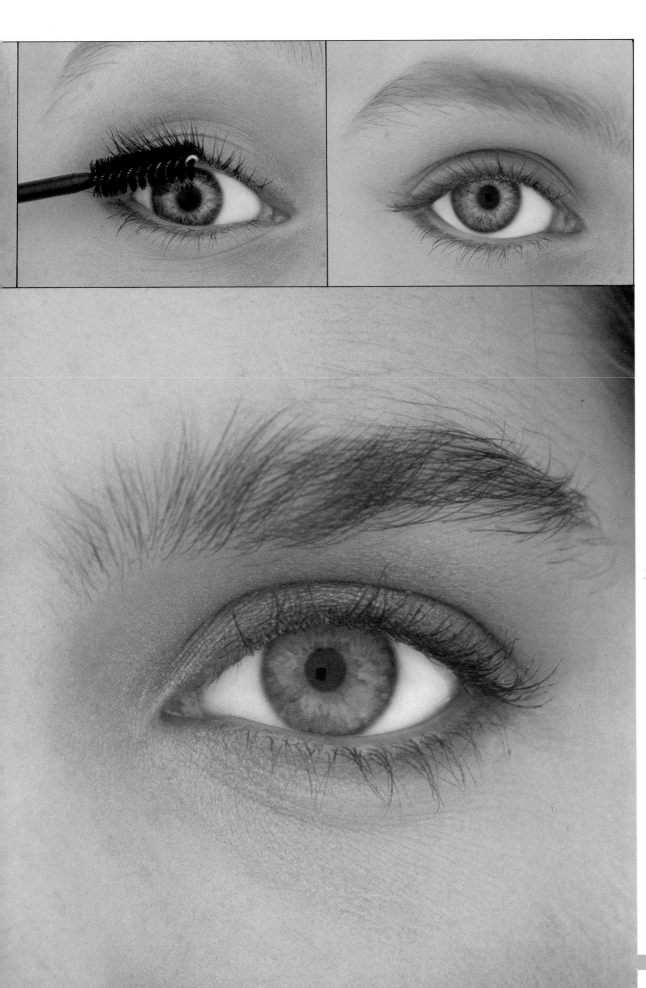

Lift droopy eyes by drawing a thin line at the inner corner of upper lid and steadily widening it so that it covers the outer corner of the lid entirely.

Widen eyes set too close together: shade a dark triangle across the outer corners of the upper eyelid.

Minimize the space between the eyes if they are wide-set, by blending shadow across the inner halves of upper lid and up towards the browbone. Slant shadow on outer corners of lower lid.

Make small eyes appear larger. Line inside of lids with soft white pencil. Use a smoky grey or brown pencil underneath lower lashes. Finish with black mascara.

Elongate round eyes by lining insides of upper lids, outer half of lower ones. Apply shadow at corner, as shown.

Bring deep-set eyes forward, by lining outer halves of upper and lower lids with darkish pencil, widening line as you go. Then apply a lighter shadow over the pencil and smudge out.

lipslipslipslipslips

Lip pencils, lip brushes, lip colours and lip gloss will add the finishing touch to your make-up. Prime first with a good base. Smooth foundation on to lips – medicated foundations are particularly good as they dry the lips out and help lip colour to last. If lipstick tends to 'bleed', apply lip colour twice – once before and once after the powder.

Outline lips with a soft lip pencil just a tone or so darker than your chosen lipstick shade. Blot with a tissue to soften the line, recontouring the mouth if necessary. Lift a droopy expression by extending lower lip at corners and 'raising' slightly. Match the length of top and bottom lips by filling the area with a pencil.

Now fill in the mouth with your chosen lip shade. Use an applicator or lip brush to apply the colour. Finish with a transparent gloss.

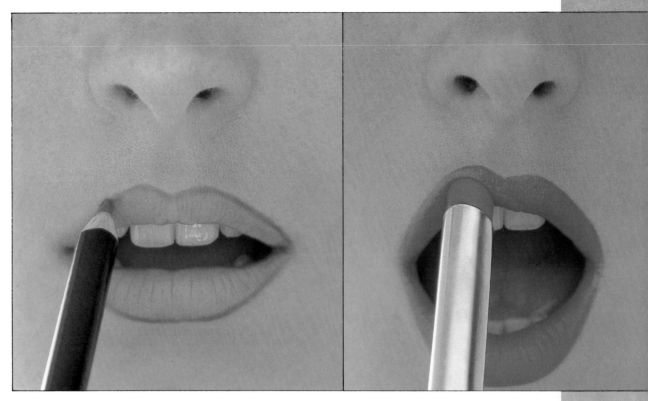

To line lips, place fore and middle fingers at each corner of the mouth so that the lips are taut. You will find it much easier to draw a steady line.

To make your upper or lower lip less full, line just inside your natural lipline with a colour as close to your own natural colour as possible. Then fill in.

To make the whole mouth less prominent, use two lipstick shades. Fill in the centre section of both lips with the darker tone of your chosen lip colour. Apply the lighter one to either side and blend inwards with a clean lipbrush.

To add fullness to the upper or lower lip take a white pencil and draw a line just outside your natural lipline. Go over the line with lipstick and fill in.

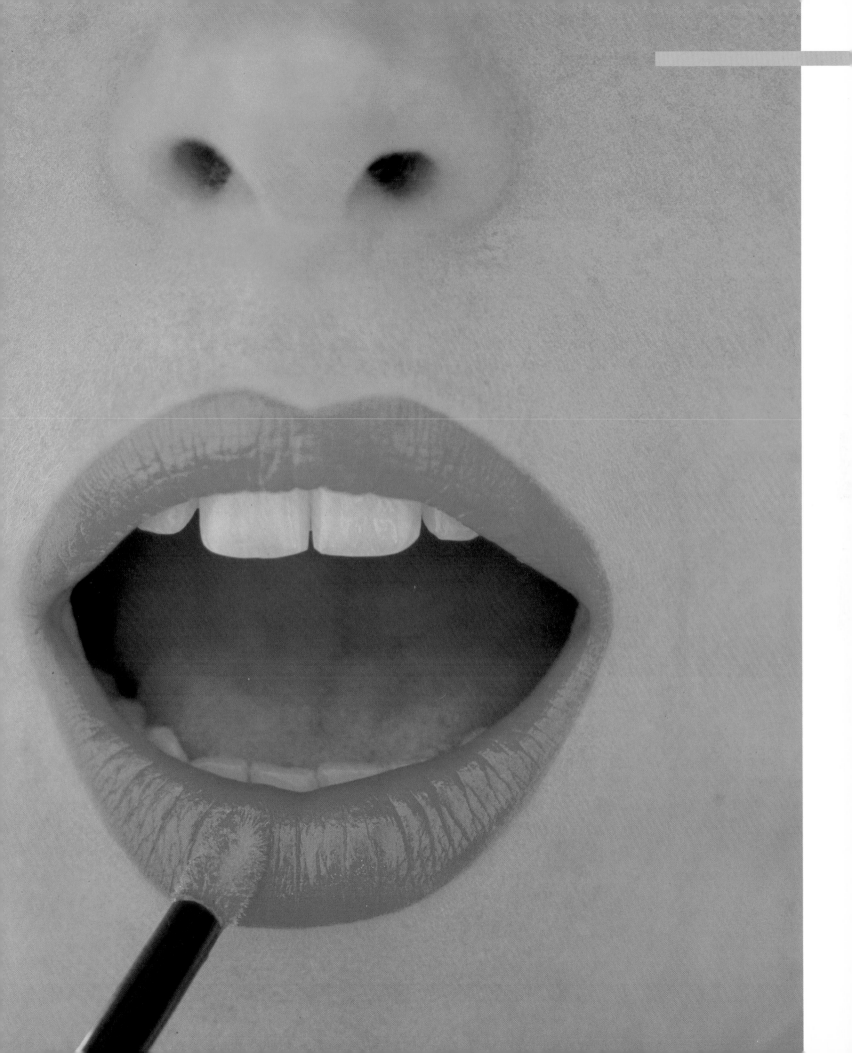

The key to a successful daytime make-up: restraint. Concentrate on evening out skintone, add a touch of colour to the face and definition to the eyes and mouth for an effective and completely natural 'no make-up' look. Here, a light moisturizing foundation is smoothed over the skin and dark circles around the eyes are concealed. A soft pink blusher is brushed over the cheekbones and across the browbone and lightly whisked around the temples and the hairline for a healthy glow. Eyes are defined with a neutral brown below and a gentle cinnamon above, and smudged slightly with a cotton wool bud to soften the effect. The lashes are emphasized with brown mascara. A light natural pink lipcolour adds the finishing touch.

The key to a successful evening make-up: emphasis and shine. Build on blusher, lip and eye colours to intensify the effect, remembering that artificial light tends to flatten colour tones in the skin. Add glamour with iridescent highlights and gleaming lipcolour.
Here, exactly the same foundation and blusher shades are used as for daytime (see above). The difference: the blusher is intensified over the cheekbones and dabbed lightly on to the tip of the nose and the chin for a warm 'party' look; a light dusting of pearly translucent powder adds shine.
The eyes are defined in dark bronze, which is continued over the upper lid, into the crease and out to the corners of the eyes, above and below, to emphasize their natural shape. The lids are then lined with black and the browbone highlit with shining gold. The lips are outlined with a deep red lip pencil and filled in with lipcolour in a similar shade.

The 'mousy' colouring of the dark blonde lends itself beautifully to highlights in the hair and to almost any colour make-up. Make the most of this versatility.
Here is a warm look: honey-toned foundation gives a golden feel to the skin, while terracotta blush at cheeks and temples and a deep coral on the lips adds depth. Eyebrows are softened in brown and eyes are defined in deep green, shading out into bronze and gold across the browbone.

Alternative make-up: try a sultry look. Emphasize the eyes in dark grey, shade silver over the lid and crease, use a tawny red on the cheeks and lips. For an exotic 'special occasion' look, define eyes in black, add depth at the crease in charcoal, shade gold over lids, across browbone and above cheekbones and onto the tip of the chin. Try a rich red on the lips and brush lightly with gold for extra shine.

mousemouse

If you have fair hair and a fair skin, you must beware of looking over made-up. As a rule, keep make-up natural and soft and avoid harsh colours and contrasts. Here, a happy medium for evening. Eyes are emphasized with green to reflect the tone of the clothes, shaded in brown across the upper lid and blended up over the crease to a browbone highlit with creamy beige. The cheeks are blushed with apricot and the lips defined in a deeper shade.

Alternative make-up: keep the whole look soft and natural for daytime. Define eyes with brown or grey, shade with pink or silver. Add mascara to the lashes, a touch of rose pink blush to the cheeks and finish with a clear or rose pink lip gloss.

fairfairfair

orientaloriental

The classic oriental face: creamy skin, silky black hair and dark eyes beneath a prominent browbone. But skin tone can look sallow. Brighten with clear cheek and lip colours or add warmth, as here, with a peach blush and toning old rose lipstick. Eyes need careful shading, especially in the socket. Here they are shaded with indigo. The colour is deepest on the lids, softens over the crease, where it is blended up and outwards to emphasize the almond shape of the eyes. A deep blue adds definition along the lower lid. The browbone is highlit with pearly white and the look is finished with lots of black mascara.

Alternative make-up: emphasize the eyes in black, add bright blusher to brow and cheekbones and a strong red to lips; for more subtlety, try green over the eyes, soft pink on the cheeks and lips.

redredred

Redheads should make the most of their natural colouring, particularly if they have freckles. Use the lightest textured foundation or a simple tinted moisturizer for daytime to let them show through. Shape eyes with shades of brown, from bitter chocolate through bronze to pale apricot and gold. Add a touch of tawny blusher and paint the lips a dusty pink.

Alternative make-up: for evening, go for a creamier skin tone and translucent powder to cover. Experiment with deep violets to define the eye, soft mauve for shading and colour. Add an iridescent touch of lilac on the inner and outer corners of the eyes and reflect in a luminous highlight across the brow and above the cheek. Finish with deep pink cheeks and lips.

Black skins tend to have uneven skin tones. Correct with a tinted moisturizer or dark shade of foundation. If necessary, blend your own from two or more different shades until you get the appropriate depth of tone. The result should even out skin tone while giving a polished sheen to the face. Add highlight to intensify the effect, using transparent white or pink over the cheekbones and temples in place of blush.

A neutral daytime make-up is chosen here, with the coral accessories in mind. Eyelids are shaded brown with a hint of green, blended into pink across the brow and defined well with black mascara. Blush and lips are complementary tones of gleaming amber. Alternative make-up: shade eyes in strong peacock shades (bright pinks and blues), cheeks and lips a deep fuchsia or raspberry pink. Try dark burgundies and purples around the eyes for greater depth, silver and gold for an exotic evening look.

blackblack

As you get older and start to lose colour in the skin and hair, you should reappraise your make-up colours and techniques regularly – at least every five years – to check that they are still appropriate for you. As the face becomes drier and more lined, foundation may tend to sink into the skin and to accentuate lines around the eyes and mouth. Use the lightest 'hydrating' foundation on top of a good moisturizer and match the tone carefully with your skin. Choose subtle, positive colours for eyes and lips to counteract greyness.

Here, skin tone is smoothed with its matching foundation and the lightest dusting of powder on the centre of the face (not around the eyes where lines are all too easily emphasized). The soft peach tones of the shirt are reflected in the soft peach cheek colour and slightly richer lip shade. Eyes are shaded to their natural colour – grey/green – and emphasized with mascara, brown not black.

Alternative make-up: define the eyes in soft brown or grey and add colour to lift and enliven face. Try pinks and lilacs or mauves across the eyes, with peaches, corals and soft pinks on cheeks and lips.

greygrey

darkdark

This unusual combination – dark hair with pale skin and light eyes – positively invites contrasts. Use an ivory tinted foundation to match skin tone, a light blush on cheeks, and try soft brown shading for emphasis around the eyes blending into a rosy pink with a white highlight over the browbone. Add brilliance with poppy red lips.

Alternative make-up: emphasize the eyes with darker shading. Try charcoal for definition, soft pink for shading over and above the crease, a deeper tawnier shade in the socket. Add bright sugar pink to cheeks and lips or keep the mouth soft with a simple gloss.

scent
The invisible difference

'One is aware of a woman's perfume before one sees her and her perfume creates the first impression. If I do not know her, I can imagine her. If I do know her, it is a lovely reminder.'

Marcel Rochas, creator of *Femme* (1942) and *Madame Rochas* (1960).

The word perfume literally means 'through smoke' and it was by walking through the smoke of a fire, on to which a fragrant pot-pourri of scented woods and spices had been thrown, that the earliest perfumes were worn. Later, incense was burned in temples and on altars and the fragrant wreath of smoke offered up as a gift to please or propitiate the gods. Indefinable and invisible like the deities themselves, the essences were not only inconceivably precious — only one of the Magi brought gold, the other two brought frankincense and myrrh, both aromatic gum resins from Arabia — but were thought to possess almost magical properties. They were used to cleanse and purify the spirit, lift the soul and soothe and heal the body.

Today the context may have changed, but much of the magic remains. Perfume speaks its own language. The language may be soft and subtle, fresh and surprising, mysterious and exotic, but the most important thing is that, because perfume develops and changes on your skin, it is a language that is entirely your own.

If you think of a perfume, any perfume, as a bunch of flowers, you will see that the hands holding them will determine whether they remain an indifferent assortment or are transformed into a beautiful bouquet. Just as it takes an artist to arrange a perfect bouquet, so it takes an artist to create a perfect perfume: one that will never overpower or cloy, that will make its own expressive statement as it changes and develops on your skin and that will last and last and, as it gradually fades, will leave the faintest trace of a fragrance that is still absolutely true to itself. These are the hallmarks of all great or 'classic' scents. Such scents are built, note by note, through all the stages of the evaporation scale (see right). At every stage of the process, different essences will be combined, one on top of the other, until the perfumier gets the combination he is after. Some of the essences used may not be natural at all, but synthetic. These are not inferior in any way. Rather, they are a means of allowing the great perfumier, or 'nose', to indulge his imagination and to create an entirely new smell that has all the freshness and sweetness of a midsummer bouquet but could never be found in one, however artfully arranged. This use of synthetics has enabled scientists to create a 'truer' rendering of fragrances that lose their purity of smell when the essence is extracted in the traditional way — hyacinth and lilac are examples of scents that smell delicious in the garden, but disappointing and almost unrecognizable when the pure perfume is extracted from them. Even more important, it has enabled perfumiers to make use of fixatives — the stronger, longer-lasting smells derived from animals, such as the musk deer and civet cat — without having to endanger the animal kingdom to find them.

All scents are built note by note, according to an evaporation scale, so that together they will create an amalgamated 'chord' and a tangible whole.

The top note is the most volatile part of the fragrance. It has the most immediate effect on the sense of smell, evaporates into the air in seconds, gives the first fleeting impression and remains for about 10 to 20 minutes, before gradually subsiding as the lower notes develop. Examples: bergamot, lemon, lavender, mint, *bois de rose*, coriander.

The middle note is the 'heart' of the perfume. This melts into and transforms the top note and carries the perfume for about 20 to 30 minutes, while the base note is developing. It usually takes 10 to 20 minutes to develop and lasts for two to three hours. Examples: *Rose de Bulgarie*, jasmine, neroli, orange flower, galbanum, verbena, thyme, lily-of-the-valley, rose absolute, lavender absolute, ylang-ylang, 'synthetic' aldehydes C8, C9, C11 and C12.

The base note determines the holding power of a fragrance and is the true characteristic from which the rest of the smell will be created. Initially strong and unpleasant smelling, base notes can take up to half an hour to develop their 'true' smell, when they will be quite beautiful. The base note lingers for six hours or more and, once all evaporation has taken place, a small residual part of it will remain for months or even years. This is known as the dry-out. Examples: patchouli, vetivert, oakmoss, orris, jasmine absolute, sandalwood, cedarwood, artificial musks, ambergris, civet and castoreum.

WEARING SCENT

There are no hard and fast rules about wearing scent. Every scent you buy becomes emphatically your own from the moment you spray it over you. Your 'body chemistry' is the main factor that will determine whether a fragrance works well for you. Once you have found one that does, however, bear the following in mind.

Where to wear it

'Perfumes smell sweetest,' wrote Apollonius of Herophila in a *Treatise on Perfumes* in about 420 BC, 'when the scent comes from the wrist.' Over 2000 years later, Coco Chanel advised that it should be worn wherever one intended to be kissed. They were both right. You can wear scent wherever you choose, but do remember the pulse points — those places where the blood vessels are nearer the surface of the skin and body temperature is therefore slightly warmer. Warmth encourages evaporation and allows the full bouquet of the perfume to develop.

Pulse points are around the hairline, the nape of the neck, behind the ears, under the breasts, in the crook of the arm and inside the wrists and knees and on either side of the ankles. Dab a small amount of the pure perfume *extrait* or a more liberal dash of *eau de toilette* on each of these and let the fragrance wrap itself around you. Avoid overdosing around the neck or in the cleavage because, as the scent rises, it will suffocate your sense of smell — a pity because scent should be worn as much for your own pleasure as for anybody else's.

You can also spray a *parfum* or *eau de toilette* on to your hair and inside the lining of your clothes. But do not spray directly on to fabrics — furs, silks and light materials in particular — as the dry-out, or residual oil, will stain them.

In summer, avoid spraying scent on to parts of the body exposed to bright sunlight. If the scent contains bergamot, a citrus note and a common ingredient in many fragrances, it may stain the skin, leaving a dark ring where scent and sunlight have mingled. In hot weather, apply scent to areas that will not be directly exposed to the sun, such as the palms of the hands, the soles of the feet, the insides of the heels, the hair and the armpit. (Be careful though — this will sting. A good idea is to dab a small amount of the fragrance on to a piece of cotton wool, wave it around for a few moments to let the spirit evaporate and then apply it.)

What to wear it with

Avoid mixing different fragrances. As any fragrance takes about six hours to 'clear', this includes scented soaps, bath oils and body lotions. If you want the fragrance to remain true to itself, use unscented soaps and lotions, baby oil and talcum powder or go for the range of bathroom accessories that matches your scent. If you do want to use a bath essence, go for a floral-based, not a herbal one. Deodorants can collide unhappily with fragrances. Use an unscented deodorant or anti-perspirant and, for sweet-smelling armpits, apply the fragrance there afterwards, as detailed above. Two more killers are strongly scented hair sprays (use an unscented one) and smoking — any fragrance will be smothered by clouds of smoke.

When to wear it

Wear it all day long, from the moment you get up to the moment you go to bed and there too, if you like. Pure perfume *(extrait)* lasts longer than *eau de parfum*, which, in turn, lasts longer than *eau de toilette* or *Cologne*. As a general rule, repeat the application of scent every four hours. This will give a fresh burst of the fragrance and keep it going throughout the day. As body heat and sweat intensify a fragrance and speed up the rate at which it 'lifts' or evaporates into the air, you will need a lighter fragrance and more of it in hot weather. If you are going somewhere special, bear the temperature rule in mind. Allow the scent 20 minutes to develop in warm weather and up to an hour when the weather is cooler or you happen to be feeling cold.

To avoid a collision of perfumes during the day, take one of three options.

1. Start in the morning with a light *eau de Cologne* or *eau de toilette* and repeat the application every few hours. At lunchtime and in the early evening, dab on a few drops of the more concentrated *extrait* of the same perfume to intensify the effect. Thus, you will build on your fragrance as the day develops.

2. Break up the day with a bath or shower — either using unscented products, so that you present a totally blank canvas for the new fragrance, or its matching accessories — and a complete change of clothes. Any daytime fragrance, even the lightest *eau de toilette*, will 'dry-out' and cling to your clothes for some hours or even days. Then spray or dab liberally with the new scent.

3. Most people find that the different fragrances produced by one House will mix fairly happily and harmoniously. This is because they are characterized by a single signature, from which all the separate scents are then built. If you find two scents that you like and they are both made by the same perfumier, start off the day with the lighter, fresher one and switch to the deeper, woodier one for the evening.

CHOOSING AND BUYING SCENT

All scents are expensive and mistakes can be expensive too. You should choose a scent with the same, or even a little more, care and thought that you put into buying clothes. While the first impression you receive when trying on new clothes is likely to be an enduring one, the same is not true of scent, which takes at least 20 minutes to develop on the skin and to give off its true smell. A quick over-the-counter spray on and a sniff will tell you nothing about the complete perfume. Bear the following in mind when trying, or buying, a new fragrance.

● Apply a small, concentrated spot of the scent. Smell it, leave it and smell it again after half an hour, when the heart of the fragrance is developing. This will give you a real idea of its character and how well it develops on, and is likely to suit, you. Then decide.

● If you can, take a small sample of the pure perfume *extrait* away with you (most companies now make samples expressly for this purpose), live with it for a day or two, ask your friends what they think and see how you like it. Because perfumes develop at different rates according to their concentrations, it is quite possible that you will change your mind about a smell once you have worn it for a while. If this is not possible, go for the smaller-sized, less expensive *eau de toilette* and use it over a period of days or weeks before buying the perfume proper.

- When trying scent, keep your field of experimentation down to four scents or less. Spread each testing area as far away as possible from the others — a dab at each wrist and in the crook of each arm, for example — to avoid creating a 'stew' that will tell you little or nothing about the individual character of each scent. It is also a good idea to make a note of which perfume you put where. Once you have had them on for some time, you may forget which is which.

- Try to avoid smelling new perfumes on smelling strips or to be influenced by the way a perfume smells on somebody else. This is not the way they are going to smell on you.

KEEPING SCENT

All perfumes are delicate and will deteriorate on exposure to air, heat, moisture and sunlight. Store scents in a cool, dark, dry place and always make sure that you replace the stopper firmly after use.

When a perfume 'goes off', it breaks down into its constituent parts and therefore changes in character. The volatile top note is the first to be lost. You will know that this has happened when the perfume darkens in colour. Once you have opened a bottle of a pure *extrait* you should use it frequently. Because it has a higher proportion of oil to alcohol and water, it is more susceptible to contamination than the more dilute *parfums* and *eaux de toilette*.

Never decant scent into a plastic container, because the plastic will react chemically with it and may alter its character quite considerably. Decant it, instead, into a glass bottle, preferably made of opaque or frosted glass which will protect it from the damaging effects of bright sunlight.

To refill a scent spray or decant a perfume: rinse the container in warm soapy water, fill with half alcohol, half water and allow to stand overnight. Rinse it thoroughly with fresh water and fill.

TYPE	COMPRISES	LASTS
EXTRAIT or **PARFUM**	15-20 per cent perfume; 80-85 per cent spirit.	Two to six hours, depending on your body chemistry. The *extrait* is the truest expression of the perfume. Sometimes, part of the spirit (alcohol) content is replaced by an oil, in order to increase the 'staying power' by slowing down the rate of evaporation.
PARFUM DE TOILETTE	12-15 per cent perfume; mostly spirit; some water.	Two to five hours. This was developed in the USA to provide a stronger and longer lasting alternative to the *eau de toilette*.
EAU DE TOILETTE	5-12 per cent perfume; more water than spirit.	Two to four hours. The higher water content and greater degree of dilution make for faster evaporation. Dab or spray on lavishly.
EAU DE COLOGNE	2-6 per cent perfume; predominantly water; some spirit.	One to two hours. *Eaux de Cologne*, which developed out of the original *Kölnischwasser*, are created to give only the lightest veil of fragrance. They are refreshing, delicate and marvellously revitalizing.

cosmetic surgery

The art of the possible

'For five days I lie in secret
Tapped like a cask, the years draining into my pillow
Even my best friend thinks I'm in the country…'

Sylvia Plath

Greek myth tells the story of Pygmalion, a sculptor on the island of Cyprus, who one day made a statue of a woman so breathtakingly beautiful that he promptly fell passionately in love with it. In vain he embraced it until the goddess Aphrodite, seeing his distress, brought the statue to life. It moved, perfection became reality and Pygmalion and his creation, Galatea, were united at last.

Cosmetic surgeons sometimes tell this story to illustrate what they call a 'Pygmalion complex': the desire to create perfection, not out of marble, but out of human flesh. In reality, however, their aims and their art are very different. Cosmetic surgery is, above all, the art of the possible — not for those in pursuit of perfection, but for those in a realistic search of a better profile, more youthful facial contours, fewer wrinkles or larger or smaller breasts. It has a great deal to do with reality — the reality of what you have or have not got and of what can be done to improve it.

Derived from the Greek word *plastikos*, meaning 'capable of being moulded', plastic surgery embraces a range of reconstructive surgical techniques that were originally developed to help repair the injuries of soldiers wounded in the First World War. These were subsequently expanded to include a series of operations, both for corrective purposes — 'mending' hare lips and cleft palates and lessening the damage inflicted by severe burns, accidental injuries and birthmarks — and for purely cosmetic ones.

It is the cosmetic side of plastic surgery that has become a minefield of medical ethics. Its image is not improved by the handful of surgeons prepared to carry out almost any operation a patient requests, regardless of the possible outcome, as long as the fee is high enough. If you are considering cosmetic surgery, you must ask your doctor or a reliable medical source to refer you to a qualified and competent surgeon.

Although some types of cosmetic surgery sound deceptively simple, it is important to recognize that any surgery, elective or otherwise, involves an operation under anaesthetic, a number of stitches, a certain amount of scarring, a period of convalescence and a risk, however slight, of post-operative bleeding, infection or swelling. With these factors in mind, it is possible to divide the various types of cosmetic surgery available into four categories.

1. Operations carried out on an out-patient basis under local anaesthetic; results are usually good, discomfort minimal and complications rare.
Examples: pinning back the ears (otoplasty) and straightforward eyelid surgery (blepheroplasty).

2. Operations carried out under general or local anaesthetic, with a short stay of three days or less in hospital; discomfort

small, results usually good, scarring concealed and complications rare.
Examples: nose surgery (rhinoplasty), most face-lifts.

3. Operations carried out under general anaesthetic, with a stay of up to a week in hospital; period of general discomfort and/or restricted mobility, some visible scarring, together with some risk of complication; results usually justify the risk where the need is indicated.
Examples: all cosmetic breast surgery, abdominal lipectomy (removal of excess fat and folds of skin around abdomen).

4. Operations carried out as above (3), but with considerable discomfort and/or a tendency to disappointing results; scarring tends to be visible and may be extensive.
Examples: breast reconstruction after radical mastectomy; 'recontouring' buttocks, upper arms and thighs.

DECIDING ON COSMETIC SURGERY

Before you embark on cosmetic surgery, and certainly before you seek the advice or assistance of a cosmetic surgeon, ask yourself the following questions.

● What is wrong with my appearance? Look at yourself really objectively in the mirror and try to be as specific as possible about what you feel needs changing. While cosmetic surgery can improve features on the face and body, it cannot change an attitude, reverse a body image or necessarily alter the way you fundamentally feel about yourself and the way you look.

● Who/what am I having the operation for? Again, while a cosmetic operation may be able to redefine a profile, lift a sagging chin or add to your bust measurement, it does not claim to be able to repair a marriage, salvage a broken relationship, reattract an errant lover or secure a job promotion. So be honest with yourself and examine your motives for having the operation. Have it for yourself or not at all.

● What do I expect from surgery? Are you being realistic? If you are 40, nothing is going to make you look 20 again or, if you are habitually shy and retiring, no amount of adding or subtracting is suddenly going to make you the life and soul of the party. The happiest results of cosmetic surgery tend to owe more to the basic outlook of the patient — a mix of realism and optimism is probably ideal — than to the technical skills of the surgeon, although these are obviously important too.

● Can I afford it? Even minor cosmetic surgery is very expensive. In Britain, under some circumstances, an operation may be carried out under the National Health Service or one of the private medical insurance schemes (the latter also applies to the USA). Examples are rhinoplasty, where the shape and structure of the nose interferes with breathing; breast reduction, if the size of the breasts is great enough to cause physical inconvenience, backache or psychological embarrassment; blepheroplasty, if drooping eyelids interfere with vision; and, occasionally, abdominal lipectomy, if muscles have ruptured following a pregnancy. Cosmetic surgery for major disfigurements as a result of injury or accident is, of course, almost always available on the NHS.

165

• Do my family and friends know that I am contemplating cosmetic surgery? If so, what do they think about it? If I do decide to proceed, who am I going to tell? To some people, cosmetic surgery is an intensely private affair; to others, it is no more secret than going to the dentist and having a tooth out. Most people tend to fall somewhere between the two extremes, seeking advice and/or support from a close friend or member of the family and telling others afterwards, only when the subject arises. Problems can occur if someone close to you is either over-enthusiastic in encouraging you to have the operation or adamantly set against it. In these circumstances, it is difficult to remain uninfluenced by what they think. But, as a general rule, try not to be persuaded either into or out of surgery by someone else.

Whether or not people will be able to detect that you have had cosmetic surgery, depends largely on the type of operation you have. Most of the popular types of cosmetic surgery, if well done, are not easily detectable and this is particularly true of facial surgery. A good face-lift, nose 'job' or pinning back of the ears can make the face look younger or more harmonious but most people will be conscious only of an indefinable improvement in appearance and will not be able to say exactly what has changed. Additional ways of fending off curiosity are to explain the change by growing your hair or adopting a new hairstyle, by saying that you have been away on holiday or that you have lost weight.

Other types of surgery tend to vary widely in detectability and it is usually the degree and extent of the scarring that is the deciding factor. The more bizarre fringes of cosmetic surgery or 'body contouring' — the operations for buttock, thigh and upper arm reduction — tend to be less satisfactory and to leave quite considerable visible scarring. They are no substitute for losing weight through dieting and exercise and results tend to be disappointing. For this reason, details of such operations are not given below.

The first step

During the initial consultation with a cosmetic surgeon, do not be afraid to ask about anything that may be troubling you. In particular, ask your surgeon:

• For his or her assessment of what is required. And be prepared to listen to it. The aim of all cosmetic surgery is to restore harmony and proportion to the face or body and the surgeon is more likely to know how to achieve this than you are. While you should never let yourself be bulldozed into accepting a nose or a breast size that you do not want, you should think twice, for example, about having a snub nose in place of your Roman one, if the surgeon advises against it. It might end up looking totally out of place.

Be wary of a surgeon who is prepared to do exactly what you ask, without first taking a full medical history, giving you a thorough examination and asking your reasons for seeking surgery. This is not prying — it is the professional concern of a highly qualified specialist, only prepared to carry out the operation if he or she genuinely believes that the result will be a happy one.

• What degree of improvement you can reasonably expect. A good cosmetic surgeon will outline all the possible com-plications and roughly assess the chances of any of these happening to you, together with the likely degree of scarring and the time the wound will probably take to heal. For your part, remember that, while you are entitled to honest and straightforward answers to your questions, you cannot expect the surgeon to be clairvoyant. No-one knows for certain how well scars will heal. All people heal differently and even different parts of the same body do not heal at the same rate. Incisions made in the area between the neck and the nipples, for example, do not tend to heal as well as those made elsewhere on the body. This is one reason why dermatologists are often reluctant to remove moles on or in between the breasts if they are situated above the nipple line, and why all cosmetic breast surgeons attempt, wherever possible, to undermine the flesh from the lower quadrant of the breast.

• Where the incision(s) will be made. Any incision leaves a scar and the most successful types of surgery are therefore those where the incision is either totally concealed or rendered inconspicuous. With rhinoplasty, or the nose operation, the bone, cartilage and tissue are undermined from within and there is no external scarring whatsoever. With some other operations, the scar is hidden by a crease or fold in the skin or by a head of hair. Men should be wary about brow lifts that 'bury' the incision mark in the hairline. If the hairline subsequently recedes, the scarring may well become visible.

If the scar is going to be subject to tension (that is, it will not run along a natural fold in the skin), there is about a 10 per cent risk of developing what is known as hypertrophic scarring — an angry, red, raised scar, which can take many years to fade out in the manner of normal scars and may occasionally never fade at all.

• What stitching technique will be used. An incision closed by the traditional 'cross stitching' method will leave a coarser, more noticeable scar line than one closed with stitches buried beneath the skin.

• What the likely degree of postoperative discomfort will be, how long you should set aside for your recuperation and in what ways your lifestyle may be restricted or affected. Any operation involves a certain amount of shock to the system and you will certainly be cheating yourself if you expect to get away absolutely painlessly. So do make sure that you know as closely as possible what you are letting yourself in for.

• What you should do, or avoid doing, in order to make the healing as swift as possible. This will usually include avoiding all sunbathing for at least six weeks (after which, cautious sunbathing may help to 'weather' the scars by giving them a more natural colour), controlling your smoking and drinking as both can increase post-operative bruising and so slow recovery, avoiding rapid weight gains or losses and not attempting or expecting too much during the first few weeks. Bruising and swelling can take some weeks to fade and results are usually seen at their best six months or so after surgery. Finally, keep to all the instructions given to you by your surgeon.

cosmetic surgery

THE OPERATIONS

Face-lift (rhytidectomy)

'Face-lift' is a single, very general term covering a number of different surgical procedures and techniques. Many cosmetic surgeons now have an impressive and flexible repertoire, which can be adapted to each new patient in the light of what needs doing.

For surgical purposes, the face divides roughly into three parts: the upper third being forehead and eyebrows; the middle third being the skin tissue around the eyes and on the cheeks; the lower third being the mouth, jawline and neck. Although the middle section is the one most commonly chosen for the partial or 'mini' lift, the other two can both be lifted independently, if required. Blepheroplasty (eyelid surgery) may sometimes be indicated at the same time, especially if there is excessive wrinkling, puffiness or bagging of the skin tissue on and around the eyelids. Dermabrasion and chemical face peeling procedures should never be carried out at the same time as a face-lift, though they may be carried out three months or more afterwards where the need is indicated.

The idea of a face-lift is not to remove all the lines from the face. Rather it is to eradicate the lines of wear and tear that suggest age, exhaustion or ill health, while leaving — though softening — the natural expression lines. The art lies in creating just enough tension for the 'lift' to hold its new contour, while avoiding the mask-like expressionlessness that can be one of the greatest give-aways of this type of surgery.

As a general rule, the incisions made by the surgeon run parallel to the scalp margins, but about 2 or 3 centimetres (¾ or 1 inch) further back, so that any scarring will be buried in the hairline and thus invisible to the eye. During the face-lift, excess skin and fat are undermined (cut free) and the underlying muscles and supporting tissue pulled backwards and upwards at right-angles to the incision. The operation takes about two hours. Stitches around the eyes are removed after two or three days, around the ears after about a week and on the scalp after 12 days to a fortnight.

As facial skin reacts dramatically to any kind of trauma, all face-lifts are accompanied by a certain amount of bruising, swelling and temporary feelings of numbness and tightness, particularly around the ears, over the eyelids and on the neck. These will usually soon subside, but it will take about six months before the results are seen at their best. The effects last between five and 10 years or more, depending on such factors as hereditary ageing patterns, general lifestyle and freedom from illness, stress and rapid weight fluctuation.

Finally, be wary of surgeons offering an apparently easier method or claiming to be able to tighten slack muscles and remove excess skin tissue in a matter of minutes. This type of treatment can leave a legacy of stretched and sagging skin tissue after only a few months.

Eyelid surgery (blepheroplasty)

Blepheroplasty is carried out both for medical and cosmetic reasons. The puffing and bagging of the upper or lower eyelids that interfere with vision is an inherited trait known as

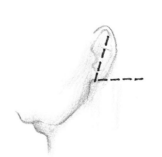

Brow lift
The incision is made across the top of the hairline on the forehead. The skin is undermined back and up to smooth out 'worry' lines and wrinkles running across the brow. There is no visible scarring in women; scarring may become visible in men if the hairline recedes.

Jawline and neck
The incision runs behind the ears and down just behind the hairline away from the chin. Sagging skin, excess tissue and slack muscles are undermined and tightened to give a firmer, cleaner jawline and to iron out some, but not all, of the wrinkles around the mouth and on the neck.

Mid-face: the mini or 'mannequin' lift
The incision runs inside the hairline at the sides of the eyes and down in front of the ears, where it is hidden by a natural fold in the skin. As the incision does not extend behind the ear, it will do little to affect skin tissue around the jawline and neck and will have minimal effect on lines and wrinkles above the lip or around the eyes. However, it will tighten sagging muscles and drooping skin around the middle and upper face. It is most successfully performed on a patient who has just started to show the first real signs of ageing and does not yet require the full lift. It can last as long as the full lift, after which time it can be repeated or, if indicated, a full lift given in its place. This operation may be slightly complicated by a small amount of residual scarring.

blepherochalasis and is considered a medical problem. The bagging and wrinkling that appears with age is considered a cosmetic problem. In both cases, surgery tends to be straightforward and healing rapid — the stitches being removed after only two to three days. It may involve a short stay in hospital or, if the case is uncomplicated, be carried out under local anaesthetic on an out-patient basis. Scarring is usually imperceptible but a certain amount of bruising and swelling makes the wearing of dark glasses advisable for about a fortnight. As the scars are still very delicate during this time, you should not wear eye make-up for at least two weeks and may feel some tightness over the eyelids for up to six weeks after the operation.

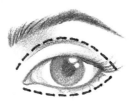

Eyelid surgery
The incision for the upper lid follows the upper eyelid fold and extends out to the outer corner of the eye, where it is buried by the smile lines. Sagging skin on and above the lid and to the side of the eye is cut away and brought down so that the remaining skin tissue is smooth and unlined. The incision for the lower lid is made just beneath the eyelashes. Excess skin and subcutaneous fat are undermined and drawn upwards, before being stitched. An incision should never be made above the eyebrow, as this leaves a visible scar.

Nose surgery (rhinoplasty)

One of the most popular and most successful types of cosmetic surgery, rhinoplasty can do much to restore a sense of harmony and proportion to the face, while leaving none of the tell-tale signs of surgery. The first recorded case of reconstructive surgery on the nose was that carried out by the Hindu surgeon, Susrata, in 6,000 BC. But only in the last 30 years have advanced techniques enabled surgeons to straighten, shorten and reshape the nose from the inside, by undermining and remodelling bone and cartilage. The nose can also be lengthened by the introduction of plastic or bone implants, which are grafted on to the existing bone.

The nose may be altered for medical reasons, such as chronic sinusitis or difficulties with breathing, or for cosmetic reasons. It should not be done until growth has finished at around the age of 15 in girls and 16 in boys. The operation is performed under general or local anaesthetic ('twilight sleep') and usually involves a short stay in hospital. A plaster is worn for up to two weeks after the operation. Although any bruising and swelling should soon subside, breathing may take several weeks to return to normal. The full result is seen after a period of about six months and will, of course, be permanent. Possible complications are nose bleeds, excessive bruising or infection.

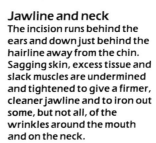

Chin implant
The incision is either made across the lower gum inside the mouth or underneath the chin. A high-grade plastic implant is then inserted to bring the chin forward.

Ear surgery
The incision is made just behind the ear. Cartilage and excess skin are removed and the skin restitched.

Chin implant

A chin implant may either be performed on its own for a recessive chin that throws the profile out of balance, or in conjunction with rhinoplasty to restore the relationship between nose and chin. It may be carried out under general anaesthetic but an operation under local anaesthetic on an out-patient basis is more usual. A tight chin bandage is worn for about 10 days and the diet restricted to soft foods only in order to keep the jaw and chin as immobile as possible.

Possible complications are rejection, infection or slippage of the implant, but these happen in less than three per cent of cases and can usually be rectified.

Ear surgery (otoplasty)

Otoplasty involves 'pinning back' over-prominent ears by removing the bands of cartilage behind them which are forcing them to jut out. Most otoplasty is carried out on an out-patient basis under local anaesthetic. A dressing, wound round the head like a wide hairband, must be worn for a week.

Any postoperative discomfort can usually be successfully relieved by painkillers. Stitches remain in for seven days and results are usually excellent.

Dermabrasion (surgical skin planing)

Dermabrasion is a surgical procedure carried out on the face during which the top layers of the skin are removed right down to the deeper dermal layer. It can be effective for some types of facial scarring, particularly pitted acne scars, and for improving the texture of an ageing skin. The operation is carried out under general anaesthetic and involves a two- to three-day stay in hospital. Afterwards, the face is protected by a fine, colourless dressing that gradually peels off as the new skin heals. To begin with, the new young skin will be pink and very tender to the touch. You must not wear make-up for at least three weeks and all sunbathing is outlawed for the first three months, as exposure to ultraviolet can result in patches of permanently altered skin pigmentation. There is a similar risk if you are taking the contraceptive pill. Anyone undergoing dermabrasion should therefore use an alternative method of contraception for at least one month before and two months after surgery.

Although results are often effective, dermabrasion will not remove deeper facial scars and there is a possibility of developing crusts or small white spots while the skin is healing. Allow at least three weeks to convalesce before resuming normal activity.
N.B. Although dermabrasion sounds less drastic than having a face-lift, it is still a surgical procedure and, if not carried out competently, can leave the skin very damaged, even scarred. So make absolutely sure that you go to a reputable doctor.

Chemical face peeling

Chemical skin peeling is less drastic than dermabrasion and can be performed without anaesthetic or hospitalization. While it will not remove small scars, it can improve and refine the texture of the skin and soften fine facial wrinkles. If you have had a face-lift let at least three months elapse before having a chemical peel.

Chemical paste is applied to the skin or to areas of the skin, such as the upper lip, producing a burning sensation, rather like having had too much sun. A dressing is then applied for 48 hours. This is followed by a powder and antibiotic ointment to soften the dry crust of skin which will have formed. This crust gradually peels away to reveal the new, pink skin underneath. As with dermabrasion, it is probably best to keep out of circulation for about three weeks, while the skin is healing and fading to its normal colour. Avoid strong sunlight for six months and do not use any make-up on the area until the healing process is complete.

Breast reduction

Reducing the size of over-large or pendulous breasts is a major procedure that involves an operation under general anaesthetic, a three- to four-day stay in hospital, bed convalescence at home for at least seven days, taking life gently for three weeks and avoiding any strenuous activity for six.

Scarring from breast reduction is more extensive than from breast augmentation, but it will usually fade out quite well after a year or so. However, it will continue to be visible at close range or under bright light. As the scars are not buried in natural folds of skin tissue and are therefore subject to tension, there is an increased risk of unsightly, hypertrophic, scarring in about 10 per cent of patients. Other complications include permanent loss of sensitivity in the nipple (temporary loss is quite normal and usually lasts for no more than three months) and/or the ability to breastfeed, if the operation is not correctly carried out. Future pregnancies can also result in a loss of shape and firmness to the breast and, in some cases, surgical revision might be necessary to rectify this. But, for most people, the dividends of being relieved of such a physical and psychological burden outweigh any of the possible disadvantages.

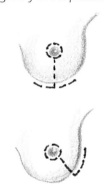

Breast reduction
Incisions are made around the nipple, down to the base of the breast and across the fold beneath, leaving a scar like an inverted 'T', or to the side, as shown. The path taken will depend on the size and shape of the breasts. Breast volume is reduced by removing fat and surplus skin, while leaving blood and nerve supply to the nipple intact, in order to preserve sensitivity and ability to breastfeed.

Breast augmentation

One of the most popular of all cosmetic surgery procedures, breast augmentation is achieved by the insertion of either an inert, soft, silicon gel implant or an 'inflatable' implant, which is filled with saline after insertion into the breast. The operation usually involves a two-day stay in hospital and a general anaesthetic, though in some US practices it is now being carried out on an out-patient basis under local anaesthetic. The stitches and dressing are removed one week to 10 days after the operation and, until then, patients may be aware of some soreness. Life should be taken very carefully for three weeks and violent exercise avoided for at least six.

Results are often extremely good. The breast feels supple, moves naturally and there is no loss of sensitivity in the breast or nipple. The operation will not interfere with ability to breastfeed, nor will it increase the risk of developing breast cancer or interfere with its detection. There is, however, one significant complication: in about 25 per cent of cases (a very general figure which is higher in some practices, lower in others) the implant can harden, causing the breast to become unnaturally firm and immobile. Practices with low 'hardening' rates tend to place the implant at a deeper level, actually behind the pectoral muscle, and encourage their patients to massage their breasts daily for at least six months after the operation. This persuades the implant to flatten out and counteracts the formation of hard scar tissue around it. In the event of hardening, about 50 per cent of cases can be dealt with through manual compression of the breast by the surgeon. For the rest, surgical revision may be necessary and, in a few cases, the implant may have to be removed entirely. A newer type of implant, known as the double lumen, consists of an outer membrane around an inner core of silicon gel. This counteracts the risk of hardening significantly because antibiotics and corticosteroids can be injected into the space between the layers, thus inhibiting the formation of scar tissue. It will not, however, eliminate the risk altogether.

Breast augmentation

A 4-5 cm (1½-2 inch) incision is either made under the fold of the breast, or in the hair-bearing skin of the armpit, where the scar is effectively rendered invisible, though the operation itself is more difficult as the surgeon is inserting the implant 'blind'. Although incisions are sometimes made around the outer circumference of the nipple, this is not recommended because it may interfere with sensitivity. The implant is inserted into the breast, just behind the existing breast tissue and the nipple. It may occasionally be inserted behind the pectoral muscle.

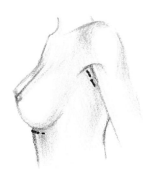

Lifting ptiotic (drooping) breasts

Breasts that have sagged due to pregnancy, fluctuations in body weight or as a consequence of the natural process of ageing can be elevated by an operation which involves moving the nipples upwards, while still attached to the underlying breast tissue, and cutting away the excess folds of skin. Although this type of surgery will improve or 'rejuvenate' the natural contours of the breasts, it will not fill out breasts which have shrunk in size. In this case, the operation can be carried out with breast augmentation.

The surgical procedure and after-care are as for breast reduction (see opposite). The incisions also follow the same lines. Possible complications are a risk of developing red, inflamed hypertrophic scars (as for breast reduction) and of the breasts sagging anew after a subsequent pregnancy. For this reason, it is advisable to wait until you have had all the children you anticipate before undergoing surgery.

Breast reconstruction after mastectomy

Reconstructive surgery for women who have had part or all of a breast removed, following the detection of a cancer, is still in its early days and the results of the operation depend very largely on the kind of mastectomy that has been carried out. The best results are achieved when a simple subcutaneous mastectomy has removed underlying breast tissue, but has left the surface skin, together with the nipple and the areola, intact. In this case the procedure for reconstruction largely follows the principles of straightforward breast enlargement or augmentation. In the event of more radical mastectomy, where the entire breast has been removed, often along with the lymph glands and much of the chest muscle as well, it is much more difficult to achieve an effective and lifelike result. The breast literally has to be rebuilt, nipple included, and this usually involves a series of operations and skin grafts.

Abdominal lipectomy

Abdominal lipectomy is a major operation, in which excess tissue and folds of skin, left by pregnancy or large fluctuations in body weight, are removed, the muscles and subcutaneous tissue undermined and a new navel constructed. This radical procedure involves a three- to four-day stay in hospital, a week's convalescence in bed and at least four weeks of gentle recuperation. Anyone considering undergoing this type of surgery should first get down to their optimum weight and stay there. Both dramatic weight increase and subsequent pregnancies can reverse the results of the surgery, causing the skin tissue to slacken again. Scarring tends to take about two years to fade.

Possible complications include developing hypertrophic and inflamed scars (about 10 per cent), infection (rare) and swelling or numbness of the skin. This is fairly common and can last for up to six months.

Fat aspiration ('body sculpture')

Although this cosmetic procedure is not strictly surgical, it <u>must</u> be carried out by a competent surgeon under a general anaesthetic. It involves first injecting a non-toxic enzyme into an area of the body (commonly buttocks, abdomen or thighs) to liquefy the fat-forming cells and then introducing a narrow tube and literally sucking the fat out. Although up to 2 kg (4½ lb) may be removed, this is not a means of weight reduction but a means of eliminating stubborn areas of fat. The art lies in removing just enough to iron out the lump or bump, while leaving enough to preserve the natural contours of the body and to match up thigh with thigh or buttock with buttock. Inexpert or over-ambitious aspiration may result in uneven contours, even dents or ridges, where too much fat has been removed. The procedure involves a two-day stay in hospital. Immediate after-effects are bruising, puffiness and oedema (water retention) but these are temporary. After-care includes wearing a dressing for 10 days and having regular massages to help stimulate the blood circulation and to break down fat nodules. The scar is no wider than a fingernail. One possible complication: ridging of the area if the skin is not sufficiently elastic to readjust to the new shape. This is more likely in patients over 40.

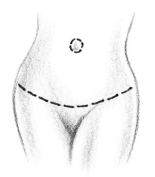

Abdominal lipectomy

A horizontal incision is made right across the lower abdomen, just above the pubic hair. Excess skin, fat and muscle are then undermined all the way up the rib cage and pulled down so that the correct level of tension in the skin can be re-established. A new navel is made in the correct place and the skin drawn together and stitched. Up to 6.8 kg (15 lb) of surplus skin tissue and fat may be removed during the course of the operation.

cosmeticsurgery

lifestyle

'What is freedom? Freedom is the right to choose and the right to create for yourself alternatives of choice.'
Archibald MacLeish

Your lifestyle has as much to do with beauty as any of the more specific routines you may adopt. You can fast on orange juice for two days out of every seven, exercise frenetically from dawn to dusk, apply your make-up with scrupulous care but, if you do not know how to relax and how to enjoy the 'highs' and manage the 'lows' of life, you will never look or feel your best.

Beauty is wellbeing. It is feeling fulfilled in whatever sphere of life you have chosen, feeling confident about your relationship with the world and its relationship with you, being able to distinguish between the things that matter to you and the things that do not, pursuing the things that you can change and accepting the things that you cannot. It is feeling <u>positively</u> well. Such wellbeing may be reflected in the mirror, but it goes much deeper. It means sleeping well, eating properly, recognizing when you are tense, learning to relax, making some time for yourself in your day, accepting challenges but not expecting to achieve the impossible, taking control of your life and not relying on false stimuli or sedatives such as cigarettes, alcohol, sleeping pills, tranquillizers or other drugs to prop you up. A long list perhaps, but it is the small changes in lifestyle, not the major upheavals, that make the difference. Such changes are within your own control.

Guidelines to help you consider certain aspects of your lifestyle and, if necessary, to revise them can be found in the following pages, but they are only guidelines. First you must ask yourself what you want out of life, what you think is important and where your priorities lie. Take a long critical look, take your Stress Test on page 23 and, if appropriate, complete the smoking and drinking questionnaires in the Personal Profile, then read this chapter and put it into the context of your own life.

Flexibility is important. If you have become entrenched in a certain way of living or manner of doing things, it is all the more important that you should aim to get a new perspective on your lifestyle. Examine your day-to-day habits and question your reasons for doing things, especially things that you do automatically. Examine the way in which you schedule your day and ask yourself how productive it is. Be objective.

Inevitably, things will happen throughout your life that will disturb your equilibrium — most temporarily, sometimes more permanently. But if you can organize your priorities around the things that matter to you and, recognizing what you want to achieve, have the courage and confidence to pursue your aims, you will be able to regain your balance and come out on top.

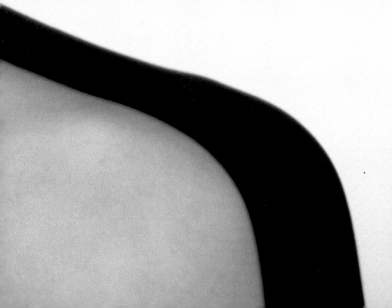

stress

'We boil at different degrees...'   Ralph Waldo Emerson

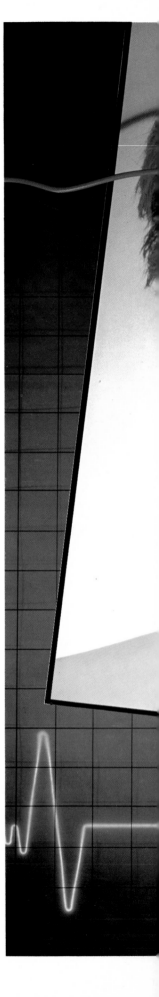

A writer once likened life to sliding down a razor blade. If you could smooth down the edges, he said, much of the pleasure would disappear with the pain. Stress provides these edges and they can be very productive, giving you the drive to create, to strive and to achieve. It is too much stress that can lead to tension and ill health. Balance is the key.

MANAGING STRESS

• <u>Distinguish between positive and negative stresses and establish your own optimum stress level.</u> A confrontation at work, a tight deadline, the prospect of an evening out among strangers ... There is no single definition of what makes one situation stressful and another not. The situation, while important, is not the major determining factor. The person is. Very similar situations can generate very different degrees of strain. Whether such a strain turns out to be positive or negative will depend principally on what Professor Hans Selye, a leading expert on stress and stress-related ill health, has called the 'optimum stress level'. This level varies from person to person according to personality and methods of handling stress.

Experience is the best yardstick. The stress that will work for you is the one that will take you up to, but not beyond, your limits. At this point, you will be performing most efficiently, will feel most stimulated and will be at your happiest and most self-confident. This is your optimum stress level. If you let stress rise much above this level, you will feel tense, agitated and unable to think or act clearly. If you let it fall much below this level, you will feel bored, unfulfilled and drained of energy and enthusiasm. Being under-challenged, that is, living below your optimum stress level, can be just as stressful as being over-challenged and living above it. In 1981, a British survey revealed illness rates among the unemployed to be significantly higher than among the working population. Elsewhere, too, lower recorded cases of ill health have been noted among women going out to work and running a home than among women doing just one, or neither, of these things.

If you are constantly living below your optimum stress level, fend off boredom with variety and challenge. Seek out new goals and think, perhaps, of changing your job or revising certain aspects of your lifestyle so that you regain your interest and enthusiasm. If you are constantly living above your optimum stress level, modify your goals, take time off to give yourself a breathing space. Immerse yourself in something quite removed from all the pressures and demands exerted upon you at work or at home. Walk, jog, paint, take classes in drama or china restoration, learn a new language, start developing your own photographs. Seek an outlet that is enjoyable and creative — not competitive —

and put the pressures of life aside for a while.

If you have type 'A' personality traits (see test on page 24), are highly competitive and ambitious and tend to thrive under pressure, you should make a particularly determined effort to do this. Studies in the USA, by physicians Dr Ray Rosenman and Dr Meyer Friedman, have shown a consistent and significant link between these personality traits and incidences of stress-related ill health — from tension headaches all the way through to coronary heart disease and complete physical and nervous breakdown. In addition, analyses of the data obtained from a long-term study on health patterns in general and the effects of excessive stress in particular, have recently revealed that women may actually be more stress-sensitive than men. The type 'A' woman is now thought to be four times more prone to stress-related ill health than her more easy-going type 'B' counterpart, while the type 'A' man, the traditional victim, appears only twice as prone.

• <u>Defuse the negative effects of stress by taking more exercise and practising relaxation techniques.</u> The stress response is a highly physical one. It gears the body and the mind to react to a state of physical, not mental, emergency. This is unfailingly appropriate in cases of immediate physical stress, such as finding a bus coming straight towards you when you start to cross the street. (It gives you the energy and the impetus to jump out of the way.) It is less appropriate in cases of longer-lasting psychological stress, such as being caught in a traffic jam for 20 minutes or mentally replaying the previous night's argument and preparing for the next.

Any type of stress alerts the body for action (see following page). If none follows, relatively large amounts of the stress hormones, together with their more dangerous by-products (such as free fatty acids which can raise cholesterol levels) are left circulating in the bloodstream with no chance of being burned off. In such cases, it is up to you to restore the balance. Remember the old adage, 'when in danger, when in doubt, shout and scream and run about', and whenever you feel anxious, aggressive, hostile or tense, let off steam by taking more exercise. This is much more productive than politely suppressing your feelings or losing your temper. It has another advantage too: by taking more exercise, you will be keeping physically fit and experiments have repeatedly shown that a healthy resilient body makes for a healthy resilient mind.

A second way of defusing stress is to practise the relaxation, meditation and breathing techniques outlined on pages 176-8 and so 'switch off' the stress signal in the brain. Anything that calms a restless agitated mind will also quieten a restless agitated nervous system. Relaxation and meditation, essential recreation for mind and body, are two

of the best ways of persuading the sympathetic 'fright, fight and flight' stress response to switch off and the para-sympathetic 'rest and digest' response to switch on. With a bit of practice and mental agility, the techniques involved can be learned by anyone.

● <u>Avoid adding unnecessarily to your stress burden.</u> Cigarette smoking, caffeine (found in tea, coffee and cola drinks), cold conditions, competitive behaviour and car driving all have one thing in common. They act on the brain to release the hormone noradrenaline (norepinephrine in the USA) into the system. This hormone (see following page) has wide-ranging physiological and psychological effects. It releases fat for fuel, puts the body into overdrive and makes the brain buzz. It is also highly addictive. Noradrenaline 'addicts' are stress seekers. The 'highs' they seek — and find — are generated by a rush of nervous energy. It is usually only when this energy exhausts itself, that the real ill effects become apparent.

● <u>Control the amount of change in your life.</u> We all thrive on change and variety. But too much change disorientates and distracts and may multiply the negative effects of other, not necessarily related, stresses that you encounter — particular-ly if the changes threaten to disrupt or substantially to alter your present way of life. Study the list of life change units on page 23 of the Personal Profile, add up your score, be aware of the major changes that may contribute to a high stress count and, as far as possible, take the big events in your life singly — not all at once.

Remember, too, that changes, good and bad, sought and unsought, will be less easily accommodated if your present lifestyle is rigid and inflexible with an outlook and attitudes to match. Flexibility is crucial. Learn it by practising it. Brush aside the cobwebs of habit from time to time by getting up at a different hour, taking a different route to work, reading a paper you would not normally read, seeking new interests, going away on holiday at a different time of year and to a different place.

● <u>Preserve a sense of proportion in the running of your day-to-day life.</u> If every minor setback that you encounter becomes a major crisis, you are making yourself needlessly anxious. So save your energy, and your anxiety, for real crises and emergencies and introduce a healthy sense of distance into your life. Achieve the necessary objectivity by bearing in mind Boswell's sage advice to Johnson: 'Sir, consider how insignificant this will appear in a twelvemonth hence.' Or imagine yourself recounting the event to a friend and, if you can, laughing over it. Most of the minor disasters of life have a distinctly funny side and you often do not have to search far to find the humour. Laughter is marvellous therapy and, like tears, a reliever of stress in its own right. Both erupt on the moment and act as valuable distractions by interrupting the serious, often self-defeating, process of thinking and worrying. Mark Twain, himself a great humorist, gives a memorable insight into the positive effects of laughter in *The Adventures of Tom Sawyer:* 'The old man laughed loud and joyously, shook up the details of his anatomy from head to foot and ended by saying such a laugh was money in a man's pocket because it cut down the doctor's bills like anything...'

WHAT HAPPENS DURING STRESS?

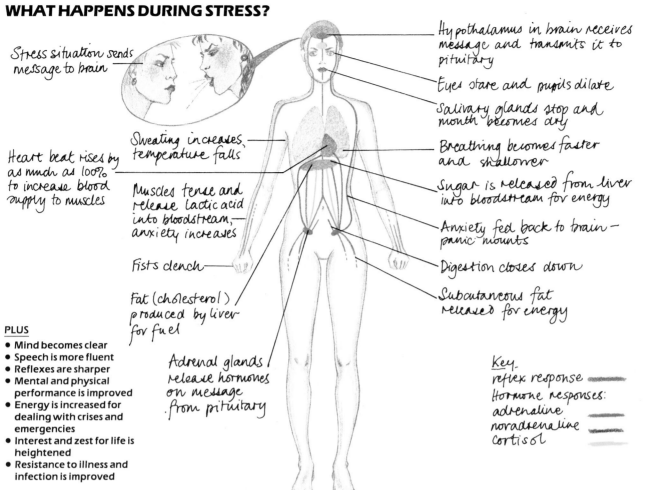

Stress situation sends message to brain

Hypothalamus in brain receives message and transmits it to pituitary

Eyes stare and pupils dilate

Salivary glands stop and mouth becomes dry

Heart beat rises by as much as 100% to increase blood supply to muscles

Sweating increases, temperature falls

Breathing becomes faster and shallower

Muscles tense and release lactic acid into bloodstream; anxiety increases

Sugar is released from liver into bloodstream for energy

Anxiety fed back to brain — panic mounts

Fists clench

Digestion closes down

Subcutaneous fat released for energy

Fat (cholesterol) produced by liver for fuel

Adrenal glands release hormones on message from pituitary

Key.
reflex response
Hormone responses:
adrenaline
noradrenaline
cortisol

PLUS
- Mind becomes clear
- Speech is more fluent
- Reflexes are sharper
- Mental and physical performance is improved
- Energy is increased for dealing with crises and emergencies
- Interest and zest for life is heightened
- Resistance to illness and infection is improved

MINUS
- Mind becomes flustered
- Body is tense and unresponsive
- Speech is confused with liability to stammer and to become tongue-tied
- Mental and physical performance is impaired
- Energy is depleted for dealing with crises and emergencies
- Interest and enthusiasm are low
- Resistance to infection – colds, 'flu, other viruses, possibly even cancer – is lowered

Specific symptoms
- Tension headaches
- Tense, sore muscles – backache, cramp
- Digestive problems – indigestion, frequent attacks of diarrhoea, gastric ulcers
- Physical fatigue and nervous exhaustion
- Insomnia
- Irritability
- Palpitations, panic attacks, raised blood pressure, increased susceptibility to stroke or coronary heart disease

● Control your time, do not let it control you. Time is like money — it goes. The answer, as with money, is to spend it wisely not frivolously. You will then find that you always have something in reserve for the occasions when you really require it.

Spending your time wisely does not mean being ruled by the clock or having to fill every available moment of the day, but being decisive about the way you wish to spend it. If you want to work, to relax, to eat, to watch television or to go away on holiday, make a conscious decision to do so and then follow that decision wholeheartedly. Try not to 'end up' doing something that you do not feel positive about, simply because you are so overwhelmed by the mass of other things to be done that you cannot actually get round to doing any of them. Nothing is more tiring, or more stressful, than not doing the things you intend to do.

● Be single-minded and acquire the art of concentration. A certain amount of pressure can be beneficial. It channels thought and focuses the mind. But too much pressure and too many conflicting demands on your time will lead to panic, confusion and an inability to think or to act clearly. So be selective, decide what you are going to worry about and forget about the rest. No-one, however competent, can do more than one thing at a time. Focus the mind on the one thing that needs doing and needs doing first — and do it. This requires concentration and, for most of us easily distracted by the smaller details of life, concentration requires practice. 'As every divided kingdom falls,' Leonardo da Vinci observed, 'so every mind divided between many studies confounds and saps itself…'

● Establish an order of priorities each day by writing down everything that you intend to do. This includes everything that you would like to do as well as everything you feel you ought to do. Arrange them in order of importance. If you feel it helps, put approximate times beside each one to indicate when you think you are going to be able to do them. Then do them — but singly and in the order in which they appear on your list. If something has been preying on your mind for days, or even weeks, promote it to the top of the list and get it done before turning your attention and energies elsewhere.

At the end of the day, run through your list and see what you have managed to achieve and what still remains to be done. By noting down how much you manage — or fail — to do, you will become more realistic about what you can expect to achieve. This will then enable you to undertake only those tasks or commitments that you know you have a reasonable chance of completing comfortably.

As you become more practised, you will find that you can only expect to control a part of your day — perhaps no more than an hour if you have a family and children or a particularly demanding job. This is fine, as long as you make that hour your own, protect it and make use of it. Making space for yourself during the day and taking time off from everyone else's demands on your time is an investment, not an indulgence, and one of the best possible ways of keeping the amount of stress in your life within reasonable limits.

On reception of the stress signal, a primitive survival response comes into action. It is known as the 'fright, fight and flight' syndrome and it equips the body to meet the challenge just as though it were going to war. Three key hormones – adrenaline (epinephrine), noradrenaline (norepinephrine) and cortisol – pour into the bloodstream and produce the wide range of biochemical and physiological changes shown above. This stress response is part of an age-old defence mechanism better suited to the stone-age lifestyle of our ancestors than to the space-age one of today. For us, the 'frights, fights and flights' of life tend to be psychological rather than physical, prolonged rather than immediate. This can result in a state of continual arousal or emergency. The consequences: prolonged physical and mental tensions which may place an unacceptable strain on the body.

ANXIETY AND DEPRESSION

Many of us are anxious about something much of the time. Often we may not even know what we are anxious about. A universal experience, anxiety has been described as 'not a fear of illness, pain or death, but a fear of fear...' Such apparently 'free-floating' anxieties often turn out to have the most concrete of causes. In such cases, simply being able to identify the cause may be enough to help the anxiety to subside. Most spectres become infinitely less frightening once they become familiar.

In moderation, anxiety can be a very productive form of stress. It can act as a stimulant — providing the drive to do well under pressure and the acumen to size up a potential threat and to take the appropriate action. But if the threat appears disproportionately large, the anxiety may become excessive and the action inappropriate. In extreme cases, such anxiety may lead to panic 'attacks' or, more specifically, to phobias — inordinate fears of apparently innocuous things, such as cats, thunderstorms or the necessity of leaving the safety of the home environment for the insecurity of the world outside. Such fears can often be alleviated through counselling, sometimes combined with the prescription of certain drugs. Anyone suffering from panic attacks or phobias should not hesitate to seek help.

Anxiety usually emerges in response to a future situation or possibility, depression as a consequence of a past event. They are, however, similar in one essential: just as nobody goes through life without experiencing some degree of anxiety, so nobody goes through life without experiencing some degree of depression. Depression ranges from mild transitory feelings of unhappiness to the much rarer severe depressions which require emergency treatment.

Depression has been dubbed the 'common cold of psychiatry'. It is not a good comparison. Colds are rarely serious, while depression frequently is and must always be taken seriously, whether or not there is a clear underlying cause.

Depressions can be divided into five main groups. The first and most common type is known as 'reactive' depression, because it has a cause and is partially, if not totally, understandable in the light of past events. Most reactive depressions can be traced back to a loss or separation of some kind — loss of self-esteem, of a job, of a close friend, of a long-standing relationship, even of an ideal. The second type is endogenous depression, also known as 'the misery syndrome' because, in this case, there is usually no clear cause for the depression — it is just there. If it is profound, it may linger for months, or even years, before it subsides. It can sometimes, but not always, be successfully treated with anti-depressants. A third type of depression may be said to be caused by hormonal disturbances. Although the influence of hormones on mood is extremely difficult to assess, it is likely that changing levels at critical times of life or, for some women, stages of the month — during or after a pregnancy, over the menopause, before a period — do have a profound effect. While it can be difficult to separate hormonal causes from other factors that may be causing or contributing to the depression, carefully prescribed hormone and vitamin therapy can sometimes have very positive results. Depression can also occur as a 'side-effect' of certain drugs, such as those sometimes prescribed for rheumatoid arthritis, hypertension, or even slimming. Occasionally, severe depressions may be symptomatic of an underlying disorder, such as true manic depression or schizophrenia.

Tranquillizers and anti-depressants

Women use a much wider range of psychotropic ('mood-changing') drugs than men do. A New York survey revealed that women account for 72 per cent of all minor tranquillizer prescriptions, 80 per cent of all amphetamines (principally diet pills), 70 per cent of all anti-depressants and, probably, an equivalent proportion of sleeping tablets. British surveys have produced similar figures. Almost inverse proportions for figures quoted on alcohol abuse (about twice as many men as women) suggest that men tend to use alcohol to sedate themselves from the stresses and strains of life, while women tend to use these drugs.

When carefully prescribed, tranquillizers, anti-depressants and sleeping pills have their advantages in the treatment of some, but not all, types of anxiety or depression. They have their disadvantages too. As these become more apparent, it is being increasingly recognized that these drugs must be prescribed, not in isolation, but in combination with the enlightened support and active therapy of doctor, family and friends. Taken in this way, they can give the depressive time to come to terms with the underlying cause of the depression while alleviating those symptoms that interfere with his or her ability to do so.

Anti-depressants are less frequently prescribed than tranquillizers, because of their limited effectiveness on all but the chronic types of depression. These drugs have a curious action on the brain and central nervous system. While they may make someone who is chronically depressed feel more 'cheerful', they will not produce a 'high' in someone who is not. They will merely make her feel drowsy and ill. Even patients considered suitable candidates for anti-depressants may suffer side-effects, such as blurred vision, drowsiness, lowered concentration, tremors and sleeplessness. In fact, some patients stop taking the drug soon after prescription because they find the depression preferable to the side-effects.

Tranquillizers tend to be more generally effective than anti-depressants and are, therefore, prescribed much more widely. In fact, one of them, Valium, is the most widely prescribed drug in the world. When prescribed for about three to six months, tranquillizers may help in relieving some, but not all, cases of reactive depression. But they should work quickly and effectively. If they do not, an alternative course of action should be considered. Tranquillizers, unlike anti-depressants, can produce a dependency when taken over long periods of time. Withdrawal symptoms are heightened anxiety, raised sensory thresholds — lights appear brighter, sounds louder and tastes metallic — trembling, dizziness, nausea, headache and impaired memory or concentration. If tranquillizers have been taken for a relatively long period of time, they should never be stopped abruptly. A gradual reduction of the dose is essential if side-effects are to be minimized or avoided entirely.

RELAXATION

The secret of relaxation, whether snatching a few minutes out of a busy working day or floating off before going to sleep at night, is not to try too hard. Relaxation, like sleep, is a passive exercise, not an active one, and a human necessity, not an achievement. But the most natural things in the world can be some of the most elusive. The difficult art of doing less and less becomes twice as hard in a world that places ever-increasing importance on <u>doing</u> rather than <u>being</u>, and on <u>making</u> rather than <u>letting</u> things happen. If, like many people, you find it difficult to relax, the yoga and breathing exercises on the following pages, together with one of the following relaxation and mind 'switching off' techniques, may help.

Progressive relaxation

This is a tried and tested technique which involves a mental and physical journey through the body, from the toes up to the head, in which you tense and then relax each part in turn. It works on the sensible basis that you have to be able to identify and recognize a tense, contracted muscle before you can recognize — and acquire — a relaxed, extended one. Do you know what a relaxed muscle feels like? Clench your fist hard and hold the pressure until you become aware of a dull, taut feeling running from your hand, through your wrist and up towards your elbow. Now release it and feel the sensation subside. That is relaxation.

To relax 'progressively' lie down on your back on the floor, with your legs falling comfortably away from each other, your arms away from your sides, your palms facing the ceiling and your head straight. Now you are ready to start. (You may find it helpful to have a friend read the passage through to you so that you can concentrate on the exercise.)

Stretch out your legs, pointing the toes down towards the floor as far as they will go. Hold the stretch for a few moments, then stretch again and release. Feel the tension gradually ebb away. Concentrate on the sensations you receive. This procedure can be applied all the way up the body. Pull your buttocks close together, hold them there and release. Pull your abdomen and pelvis down into the floor, press, hold, press again then release. Clench your fists, feel the tension running along your lower arms, hold and release. Pull your shoulders up towards your ears, hold them there, and release. Press your head into the floor and release. Clench your jaw, clamp your teeth together, press your tongue hard against the roof of your mouth and feel the tension radiating outwards towards your ears. Release, let your mouth drop open and your tongue lie flat. Swallow and feel your throat soften as the tension subsides. Close your eyes tightly together and release. Close them again. Turn your eyes up to 'look' at your eyebrows, down to your toes, to the left and to the right. Lift your eyebrows up as far as possible and, as you release them, feel your forehead open and widen as the muscles relax. Imagine all the lines of worry being smoothed away. Take a deep breath, hold it for a few moments and then let go in a long, drawn-out sigh. Finally, check every part of your body for signs of tension — feet, hands, shoulders and mouth in particular. Then let your mind relax. Think cool, white thoughts and drift.

Autosuggestion and autogenics

These techniques work on the principle that you can talk your body into a state of relaxation. At its simplest, this is achieved by the slow and rhythmic repetition of a two-syllable word, like re-lax or hea-vy. Allow your breathing to follow its own rhythm (the second syllable should fall on the out-breath) and you will find that you can soothe your mind while simultaneously encouraging your body to unwind.

A much more sophisticated version, known as autogenics ('generated from within'), was developed by a German neurologist Dr Johanne Schultz in the 1930s. This involves persuading different parts of the body to generate their own specific sensations — starting with heaviness and warmth in the limbs and progressing to calmness and regularity of the heartbeat, awareness of a natural breathing rhythm, warmth in the abdomen and, lastly, coolness over the forehead. The complete technique takes time, practice and the guidance of a trained teacher. A simpler, abbreviated technique is therefore given below.

Start by thinking yourself heavy. Turn all your attention to your right arm. Say 'my right arm is heavy', repeating the phrase to yourself until you feel your arm becoming increasingly heavy and more immoveable. Repeat the exercise with your left arm and, once you can generate sensations of heaviness quite easily, extend the exercise to your legs ('my right leg is heavy', etc). If you find that you can achieve a good state of relaxation, progress to thinking yourself warm. But do not rush it. Try to acquire what Schultz termed an attitude of 'passive concentration'. Listen without judging, observe your body without thinking 'good' or 'bad' and concentrate simply on producing the appropriate sensation.

Biofeedback

This is an excellent and practical aid to relaxation, if you have access to a machine. It works like a lie-detector, using tiny electrodes on the skin to measure resistance or temperature

Neck, shoulders and upper back are commonly tense. Release the tension by giving yourself a massage. Place an orange between you and a wall or door and roll it around, by bending and straightening the knees. Concentrate on tense and painful areas – between the shoulder blades, along the spine, up across the shoulders and the neck ... (This is not an exercise for smart walls and precious wallpapers, as the orange may stain them.)

and to relay the 'message' as a series of lights on a screen or as audible bleeps. The more tense you are, the greater your skin resistance (or the lower your temperature) and the more numerous the flashes and the bleeps. The idea is to try to widen the intervals between them by using whichever relaxation method you find effective. Because the machine gives constant information (feedback) on how well you are doing, it is usually only a matter of minutes before you find that you can exert some control over the frequency of the flashes or bleeps. Biofeedback is valuable both because it shows you that you can relax, and you are not alone if you are convinced that you cannot, and because it encourages you to adapt your methods to the machine and so helps you to select the technique that suits you best.

Massage

Massage is an excellent aid to relaxation. The most profitable areas of the body to concentrate on: the neck (left), the foot and the stomach. Many of the nerve endings of the body lie in the sole of the foot and, when stimulated or soothed through massage, can generate a strong sense of wellbeing throughout the body. Take a ball and roll it under your foot, varying the pressure as you go. Imagine that it is coated with ink and that you must cover every centimetre of the sole with it.

A good stomach massage is extremely calming. This one centres around the ancient Chinese acupuncture point known as the *Hara*, or 'Sea of Energy', and is situated three fingers' width below the navel. Lie on your back with your knees bent so that your abdominal muscles are fully relaxed. Massage the stomach with the palm and fingers. Move in a clockwise direction. Breathe out and apply more pressure as you stroke down and across the *Hara*, breathe in and release the pressure as you move up and over the navel.

Mind control

This refreshingly down-to-earth means of quietening the mind simply involves starting at the number 100 and counting backwards to zero. Breathe out as you mouth each number and let the numbers follow the rhythm of your own breathing. If other thoughts intervene do not chase them away. Watch them passing across your mind and disappearing out of view, rather like a train travelling through a landscape. Then return to your counting, picking up where you left off. As you get more practised, you should find that sequences are longer, interruptions fewer and that you can achieve the same degree of mental relaxation counting from 25 as you did from 100.

Meditation

Meditation can be an extremely effective way of controlling restless, fragmented thinking, overcoming anxiety, releasing tension and refreshing the mind.

You do not need a guru, or even a particular philosophy, in order to meditate, although some guidance may be helpful initially. You do need 15 to 20 minutes when you know you will not be disturbed. You must also be comfortable — or you may find yourself meditating on your own discomfort.

Sit with legs crossed and hands folded in your lap so that your body makes a circuit around which your energy can flow. Close your eyes. Quieten your mind by allowing it to dwell on an object. Let the object be all-absorbing. Visualize a symbol, focus on a rhythm of breathing (see following page) or repeat a single word or phrase. Some sanskrit words and phrases known as mantras, while meaningless to Western minds, have a remarkable resonance. Try the ancient Siddha Yoga mantra *Om Namah Shivaya* or simply repeat the word 'One'. As you do so, retreat a step and watch your mind at work. Become a passive observer. Meditate.

Yoga

Yoga postures (*asanas*) and breathing exercises (*pranayama*) are a practical and effective way of counteracting stress and tension. The straightforward steps here can be practised by anyone. Although some of the positions may appear awkward or difficult, they are not contortions and should be practised with gentle and precise movements — not with great athleticism. The postures are designed to refresh the body after an inactive day, increasing muscle tone and bringing oxygen to every cell in the body. Although they may appear to be static, you will soon discover that the spine and limbs will continue to stretch as the muscles relax. The postures can be held for some seconds, even minutes.

The yogic practice of deep breathing takes time to acquire and is best taught by a qualified teacher. Beginners should concentrate on establishing a steady rhythmic breathing. Draw the breath in from the pelvis so that the abdomen is pulled back towards the spine and the chest expands as the lungs fill. The exhalation should be smooth and the air gradually released, not consciously pushed, from the lungs. Practise the breathing separately at the end of the session and you will find that, as the breath is deepened and controlled, the nerves are soothed and the brain refreshed.

Basic rules

1. Practise in a well-ventilated room.
2. Progress slowly and methodically, studying each picture, together with the instructions, before attempting the poses.
3. Practise on an empty stomach.
4. Practise the postures regularly, preferably every day. Enjoy it. Do not force the postures. Go as far as feels comfortable.
5. If in doubt about your health, consult your doctor first. Do not use these postures as a curative. While yoga can do much to improve the many minor ailments that result from poor posture and wrongly used muscles, some of the claims made for it have been greatly exaggerated.

Breathing

Breathing techniques provide some of the most rapid routes to relaxation. Here are two of the simplest.

The first is an emergency technique which works first by distracting, second by soothing, the mind. Use it whenever you feel anxious or agitated. Standing if possible by an open window, breathe in through your nose, steadily and deeply, over a slow count of 12. Hold for 12. Then open your mouth and produce an audible 'haaah' as you release the air from your lungs. This invaluable instant calmer should not be repeated more than two or three times as the depth of breathing may make you dizzy.

The second breathing technique is much gentler and can be practised indefinitely. It is Chinese in origin and is known as the 'Breathing of Selflessness'. It makes a useful adjunct to any of the relaxation techniques described earlier and entails breathing through your nose throughout. Breathe in to a count of four and out to a count of 12. Keep the rhythm so smooth and so gentle that a feather would not stir if it were held in front of your nose. Continue counting until the breathing falls easily and automatically into the rhythm you have established and a deep state of relaxation is reached.

Start by taking up *tadasana* (mountain pose) (1). Stand with heels and toes touching, toes spread as wide apart as possible. Pull up knees, tighten buttocks, stretch spine, drop and relax the shoulders. The chest will open as a result of the spinal stretching. Breathe evenly and deeply several times before taking up *vrksasana* (tree pose) (2). Point elbows out away from the body, press palms together, and rest the foot on inner thigh. Relax into it, maintaining the stretch in the spine. Breathe evenly and deeply and remain there for as long as you feel comfortable. Then change legs.

Jump the feet about three feet apart and hold the arms out at shoulder level (3). Turn the left foot in and the right foot out, so that the whole leg turns outward from the hip. Align right heel with the middle of the arch of left foot. Breathing out, extend the spine to the right (4). Turn the head and look up at the outstretched hand. Repeat to other side, trying to make an absolutely vertical line with the two arms. This pose, known as *trikonasana* (triangle pose), will relieve stiffness in legs and, as long as the head is held correctly, will help unlock sore neck muscles.

Taking up starting position (3) again, but with the feet wider apart, go into *virabhadrasana* II (warrior pose) (5). Bend knee (keeping it over the ankle and aiming, eventually, to form a right angle there) and stretch spine upwards. The weight should be evenly balanced. Repeat to other side. Starting in *tadasana* (1), join the palms together between the shoulder blades. If you cannot manage this, hold the elbows as shown (6). Jump the feet

three feet apart and turn the legs and trunk to the right. Stretch the spine fully. Breathing out, bend forward from the hips and stretch out to the chair (7). This pose, known as *parsvottanasana* (lateral extension), helps to remove stiffness at hips, correct rounded shoulders and also gives the spine a good stretch. *Virasana* (hero pose) is performed keeping the knees together and sitting on the buttocks inside the feet. If the knees are weak, avoid this exercise; if the hips are stiff, use a cushion as shown (8). Place hands on soles of feet. If you find this difficult to do, sit in simple cross legs (9), interlocking the fingers for a more intense effect and stretching the arms up over the head. Finish with *bharadvajrasana*, a spinal twist. Bend the legs aside and keep the knees aligned with the hips (10). Rotate the trunk to face the outer thigh and catch the knee. Support the trunk with the other hand, stretch the spine and turn the head to look over the shoulder.

sleep

'How do people go to sleep? I'm afraid I've lost the knack...'   Dorothy Parker

'Don't go to bed,' advised Mark Twain, insomniac and humorist, 'because so many people die there.' But the truth is that, if you did not, you would soon find yourself yearning for cool sheets and a soft pillow. Sleep is essential to all living things, which have their own cycles of waking and sleeping, activity and rest, stop and go. It is the balance between them that generates energy and interest. During sleep, the body gathers its resources, regenerates its energies, rebalances its metabolism and orders its psyche. Just how much it refreshes the brain and the body becomes apparent as soon as you are deprived of it. Lack of sleep quickly diminishes the quality of life when awake.

Fortunately, this does not happen very often. Sleep is so natural and vital that the body tends to take just as much, or as little, as it needs — 14 hours or more as a baby, six hours or less as an octogenarian. But it is not just age that determines your sleep requirements. The amount of sleep needed varies considerably from person to person and with the state of the mind and emotions. The 'eight-hour rule' stands corrected: experiments in sleep laboratories have consistently shown that some people need as few as five hours sleep before waking refreshed and alert, while others may need as many as 11. Body and brain seem to restore themselves at different rates in different individuals.

If you are worried that you are not getting enough sleep, consider first that you may, in fact, be getting all the sleep that you need and that you are only suffering from unreal expectations. Use your diary to record how much sleep you got, or thought you got, over a two-week period and how you felt the following day. If you habitually wake up feeling unrefreshed and carry on feeling excessively tired throughout the day, then you may not be getting your full quota.

You should bear in mind, too, that if you are going through a particularly demanding phase in your life and are getting very little sleep, you do not have to 'make it all up'. Studies on students kept up for three nights in a row at the University of Florida, USA, showed that they only needed three to four hours extra sleep to make up for the 24 that they actually lost.

GETTING TO SLEEP

Sleep cannot be forced. It is easy and effortless and seeks you out. It does not come with 'trying', still less with anxiety. As worrying about not getting off to sleep is almost certain to keep you awake, relax using any of the methods detailed on the previous pages and let sleep surprise you. It almost certainly will.

Even so, there will be times in most people's lives when sleep is elusive. You may take hours to go off to sleep and then find that your time asleep is disrupted by periods of wakefulness. Or you may wake up at dawn, overcome with

tiredness, and yet find it impossible to drop off again. You may get up in the morning and somehow struggle irritably through the day, only to go to bed at night to find that exactly the same thing occurs. Sleeplessness has become a pattern. While it is a pattern that usually resolves itself spontaneously, prolonged periods of insomnia can lead to considerable strain and should be discussed with a doctor, in order to rule out any medical cause.

If you are suffering from sleeplessness, do not automatically reach out for the sleeping tablets. These should be a last, not a first, resort and should be prescribed only for a short period of time in order to help you ride through a particularly difficult period. Despite their evident drawbacks, however, sleeping pills (hypnotics) are still widely prescribed. In fact, it has been estimated that every tenth night's sleep in the UK is hypnotically induced. While the newer generation of sleeping tablets may be safer than the previous ones (the barbiturates and the highly addictive Mandrax), they still work in large general areas of the brain, often depressing the central nervous system in amounts above that simply required to produce sleep. They may linger in the system long enough to give feelings of 'hangover' on awakening together with impaired concentration and alertness the following day. In addition, these sleeping tablets, which are almost identical in chemical composition to tranquillizers, can lead to dependency. With long-term use, it becomes increasingly difficult to get to sleep without them — so treat them with respect.

Countdown to sleep

● Go to sleep when you are tired, not when it is time for bed. If you feel wide awake, stay up. Capitalize on having a little extra time. Write letters, read a book or take a short walk. Fresh air and gentle exercise are two of the best sleep inducers, particularly if taken an hour or so before going to bed.
● Get up earlier. One of the most effective ways of counteracting difficulties in getting off to sleep at night is to get up an hour earlier in the morning. It takes a certain amount of discipline, but persevere and you will soon find that you start feeling sleepy at bedtime — if not before.
● Avoid over-loading the stomach just before going to bed. Meals are best eaten early in the evening and proteins, despite their unearned reputation for causing bad dreams, make much better bedtime foods than carbohydrates. Cheese, milk and yogurt are all good, late night foods. Milk is especially suitable because it contains high levels of an amino acid (tryptophan) that seems to play a significant part in mobilizing the sleep-inducing chemicals in the brain.
● Make sure that your system is not running on overdrive by the time you go to bed. Question your intake of all stimu-

Being asleep has much of the complexity and variety of waking life. During an average night's sleep, you will pass through cycles, each composed of four or five distinct stages (see below) and lasting for about 90 minutes. You will change position about 40 times – considerably less if you have taken sleeping pills or an excessive amount of alcohol, considerably more if agitated or depressed. You will 'wake up' several times, but will pass so rapidly through the sleep/wakefulness threshold that you will remember nothing about it. Your brain waves, if recorded, would travel about 6 km (3½ miles). You will probably dream.

The Stages
Sleep threshold: known as the state of relaxed wakefulness. The muscles are relaxed, the breathing is shallow and the mind tends to wander. Brain waves follow the alpha rhythm – about 10 cycles per second – but will shift to a higher level on arousal or a lower one on going to sleep.

Stage 1: a very light stage of sleep from which you are easily awakened. Temperature starts to fall, the pulse rate slows and becomes more regular and the brain waves become smaller, slower and more uneven.

Stage II: a slightly deeper level of sleep, from which you will be easily awakened by sounds. Blood pressure, body temperature, pulse rate, breathing and body metabolism continue to slow. The eyes may roll from side to side. Brain waves become larger with irregular peaks.

Stage III: moving into deep sleep. A louder noise is required to awaken you. Brain waves become much larger and slower – between one and three cycles per second. Dreams are rarely recalled on awakening. All body processes continue to drop.

Stage IV: the deepest stage of sleep. The body temperature is at its lowest and breathing at its slowest and most even. It is difficult to arouse the sleeper out of this stage and dreams are very rarely recalled. This is the period of sleep walking and night terrors – the most terrifying dreams of all. Brain waves follow the delta pattern – very large, slow and jagged. Because restoration of body and brain is thought to be at its most intense during stage IV sleep, it is traditionally considered to be the most valuable. Onset usually occurs within the first hour of sleeping and may not be repeated for the rest of the night. Insomniacs and people who take sleeping pills will miss out on this stage entirely.

REM (Rapid Eye Movement): the busiest period of sleep. Brain waves resemble the waking alpha pattern and the more adventurous type of dreaming occurs. These dreams are often vividly recalled on awakening. Blood pressure, pulse rate and breathing become faster and irregular. The need for REM sleep varies greatly with age. Children, especially babies born prematurely, need most. There have been speculations that the foetus spends all its sleeping time in REM. People taking sleeping pills have little or no REM sleep and on ceasing to take them, go into what is known as 'REM rebound' – compensating by having more on subsequent nights until the shortfall has been made up.

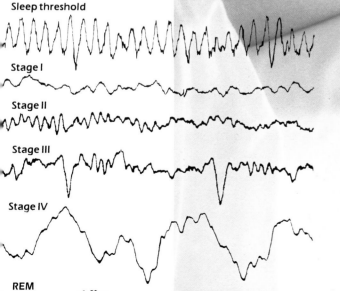

Sleep threshold

Stage I

Stage II

Stage III

Stage IV

REM

lants, including alcohol, sugar, salt, coffee, tea and cola drinks. The caffeine present in the last three speeds up the metabolism and its 'buzz' may last for up to seven hours. If you go to bed at midnight, coffee or tea drunk at six o'clock in the evening could well be keeping you awake. While caffeine tends to interfere with sleep in the early part of the night, large amounts of alcohol, though sleep inducing, will cause you to wake early. Because the alcohol is still in the process of being metabolized, it can react upon the digestive and nervous systems, causing restlessness and gastritis — not to mention hangover.

● Take a warm bath before going to bed. Use an aromatic essence to soothe and relax you. Some of the pure, essential oils, such as chamomile, melissa and orange blossom, are deliciously relaxing. As you soak, try going through a simplified progressive relaxation procedure, or simply lie there and enjoy it, letting your mind drift. Do not drift off altogether, though.

● Make yourself a sleep pillow. Place a pot-pourri of herbs — dried hops, lime blossom, rosemary, lavender, jasmine and chamomile — in a flat linen 'envelope' and tuck it inside your ordinary pillow. Hops and lime blossom, in particular, have very strong sleep-inducing properties.

● Check that you are comfortable in bed. This may sound obvious, but it is crucial. There are no hard and fast rules about what makes one bed and bedroom preferable to another — it is your own comfort that counts. If you find you tend to sleep better in other beds, your mattress may be too soft or too hard, or your bedroom too cold or too hot. The ideal temperature is thought to be 15.5-18°C(60-64°F). Consider these points and, if necessary, change them.

● Is your sleep disturbed by background noise? Some people find sound, whether the indistinct rumble of traffic or the louder ticking of an alarm clock, conducive to sleep. Others find it infuriating. In addition, there is the possibility that your sleep is being disturbed by noises of which you are unaware. If you do find it difficult to get off to sleep, keep waking up during the night, or feel excessively tired the following day, embark on an anti-sound strategy. Move to another bedroom away from street noise, have double-glazing fitted to bedroom windows, or buy a pair of earplugs.

● If sleep still eludes you, try building up the amount of carbon dioxide in your body. It is easy to fall asleep in a crowded room when the windows are tightly shut, because the amount of oxygen available is gradually being displaced by carbon dioxide. Carbon dioxide acts as a natural tranquilizer (in excess as a poison too, of course), numbs the brain, slows the body responses and produces a range of 'symptoms' identical to Stage I sleep. This breathing technique will temporarily raise your carbon dioxide levels, without dangerously depriving you of oxygen. Take three deep breaths and, at the end of the third, hold on to the outward breath for a count of six, so that the lungs are completely emptied of air. Repeat this twice. Then do it once again but, this time, having exhaled as deeply as possible, breathe 'minimally', not gulping for air but breathing from the top of your chest in short, shallow breaths. This will increase the amount of carbon dioxide in your system and can be repeated every 10 minutes or so — if you are still awake.

182

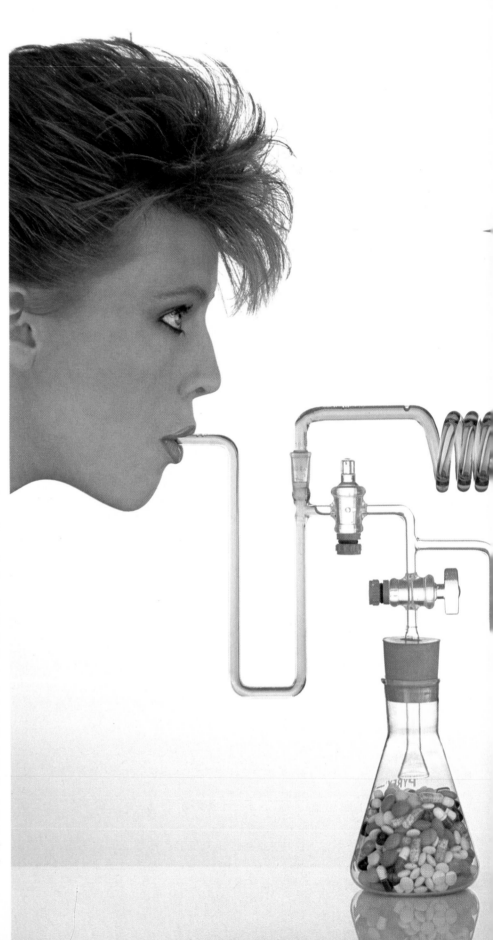

drugs and dependencies

'The chains of habit are too weak to be felt until they are too strong to be broken...'
Samuel Johnson

None of us likes to feel that our lives are bound in and circumscribed by habit. Yet we order our days within its comfortable, reassuring framework. From the moment we wake in the morning, we run through a habitual pattern of doing things — getting up at a certain hour, dressing in a certain order, having a certain type of food for breakfast, reading a certain daily newspaper, taking a certain route to work... All these are habits. Try changing a few of them to see how odd and 'wrong' they feel.

While it would be ridiculous to suggest that such habits are harmful, a second set of habits does require more careful attention. These are the dependencies. They can be physical, emotional or psychological — sometimes all three at once. A psychological or emotional dependency can be defined as an overriding need for something or someone without the involvement of a drug. The dependency of an infant upon its mother is an obvious example. This early and natural dependency may later be exchanged for others in adulthood that are not only inappropriate but are also, often, potentially harmful. You can become dependent on almost anything — gambling, people, eating, television, noise, slimming pills, sleeping tablets...These are not simply habits, but props used to bolster up confidence, to give a sense of security, to add excitement or to provide a refuge from the pressures, miseries and frustrations of life.

Of all the dependencies, the most dangerous are the drugs, because theirs is a physical as well as a psychological dependency and one which may end up by destroying your health, if not by actually killing you. In medical terms, drug use is said to constitute a dependency when two factors are present. The first is a tolerance to the drug at doses that non-users would find unacceptable or unpleasant and the second is physical signs of withdrawal if the drug is denied. The obvious drawback: many drug users are not aware either of their tolerance to the substance or of their possible susceptibility to withdrawal symptoms while continuing to take it. It is, therefore, crucial to recognize and to break the chains of these drug habits before they become too strong to be broken or, at least, to be broken easily.

It is extremely difficult to quantify the effects of many drugs. Some, like LSD and other hallucinogens, may not lead to addiction but may still cause irreparable mental or physical damage. Others, like marijuana, cause no apparent physical damage but the 'high' they produce can lead to a strong psychological and social dependency. In addition, marijuana produces distortions of time and space that could be potentially dangerous when driving. Although some drugs have their uses, it is important to recognize what these are, together with their limitations, and to examine your own reasons for using them.

SMOKING

'Most people who drink alcohol or take sleeping pills are able to do so in moderation or on special occasions and can tolerate periods without them, but the most stable and well-adjusted person will, if he or she smokes at all, almost inevitably become dependent on the habit...' The British Royal College of Physicians

Smoking is not only one of the most habit-forming activities there is; it is also one of the most dangerous habits on which to become dependent. The main dangers are cancer of the lung, mouth, throat, oesophagus, pancreas and urinary tract; stroke and coronary heart disease (the risk of sudden and fatal heart attack is up to five times greater if you smoke); chronic bronchitis (95 per cent of sufferers are smokers), emphysema and pneumonia. These health risks should not seem remote. If predictions are right, the lung cancer rate for women will have exceeded that for breast cancer by the end of the decade in both Britain and the USA. No woman is complacent about getting breast cancer, yet millions invite lung cancer every time they light a cigarette.

There is another aspect to consider if you smoke: other people. Smoking during pregnancy presents a known and established hazard to the foetus (see page 200). Less well known are the perils of 'sidestream' smoke. This is emitted into the air from a smouldering cigarette and sometimes contains carcinogens (cancer-producing substances) in higher concentrations than those inhaled directly by a smoker. Two important studies, one in Japan and one in Greece, have shown that the risk of lung cancer among non-smoking women is higher if they are married to smokers. Such findings are likely to make 'passive' smoking the health issue of the decade.

If you smoke at all, answer the questionnaire on page 25 of the Personal Profile. Consider your reasons for continuing to smoke and the reasons why you should stop and write them down in two columns. If the second outweighs the former, make a really determined effort to stop. In addition, consider the following.

Stopping smoking: guidelines to giving up

● Is a low-tar cigarette really better for you? Yes, if you take notice of the advertisements with their emphasis on 'wising down' or 'adopting a low profile'. Not significantly, if you listen to the scientists, whose research results show almost unanimously that, if you change your brand of cigarettes from a high to a lower tar variety, you will also tend to change your manner of smoking. In other words, you will compensate for the loss of nicotine, either by inhaling each cigarette more deeply and more often or simply by smoking more of them. The difference, then, is probably smaller than it has been made out to be, unless you smoke high tar unfiltered cigarettes. In this case, a lower tar count and a filter will certainly work in your better interests. If a cigarette is to work in your best interests, however, you must leave it in the packet.

● Will cutting down the number of cigarettes you smoke each day or week help you to give up? Perhaps, but only if you have tremendous reserves of self-discipline, in which case giving up right away should present no problem. In most cases 'cutting down' is simply a euphemism for not giving up entirely and is unlikely to work, because the rules you set yourself are too flexible: if people know you are cutting down, they will not exclaim when they see you with a cigarette in your hand, but they will if they know you have made a resolution to give up. Many 20-a-day smokers, reluctant to give up completely, talk of embarking on a 'cutting-down' strategy until they reach a point where they are smoking one or two cigarettes a day. This rarely, if ever, happens. The truth is that occasional smokers account for less than two out of every 100 smokers and do not have a history of heavy smoking.

If you do want to 'wean yourself' off nicotine, stop smoking and chew nicotine gum instead. This is available on prescription in the UK and, at the time of writing, under trial in the USA prior to sales there (nicotine lozenges are currently available across the counter without a prescription). Although the taste of the gum is initially unpleasant, it is worth persevering because it satisfies your cravings for the drug, while minimizing the effects of withdrawal, and thus enables you to break the smoking habit. In the UK, trials for the year 1980-1981 showed the gum to have a success rate of nearly 50 per cent after 12 months. This is an impressive figure when compared with the five per cent who manage to give up on their own for an equivalent period of time. Other therapies that can help you to negotiate some, but not all, of the early hurdles include acupuncture, hypnotherapy and aversion therapy (smoking yourself sick). All of these can work well, provided that the desire to stop and to stop permanently is there in the first place. No technique is yet available to help the smoker who does not want to stop — nor is there ever likely to be.

● Is there such a thing as a 'right' time for giving up? Yes, it must be when you wholeheartedly want to stop. Anything less than complete commitment is likely to come to grief. No-one ever claimed that giving up was easy. It can be extremely difficult and the longer you have been smoking and the more ingrained the habit has become, the more difficult you are likely to find it. Good times for giving up are, first and foremost, the moment you really decide you want to, without delaying until tomorrow morning, next week or the New Year; after an illness or a cold, when the desire to smoke has temporarily disappeared; when embarking on a relationship with someone who does not smoke and dislikes the fact that you do; on holiday when you are temporarily removed from most of the everyday cues that fuel your desire for a cigarette; before you become pregnant.

● Once you have made the decision to give up, how can you keep to it? Reinforce your resolution by making it as public as possible. Make sure that everyone you know is aware that you have given up and ask them to support your non-smoking. Every time you resist the urge to smoke, count it as a victory and remember that each victory becomes progressively easier to achieve. Be aware, too, of all the positive aspects of giving up — how much better you are feeling, how much money you are saving, how much healthier you will be in 10 or 20 years' time and how much younger your skin will look.

● Will giving up smoking cause you to put on weight?

Possibly in the short term, not significantly in the long term.

Three factors are thought to be responsible for a gain in weight after giving up smoking. The first is that you start to feel hungry: your palate wakes up, your sense of smell becomes more alert and your appetite more suggestible. In addition, the hand-to-mouth habit dies hard. Eating in general and snacking in particular are the closest substitutes for lighting and smoking a cigarette. Fight against this by being on your guard. Find something else to occupy your mind and your hands. The third factor may be physiological. Some studies have shown that smoking raises the metabolic rate by reducing the rate of oxygen consumption. After giving up, the metabolic rate drops so that, even if the amount of food eaten remains constant, you absorb more of it because you metabolize it more slowly.

Some weight is commonly put on over the first three months of non-smoking. In the USA, the largest single study on the long-term effects on weight of giving up smoking among women (a 42-year trial) revealed that the immediate weight gain varied from smoker to smoker and correlated closely with the amount smoked — the heaviest smokers gaining up to 13.5 kg (30 lb) while the lightest ones gained less than 2 kg (4½ lb). Encouragingly, this survey, in common with others in Britain and Europe, revealed the greater part of the weight gain to be temporary. Over a lifetime of non-smoking, it levelled out to just 1.8 kg (4 lb). The heaviest smokers must have subsequently lost considerable amounts of weight.

If you are one of the millions of women who use cigarette smoking quite consciously as a means of suppressing your appetite and so controlling your weight, review your priorities. The prospect of gaining a few pounds should not seem more terrible than the prospect of succumbing to one of the diseases listed earlier. So take a long-term view. Be aware of the pitfall of 'substitute eating' but do not be too censorious with yourself — enjoy the new appreciation of flavour you are experiencing instead. If you are a heavy smoker, you may find nicotine gum (or lozenges in USA) helpful. This not only helps you to break your habit in stages but also seems to have a positive effect on weight. The four studies on the subject have all shown that gum chewers gain up to 50 per cent less weight than average over the first six months of non-smoking.

● Are there any ways of minimizing the dangers of smoking, if you are not yet confident about your ability to give up? Yes, with reservations, since the only safe cigarette is the one that you do not smoke. There are ways, however, of making one cigarette less unsafe than the next. Take fewer puffs, try not to inhale, put your cigarette out earlier and never relight it. Never smoke a cigarette right down to the filter. All the toxic substances in the tar are at their most concentrated in the last third.

Try to cut down the number of cigarettes you smoke. If you are a 'packet-a-day' person, buy them in packets of 10 not 20. Start smoking later in the day. Analyze your desire for each cigarette you take out of a packet, and cut out those you would have smoked 'automatically' and without enjoyment. As you find yourself smoking less and less, ask yourself whether you would not be better off giving up altogether.

DRINKING

'The first draught serveth for health, the second for pleasure, the third for shame and the fourth for madness…' Anarchasis

Alcohol is a relatively simple chemical substance easily produced in decaying vegetable matter. It is found naturally in the body as a by-product of the breakdown of food in the gut. It is a powerful sedative and reinforcer of mood and has been used throughout the ages for its deliciously intoxicating effect.

Alcohol has a curious two-fold effect on the brain and central nervous system. First it stimulates — releasing inhibitions and generating mild feelings of elation and wellbeing. Then it depresses — slowing responses, causing speech to be slurred, coordination to be lost and sexual desire to evaporate. In moderate amounts, alcohol will send you to sleep. In massive quantities, it can lead to coma and even to death.

Drinking is enjoyable and relaxing, promotes a sense of wellbeing and can contribute hugely to the enjoyment of any meal. In excessive quantities, however, it is both poisonous and highly addictive and can leave a massive trail of destruction in its wake — broken marriages and homes, financial crises, psychological and physical breakdown and innumerable symptoms of ill health. Because alcoholism is 20 times more prevalent than all other forms of drug addiction put together and because we are all at risk, we must choose what role we are going to let alcohol play in our lives — how much we are going to drink, in what manner and towards what end.

If you have not already done so, check your responses to alcohol and your reasons for drinking in the questionnaire in the Personal Profile. Start counting the amount you drink rather as you would the number of calories you eat or cigarettes you smoke. For the purpose of counting, alcoholic drinks can be divided into units. One unit is a centilitre of alcohol, contained in 284 millilitres (half a pint) of beer or its equivalent. Hence, 1 unit of alcohol = 284 ml (½ pint) beer = 1 glass wine or champagne = 1 sherry glass fortified wine (sherry, port, vermouth, etc) = a standard single measure whisky, gin, vodka or brandy. The size of the glass or measure is obviously important. Some wine goblets can hold twice as much as the smaller, standard glass and allowances must, therefore, be made for this.

Drinking habits

Light drinking (occasional or weekend drinking; no more than two or three units a day). Drinking for enjoyment on special occasions or restricting the amount you drink to two or three glasses of wine (or their equivalent) a day will enhance mood and reduce tension. This type of drinking can be positively beneficial, particularly if the alcohol is taken with a meal, because it relaxes you and gives your digestion a chance to work properly.

You should be especially careful when driving though. As few as two units of alcohol will impair your judgement to some extent.

Moderate drinking (frequent drinking; between four and

seven units a day). Although medical experts are reluctant to draw up hard and fast rules about how much anyone should drink (tolerance varies from individual to individual as does susceptibility to physical dependency and/or damage), four units is generally agreed to be the amount of alcohol people can consume daily without putting their health at risk. Even so, if your intake is habitually closer to five than, say, three, certain chemical changes in the blood will be detectable and the burden on the liver will be increased. Women are particularly at risk of liver disease. A woman who regularly drinks seven or more units of alcohol, particularly if it is on a daily basis, has a significantly higher chance of developing hepatitis or cirrhosis than a man.

At five units, your blood/alcohol level will almost certainly have risen to a level that will make you unfit to drive in the legal sense in Britain and in many states in the USA.

Heavy drinking (daily or 'binge' drinking; eight or more units a day). Drinking in this quantity may lead to the formation of a strong habit. Even if there is no physical dependence on alcohol, there is likely to be a strong psychological one.

Heavy drinking increases your susceptibility to a number of hazards — physical, emotional, social and professional. These include aggressive or withdrawn behaviour, tearfulness and loss of confidence, poor work performance, absenteeism, loss of interest, loss of memory, anaemia, digestive upsets, frequent bouts of colds or 'flu, ulcers of the stomach and digestive tract, heart disease, pneumonia and the diseases of the liver mentioned above. Heavy drinkers should make a positive and determined effort to reduce their consumption to that of the moderate or light drinker (preferably the light one). If they find this difficult or impossible, they should seek medical help.

At 10 units, your blood/alcohol level is almost twice the British legal limit and your judgement is substantially impaired. The likelihood of your having a car accident is 25 times greater than if you had drunk nothing at all.

Excessive drinking is not so much a question of the amount as the manner of drinking. Excessive drinkers may drink furtively or in secret, will create excuses and seek outlets for their drinking, and will continue to drink, and to become drunk, even when they know they should not. Excessive drinkers need to drink. For them, alcohol is one of the most important, if not the most important, aspects of their lives.

If you drink excessively, and continue to do so, some degree of ill health is inevitable and physical dependence is likely. Do not wait for double vision, with or without hallucination, loss of sensation in the hands and feet, trembling of the hands (*delirium tremens*) or nightmares before you do something. Cut your drink consumption right down. If you find it impossible, seek help right away.

Drinking codes

- Stop when your drinking exceeds the safe unit count.
- If you can, eat when you drink, so that the alcohol is absorbed more slowly into your bloodstream. If you will not be eating, have something to eat or a glass of milk first.
- Avoid unfamiliar drinks and avoid mixing your drinks.

When you drink, alcohol passes through the stomach into the intestine where it is rapidly absorbed into the bloodstream. The rate of absorption is determined by the strength of the drink (diluting slows it down), the amount of food eaten (drinking on an empty stomach more than doubles it) and your body weight (the lighter you are, the more rapid it is).

Once in the bloodstream, alcohol is oxidized (broken down) at a rate of about one centilitre an hour – the equivalent contained in a glass of wine or a single measure of spirits. Oxidization renders alcohol harmless by releasing toxins which are, in turn, potentially damaging to the liver cells. Excessive drinking can lead to liver diseases such as hepatitis and cirrhosis. Women are particularly susceptible.

Water... satisfying, refreshing, 100 per cent natural and absolutely calorie free. Acquire a taste for it – become a water expert. Run through the ranges of bottled mineral waters from the great spas or volcanic regions of Europe or the USA. True connoisseurs can identify waters by their taste, just as wine experts can identify wines by their bouquet...

● Drink slowly and sip rather than gulp. Slake your thirst with water or soft drinks, not with alcohol. Do not keep your drink in your hand, put it down on a nearby table. You will then be drinking when you really want to and not just because it is 'there'.

● Do not drink spirits neat — dilute them. Still 'mixers' are preferable to carbonated ones, as the effervescence can speed up the rate of absorption into the blood. Both red and white table wines can be diluted with water and lose surprisingly little of their taste and colour. Top up white wine with soda water and ice and you have a deliciously cool summertime drink.

● Beware the continually topped-up glass, because you will certainly be drinking more than you think you are. If you are doing the topping up, do not fill glasses before they are empty. Never rush to fill a glass if someone is drinking too fast.

● Develop a positive attitude towards non-drinking, both in yourself and in others, particularly those who have determined not to drink. Never press people to drink more than they want and do not allow yourself to be pressed either. Always provide soft drinks and/or mineral water when entertaining. Recipes for non-alcoholic cocktails are given over the page.

● If you go to a party and you are not drinking alcohol, get a soft drink in your hand as soon as possible. If you are holding a glass, no-one will worry about what is in it. They are much more likely to be concerned about what they are drinking than about what you are not drinking.

IS SOMEONE CLOSE TO YOU DRINKING TOO MUCH OR TAKING DRUGS?

If you think that someone close to you is drinking too much or is taking drugs or is obsessively concerned with not eating (*anorexia nervosa*, see also page 77), you have two options. You can stay silent or speak out. If you elect to do and say nothing, you must recognize that the situation will probably not improve. It will merely drift on. If, on the other hand, you elect to confront the person with your feelings, bear in mind that confrontation does not have to be hostile, antagonistic or tearful. Well-managed, it can be diplomatic, tactful and caring. But before you do anything, examine your own feelings and fears. Ask yourself whether your suspicions are reasonable and how far you are prepared to offer your support. It is also a good idea to get as much information on the subject as you can so that you know what you are dealing with.

Choose your time carefully. Do not bring the subject up after a difficult scene or an argument and never confront an alcoholic when drunk, or a drug user when 'high'. Try, if you can, to lead the discussion round after you have been laughing together or sharing a confidence.

Even when the mood is right, you must expect a brush-off. Whoever you are talking to and whatever the problem, he or she is likely to feel caught out or cornered and to see your concern, however well meant, as an intrusion. But, behind the defensiveness and the denial, they are likely to be feeling unhappy and isolated, racked with fear and guilt and to be suffering a complete lack of self-esteem. So tread very carefully and do not make accusations. Show your concern and offer your support instead: 'I know you have been taking drugs/eating nothing/drinking too much, and that upsets me. Why don't you see the doctor and talk it over? I'm prepared to go with you.' If you are met again by denial, try to think of things that have happened as a result of the problem and mention them — the absences from work, the loss of enthusiasm for old interests, the loss of a licence because of drunken driving, the consistent complaints of feeling unwell. Ask why they have happened and point out that not only do you want to know but that you are confused and want to understand: 'I love you, I'm concerned for you. Please help me to know what is wrong so that I can understand.'

Do not expect miracles the first time you try this approach. Take it carefully and in stages. The first step is to show your concern, your support and your willingness to talk openly and reasonably. The second is to encourage them to talk and to try, if possible, to get them to admit that they are alcohol/ drug dependent or, more simply, that they are unhappy or have been feeling unwell. The third is to give them the confidence that they can get better and to persuade them to seek help. This is important: most help and referral agencies do not accept appointments made on someone else's behalf, rightly recognizing that recovery starts from personal motivation and cannot be achieved by 'proxy'. Finally, do not lose sight of hope. There is cause for optimism, particularly in the early stages of a dependency. No drink or drug problem is untreatable and people who have once been totally dependent frequently recover.

non-alcoholic cocktails

Whole Lemonade

Metric/Imperial/American
3 lemons
3-4 tablespoons clear honey or liquid
   sweetener to taste
900 ml/1 ½ pints/3¾ cups cold water
slices of lemon or lime, to decorate

Cut each of the lemons into eight pieces, removing the pips but leaving the peel. Place in a blender or food processor with the honey (or sweetener) and half the water. Blend thoroughly, then add the rest of the water. Strain and serve, decorating each glass with a slice of lemon or lime. *Serves 4.*

Sunrise

Metric/Imperial/American
4 oranges
2 lemons
300 ml/½ pint/1 ¼ cups soda water
150 ml/¼ pint/⅔ cup Grenadine
crushed ice

Squeeze the oranges and lemons and pour into a jug (pitcher). Add soda water (for special occasion imbibing, you can substitute champagne) and stir in the Grenadine. Place crushed ice in tall glasses and add the cocktail. *Serves 4.*

**From left: Whole Lemonade;
Banana and Hazelnut Flip;
Redcurrant, Orange and
Almond Drink; Sunrise;
Avocado and Cucumber Cup;
Peach, Apple and Ginger Fizz;
Caribbean Cocktail; Clam and
Tomato Cocktail; Chestnut
Flip.**

Iced Mint Tea

Metric/Imperial/American
600 ml/1 pint/2½ cups water
3 sprigs of mint
1 tablespoon honey (optional)
2 teaspoons China tea (or 2 teabags)
mint leaves and lemon slices, to decorate

Place the water in a pan, add the mint and the honey, if using, and bring to the boil. Then pour on to the tea and leave to cool. Pour the infusion into a jug (pitcher) and place in the refrigerator until ice cold. To serve: strain the mixture and serve in tumblers decorated with fresh mint leaves and lemon slices. The colder the cocktail the better it tastes, so make well in advance. *Serves 4.*

Clam and Tomato Cocktail

Metric/Imperial/American
2 medium carrots, scrubbed and chopped
4 sticks celery, scrubbed and chopped
600 ml/1 pint/2½ cups tomato juice
300 ml/½ pint/1 ¼ cups clam juice
good dash of tabasco
2 tablespoons Worcestershire sauce
squeeze of lemon juice
celery salt
generous grinding of black pepper
olives, to garnish

Combine all the ingredients in a blender or food processor, then chill in the refrigerator or add ice, if preferred. Serve in tumblers garnished with an olive on a cocktail stick (toothpick) balanced across the top. *Serves 4.*
Note: Clam juice is available from good delicatessens and most large supermarkets and makes an interesting combination with the tomato. This cocktail makes a particularly good pre-lunch apéritif. But, if you do not like the taste, or have difficulty finding the clam juice, you can leave it out and still have a delicious tomato and vegetable drink.

Peach, Apple and Ginger Fizz

Metric/Imperial/American
2 medium peaches, peeled, stoned
   (seeded) and chopped
1 ½ eating apples, peeled, cored and
   chopped (or 120 ml/4 fl oz/½ cup apple
   juice if a thinner consistency is required)
½ tablespoon chopped stem ginger
600 ml/1 pint/2½ cups chilled ginger ale
crushed ice
apple slices, to decorate

Place the peaches, apples and ginger in a blender or food processor with 2 tablespoons of the ginger ale and blend thoroughly. With the machine still running add the rest of the ginger ale. Pour into tumblers over crushed ice and decorate each glass with a slice of apple. Drink while still frothy. *Serves 4.*

Redcurrant, Orange and Almond Drink

Metric/Imperial/American
300 ml/½ pint/1¼ cups redcurrant 'nectar'
6 tablespoons frozen orange concentrate
juice of ½ lemon
300 ml/½ pint/1¼ cups dry ginger
small teaspoon almond essence (extract)
salt or sugar

Combine all the ingredients in a jug (pitcher) or cocktail shaker and pour into cocktail glasses, having dipped the rims first in water and then in salt or sugar so that they have a fine white dusting around the top. *Serves 4.*
Note: Redcurrant nectar is available from delicatessens and most supermarkets. Alternatively, use redcurrant concentrate diluted and sweetened to taste.

Banana and Hazelnut Flip

Metric/Imperial/American
2 eggs, separated
2 teaspoons honey
600 ml/1 pint/2½ cups milk
2 ripe bananas
40 g/1½ oz/⅓ cup chopped hazelnuts (optional)

Whisk the egg yolks until frothy. Add the honey and, when blended, gradually incorporate the milk. Allow to stand and to chill in the refrigerator for an hour, then blend the mixture with the bananas and the hazelnuts, if using. Whisk the egg whites until stiff and fold into the banana mixture. Pour into chilled tumblers. *Serves 4.*

Chestnut Flip

Ingredients and method as above. Simply substitute 325 g/11 oz can chestnut purée (unsweetened) for the bananas and hazelnuts, pour into cocktail glasses and decorate with grated nutmeg. *Serves 4.*

Avocado and Cucumber Cup

Metric/Imperial/American
2 small avocados, peeled, stoned (seeded) and chopped
juice of 1 lemon
1 teaspoon horseradish
¼ cucumber, chopped
sprig of parsley
3 teaspoons mayonnaise
generous grinding of black pepper
pinch of sea salt
2 ice cubes
250-350 ml/8-12 fl oz/1-1½ cups chicken stock, chilled
cucumber slices and parsley sprigs, to garnish

Combine all the ingredients in a blender or food processor, ice cubes included, and adding chicken stock gradually until the cocktail is the consistency you require. Adjust seasoning, if necessary, pour into chilled tumblers and garnish with cucumber and/or parsley. *Serves 4.*

Caribbean Cocktail

Metric/Imperial/American
1 thick (1 cm/½ inch) slice ripe pineapple or scooped flesh of 2 mangoes
2 ripe bananas
juice of 3 oranges
8 ice cubes
2 tablespoons crème de coconut (optional)
good squeeze of lime juice
crushed ice

Combine all the ingredients, except the crushed ice, in a blender or food processor. Pour into tall glasses over crushed ice. *Serves 4.*

Passionfruit Cooler

Metric/Imperial/American
3 passionfruit or 200 ml/⅓ pint/⅞ cup passionfruit 'nectar'
600 ml/1 pint/2½ cups soda water
good dash of angostura bitters
ice cubes

If using passionfruit, cut them in half and scoop out the flesh. Combine the flesh (or 'nectar') with soda water and a dash of angostura. Mix thoroughly. Serve 'on the rocks' in tall glasses. *Serves 4.*

biological body clock

'I know the melody now — it is the rhythm that escapes me . . .'   **Confucius, 600 BC**

We are aware of time and yet oblivious to it. We are aware of a gradual change in the seasons, of the ceaseless alternation of night and day, of light and dark. We are aware usually to the hour, often to the minute, what o'clock it is. Yet we are strangely unaware of a corresponding rhythmicity within ourselves. We become oblivious to the ebbs and flows of our own inner rhythms, we even tend to live at odds with them.

Bodies observe a set of very precise temporal laws of their own. Vitality, fatigue, mood, irritability, hunger, blood/sugar levels, body temperature, the rate of urination, sensory awareness…all rise and fall according to their own separate cycles over the course of a 24-hour day.

The pages that follow concentrate on this inside story. Understanding and observing how your body works can help to put you back in touch with your natural rhythms. As you get more attuned to them, you will find that you can predict some changes in advance, and, by so doing, protect those times when you are lacking in energy or feeling lower than usual. You will also be able to exploit those stronger moments when your energy and vitality are high. A chart to help you in your introspection can be found on page 27.

Being in tune with your inner rhythms has another advantage: it enables you to distinguish between naturally occurring changes and other unfamiliar changes that may signal anything from early pregnancy to a benign breast cyst. This is self-help because you can then go on to seek professional help and advice at the earliest possible stage.

PUBERTY AND ADOLESCENCE

'There is nothing so wonderful as youth,' enthused *Vogue* in 1938. 'Youth can do anything; it can even apply its paints in round patches wherever it pleases . . . ' In fact, if youth were to do any such thing, it might soon find that its paints were aggravating a far from wonderful tendency to oiliness and spots.

In addition to acting on specific 'target' sites, such as breasts and ovaries, the hormones produced at puberty affect the functioning of a wide range of glands and organs. The eyeball expands slightly in size, the apocrine glands start to function for the first time and the sebaceous glands, previously small and dormant, enlarge as they increase their output. The results are possible long-sightedness, a tendency to perspire more and in a different way, as the neutral smell of childhood changes into the individual one of adulthood, and increased oiliness of body, face and hair. Although acne is a major teenage problem, few teenagers (probably less than two per cent) seek medical help . While severe acne may need treatment with drugs, the milder type can be treated by washing with a medicated soap and using a grease solvent lotion afterwards. Many excellent lotions and creams are now available across the counter. Those containing retinoic acid or benzoyl peroxide are particularly good.

If you have an oily skin, bypass elaborate cover-up strategies. These will only contribute to the problem by clogging the fine pores of the skin with particles of incompletely removed make-up. If you need camouflage, be area specific. Use a special concealer stick applied to the pimple with a fine brush (see page 147). The best contain an astringent or antiseptic to help dry spots out. For more cover, use a matt, medicated foundation and 'set' with powder to prevent breakthrough shine. Attend particularly to the T-zone of the face, where the sebaceous glands are more numerous and oil more abundant. Apply powder across the forehead, central panel of the face and chin, pressing firmly down as you go.

Changes in weight and shape

Of all the changes at puberty, the most noticeable is a change in shape. Breasts develop, contours become softer and rounder as the distribution of fat shifts from waist to hips and the pelvic bones widen. These changes are always preceded and accompanied by a gain in weight. About 5.5 kg (12 lb) is gained in the year before puberty starts and the same amount again in the following two years. This is an integral part of puberty and may be a major trigger mechanism for it. One theory, known as the 'critical' theory of body weight, actually maintains that weight is not only a crucial determinant of the timing of puberty, but also that nearly all girls start puberty at the same weight of 48 kg (106 lb). While surveys have tended to discredit this theory, a more plausible offshoot — namely, that each girl must achieve her own trigger weight — is now widely accepted. Even so, there are two important provisos — the ratio of fat to muscle and bone must be high enough and the psychology must be ripe.

Psychology is probably the greatest determining factor. The mind governs the endocrine system to a considerable extent. It can override all physical cues, working via the higher centres of the brain to inhibit biological responses and delay time signals. This is true at puberty and throughout adult life, when it can postpone periods, suppress fertility and produce physical symptoms, such as stomach ulcers and skin rashes. Its effect should never be underestimated.

The weight factor, too, can continue to be important after puberty. One of the first clinical signs of *anorexia nervosa*, the 'slimmer's disease', is amenorrhoea, or failure to menstruate. Smaller weight losses can also have the same effect, particularly if the weight is lost very quickly. The theory is that by crash dieting, the dieter 'crashes' through the barrier separating childhood from adulthood and so becomes, biologically speaking, a child again. According to some doctors, 'reproductive' anorexia is very common among girls in their teens and early twenties. Any diet that inhibits or disrupts menstruation over more than one cycle is too meagre and should be increased until the hormones controlling menstruation are switched on again and a regular cycle re-established.

Adolescence is a time of psychological as well as physical change. A rapidly changing body brings with it a rapidly changing body image. It is usually not long before the second temporarily overtakes the first. In one experiment at a London teaching hospital, a group of adolescent girls was asked to estimate the size of their waists and thighs. Nine out of 10 judged them to be larger by up to 70 per cent than they really were. While the shape of a stranger standing nearby was judged quite accurately, the shape of a best friend was, interestingly, over-perceived to much the same degree as the subject over-perceived herself. Other independent studies have shown that adolescents commonly see themselves as larger than they really are and that real size and perceived size only finally tend to mesh in the late teens or early twenties.

THE MENSTRUAL CYCLE

While a man's hormonal profile might be visualized as a straight line that starts at birth, is underlined at puberty and then stretches indefinitely onwards, a woman's is characterized by a series of even, regular loops that begin at puberty, run in approximately 28-day cycles, revolve around one key event — ovulation — affect every single cell in her body and can have considerable repercussions on the way she feels and looks.

The word 'menstrual' derives from the Latin *menstruus*, meaning monthly, but, in fact, few cycles run the classical 28-day course. Some may run for as many as 35 days, others for as few as 21. All are normal. There are wide variations, too, in the length of time the period lasts and the amount of blood lost. Some last for just a day or two (they are especially likely to be brief if you are taking the combined contraceptive pill) while others may persist for up to 14 days — actually half the cycle. This condition can be aggravated by the IUD (coil) and, if bleeding is excessively heavy, may even lead to anaemia (see A-Z).

The average woman can expect to menstruate for 30 to 35 years of her life and, in that time, to menstruate between 300 and 500 times for between two and five days at a time. In almost all periods, 90 per cent or more of the menstrual

blood will be lost in the first three days. Although periods may be infrequent and/or irregular in early adolescence while the body is switching to a new hormonal gear, a regular pattern of intervals between each bleeding should soon establish itself. The cyclical nature of the menstrual cycle is caused by fluctuations in the hormones controlling it (see below).

The premenstrual phase

It has been estimated that nine out of 10 women have some clue that a period is on its way. Common signs are poor concentration, a dragging feeling or ache in the abdomen, weight gain, loss of libido and sore, tender breasts. These, together with tension, irritability, tearfulness, bloating and headache, constitute the major symptoms collectively known as the premenstrual syndrome (PMS). These symptoms are suffered in moderate to severe form by about 10 per cent of women.

Ever since the term 'premenstrual tension' was coined in 1931, more and more symptoms, both vague and specific, have been attributed to the fluctuating hormone levels over the three to 10 days before the onset of menstruation. The withdrawal of the ovarian hormone progesterone (see below) is most commonly thought to be the aggravating cause. Before 1931, the tendency was to blame menstruation rather than the few days preceding it. The 1892 *Dictionary of Psychological Medicine*, for example, lists the following 'side-effects' of menstruation: 'Kleptomania, pyromania, dipsomania, suicidal mania, erotomania, nymphomania, delusions, acute mania, delirious insanity, impulsive insanity, morbid jealousy, lying, calumny, illusions, hallucinations and melancholia…'. Apart from melancholia, PMS is unlikely to be the cause of any of these.

Less dramatic but, nonetheless, disruptive physical and psychological symptoms may indicate PMS, if they appear regularly each month over the premenstrual phase. If you think that you suffer from PMS, chart your symptoms, using the symbols suggested on page 27, on the day or days they occur in a special diary. But bear in mind that your symptoms may have no connection with the cycle at all. Research has shown that women encouraged to believe that they are entering the premenstrual phase tend to ascribe unconnected problems to the syndrome. If you do spot a definite cyclical connection, see your doctor and take the diary with you. PMS can be effectively treated both through hormone and vitamin therapy and with diuretics, if bloating is a problem. Find further details in the A-Z. Self-help can also do much to relieve tension. Keep as physically fit as possible throughout the month and protect the few 'bad' days before your period by keeping them as free as possible. Arrange exacting appointments, interviews and tasks for other days when you are likely to be feeling stronger.

Other effects of the premenstrual period may include an increased tendency to oiliness of the skin and hair due to extra hormonal stimulation of the sebaceous glands. If you suffer from spasmodic outbreaks of acne, it may be worth charting the appearance and disappearance of these spots. If there is a cyclical link, try adapting your beauty routines about halfway through the cycle. Use a medicated soap

and/or a fairly strong astringent from about the tenth day after your last period finished and see if you notice an improvement.

The premenstrual phase is not a 'bad' time of the month for all women. One study, analyzing the standard of work in a girls' boarding school and correlating the results with the stages of the cycle, revealed that, while 27 per cent of the girls showed a drop in standard over the premenstrual period, over 50 per cent showed no appreciable change and 17 per cent actually showed an improvement. Such apparent contradictions indicate that different women respond differently to the monthly ebb and flow of key hormones, such as oestrogen and progesterone. The hormone levels do not appear to differ greatly from woman to woman. The threshold of sensitivity is probably the determining factor. This is borne out in clinical practice, where analyses of the blood of patients with very severe PMS often do not reveal anything demonstrably 'different' or 'wrong' with the hormones themselves. Nevertheless, their symptoms will

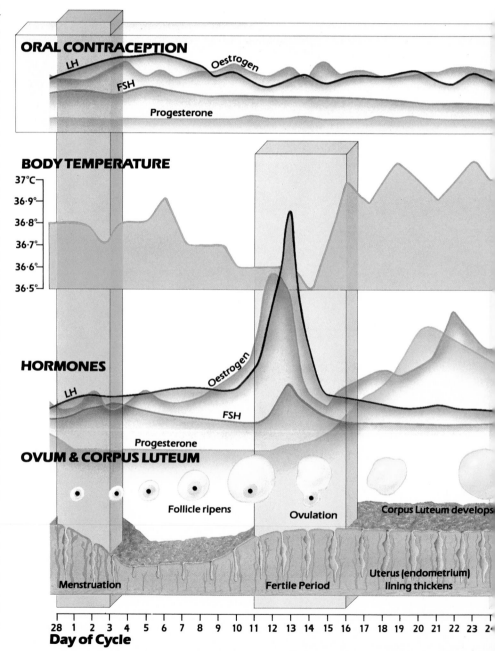

ORAL CONTRACEPTION

LH Oestrogen

FSH

Progesterone

BODY TEMPERATURE

37°C
36·9°
36·8°
36·7°
36·6°
36·5°

HORMONES

LH Oestrogen

FSH

Progesterone

OVUM & CORPUS LUTEUM

Follicle ripens   Ovulation   Corpus Luteum develops

Menstruation   Fertile Period   Uterus (endometrium) lining thickens

28 1 2 3 4 5 6 7 8 9 10 11 12 13 14 15 16 17 18 19 20 21 22 23 24
Day of Cycle

rhythmsrhythms

often improve when these apparently normal hormone levels are adjusted through carefully prescribed therapy.

A mild 'down' at the end of the cycle is not uncommon. Probably as many as 75 per cent of women feel that they are not functioning at their best over this time. But such low points are usually balanced by 'ups' elsewhere in the cycle, often over ovulation. Pinpoint this time for yourself, using the chart in the Personal Profile to help you, and capitalize on it.

Changes at ovulation

As well as its very variable effects on mood, performance and appearance, the menstrual cycle produces two other changes, which can be observed around the time of ovulation at mid-cycle. The first is a change in the appearance and consistency of the cervical mucus, which thins out and becomes stretchier and more elastic as ovulation approaches; the second is a slight dip in resting (basal) body temperature at ovulation, followed by a rise of about half a degree until the end of the cycle and the onset of menstrua-tion. Although the dip in temperature may be so small as to be imperceptible, a temperature that does not rise or that remains absolutely stable throughout the cycle almost certainly indicates that the cycle was anovular.

Occasional anovular cycles are not unusual among normally fertile women. In fact, they tend to become more frequent after the age of about 25, when the ovaries and reproduction system have passed their peak of efficiency. A succession of anovular cycles, however, will indicate one of four things: that you are pregnant or taking the contraceptive pill (both inhibit ovulation by maintaining hormones at a constant level), that you have been through the menopause or that you have an ovulatory disorder.

These two changes offer a natural method of birth control, which can be up to 97 per cent reliable when taught by skilled medical personnel to motivated couples. Equally important, couples who are having difficulty conceiving can time their lovemaking to coincide with ovulation and so maximize the chance of pregnancy occurring.

Nearly every month between the years of puberty and the menopause, the body prepares for a possible pregnancy. The major exceptions: when pregnant already or when taking oral contraception (see left), which flattens out hormonal levels to produce an arhythmic, anovular cycle.

Follicular phase. A number of follicles in the ovaries develop and ripen under the influence of the follicle stimulating hormone (FSH), released by the pituitary gland in the brain. As the cycle progresses, and usually by the eighth day, most of these follicles die or cease to develop. One, occasionally two, continue to develop and the immature egg within to ripen. Throughout this time, oestrogen is being produced by the ovaries. Once it reaches a critical level, it stimulates another pituitary hormone, luteinizing hormone (LH). This triggers the release of the egg.

Ovulation usually occurs between the fifteenth and thirteenth day before the next period begins. The body temperature dips slightly and then rises by about 0.5°C (0.9°F) and cramp-like pains, known as *mittelschmerz* (literally 'middle pain'), may be felt in the lower back and abdomen.

Luteal phase. The egg is transported down the Fallopian tube towards the uterus. Fertilization can take place at any point within the next 24 hours (it is also viable up to three days before ovulation as sperm can survive for up to 72 hours). Progesterone, responsible for preparing the lining of the womb (endometrium) for the implantation of the fertilized egg is produced by the ruptured follicle (corpus luteum). It surges with oestrogen about eight days after ovulation. If fertilization occurs, they continue to rise and effectively to maintain the pregnancy. If fertilization does not occur, they subside and the endometrium disintegrates and is shed.

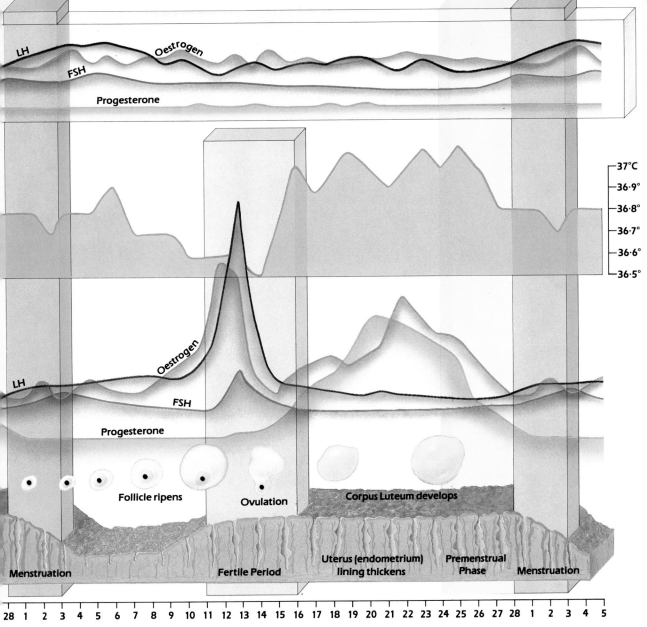

LH
Oestrogen
FSH
Progesterone

37°C
36·9°
36·8°
36·7°
36·6°
36·5°

LH
Oestrogen
FSH
Progesterone

Follicle ripens
Ovulation
Corpus Luteum develops

Menstruation
Fertile Period
Uterus (endometrium) lining thickens
Premenstrual Phase
Menstruation

28 1 2 3 4 5 6 7 8 9 10 11 12 13 14 15 16 17 18 19 20 21 22 23 24 25 26 27 28 1 2 3 4 5

sexuality

'i like my body when it is with your body. It is so quite new a thing. Muscles better and nerves more...'

e.e.cummings

Sexuality is enormously complex and individual. Much more than just an outward aspect presented to the world or an inward one preserved for your private life, it is an intrinsic part of your personality, reflected in the way you respond to other people and the way you feel about yourself. There is no such thing as 'good' or 'bad' in sex. Good sex is what is good for you — and for your partner.

Sexuality fluctuates according to mood, season, circumstance, even to the time of the day or month. Although sexuality is more than 'just sex', sex is its ultimate expression. Early sexual encounters are often fraught with anxiety, but ironically, the two principal anxieties, appearance and performance, have little to do with sexuality. Novelty, on the other hand, does. It is a powerful aphrodisiac and a powerful awakener of a usually hidden, more vulnerable self. Most people, men and women, remove their defences with their clothes.

Where anxiety can make you vulnerable or tense, relaxed, happy sex can make you feel and look marvellous. That vibrant and visible aura of wellbeing may have much to do with the fact that sex is the best 'de-stresser' of all, combining vigorous physical exercise with straightforward mental release. As feeling takes over from thought and instinct from conscious decision, tensions, frustrations and anxieties are dispelled. This can happen as much during the lingering pleasure of foreplay as in the final rush of feeling at orgasm.

Sexuality is individual. There is no one prescription for 'successful' loving. All things to all people, sex can be casual or committed, abandoned or inhibited, gentle or intense, pleasurable or painful, exciting, disappointing, all eventful, even boring. Times when sex tends to be not so good include when you are insecure about what one of you is feeling, when you are tired, preoccupied or anxious about how reliable your contraceptive method is and at some more specific phases of life, such as after birth, when the pelvic floor muscles are stretched and need tightening (see contracting exercises on page 205) and at the menopause, when falling levels of oestrogen produce a thinning of skin tissue and dryness in the vagina that may make penetration difficult. Hormone replacement therapy (see page 213) can often help to counteract this problem.

Sex can and should be a happy, relaxed and enjoyable experience whether you 'come' separately, simultaneously or not at all. In fact, for most people the emotional intimacy and the sharing aspects of sex are held to be just as fulfilling as orgasm alone, if not more so. Even so, failure to reach orgasm blights many otherwise happy relationships and is the most common reason for women seeking help from sex therapists. Anxiety not only tends to forestall the event itself but also interferes with the considerable pleasure that might have been derived without it.

In addition, old attitudes die hard. The comprehensive surveys carried out in the USA strongly suggest that, for all the new liberation, many women are still reluctant to assert themselves sexually or to indicate what they want in bed. If there is an absence of communication and encouragement, sex usually proceeds at the pace determined by the male. In such cases, it is hardly surprising that orgasm is elusive: men can be aroused and ready for intercourse in seconds, while women usually take much longer to become aroused and will take an estimated 10 to 20 minutes of intromission (penetration) before they reach the point of orgasm.

The time factor is the most critical difference between the sexes. In fact, it is now widely held that, in almost every other respect, there is less dissimilarity between the sexes than there is individual variation among members of the same sex. Sexual preferences, it seems, have more to do with personality than they do with gender. Physiologically, men and women share the same erogenous zones and, with the exception of ejaculation, go through identical stages of arousal and orgasm. There also seems to be a definite correlation between length of arousal and intensity of orgasm, particularly if the orgasm is delayed with repeated stimulation up to points of near climax, followed by a drift back to that state of limbo-like suspension that sexologists call the 'plateau' phase. Such a leisurely preamble not only makes for a more rewarding and intense orgasm for both sexes but is, for many women, the only way to achieve one.

Many women find that they first climax on their own, when they can explore their own responses to touch without the pressure of having to perform for, worry about or hurry for someone else. Masturbation can be helpful, because it enables you to concentrate on what you like, to discover what pleases you and to show your partner — either silently through touch or through words and sounds.

Communication is very important. Your mutual pleasure is, after all, your mutual responsibility and intuition is only a small part of lovemaking. If you find that you cannot express what you like or dislike, or what you are feeling or not feeling, you should begin to examine your relationship in more depth.

The relationship is critically important. A stale relationship, which has exchanged love for habit, will diminish pleasure in sex (even if, as sometimes happens, it is the only pleasure which remains), as will most casual encounters. The pleasure that is derived from complete physical and emotional intimacy, on the other hand, can be one of the richest and most rewarding areas of human experience.

Choosing a contraceptive method is not always easy. All the methods currently available have their drawbacks as well as their advantages.
This chart should enable you to weigh up the drawbacks against the advantages and to choose a reliable method that will work for you. Factors to consider: your age, your relationship, your degree of motivation, your medical history, your personal attitudes and religious beliefs. The chart does not include details of the following:
1. The use of spermicidal creams, foams and pessaries on their own.
2. The 'rhythm' or 'calendar' method, which calculates 'safe' and 'unsafe' times for intercourse on the risky assumption that ovulation always happens in the middle of the menstrual cycle ('natural' contraception, see chart, is quite different).
3. *Coitus interruptus* (withdrawal), which is both frustrating and unreliable because some sperm are almost always released in the seminal fluid prior to ejaculation.
No family planning clinic would endorse any of these methods and, for this reason, they are not given here.

CONTRACEPTION: the alternatives

METHOD	DESCRIPTION	DRAWBACKS	COMMENTS
Combined oestrogen/progesterone contraceptive pill (Effectiveness with conscientious use: 99.7%)	Method used by about 70 per cent of women at some time in their lives, and, at present, by 50 million women throughout the world. There are at least 20 different types. The smallest dose oestrogens are 'triphasic', that is, tailored to specific stages of the cycle. Usual dose of 35 mcg oestrogen may be increased to 50 mcg in the event of breakthrough bleeding. The pill works by altering hormonal behaviour, so that there is no 'true' menstrual cycle and the body is 'fooled' into thinking itself pregnant. It has four specific actions: 1. It prevents ovulation. 2. It reduces the 'motility' (muscular movement) of the Fallopian tube so that, if ovulation were to occur, the egg could not pass from the ovary to the uterus. 3. It prevents the thinning of the cervical mucus so that it remains sperm-resistant. 4. It inhibits the build-up of the lining of the uterus.	In susceptible women, oestrogen may cause excessive blood clotting, which can lead to thrombosis, stroke or heart attack. Risk is now only thought to be appreciable in women over 35, especially if combined with other risk factors – smoking, overweight, high blood pressure. Liver tumours, gall bladder disease and cervical ulcers have also been implicated with the combined pill, as is an increased susceptibility to thrush and, rarely, difficulties in conception on ceasing to take it (about two per cent). Mild to moderate side-effects may include headache, depression, weight gain, nausea, chloasma (melasma), and raised blood pressure. You are unsuitable for the combined pill if: 1. Two or more of the risk factors described above apply to you. 2. You have had a thrombosis. 3. You have a hormone-dependent cancer. 4. You have a serious liver disease. 5. You suspect you may be pregnant. 6. You are breastfeeding. 7. You are about to undergo surgery. All surgery carries increased risk of thrombosis.	The most reliable and convenient of all contraceptive methods bar sterilization. However, bouts of diarrhoea or sickness may mean that the hormones are not in the bloodstream long enough to guarantee contraceptive effect. Consult a doctor, and, if in any doubt, use additional means of contraception for 14 days. The same applies if more than 36 hours elapse between taking pills. Future possibilities: 1. The use of surgical implants for continuous, slow release of oestrogen and other hormones to give protective and reversible cover for up to five years. 2. The development of a vaginal 'ring', which would have a similar action (already available in progestogen-only form). 3. Immunization against pregnancy, using a protein or hormone produced during pregnancy, to guarantee reversible immunity for up to five years. 4. Nasal contraceptive sprays to inhibit the release of hormones initiating ovulation. 5. A male pill has already been developed in China but has significant drawbacks and toxic side effects.
Progesterone only contraceptive pill, also known as POP or the 'mini' pill (Effectiveness with conscientious use: 98%)	This pill is taken daily throughout the cycle, even when menstruating, and must be taken at the same time each day. It has three actions: 1. To prevent thinning of cervical mucus so that it does not become sperm receptive. 2. To render the lining of the uterus inhospitable to the egg, should fertilization occur. 3. To prevent ovulation in about 40 per cent of cycles.	Not as effective as the combined pill. Higher incidence of breakthrough bleeding and irregular menstrual cycles. May provoke migraine in susceptible women. You must be conscientious about taking it, and if more than three hours have elapsed since your last pill was due, you must take additional contraceptive precautions.	The main advantage is the considerable lowering (some even maintain elimination) of the risk of blood clotting and subsequent thrombosis in high-risk women. It is, therefore, an extremely useful alternative to the combined pill in women over 35, especially if other risk factors are already present (see above). POP is also sometimes prescribed for women experiencing side-effects on the combined pill.
Progesterone injections (Effectiveness with conscientious use: 98%)	Single dose progesterone gives contraceptive protection for three months. It works in the same way as the progesterone-only pill (see above).	Outlawed as a means of long-term contraception (more than three months) in the UK and the USA, after it was found to cause breast tumours in beagles, but still widely used in the rest of the world. Also linked with primary (temporary) infertility after long term use.	Useful means of contraception for the highly forgetful and for partners of men who have had vasectomies, as the operation takes three months to become effective (see opposite).
Inter uterine device (IUD) or 'coil' (Effectiveness with conscientious use: 98.3%)	Copper-and-plastic or plastic-only devices, fitted into the uterus with a loose thread so that you can check it is still in place. Any foreign body in the uterus seems to inhibit conception. Copper devices release minute traces of the metal into the system and have simultaneous effects on the sperm, the cervical mucus and the lining of the uterus. They are more effective than the plastic-only devices.	The presence and pressure of the IUD in the uterus can cause pain and heavy, prolonged periods together with an increased risk of anaemia, due to excessive loss of iron in the blood. Occasional expulsion. If a pregnancy does occur, there is an increased risk of miscarriage (25 per cent) and of ectopic pregnancy (five per cent). The IUD is not suitable if you have an acute pelvic infection or undiagnosed vaginal bleeding. It may be inadvisable if you have a history of pelvic infection.	More suitable for older women and/or women who have had a pregnancy, both because they are less likely to have menstrual difficulties and because they are less susceptible to pelvic infection. For maximum contraceptive effectiveness, the copper devices should be replaced every two years. Provided there are no complications, the plastic ones may be left in indefinitely. IUDs are also sometimes fitted as a means of post-coital contraception (see opposite).

cautioncautioncaution

METHOD	DESCRIPTION	DRAWBACKS	COMMENTS

Diaphragm or 'cap'
 	
(Effectiveness with conscientious use: 98%)
	Vulcanized rubber membrane with flexible rim fits over the cervix to block access of sperm to uterus. It should be used in conjunction with spermicidal creams or pessaries and left in place for six hours after intercourse. An increasingly popular method of contraception, partly because of the degree of control it offers a woman over her own body and partly because of the side-effects and bad publicity connected with the pill.	Requires a certain amount of premeditation before intercourse and a lot of motivation. Some women also find the creams and pessaries messy and unpleasant and this may inhibit their sex lives. Not an ideal method if you are a forgetful, easy-going, risk-taking type of person or if you are very sexually active.
		    May aggravate recurrent cystitis.
			The size of diaphragm depends largely on the amount of intra-pelvic fat, so always have it refitted after losing or gaining more than 4.5 kg (10 lb) in weight or after a pregnancy. Fill it with water or hold it up to the light regularly to check for holes or defects in the rubber.
			    Imminent advances: a sponge diaphragm, pre-treated with a spermicidal agent, and a 'made-to-measure' extended wear cervical cap with a one-way valve to allow for the downward flow of menstruation while preventing the upward one of sperm.

Condom (Effectiveness with conscientious use: 97%)	Vulcanized rubber sheath that slips over the penis. Still the most common method of contraception. According to one survey it is used by 25 per cent of all married couples in the UK.	Loss of sensitivity during intercourse for the male. High risk of pregnancy, if used irresponsibly or if the sheath slips off or breaks during intercourse.	Invented by men for men, not as a precaution against pregnancy but as a protection against venereal disease. The sheath still confers a higher degree of protection against this than any other method.

'Natural' contraception
 	
(Effectiveness with conscientious use: 85%)
	A highly scientific method (not the riskier rhythm or 'calendar' method or *coitus interruptus*). It works by:
	1. Assessing the consistency of the cervical mucus, which thins out just before ovulation.
	2. Taking and charting your basal (resting) temperature over the menstrual cycle.
		A complicated and time-consuming method, at least initially, that requires a high degree of motivation. Until you become more practised, sex is often accompanied by anxiety that you have failed to identify signs of ovulation correctly. Anyone interested in the method should receive specialized instruction at a 'natural' family planning clinic.
		    Other disadvantages:
		1. The temperature method cannot predict ovulation in advance.
		2. The period of abstinence over the unsafe time may place strains on the relationship.
			As new and more accurate ways of identifying the fertile period are developed, this method is likely to become increasingly popular. It is particularly suitable if personal, health or religious reasons make other types of contraception unacceptable.
			    One advance is the 'intelligent' thermometer which records body temperature and assesses chances of ovulation. Future possibilities include:
			1. Home urine or saliva sampling kit to assess fluctuating hormone ratios.
			2. A 'bionic' bra to register dip in temperature at ovulation.

Sterilization
 	
(Effectiveness: approaching 100%)
	The ultimate answer to fertility control.
	    Male sterilization (vasectomy) involves minor surgery to cut or tie the *vas deferens*. Fertile sperm may be left circulating for up to three months so contraceptives must be used for some time after. Female sterilization uses one of two methods.
	1. Diathermy or excision to destroy all or part of the Fallopian tubes.
	2. Blockage of the tubes, either by tying or by means of clips or rings.
		Any of the risks of normal surgery applies here, plus an increased risk of pelvic infection.	Advances in microsurgical techniques for female sterilization mean less damage to body tissue in order to ensure complete sterilization. The failure rate (just a fraction of a per cent) is also substantially lessened.
			    When in doubt – DON'T. The numbers of both men and women seeking reversal of sterilization are increasing.
			    NEVER combine abortion with sterilization. These two momentous and possibly traumatic decisions should always be made independently.

Post-coital or 'morning after' contraception
 	
(Effectiveness: to be assessed)
	Methods of counteracting the possibility of pregnancy, once intercourse has taken place, include taking relatively high doses of oestrogen within 36 and preferably 12 hours of intercourse and having an IUD fitted. Both methods work in an interceptive capacity to prevent implantation of the fertilized egg in the uterus.	Both methods are still relatively new and therefore not widely available.
		    Oestrogens may produce nausea.
		    Some gynaecologists would not recommend fitting an IUD as the chances of infection may be too risky under certain circumstances. Chance of IUD producing an ectopic pregnancy in the event of fertilization has yet to be assessed.
			The timing, dosage and right type of oestrogen are essential, so seek the assistance of a doctor or family planning clinic.
			    The IUD works within 60 hours of intercourse and therefore makes a better 'late' choice than the course of oestrogens. It can also be left in place, offering long-term method of birth control once the crisis is over, in which case drawbacks will apply as above.

pregnancy

'Irrefutable, beautifully smug...the women/ Settle in their belling dresses.
Over each weighty stomach a face/ Floats calm as a moon or a cloud...
They listen for the millennium,/ The knock of the small, new heart.'

Sylvia Plath

PREPARING FOR PREGNANCY

The healthier and fitter you are before you conceive, the better your chances of having an uncomplicated pregnancy and a healthy baby. If you are sleeping well, taking regular exercise and eating in a balanced way, you will be more able to meet the considerable demands of the growing foetus. Many doctors believe that the present system of antenatal care, which usually begins in the twelfth week of pregnancy, starts much too late. By this time all the critical stages of development are well under way. The foetal heart, for example, has started to beat by the eighth week. The mother-to-be, meanwhile, may not even know she is pregnant.

● To ensure that your baby has the best possible start in life, become as fit as you can before you attempt to conceive. Allow yourself a minimum of three months. Take at least 20 minutes exercise every day and revise your diet, if necessary. Make sure that you are getting plenty of fresh food and include 600ml/1 pint (2½ cups) of milk, three slices of wholemeal bread and plenty of fresh vegetables a day. Balance your intake of protein and fats against carbohydrates. Recent studies on morning sickness and diet prior to conception suggest that a high protein diet may predispose towards sickness in pregnancy, while a well-balanced diet with adequate carbohydrate may protect.

● Make sure that you are at a healthy weight. Being underweight is probably a greater hazard to your own health and to that of your baby than being slightly overweight. If you are very overweight, however, the pregnancy may be complicated by a tendency to higher blood pressure, fatigue and even diabetes. Pregnancy is not a time for strict dieting. Erratic and compulsive eating patterns are also unwise, so straighten yours out well in advance.

● Avoid taking any unnecessary drugs both before and after conception, when you might find some of the 'alternative' homeopathic remedies for minor disorders worth exploring. Although you should avoid all unprescribed drugs during the first 56 days of pregnancy, there is no need to become drug phobic. If you are unwell, consult your doctor and let him or her know that you are pregnant. If untreated, some illnesses present a much greater health risk than the properly prescribed medication.

Unnecessary drugs also include smoking and drinking large quantities of alcohol, coffee or tea and excessive use of common drugs, such as aspirin and even laxatives. 'Hard' drugs, such as cocaine and LSD, are very dangerous and their harmful effects on the developing foetus are well-established. 'Soft' drugs are also inadvisable. Marijuana, for example, is now thought to depress the activity of the sperm, so possibly reducing the chances of conceiving easily.

● Of all the common 'environmental' hazards, cigarette smoking is undoubtedly the most dangerous. Smoking reduces the blood supply to the placenta, so interfering with the nutrition of the baby, passes on toxic chemicals contained in the tobacco smoke and reduces the amount of oxygen available. This may produce an acute rise in the baby's heart rate. Rises of as much as 30 per cent have been recorded during cigarette smoking and are considered a definite sign of foetal distress. The consequences of smoking during pregnancy include lower birthweights, higher rates of miscarriage, stillbirth and foetal death, lowered resistance to infection, particularly respiratory infection, during the first years of life, and even retarded physical growth and mental development. The rate of foetal death alone rises by 35 per cent in women who smoke 20 or more cigarettes a day. If you do smoke, make a concerted effort to give up before you plan to become pregnant. If you find this impossible, cut down to five cigarettes a day or less.

● While heavy drinking during pregnancy is almost certain to affect the foetus, there is now thought to be a link between moderate drinking and minor defects, particularly those affecting heart, face and limbs. Either abstain entirely or limit your drinking to an absolute maximum of two drinks a day. Restrict your intake of caffeine similarly. Make three or four cups of tea or coffee a day your upper limit.

Much of the evidence of the effects of taking these and some other drugs is circumstantial, but it is significant that many women develop an aversion to tea, coffee, alcohol and cigarette smoke well before they discover that they are pregnant. Such aversions are probably regulated by powerful biological factors working to protect the foetus from potentially harmful influences and are well worth heeding.

● Two diseases, rubella (German measles) and venereal disease, can affect your developing baby. Ask your doctor for a blood test to check whether you are immune to the rubella virus well before you plan to conceive. If you are not, you can be immunized against it, but you must continue with contraception for three months afterwards, as you will still be susceptible to the virus. Sexually transmitted diseases, such as gonorrhoea and syphilis, may also affect your baby. If you or your partner have or suspect an infection, go to your doctor or to a clinic for a check-up. If one of you is infected it is essential that you are both treated and that you continue to use contraception until you receive confirmation that the infection has completely cleared.

Finally, in cases where one or both potential parents has a family history of genetic disorder, pre-pregnancy genetic counselling clinics and chromosome screening facilities are available, so that some assessment can be made of the chances of having a healthy baby.

posturesposturespostures

Keeping fit is important during pregnancy, when a good regular exercise programme combined with a gentle sport, such as swimming, can do much to help prepare you for the birth by keeping muscles strong and joints flexible. Posture is critically important, too, and can make all the difference between nine months of joyful burgeoning and nine months of aches and pains that seem to increase in direct proportion with your size.

The exercises given here are not intended to comprise a 'keep fit' routine. They are simple postures designed to help ease specific problems, such as lower back pain or cramp, together with some of the more general aches and pains

that you may become aware of as your pregnancy progresses. You may also find these postures helpful for the early stages of labour.

Modified versions of some of these postures, the squatting position in particular, are sometimes used for the delivery of the baby during natural childbirth. Whichever way you decide to have your baby, however, the most important thing is to feel comfortable and relaxed. Recent research strongly suggests that fear and anxiety can block the production of key hormones, such as oxytocin, that help labour to progress, and can also inhibit the production of endorphins (see page 128), the body's own natural painkillers.

4 **5** **6**

Sitting, though apparently comfortable, can be a major contributor to backache. Take the strain off your back by sitting cross-legged, tailor fashion (1).

Sleeping can also be a problem in later pregnancy. Lie on your side, keeping the knee raised on a pillow (2). This will give the abdomen more space, take the pressure off the uterus and enable the blood to circulate more freely round the pelvis.

Squatting is one of the most comfortable and restful positions, once you get used to it. Practise from your early pregnancy, supporting your heels and bottom with a folded towel if you need to (3). An adaptation of this, in which the mother is supported beneath her upper arms and elbows, is the most widely practised of all the upright postures during childbirth, because it greatly increases pressure in the pelvic area with the least possible muscular effort. The body's weight is taken by the knees and the ankles and by the person supporting. (These aspects are reversed if the mother lies on her back, as in

the conventional manner, with the uterus tipped backwards against the pull of gravity.)

Cramp in the legs is a common problem in later pregnancy when congestion in the pelvis prevents the blood circulating freely in the legs. Counteract it by holding a towel or scarf around the balls of the feet and pulling the toes upwards to stretch out the muscles at the back of the calf (4).

To overcome tension and stiffness and to help relieve backache, take up starting position (5) and arch the back (6). Then straighten it, but do not allow it to hollow. Repeat several times.

Rocking and circling movements of the pelvis, commonly seen preceding birth among primitive peoples, have been shown to help the baby down the difficult passage from the uterus into the birth canal. Even if you are not planning to incorporate rocking and circling movements in your birth programme, you will find them useful for restoring blood circulation and easing any

dragging pains in the abdomen and lower back. The pelvis can be rotated through 360°, using the belly-dancing movement (7), or rocked gently from side to side (8). Start on hands and knees and look round to either side, bringing each hip towards you as you turn to look at it.

8

PREGNANCY NOTES
First to third month

Although your antenatal care programme should ideally start from well before conception, some women find it hard to revise their lifestyles until they are pregnant. If you have not done so already, give up smoking, drink only in strict moderation, avoid all unprescribed drugs and rebalance your diet along the guidelines already given, as much for your own sake as for the baby's. During pregnancy, a priority system operates to ensure that the foetus has all the nutrients it needs, even if it means depriving the mother. If your diet is unbalanced or too meagre, you will almost certainly be undernourishing yourself, even if the baby has all the nutrition he needs.

Your doctor may advise you to take mineral and vitamin supplements. In addition to folic acid, now thought to play a vital part in protecting against spina bifida and other birth defects, other vitamins and minerals, such as vitamin D and iron, may also be prescribed. Iron may be necessary, but your doctor must determine this. The mineral is no longer routinely given in early pregnancy because too much can interfere with the absorption of other essential minerals, such as zinc. Vegans and vegetarians may well require additional vitamin and mineral supplements.

Enrol at a local antenatal class, make sure that you feel happy and relaxed with your doctor or obstetrician (you have a year's close contact ahead and it is essential that you should be able to ask any question without feelings of unease or embarrassment) and arrange to see your dentist. Important at any time, good dental care is essential now, when you are more susceptible to gingivitis and other gum infections.

During the first 12 weeks your need for rest is greatest, you are most likely to be feeling nauseous (see below) and you are most likely to miscarry. Miscarriages put an early end to one in 10 pregnancies, are most common in the tenth and eleventh weeks and are usually caused by abnormalities in the foetus. While very distressing, first time miscarriages are very unlikely to affect the outcome of subsequent pregnancies. Even women who miscarry twice or more have an 80 per cent chance of delivering a healthy, full-term baby the next time.

Nausea, with or without actual sickness, affects 70 per cent of all pregnant women. Although it is often called 'morning sickness', less that 10 per cent find that their symptoms are restricted to the early part of the day. It occurs most often on an empty stomach and is usually most severe at around the ninth to tenth week of pregnancy, when the hormone human chorionic gonadotrophin (HCG), now thought to be a contributing factor, is at its peak. Try overcoming nausea with small, bland meals at frequent intervals, a piece of dry toast, a cracker or biscuit on wakening, and 'sharp' fruit drinks such as grapefruit and lemon. If sickness persists or is severe, consult your doctor.

Pregnancy is traditionally a time of clear skin and shining hair, but the first three months can be quite the reverse. A sudden surge in hormones can produce a rush of activity in the sebaceous glands and increased oiliness on the face and hair is fairly common. Counteract oiliness on the face with a good astringent, acne with creams not drugs and oiliness on the hair by washing it frequently with a mild shampoo.

If your nipples are inverted, special nipple shields, which fit into the bra and evert the nipples, can make breastfeeding possible. It takes some time for these to work, so buy them in early pregnancy and wear them daily.

Fourth to sixth month

This is usually a time of great physical and emotional wellbeing. Any early tiredness, nausea and depression should have subsided and you will probably be feeling on top of the world. The foetus is now growing fast. In the fourth month alone, it will double in size. You, too, will be growing fast over the course of the pregnancy, you will probably gain about 11 kg (25 lb) in weight, sometimes more. This essential weight goes into nourishing the baby, building up the placenta and the amniotic fluid, enlarging the breast tissue, increasing the blood supply and creating reserves of fat and protein for late pregnancy and the post-natal period.

As you get larger, adapt your beauty routines. Your hair and skin should be looking marvellous now, so capitalize on this by wearing new hairstyles, rethinking your make-up and dressing up necklines with jewellery and other accessories. Calling attention to your top half will draw it away from your stomach.

As your weight increases, so does the strain on your abdomen. The increased blood flow to the pelvis and congestion caused by the enlarged uterus may lead to haemorrhoids (piles) and varicose veins. Protect against them by practising the rocking and circling exercise on the previous page and by following the guidelines on page 221.

As your skin stretches, tiny tears or stretch marks may occur beneath the surface. They happen in the deeper layer of the dermis, so massage creams and oils will not prevent them, though foods high in zinc and vitamin C (seafood and fresh fruit and vegetables) might. Find further details in the A-Z. If your skin feels dry, use a good, oil-based lotion to keep it supple. Get accustomed to handling your body and breasts in preparation for birth and breastfeeding. At about five months, you will notice a discharge coming from the nipples, which may cause them to become sore and cracked. Bathe them daily to remove the discharge and apply a lanolin-based cream to keep them soft and supple and to prepare them for breastfeeding. As the breasts enlarge, keep them well supported with a comfortable, well-fitting bra, to prevent any stretching of the supporting ligaments.

Between 16 and 20 weeks, you will become aware of the baby moving (quickening) inside you. At 20 weeks, the foetal heartbeat becomes audible and, by the end of this period, the foetus is 30cm (12 inches) long, weighs just over 225g (8oz), has well-formed lungs, identifiable fingerprints, an expressive face, will respond to touch and may suck its thumb.

Seventh to ninth month

By the seventh or eighth month, you may be carrying 6kg (14lb) or more of extra weight and, by the ninth month, your blood volume will be one and half times that of your

carecarecarecare

non-pregnant state. All this may lead you to feel very tired and breathless, to lose your balance and to feel dizzy. Take things slowly, ask for help getting into or out of the bath, get plenty of rest, continue with your exercises and practise your breathing techniques, so that you remain relaxed and calm. Try to avoid even moderate drinking. Recent studies have shown that mothers who drink alcohol during the last three months of pregnancy tend to give birth to restless babies who sleep less and cry more.

The final three months are a time of growth, consolidation and perfection of detail. The foetal respiratory and digestive systems become fully developed, the eyes open and the foetus becomes more acrobatic. Vigorous punches and kicks will be felt clearly and a limb, foot or elbow can often be identified. This is also the time when essential immunities to infections are passed on to your baby through the antibodies in your bloodstream.

AFTER THE BIRTH
Getting back into shape

As with pregnancy, getting back into shape after the birth will take nine months. If you are young, extremely fit, naturally lithe and slender with a supple, elastic skin tone, you might just manage it in six. But you should not rush your post-natal programme, nor should you expect too much of yourself at this extremely demanding and challenging time.

Start gentle exercises a few days after the birth with some of the stretching and limbering routines in the Shape chapter (blue leotard), graduating to the stronger exercises as you get fitter. You do not need a special set of post-natal exercises — with one exception. This concerns the internal muscles of your pelvic 'floor'. These stretch with the birth and, if allowed to remain stretched, can seriously reduce sexual enjoyment and may lead to leaking on coughing, laughing or energetic exercise, if not to actual incontinence. The pelvic floor muscles should be strong enough for you to leap vigorously up and down, while opening and closing your legs and coughing with each stride, with no leaking at all. To exercise these muscles, think of yourself 'gripping' during intercourse or stopping an imaginary flow of urine, squeeze, hold for a few moments and let down gently. Repeat this exercise whenever possible. It will pay enormous dividends.

Changes in shape and breastfeeding

All the weight gained during pregnancy does not instantly fall off after the birth. People lose weight at different rates. Many women do not return to their normal weights until they stop breastfeeding.

All breasts change shape after pregnancy, tending to lose some of their roundness at the top. This is caused by the weight-gain and change in shape during pregnancy and has nothing to do with whether you choose to breastfeed. Breastfeeding will not make your breasts droop or sag any more than they would have done naturally, as long as you wear a well-fitting nursing bra.

When breastfeeding you need plenty of carbohydrate in order to manufacture the milk, so do not let any cravings you thought you had left behind depress you. While you should

not be censorious with yourself over your eating patterns, you should remain as conscientious about your general health as you were when pregnant. Consult your doctor about vitamin supplements, do not smoke, do not take any unprescribed drugs and drink only in moderation as harmful substances can be passed on in the breast milk.

Hair care

While your hormone levels are readapting to your non-pregnant state, you may notice that your skin and hair lose condition. This is aggravated by fatigue, so try to get as much rest as you can and, if possible, some help with the baby.

During pregnancy, the hair growth phase is extended by a surge of several hormones. An increased rate of hair fall is both natural and extremely common around 12 weeks after the birth, when you start to shed the hair that would normally have fallen out during the previous nine months. It may continue to fall out for two months or more, but it will grow back. You can do much to help it regain its stability and strength by looking after your general health and by taking wheatgerm or brewer's yeast — both natural sources of the B vitamins which are important to the condition of the hair.

The first few weeks with a new baby: this uniquely rewarding and challenging time can also be extremely exhausting. Preserve your energies by taking life slowly and giving yourself a full nine months to get back into shape after the birth.

INFERTILITY

When you consider the intricate process by which a fertilized egg, no more than 0.13 mm (0.005 inch) in diameter, and considerably smaller than the size of a full-stop on this page, grows and develops into a new human being, it is surprising not that some of us have difficulties in conceiving and bearing a child, but that it ever happens at all. Even so, for one in every 10 couples, regular unprotected sex for over a year will not result in conception. While nothing is more agonizing to a couple attempting to conceive than the dawning anxiety that one of them may be infertile, the fear of a childless future is often unfounded. The treatment of infertility is one of the most optimistic areas in medicine and is now coming to the rescue of six out of every 10 couples referred to infertility clinics for further investigation.

If you have been trying to conceive for two or more years or you are older and the pressure of time is upon you, make an appointment with your doctor. In a surprisingly high number of cases, a preliminary interview with both of you will be enough to bring on conception. It may be that a return to normal, non-anxious lovemaking works the magic. But the connection between consultation and conception, about 20 per cent, is too high to be coincidental. During the interview, your doctor may suggest that you try some simple, self-help methods to increase your chances of conception.

If these methods fail or the necessary premeditation for carrying them out is placing strains on the relationship, further investigation should be embarked upon right away. It is important that both partners should be tested for possible infertility. First, the incidence divides fairly equally between men and women at 40 and 50 per cent respectively (in 10 per cent of cases, no clear reason for infertility is found). Second, tests for male infertility (sperm count and clinical examination) are considerably simpler and less extensive.

Ovulatory disorders

Ovulatory disorders are the most common cause of female infertility and, therefore, tend to be investigated first. Such disorders may be the result of inadequate hormonal stimulation or, less often, an imbalance caused by raised prolactin levels (this can be treated by a course of tablets). Or they may simply reflect a temporary difficulty in conceiving. This is particularly possible in the late twenties or thirties, as frequency of ovulation declines past the age of 25. A blood test or endometrial biopsy (scraping taken from the lining of the uterus) taken in the second half of the cycle will establish whether or not ovulation has occurred by testing for levels of the ovarian hormone, progesterone. This is the key hormone because it is secreted by the ruptured follicle once ovulation has taken place (see page 194).

In the event of ovarian malfunction, the ovaries can often be stimulated with a weak anti-oestrogen, chlomiphene citrate. This raises the level of naturally occurring ovarian stimulating hormones in the pituitary gland to induce ovulation in about 80 per cent of women. There is a six per cent risk of multiple birth, almost always twins and very occasionally triplets. If this fails, the stronger gonadotrophin hormones (LH and FSH) may be prescribed. As these act directly on the ovaries, excessive stimulation gives a higher (20 per cent) chance of multiple pregnancy. Although usually twins, these drugs are responsible for the dramatic incidences of quintuplets and sextuplets and careful assessment of the level of stimulation required is therefore essential.

Damaged Fallopian tubes

The second most common cause of female infertility, damaged Fallopian tubes, unfortunately, cannot usually be as easily or as successfully treated as ovulatory disorders. The Fallopian tubes are most commonly damaged by venereal infection, but other factors can be an ectopic pregnancy, in which part or all of the Fallopian tube is removed with the growing embryo, any type of pelvic surgery and even a ruptured appendix. Sometimes, microsurgical techniques are used in order to free blocked or scarred tissue that might be interfering with the passage of the egg from the ovaries to the uterus. This, however, sounds much simpler than it is. The Fallopian tubes are so delicate that surgery can sometimes aggravate, rather than mend, the damage.

In the future, correction of this type of infertility probably lies with the newly-developed methods of 'in vitro' (test tube) fertilization. The egg is taken from the ovary, either during natural or stimulated ovulation, fertilized by the sperm outside the body and then re-implanted in the uterus. But it is still a young science and several difficulties must be overcome before it becomes more widely available.

health care

'Nothing in life is to be feared. It is only to be understood ...' Marie Curie

Self-help methods can increase the possibility of conception by enabling you to time your lovemaking to coincide as closely as possible with ovulation. Most women ovulate on or around the fourteenth day before the beginning of their next menstrual period. Charting the length of three or more cycles should give an average. Observable signs of ovulation include a thinning of the cervical mucus one or two days beforehand, a slight (not always apparent) dip in basal body temperature as ovulation happens, followed by a rise of about 0.5°C which is then sustained for the rest of the cycle. Use a clearly marked clinical thermometer to take your temperature every morning as soon as you wake up. A rise in temperature indicates that you have ovulated, provided that you feel well and and are not succumbing to an illness or infection, and should make love within the next 24, or preferably the next 12, hours.

Knowing how your body works will stand you in good stead. Being aware of what can occur, being awake to the danger signs and having a baseline knowledge of what is and is not normal for you, means you are substantially reducing the risks, not of illness or infection occurring, but of allowing it to develop to a stage when it may, indeed, be ominous. This is your first line of defence and your most important one. It means taking the responsibility for your own good health, looking upon your body intelligently, not being frightened to find out about it and having the common sense to consult your doctor, should you find — or feel you might have found — anything potentially abnormal.

BREASTS

How women feel about their breasts largely determines how they feel about themselves as women. Because of this, breast cancer and with it the thought of losing a breast, generates more fear among women than almost any other single disease. This fear keeps the average British or American woman at home for five or six months before she consults her doctor about a lump she has found in her breast.

Not every lump, however, has to be a cancer. In fact, very few are. Even so, breast cancer is the most common form of cancer among women and afflicts one in every 17 women at some time in their lives. For this reason, it is essential to be especially vigilant — and vigilance begins at home.

Although there is a tendency to talk of breast cancer as a single disease, there are many different types. Some are very slow-growing and may not spread beyond the breast for 10 to 15 years. Others spread much more rapidly. The 'doubling' time for breast tumours (in other words, the time it takes one abnormal cell to become two and two to become four) can be as little as two months or as much as nine years. Whatever the type of cancer, the chances of successful treatment increase dramatically with early detection.

Early detection depends, first and foremost, on regular, monthly self-examinations (see page 210). The more practised you get at examining and feeling your breasts and the better acquainted you are with the natural differences and irregularities between them, the greater your chance of spotting a significant change at the earliest possible opportunity. Early detection depends, secondly, on medical screening procedures. There are two basic methods for screening the breasts, clinical examination and mammography. With advances in technology it is possible that a third — ultrasound — may provide a major breakthrough.

While it is undesirable that any screening method should carry a risk, however slight, of aggravating the condition it is supposed to be protecting against, mammography (soft tissue X-ray) is undoubtedly the earliest way of reliably detecting a breast lump before it has become large enough to be felt, by either doctor or patient. A breast lump usually only becomes 'palpable' (able to be felt) at about 2 cm (¾ inch) in size. The mammogram can detect a lump at ½ cm (⅕ inch), sometimes less, and will pick up between a quarter and a third of all breast cancers before they become large enough to be felt. As long as minimal dose radiation is used, the risks carried by the screening process are virtually negligible when set against the considerable advantages of early detection. The findings of a recent US study on the comparative risk-to-benefit ratio of mammography are illuminating. Clinical records and various established factors enabled scientists to compute that if one million women were to be screened annually for 10 years, radiation-induced breast cancers would be induced in seven — in the meantime, 138,000 early cancers would have been detected.

Breast cancer: the risk factors

Although isolating specific risk factors is difficult with any disease, the following are now regarded as being the major ones for breast cancer and the ones at the top of the list are considered to carry the highest risk. They do not suggest that you are likely to get breast cancer, accounting as they do for at least half the female population. But they do suggest that you should be especially vigilant.

● If you have already had cancer in one breast or have any other type of hormone-dependent cancer, such as cancer of the cervix, uterus or ovaries.

● If you have a close relative who has had breast cancer, particularly if the cancer occurred at an early age (35 or younger) and was bilateral (in both breasts).

● If you have never been pregnant or, particularly, if you had your first full-term pregnancy over the age of 35. While childbearing in your teens and early-to-mid twenties seems to have a definite protective effect, breastfeeding does not appear to have a significant one.

● If you are over 35. Breast cancer is extremely rare in women below this age group, when a lump in the breast is most likely to be a benign tumour or cyst (see A-Z).

● If your periods started early (at 12 or younger) and finished late (at 50 or over).

● If you have had benign breast disease. Some breast lumps, though 'benign', occasionally show signs of abnormal, pre-cancerous growth.

● If you have undergone prolonged hormone replacement therapy, after hysterectomy or over the menopause, you may be at a slightly increased risk. The progesterone component of both the combined hormone replacement therapy and the combined contraceptive pill seems to confer a protective effect against benign breast disease.

CERVICAL AND PELVIC SCREENING

Cancer of the cervix, or neck of the uterus, accounts for five per cent of all cancer deaths in women and a quarter of all such deaths in women under the age of 50. It shouldn't do. The most common type of cervical cancer, cancer *in situ*, can be detected before it actually becomes a cancer by carrying out a simple smear ('Pap') test. This involves scraping cells from the surface of the cervix with a wooden or plastic spatula and sending them to a laboratory for culture. Detected at this early stage, abnormal pre-cancerous cells can be eradicated by using cold, heat or, more recently, laser treatment. The advantages of the laser are that it works at the speed of light, can be focused with breathtaking accuracy, requires no anaesthetic and involves a simple 10-minute out-patient procedure. As the disease progresses, however so the methods of treating it become increasingly more radical. Early detection, then, is vital and it is to every woman's advantage to seek smear tests at regular intervals (see calendar, below). For, although they do not constitute an absolute guarantee against developing the cancer, they will considerably reduce your chances of doing so. Of all the British women who died of cervical cancer between 1973 and 1978, nine out of 10 had never had a smear test.

Cancer of the cervix has several clearly established risk factors. By far the largest is sexual intercourse. As sexual activity moves you immediately from a no-risk to a high-risk

Screening is controversial. Some doctors consider it very helpful, potentially life-saving and too little practised, while others consider it a potential disservice because it may either engender unnecessary alarm or a false sense of security, even complacency, by encouraging people to hand the responsibility for their health over to their doctors. Your family history and your lifestyle – your diet, your smoking and drinking habits, and how much exercise you take – may be more important in determining good health than are regular check-ups, but infections and diseases can strike the healthiest individual. Happily, some of these can now be caught early enough to increase the prospects of successful treatment quite considerably. This more than justifies screening for them. The thinking on health checks has changed over the last decade or so. No longer is the annual 'physical' the preventative prescription. Most important is to have specific tests for 'high-risk' parts – breasts, cervix, heart– as age, sex and family history indicate. Use this chart to see at a glance which health checks you should be having when.

HEALTH CALENDAR: the whys and whens of screening

WHAT?	WHEN?	WHY?
Complete physical check-up	Healthy people who carry no special risk, such as a family history of heart disease, do not necessarily need an annual check-up. A more realistic schedule would be every two years from the age of 35 to the age of 50; once every year after that.	To establish that you are fit and in good health with no obvious or incipient signs of illness, that your lifestyle is healthy and that you have no risk factors, such as high blood pressure, that can be precursors of ill health.
Breast self-examination	Every month just after your period has finished; on the first day of each calendar month, if you have been through the menopause.	To check for any changes in the breasts (see following page) that should be referred to your doctor for further investigation. Of the 100,000 new breast cancers per year in the USA, 90 per cent are detected by women themselves.
Mammography (minimal dose radiation) and/or clinical breast examination	Mammography once at the age of 35; a single view can be done annually thereafter. If you fall into one of the 'higher' risk categories, detailed on the previous page, your doctor may suggest that you have mammograms taken earlier and/or more frequently. If a female relative (mother or sister) has had breast cancer, you should start mammography screening at an age earlier than that at which the relative's cancer was detected. Clinical examinations should be carried out annually.	To give the doctor a 'baseline' reading of the normal architecture of the breast, if it is the first mammogram, against which subsequent X-rays can be referred to detect any changes; to pick up the 'high risk' breast – certain tissue patterns being linked with a higher incidence of cancer; to provide reassurance that all is well in the breast; to clarify the nature of a lump that has been found (i.e. whether it is cystic and benign or potentially cancerous) and thus occasionally avoid the need for surgical investigation (biopsy). A clinical examination entails having the breasts checked manually by medically trained personnel. This can be especially helpful for women who feel apprehensive about examining their breasts or who would like instruction on how to examine them.
Cervical smear (Papanicolaou ['Pap'] test)	Soon after the time of first intercourse and again one year later; thereafter at three-yearly intervals up to age 35 and at five-yearly intervals up to age 60. If all results have been negative, testing can be discontinued. You should have an annual smear test if you have had the herpes virus.	To detect the presence of abnormal cells on the cervix which may be pre-malignant (i.e. indicative of future cancer) and which, once found, can almost always be completely eradicated. The first smear should be followed by another one year later, to guard against the possibility of a 'false negative' result. As it takes an average of 10 years for localized (*in situ*) cancer of the cervix to spread, a three-yearly check-up thereafter should give time to detect any changes.
Blood pressure reading	Every three years up to age 35 and annually thereafter; annually, whatever your age, if you smoke, are very overweight or have diabetes; when you are pregnant; whenever your prescription for the contraceptive pill is renewed. If you already have diagnosed high blood pressure and are taking pills for it, you should have your blood pressure checked each time the prescription is renewed as the same dose of pills may not be required.	To check for high blood pressure (hypertension) which can be completely symptomless. It is important that you get your blood pressure checked regularly over the age of 35 (pressure tends to rise with age) because it is a recognized risk factor in heart disease (pumping against the high pressure places additional demands on the heart). A good average pressure is considered to be 120/80. Slightly lower than average pressure is hardly ever a problem – in fact it can be a health plus. High blood pressure during pregnancy may indicate that the pregnancy and birth will need careful monitoring. It is important to have blood pressure checked both when starting oral contraception and when renewing prescriptions, because it can rise while taking it and might make a change in birth control necessary.

screenscreenscreen

category, a smear test should always be carried out at the age when sexual intercourse is first begun, particularly if still in your teens. A young cervix is many times more susceptible to the cancer than an older one. If you have had the herpes virus (see page 216), a smear test should be carried out annually, as this is now thought to increase the risk of developing abnormal cells on the cervix.

When you have your smear test, you should also have a bi-manual pelvic examination to check for cysts, fibroids (benign growths) and early signs of pelvic inflammatory disease, though this is not always identifiable by examination. Pelvic inflammatory disease is caused by an infection that either originates or migrates beyond the cervix. The cervix protects both the uterus and the more susceptible Fallopian tubes beyond it. Any situation in which the cervix has recently been opened, such as after having had an IUD fitted, after a birth, abortion or miscarriage or after having a D and C (dilatation and curettage), can increase the risk of developing a pelvic infection. Early symptoms of pelvic inflammatory disease are tenderness, pain during intercourse, irregular or very heavy periods, bleeding abnormally between periods (a small amount of 'breakthrough' bleeding is quite common at mid-cycle; a heavier flow is not), or any bleeding six months or so after the menopause. These symptoms may or may not be accompanied by a discharge, but you should always be medically investigated.

WHAT?	WHEN?	WHY?
Chest X-ray	Chest X-rays are usually no longer included in the routine series of health checks and are not generally recommended.	Chest X-rays are now not even recommended for heavy smokers because they cannot pick up a cancer early enough to reduce mortality rates, though they can be useful for picking up infections, such as asymptomatic TB.
Lung function test	Not at all, unless you get breathless walking up two or three flights of stairs, in which case tests may be indicated.	To see how much air you can shift through your lungs by blowing into a breathalyzer-type bag, known as a spirometer; a poor result may indicate emphysema or bronchitis.
Electrocardiogram (ECG) and blood/cholesterol reading	At age 35 in men; 40 for women. As recommended – usually annually for men and less often for women, for whom the sex hormones before the menopause seem to confer an inbuilt resistance to coronary heart disease. Your blood/cholesterol levels should be screened more frequently if you have passed the menopause, smoke heavily, take the contraceptive pill or are substantially overweight, as these factors counteract the protective effect.	The ECG is considered of limited value for healthy people, but nevertheless important for getting a baseline pattern against which any subsequent deviations can be spotted. Because the ECG measures the heart's electrical activity, certain abnormalities, such as flutters, will show up. As men are especially at risk of heart disease, an ECG should be taken at regular intervals after age 35. Of potentially greater value, however, is the blood/cholesterol test. Raised blood/cholesterol levels are a recognized risk factor in coronary heart disease. By enabling preventative action to be taken (the diet adjusted, for example), a blood/cholesterol test could prove life-saving.
Dental check-up and/or visit to dental hygienist	Your teeth and gums should be checked every six months and at the beginning of pregnancy, unless your dentist specifies otherwise. You should see a dental hygienist to have your teeth scaled and professionally cleaned and polished once a year (more often if living in a hard water area).	To check for early signs of tooth decay and/or gum disease. The visit to the hygienist is important because tartar (an accumulation of plaque) calcifies and hardens on the tooth and can initiate gum disease by irritating the gum. Once calcified, tartar cannot be removed by brushing. Tartar tends to build up faster in hard water areas due to deposits of mineral salts in the water and may need removing at six-monthly rather than yearly intervals.
Sight testing	At nursery school age (four or five); thereafter as indicated by ophthalmologist or if and when problems present themselves. Most people will require a sight test at between the age of 40 and 50 when focusing at close range starts to diminish due to natural deterioration of crystalline lens inside the eye. This sight test can be combined with an investigation for early signs of cataract. Diabetics should have regular check-ups for the eyes.	To check for long- or short-sightedness; to fit reading glasses to counteract the natural tendency to long-sightedness that increases with age; to look for early signs of cataract on the eye.
Glaucoma testing for eyes	Between the ages of 40 and 50; earlier if there is a family history of glaucoma.	To check for evidence of glaucoma, a sight disorder caused by a build-up of pressure in the eye. Glaucoma leads to 'tunnel vision' through a gradual loss of peripheral vision. It is important that the eyes are checked even if the sight seems perfectly all right, because glaucoma can be absolutely painless and symptom-free in its early stages.

BREAST SELF-EXAMINATION

Examine your breasts once a month just after your period has finished. Breasts undergo glandular changes through the menstrual cycle and many people find that their breasts are naturally lumpy and tender just before menstruation. If you have been through the menopause, you should examine your breasts on the first day of each calendar month.

Most breasts are naturally asymmetrical — the shape may be uneven, the nipples may point in different directions or one breast may be significantly higher or lower or larger or smaller than the other. Study your breasts to see whether any of these apply. The key to successful, unanxious breast examination is change, so you must be aware of what is normal for you.

What to watch out for

● <u>A lump in the breast.</u> Only a very small proportion, probably less than 10 per cent, of all lumps are cancerous, but it is impossible to tell by feeling whether a lump is innocent or not. Only a doctor can decide whether or not this is the case. In order to do so, it may be necessary to remove the lump surgically (biopsy) and to subject it to various tests. This does not necessarily indicate anything ominous. Between 60 and 80 per cent of all lumps examined in this way turn out to be harmless. Even so, you should always see your doctor if you find, or suspect that you have found, a lump in your breast.

● <u>Any moles that have changed in size, shape or colour.</u>

● <u>Dimpling or puckering of the skin, an unusual prominence in the blood veins on either breast, or a retraction (drawing in) of the skin tissue.</u> Any of these may indicate the presence of a lump pressing on the ligaments inside the breast, thus affecting its contour and appearance. Again, only a doctor can decide whether or not this is the case.

● <u>Inverted nipples.</u> Some women have naturally inverted nipples or, more rarely, one nipple may always have been inverted while the other one is not. If your nipples have always been this way, you have no cause for concern. Any situation, however, in which the nipple has recently become inverted requires further investigation.

● <u>A discharge coming from one or both nipples.</u> Check for this by looking inside your bra before carrying out your monthly breast self-examination. Although a discharge is not uncommon when taking or (particularly) when coming off the contraceptive pill, just prior to menstruation, or after breastfeeding, when a small secretion may persist for some months, it should never be ignored, particularly if it is persistent, coming from one nipple only or is bloodstained. This may indicate the presence of a small wart, which, if left untreated, may lead to cancer. So consult your doctor and, in the meantime, do not squeeze or interfere with the nipples in any way. Consult your doctor, too, if you have an ulcer or sore on the nipple that does not heal.

● <u>Enlarged or inflamed lymph glands.</u> The lymph glands surrounding the breast lie on the outer sides and run up towards the armpit. They are essential for regulating the body's fluid balance and for fighting off infection. Although they may enlarge quite naturally if you have an infection or before menstruation, you should see a doctor if the inflammation has not subsided after three weeks.

checkcheckcheck

● <u>Start with a visual inspection (1)</u>. Stand in front of a large mirror with a good light placed to the side, not overhead. Now look at your breasts. If this is the first time you have carried out a breast examination, take the opportunity to note exactly how they look.

● <u>To help check the differences between the two breasts, place the hands on top of the head (2)</u> and turn slowly to the left and the right. The crossways angle of the lighting should help you to spot any irregularities or dimpling in the skin surface.

● <u>Place your hands on your hips and press firmly down and inwards (3).</u> This should tighten the pectoral muscle and, thus, help you to spot any dimpling. Then, keeping your hands where they are, lean forwards from the hips, so that the breasts fall straight downwards, and inspect them head-on. Look particularly for any tautness in the skin tissue, any change in the way the nipple is pointing, and for a nipple that becomes inverted on leaning over but everts itself naturally as you stand up again.

● <u>Lie down on a firm surface and place a folded towel or pillow beneath the shoulder of the side you examine first (4).</u> This is especially important if your breasts are large, as the breast will then sit evenly on the chest wall. Feel each breast in turn with the opposite hand and, to begin with, keep your arm by your side. Feel with the flat surface of your middle three fingers, keeping them straight, but not

tense, and the wrist flexible. The amount of pressure you exert should be firm enough for the skin surface to move with your fingers (they should <u>not</u> just glide over it) but not so firm that the natural texture becomes hard and lumpy if you press too hard. Press the breast tissue gently but firmly towards the chest wall, starting just above the nipple and tracing concentric circles radiating outwards in a spiral the whole way round the breast. Be particularly on the look-out for any fixed, hard lump that will not move away easily when you press the breast tissue between your fingers. Make sure that you feel every part of the breast, beneath as well as above.

● <u>Finally place your arm above your head so that the outer side of the breast is stretched and accessible (5).</u> Repeat the examination, as above, and pay particular attention to the upper part, or tail, of the breast which extends up into the armpit.

211

ageing

'It's not catastrophes, murders, deaths, diseases, that age and kill us; it's the way people look and laugh and run up the steps of omnibuses...'
Virginia Woolf

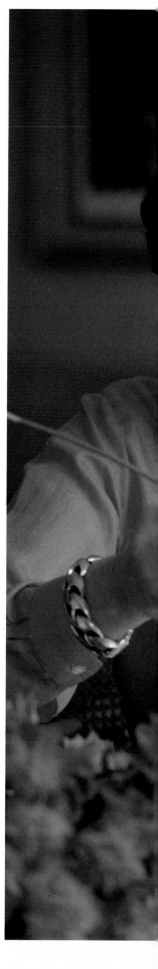

THEORIES AND THERAPIES

Ageing is an unalterable, unavoidable, inevitable fact. The degenerative process starts in the brain, spreads throughout the body, infiltrating every cell and producing all the familiar physical and mental signs of age — hair greys, skin wrinkles, eyes lose their focusing ability and other senses become feeble, joints become creaky, memory falters.

From the beginning of time, man has sought to explain this dismal process. Modern theories, often no less colourful or bizarre than those postulated by the ancients, range from a 'death' hormone, released by the brain at the time of adolescence with the awesome power of slowly starving body cells of oxygen, to an insidious invasion of bacteria in congested faecal matter in the gut — a sort of toxic constipation. Another theory, maintaining that ageing is equivalent to rusting to death and is caused by an accumulation of oxidants in the blood, made vitamin E, well-known for its anti-oxidant effect on the blood, a youth tonic overnight.

What we do know is that ageing is principally, though not wholly, a matter of wear and tear. The straightforward business of living is registered at cellular level, where it affects the process of division and renewal. The damage is cumulative. Small defects, imperceptible at first, become increasingly noticeable as the years pass by.

Genetic evidence that body cells have a finite capacity for reproduction supports this theory. Instead of dividing indefinitely, cells can only divide a fixed number of times. RNA therapy uses injections containing nucleic acids in order (theoretically) to prolong the life expectancy of these cells. But its value, if any, is far from clear. The same applies to other types of cellular or glandular extract and the numerous multi-vitamin packages currently on the market. Science may one day provide us with a means of significantly prolonging youth, but it is unlikely to happen in our lifetime.

The secret of eternal youth may elude us, but we still 'make do' with anti-wrinkle creams, cosmetic surgery, hair dyes, vitamins, youth tonics and elixirs. In our 'Keep Young' culture, we age fearfully not gracefully, associating age with inevitable physical decay and mental slowdown. We ignore the example set by great artists, actresses, designers, writers and politicians, such as Monet, Mattisse, Celia Johnson, Chanel and Churchill, whose vigour and creativity carried well into their seventies and eighties has shown abundantly that this need not be the case. Ageing is an attitude. Helena Rubinstein, convinced that you are, literally, as young as you feel, maintained that the secret was to stay committed, involved and right in the mainstream of life. 'Work,' she wrote in her nineties, 'has indeed been my beauty treatment. I believe in hard work. It keeps the wrinkles out of the mind and the spirit....'

Beauty points for 40 plus – skin, hair, make-up, health

Taking responsibility for your own health is your first priority if you want to preserve your looks from the advancing years. Start with regular exercise, concentrating particularly on the loosening and stretching exercises (blue leotard) in the Shape chapter in order to keep joints mobile. Continue with plenty of fresh air and sleep, a balanced diet, a conscientious skincare regime and regular health checks.

● Rethink your skincare programme and make-up techniques every five years from about the age of 40.

A skin that has become drier and looks flaky in patches needs a mild exfoliant once a week and a richer (greasier) moisturizer at night. The throat and neck tend to age particularly rapidly, so always start moisturizing from the collar bone up and take a preventative line with the neck strengthener exercise on page 42. Increased facial hair, due to declining levels of oestrogen, is an age-related problem. Treat it temporarily by bleaching or permanently by electrolysis.

● Cosmetics can subtract years from the look of the face but, unless applied very carefully, they are more likely to add them. Layers of foundation and face powder can be very ageing because they tend to settle into the creases of the skin, bringing out every line. So use a lighter hand when making up. Apply a thin layer of moisturizing foundation with a slightly damp sponge and cover with a translucent dusting of powder. Keep to the barest minimum around the eyes, where wrinkles are all too easily emphasized. Once past the age of 60 and provided that your skin tone and texture are generally good, use foundation only on the cheeks if red veins are a problem; powder not at all.

Bearing in mind that complexion tones change as you grow older, make sure that foundation, blusher, eye and lip shades are still appropriate. Choose a foundation that is as close to your natural colour as possible and keep blusher, lip, nail and eye colours neutral and soft. Outlaw black mascaras and eyeliners, frosted colour shadows and bright dramatic colours. All of these tend to be more ageing than effective.

● Although you lose colour most perceptibly in your hair, you also lose it in your skin. This mutual mellowing of complexion and hair colour is due to a gradual loss of the pigment in the cells of the hair and the skin. Striving to recapture your old 'natural' colour when your hair starts to go grey can produce an unhappy, jarring contrast between skin and hair tones. Capitalize, instead, on the new tones and have the lightest strands brightened a shade or two for a head of soft, natural highlights. If your own natural colour is very dark, lighten the base a shade or two for a softer effect. You can go on in this way until you are as much as 80 per cent grey. After this, you may want to consider tinting your hair.

THE MENOPAUSE

For many women, the menopause signifies the dividing line between youth and age. This feeling is reinforced by the many myths surrounding the menopause — feeling terrible, hating sex, becoming old, tired, wrinkled and depressed. These are not physical symptoms produced by hormonal changes, but psychological symptoms produced by society's attitude towards middle-aged women.

Medically, this phase of life is known as the climacteric; the menopause refers only to the last menstrual period. For most women, this occurs between the ages of 48 and 53. After this, the ovaries cease to produce a monthly egg and the levels of the hormones, oestrogen and progesterone, gradually fall. About three-quarters of women experience some symptoms while this is happening. These include a tightness and loss of lubrication in the vagina, which can make sex uncomfortable, and hot flushes (flashes in the USA). These are sudden sensations of heat, which usually originate in the chest and spread rapidly upwards, raising surface body temperature by as much as 4°C (7°F). Other effects may include thinning hair, increased facial hair, dry, flaky skin and an increased tendency to loss of bone mass and to a disease known as osteoparosis, in which the bones become thin and brittle and more prone to fractures. All women once through the menopause should take fish liver oil capsules (vitamins A and D) together with extra calcium to help keep bones strong and healthy. This is particularly important during the winter, when there is little sunlight (a major source of vitamin D).

In as many as 70 per cent of women, the tangible symptoms of the climacteric are not severe. If you do feel discomforted by hot flushes or by dryness in the vagina, consult your doctor. Responsibly prescribed hormone replacement therapy (HRT) is an effective way of treating menopausal symptoms. Natural oestrogens are taken with synthetic progesterone (progestogen) to produce a monthly bleed. HRT is most often prescribed for between 24 and 36 months, although in some cases it might be taken for longer. It should always be stopped gradually as abrupt withdrawal can exacerbate the symptoms.

The uterine cancer 'scare' of the mid-1970s has now been largely overcome by the inclusion of progesterone. In addition, the oestrogen component of HRT is now thought to confer a protective effect against coronary heart disease, a greater cause of death among women after the age of 55 than cancer of the uterus. Research figures published by the American Heart Foundation in March 1982 showed that of a sample of 2269 women between the ages of 40 and 69, the death rate for women not taking the oestrogen was nearly one per cent a year compared with three-tenths of one per cent for the oestrogen users. The current thinking is that the risks of HRT are more than justified by the positive advantages where the need is indicated. One of the most positive advantages is the fact that women on the therapy conserve their bone mass, do not lose height and do not develop osteoparosis. Research increasingly suggests that, by helping to keep women agile and active into their 70s and 80s, HRT may be our closest step yet to stalling the ageing process.

a-z of common disorders

'None of us are perfect. I myself am peculiarly susceptible to draughts...'
Oscar Wilde

This alphabetical guide is intended to give you a basic understanding of the way in which your body functions and, occasionally, malfunctions. It is also designed to help you to relieve some of the more common aches and pains by giving simple and practical notes on self help. It is not, however, intended to replace your doctor. No amount of medical 'knowledge' gleaned from reading books can replace the deep understanding that a qualified doctor gains from years of training and experience. So use this guide for interest and for reference and, if in any doubt, consult your doctor.

Acne

In the normal course of events, sebum, made in the sebaceous glands deep down in the skin, travels up the hair follicle to emerge through a fine pore on the surface. There, it emulsifies with sweat to fulfil its vital double role of lubricating and protecting the skin. However, if the sebum hardens and becomes trapped just beneath the surface of the skin, or if the dead epidermal cells stick together and clog the opening of the pore, a small pimple or blackhead will appear. If the blockage occurs deeper down, inflammation and primary bacterial infection combine to produce a much larger and angrier spot. Both are acne.

The more severe inflammatory types of acne are thought to be caused by the male hormone, androgen, circulating in the bloodstream and causing the sebaceous glands to secrete grease. Nothing is demonstrably 'wrong' in a hormonal sense: some people are simply more sensitive to the hormone than others. This sensitivity will depend on familial inheritance and skin type.

Although diet has no direct causal link with acne, an imbalanced diet can certainly aggravate it. So, too, can stress, over-zealous self 'treatment' and squeezing. The first rule is to leave your skin alone. (If you are an habitual picker or squeezer, cut the fingernails short and watch your skin improve.) Wash your skin twice daily with an antiseptic or medicated soap, use topical creams and lotions sparingly and remember that there is absolutely no virtue in fanaticism. Dirt and oil on top of the skin have nothing to do with any but the smallest of pimples—it is the oil trapped beneath that is to blame.

If you have persistent or severe acne, or are distressed about the condition, see your doctor. Acne can be treated — often extremely effectively — with a course of antibiotics, prescribed over a period of months or even years. It works by counteracting the effects of the problem, not by 'curing' it. It may be as many as three months before a noticeable improvement in the condition of the skin can be seen.

Topical acne treatments range from mild antiseptic lotions (astringents) to stronger, more abrasive chemical solutions that 'strip' off the dead layer of skin cells to unblock the pore and free the sebum. Lotions containing benzoyl peroxide, salicylic acid or retinoic acid (vitamin A) are probably the most effective. However, while they can be valuable in treating superficial non-inflammatory acne, they will not help more severe types and may even aggravate them. In addition, if these lotions are used too often or applied over-enthusiastically, they may produce redness, dryness and excessive irritation. 13-Cis Retinoic acid (at present only available in the USA), taken orally as a course of tablets, works by cutting down sebaceous activity and can be very effective. Its disadvantage, however, is that it tends to dry up the skin. Common side-effects are chapped lips and general flaking and dryness.

In the future, medical treatment of the more severe types of acne may involve regulating the hormone levels responsible for producing the condition, either by prescribing an anti-androgen, usually cyproterone acetate, or additional oestrogen, depending on the patient. While effective in combating and protecting against acne, the drug is at present being combined with an oestrogen for a contraceptive effect. Risk factors on ovulation and pregnancy have still to be assessed.

Allergy

An allergy is an exaggerated reaction to a substance, or group of substances, that is usually tolerated perfectly well. The substance itself may be inhaled (grass pollen, house dust), eaten (eggs, wheat, penicillin) or absorbed on contact with the skin (lanolin, detergents, perfume, metals). The list of these allergens, or allergy-producing substances, is virtually endless. Anyone can be allergic to almost anything.

Confusingly, too, allergies are the result of a number of paradoxes. The first is that you only develop an allergy to a substance after you have been exposed to it. Allergies to insect bites, for example, are much more common after the age of 30 as it takes at least one sting and usually more before a susceptible person becomes allergic to the venom. The second paradox is that allergies are produced by the antibodies that would normally serve to protect the body from disease by recognizing invading germs and viruses as potentially harmful and alerting the body's auto-immune (disease-fighting) mechanism. An allergic reaction occurs when these antibodies identify a completely harmless substance as being potentially harmful and dangerous. This prompts the release of chemicals, such as histamine, that are normally sealed away in the cells of certain body tissues — skin, gut, mucous membranes of the nose, conjunctiva of the eyes and respiratory system. The result is the familiar allergic reaction: running nose, sore streaming eyes, wheezing and asthma, hives (a nettle-like rash on the skin), eczema and itching and swelling. Sometimes the allergic reaction may be so severe as to cause breathing difficulties or even anaphylactic shock during which blood pressure drops suddenly and breathing, heart beat and circulation may weaken and even fail.

If you have a reaction to a substance, known or unknown, and you suspect it may be an allergy, you should see your doctor who may then refer you to an allergy clinic for diagnostic patch testing. This entails placing minute amounts of the substance in question or a number of common allergens on the skin, usually the forearm, and waiting for a local reaction, such as a series of raised bumps, to appear at the site of contact. In most cases (some food allergies are an exception, see pages 75-6), this will enable doctors to determine the cause of the allergy. Treatment will then largely consist in avoiding the offending substance and in treating the reaction symptomatically when or if it recurs. The most notable of all the drugs used for this purpose is antihistamine, which can be applied as cream, inhaled as a spray or taken in tablet form. Although anti-histamines have a reputation for making you drowsy, there are many different types of the drug and, by changing your prescription, it is usually quite possible to find one that works well for you. There is also a new drug which works like an antihistamine but has none of its potential side-effects. One word of warning: if treating yourself for allergy, do not over-medicate. This is especially important if you are using the nasal spray as it can have a rebound effect and serve to exacerbate rather than mitigate your symptoms.

One particularly common type of allergy is hay fever, or 'allergic rhinitis', a condition suffered by 15 million people in the USA and 3 million people in Britain. Hay fever is not caused by hay at all but by the pollens of various trees, grasses and moulds. Although there is no clear pattern to the allergy it tends to appear first between the ages of 12 and 20 — but it can begin after the age of 30 or later. You can also grow out of it, the condition vanishing as mysteriously as it first appeared. Most hay fever is caused by the pollen of common grasses which flower from mid-May to mid-July, reaching their peak in June. As there is a considerable amount of cross-reactivity between the various grasses, hay fever sufferers are likely to show an allergic response to all or most of them. If symptoms start much earlier or later the reaction may be due to a tree pollen (mid-January to April or May) or mould (August to October). Preventative treatments are particularly important in the case of hay fever, as grass pollen, being airborne, permeates the atmosphere — in cities as well as in the country, indoors as well as outside. Various forms of preventative treatment, if taken at the onset of an attack, can block the reaction at source (eyes, nose, throat) but, once it sets in, can take several days to relieve it. There are preparations for the eyes and lungs and a steroid spray to offset sneezing and running noses.

You can also be vaccinated against hay fever. This involves a simple course of injections in which the dose of pollen vaccine is successively stepped up, usually in three stages but sometimes more. This has made it possible to relieve symptoms and desensitize sufferers to a point where the symptoms are either greatly relieved (60 per cent, or, in a small number, cease entirely. Injections should begin in February or March so that desensitization has been completed by the time the first grass pollen is in the air. These do have a cumulative effect and it is therefore quite possible to find, after two or three years of treatment, that your hay fever is indeed a thing of the past.

Amenorrhoea
(absence of menstruation)

Between the ages of 15 and 45, the most common cause of amenorrhoea is pregnancy. Pregnancy should always be suspected if a period has been missed for more than a fortnight and sexual intercourse has taken place at any point over the preceding cycle, regardless of whether or not contraceptives were used. Stress, anxiety, changes or disruptions in your day-to-day life (such as going on holiday), crash dieting, and coming off the contraceptive pill are other common inhibitors of ovulation and may well disrupt your cycle. If you are in your 40s or early 50s, absent or irregular periods may indicate that you are approaching, or have passed through, the menopause (see page 213). If you are over the age of 16 and have never had a period or have not had a period for three months or more, you should see your doctor. Tests may be necessary in order to determine the cause.

Anaemia

Iron-deficiency (dietary) anaemia is by far the most common type and women are much more susceptible to the condition than men. In fact, in one recent study, 10 per cent of all women between the ages of 15 and 44 were said to be on the threshold of this condition, due to excessive blood (and iron) loss during menstruation. A loss of iron in the blood produces a whole range of non-specific symptoms — tiredness, breathlessness, giddiness, pallor, weakness in the limbs and, often, an overwhelming lethargy — because it depletes the amount of haemoglobin, the oxygen-carrying pigment in red blood corpuscles. Haemoglobin is responsible for nourishing and regenerating every cell in the body and for producing the characteristic 'redness' of the blood. Many cases of anaemia present two important diagnostic clues. These are nails that are 'spoon'-shaped and curl up or downwards and a lack of colour either beneath the nail or in the normally richly supplied conjunctival tissue inside the lower eyelid. Although iron-deficiency anaemia is often caused by menstrual blood loss (one of the drawbacks of the IUD is a heightened risk of anaemia in some women due to an excessively heavy menstrual flow), but it may also be caused by other types of external or internal bleeding, such as a silent and slow-bleeding peptic ulcer.

If you suspect you have anaemia, or are feeling excessively tired, you should see your doctor. You should not dose yourself with iron supplements because, if you do have the condition, commercial iron-bolstered multivitamin pills will not contain enough iron to rectify the balance. If you do not have the condition, too much iron can be as bad for you as too little as it interferes with the absorption of other essential minerals, principally zinc. For this reason, iron supplements are no longer automatically given as a routine part of ante-natal practice during pregnancy. If you want to safeguard yourself against iron-deficiency anaemia, incorporate a dark green leafy vegetable, such as broccoli, into your diet together with a helping of liver, kidney or heart each week. Eating a vitamin-C rich fruit or vegetable with your meals will also help as this vitamin has been shown to aid iron absorption in the body (see page 72).

A second, rarer, type of anaemia is known as pernicious anaemia and is caused by a deficiency of vitamin B12 or, more commonly, an inability to absorb it from the diet. As B12 is found only in foods of animal origin (meat, fish, milk, etc), strict vegetarians, or vegans, should always take additional B12. Supplements are now available in synthetic vegetable form. An inability to absorb the vitamin is hereditary and seems to occur most often in middle-age, particularly among those who are blue-eyed and white or fair-haired. Once diagnosed, the condition can be remedied by giving regular doses of the vitamin through injection directly into the bloodstream.

Athlete's foot

This infection is by no means exclusive to athletes and is caused by a fungus. Although most commonly seen on the feet, the same infection can also occur in the groin, mouth or armpits — any corner of the body that makes a moist, dark and attractive breeding ground for bacteria. The most common site of athlete's foot is in between the toes. You can protect against it by washing and drying the feet and toes thoroughly, although not rubbing harshly. If you get the infection, treat it with strong salt footbaths, apply surgical spirit twice daily to dry out the skin and one of the many anti-fungal powders available. Do not use ordinary powders as these will tend to clog. If the infection is very painful and the skin cracked and sore, anti-fungal antibiotics can be prescribed to make healing more rapid.

Back trouble

'Back trouble' is a blanket term that covers everything from the smallest twinge along the spinal column or crick in the neck to the more serious disorders of the spine and central nervous system. Four out of five people will have at least one severe attack at some time in their lives. Many will be fortunate enough to recover in a few days or weeks, but a growing number — and some experts now maintain that it is 10 per cent of the population — live in chronic pain from which they can find little or no relief.

By far the most common cause of back trouble is lumbago. This is a chronic, nagging pain in the lower back. It can be triggered off by any number of things from the single event, such as standing awkwardly over a low basin when washing your hair, to the undramatic accumulation of years of bad standing, together with all the stresses and strains of everyday living. It can also strike during pregnancy, after the birth of a child, before a period and during the menopause. Following the guidelines on posture and on safeguarding the health of your back and spine given in the Shape chapter should help to prevent the onset of back trouble and to relieve the pain if you do get it. (See pages 202-3 for positions that will help to relieve backache during pregnancy.)

If you have persistent backache or a sharp pain in your spine or neck, you should always see your doctor. Because there are so many different causes of backache, you should never do 'corrective' exercises unless these are individually tailored for you by your doctor or specialist. (See page 35 for a list of exercises you should beware of).

If your back suddenly 'gives way', stop what you are doing immediately, call a friend and lie down on your back or your side (never your front). Bend your knees and ask your friend to apply cold compresses to the injured or painful area, by wrapping a plastic bag filled with ice-cubes in a towel. Call your doctor.

Boils

Boils, or abscesses, are infected hair follicles and they can appear anywhere on the body. Adolescents are particularly prone to them. Treat boils with an antiseptic lotion, preferably povidone iodine or magnesium sulphate, and leave them well alone. Avoid squeezing them or using the old-fashioned and now outdated method of applying hot compresses, as both of these may spread the infection. If you have recurrent boils, you should consult your doctor as, just occasionally, they may be symptomatic of diabetes.

Bruising (haematoma)

Bruising is caused by a blow to the body breaking the blood capillaries beneath the skin. While nothing can hasten the disappearance of a bruise once it has appeared, prompt action immediately after receiving the blow may prevent it appearing in the first place. Apply ice packs (fill a plastic bag with ice-cubes and then wrap in a towel) or cold compresses for about an hour to lower the skin temperature and thus reduce the activity of the skin cells.

Bunions

See Enlarged toe joints.

Burns and scalds

Burns are caused by direct contact with heat, such as a naked flame or an electrical current, and scalds by the products of heat, such as steam. They are classified in order of severity. First degree burns are the least severe and you can usually treat them yourself. Third-degree burns are very severe indeed and require immediate first-aid and admission to hospital.

Fast action is essential if somebody's clothes or hair are on fire. Grab a blanket, a towel, a thick woollen jacket or an overcoat and wrap it around the body to smother the flames. Then cover with a blanket to keep the body warm (body temperature tends to drop very rapidly) and telephone immediately for an ambulance.

Minor burns or scalds should be treated by running cold water over the injured area for at least 10 minutes and then applying ice packs (put ice in a plastic bag and then wrap in a towel, never apply directly to the skin) for up to an hour. This lowers the temperature and thus the activity of the skin cells and minimizes the damage, while acting as a natural 'anaesthetic'.

Never apply butter to burns. Use a dry dressing instead and then leave to the air. Blisters should be left to themselves and will usually break spontaneously. If they do not, consult a doctor. Do not attempt to lance them yourself.

Cataracts

Cataracts are caused by a gradual clouding of the crystalline (fine focusing) lens inside the eye. As the lens becomes more opaque, so the vision becomes more blurred. Because the condition is caused by a defect inside the eye, it will not be improved or helped by the wearing of glasses. Although some babies are born with cataracts, the condition is particularly linked with advancing age. In fact, it is now thought that, by the age of 70, 90 per cent of people may have some degree of it. Everyone should have their eyes checked for early signs of cataract soon after the age of 40. Cataracts can also occasionally be caused by injury or trauma to the eye, by certain drugs, by excessive radiation or sun exposure and by diabetes. The condition can be treated surgically by removing the damaged lens and increasing the focusing power of the eye by placing the appropriate lens in, on or in front of the eye.

Cellulite

Does it exist or doesn't it? Depending on whom you talk to, cellulite is either a non-existent condition invented by the French or it is 'fat gone wrong', an exclusively female and virtually universal condition caused by sluggish circulation, congested blood vessels, accumulated toxic and metabolic waste and mineral and vitamin imbalances. The truth is probably half way between the two. Whether you call it cellulite or call it fat, there is absolutely no doubt that women do have a different type and different distribution of fat to men. For where, in men, fat is packaged in small compact compartments that are fairly evenly distributed beneath the skin, in women the cellular arrangement is not only much looser but has a marked tendency to accumulate on bottoms and thighs. This type of fat is uneven and dimpled in appearance (the French, expressively, call it peau d'orange) and can feel uneven and grainy when rolled beneath the fingers. While there is no doubt that factors hormonal and genetic are to blame for this, together with (probably) too little exercise and too much to eat, what is dubious, is the number of treatments and therapies — from wearing inflatable boots to undergoing courses of dandelion injections — that claim to be able to 'break up' or to 'mobilize' fatty deposits, 'disperse' toxic waste, 'stimulate' a sluggish circulation and so 'recontour' the body. None of these has been shown to work really effectively on a clinical basis and results, while expensive, are often disappointing.

Chloasma (melasma)

This is a blotchy darkening of the pigmentation in the skin that usually appears on the cheeks just below the eyes, above the lip, on the forehead, in the armpits, on the nipples and around the genital area. It occurs in as many as one-third of all women on the pill and is not uncommon in the last three months of pregnancy. While it will fade in time, chloasma is aggravated and rendered more noticeable by exposure to bright sunlight. Keep out of the sun as much as possible, avoid sun lamps and use an efficient sun block. You can sometimes counteract the darkening by bleaching the skin, but results are not always good and may even leave the skin looking blotchier than before.

Colds

Colds are caused by a number of different viruses and produce a range of symptoms, including sneezing, coughing, streaming eyes, a congested or running nose, sore throat and headache. A raised temperature is rare.

If you seem to have a persistent cold or suffer intermittently all through the winter months, your resistance is low and so, too, probably is your general health. Keeping fit, strong and well-nourished and avoiding sudden drops or rises in temperature (do not overheat rooms) should constitute your first line of defence. You can, if you like, also take additional vitamin C in the form of tablets, although opinion as to whether or not this is an effective safeguard is very divided. Nobel laureate Linus Pauling recommends 'mega-doses' of up to two grams of the vitamin a day (equivalent to 200 oranges) to keep the cold virus at bay, together with a further

500 mg every four hours, if you feel that you are about to or have succumbed in order to reduce the severity of the symptoms.

More traditional methods of treating colds involve relieving the symptoms. Most doctors now recommend that you do this by treating each of the symptoms independently. Take an antitussive cough medicine for a dry, hacking cough; an expectorant for a 'productive' one; lozenges containing phenol or benzocaine or gargle (½ teaspoon salt or two drops tabasco in 225 ml/8 fl oz/1 cup of warm water) for a sore throat, or suck ice which works like a surface anaesthetic by numbing the throat; a decongestant for a blocked nose, (but do not use for more than three days as it has a rebound effect); an anti-histamine preparation if your nose is runny, which works in the early stages of a cold much as it does in the early stages of hay fever (see Allergies). You should also drink plenty of fluids to replace those you are losing.

Cold sores

These can appear anywhere on the body and are transmitted on contact by a virus known as herpes, from the Greek *herpein*, meaning to creep. They may have nothing to do with colds at all. The sexually transmitted type of cold sore, for example, is caused by a quite different strain of the virus to the one that produces the characteristic sores around the mouth and may accompany a cold. These cold sores are painful and extremely difficult to cure completely, for although they tend to be self-limiting — that is, they usually disappear quite spontaneously after only a few days — the recurrence rate is high. Although the sores disappear, the virus retreats to a nerve cluster at the base of the spine and remains there until the next attack when it returns to its usual eruption site. Symptoms can often be relieved by keeping the area clean and dry — bathing with a salt/water bath solution.

Because the sexually transmitted herpes virus has now been implicated as a possible trigger for cervical cancer, anyone who has had the virus should have annual smear ('Pap') tests to check for the presence of abnormal, pre-cancerous cells on the cervix. If abnormal cells are detected on a smear, they can usually be easily eliminated in the early stages (see pages 208-9). (See also Sexually transmitted diseases.)

Conjunctivitis ('pink eye')

Conjunctivitis simply means inflammation of the conjunctiva — the thin, transparent membrane that covers the white of the eye. This condition can be caused by allergy, infection or irritation. The eyes feel sore and gritty, may water profusely, particularly if the cause is allergic, and will look red and bloodshot where the blood capillaries that bring oxygen to the surface of the eye have dilated to help fight the infection. Conjunctivitis is usually best treated by leaving the eyes well alone. If it is infective, however, it will need treating with antibiotic eye drops. In the case of allergy such as hay fever, special drops may also be prescribed to reduce the inflammation.

Constipation

A considerable amount of constipation exists only in the mind. One of the most significant side-effects of the great fibre revival of the last 10 years is an obsession with 'regularity'. But you do not have to open your bowels once a day — or even every other day — in order to be functioning normally and healthily, as long as when you do open them, you do so at regular intervals and without straining or discomfort. Straining may lead to haemorrhoids and is almost certainly an indication of constipation. So too are hard, 'bullet'-type stools. If you do find you are constipated, look first to your diet.

Although laxative tablets or medicines can be effective in the short-term, they are self-defeating in the long term because they encourage the bowel and gut to become lazy. Eat a tablespoon of bran on your cereal or in soups or stews once a day instead, increasing to a quarter of a cup if necessary, and give your body at least a month to adjust to the new regimen before you conclude it is not working and return to the laxatives or the doctor (preferably the doctor). If you have constipation that alternates with diarrhoea, or notice blood or black streaks in your stools, see your doctor.

Corns and calluses

Corns are caused by an over-growth of the top layers of the skin on the foot in response to pressure or friction, and can be considerably uncomfortable, even painful. Do not attempt to treat corns yourself beyond applying a dressing or unmedicated corn plaster to relieve the pressure. Paring away at the layers of accumulated skin may lead to septic infection and will most certainly increase the soreness. Medicated corn plasters should be avoided too, particularly if you have poor circulation or are diabetic. Seek the help of a chiropodist, who will be able to treat it and to advise on ways of avoiding a recurrence.

Calluses are more general patches of hard, rough skin that build up on areas of the body, usually the foot. Guard against getting them by looking after your feet well, by wearing comfortable shoes, by combating dryness with a daily application of moisturizer and by using a pumice stone to rub away dry spots with a little soap and warm water.

Cuts

If you have a cut that is very deep or unclean, check whether you have had a recent tetanus booster. If in doubt, ask your doctor to give you one, particularly if you are on holiday abroad or living in a hot climate. In all cases, clean the wound thoroughly under cold running water, then clean your hands thoroughly and, using ordinary soap and water or a mild diluted antiseptic solution, wash the wound, sweeping cotton wool away from it so that you are not rubbing dirt into it. Remove all visible dirt and cover with a clean dressing. Once the bleeding has stopped, the wound should be left to the air as much as possible. If it is deep enough to require bandaging, or if it does not dry up within a day or so, or if you notice pus forming and leaking from the wound, you should see your doctor. The wound may be infected. If this is the case, it can be cleared with an antibiotic preparation.

Profuse bleeding should be treated as a medical emergency. This is almost always arterial in nature and should be treated by holding your hand over the bleeding part, either by applying pressure directly over the wound (put on a tight bandage and press very firmly) or by holding the two sides of the wound together. If this fails to stop the flow, and the injury is on a limb, apply a tourniquet, using anything that can be wound around the injured part, such as a handkerchief, a belt, or a scarf. Place the tourniquet between the injury and the heart and hold it as hard as is required to stop the bleeding. Do not keep the tourniquet on for longer than fifteen minutes and always take the injury to a doctor or hospital as soon as possible. These are first-aid measures only and medical advice must be sought as soon as possible.

Cystitis

Cystitis is a urinary infection and is caused by bacteria, known as *E. coli*, and also occasionally by other germs, travelling from the anus and bowel up to the urethra and into the bladder, where they cause the lining of the bladder to become inflamed and infect the urine. Cystitis is extremely common and afflicts 60 per cent of all women (often repeatedly) at some time in their lives. It can also be very painful . Symptoms are a constant and weary desire to pass water, pain and a burning sensation when doing so together with an inability to pass more than a few drops at a time, a dragging ache in the lower abdomen and a dark or 'strong' looking urine which may be streaked with blood from the inflammation.

If you suspect you have cystitis, you should always see your doctor. Most, but by no means all, types of cystitis can be cleared up with a quick (five-day) course of antibiotics. In the meantime, there are several self-help measures you can take to help relieve the pain. On the first signs of infection, drink two glasses of cold water. Fill two hot water bottles and settle down with one between your legs (warming the skin in this way reduces the burning sensation when urinating) and the other behind your back. Then drink the following: 300 ml/½ pint (1¼ cups) liquid, such as water-based squashes, every 20 minutes for at least three hours; a cup of black coffee or tea hourly (this encourages urination); a teaspoon of bicarbonate of soda mixed with a little water hourly (bicarbonate of soda is an alkali and, by making the urine less acid, takes the sting out of it). This should help to flush out the infection. Every time you urinate, wash yourself gently from front to back with plain warm water and dab yourself dry.

If you suffer from recurrent cystitis, take the following steps to reduce the likelihood of your getting a further attack:
Drink plenty (about 2 litres/3½ pints/4½ pints) of water or a bland fluid, such as milk or weak tea, every day to keep the bladder clear of germs.
Keep your vagina and urethra extra clean — wash with plain warm water, using a separate flannel, and always work from front to back to avoid transferring germs from the anus to the urethra. Avoid bath oils, talcum powders, vaginal deodorants and antiseptics and wash carefully with plain warm water before intercourse and again afterwards. It may also help if you pass water fairly soon after intercourse in order to flush out any germs which may have entered the urethra.

Cysts

Cysts are fluid-filled capsules that can appear on any part of the body. They may be as tiny as a grain of sand or as large as a squash ball and are usually benign. In fact, sebaceous or skin cysts, which are the more common type, are always benign and are only removed for cosmetic reasons. Other types of cyst, however, may be more ominous and for this reason always require medical attention. Breast cysts often give rise to great concern, even panic, when first discovered, but they are rarely ominous and can often be both easily diagnosed and treated by a simple out-patient procedure. A common type of cyst that women get is an ovarian cyst. This is usually caused by one of the ovaries failing to release an egg at ovulation and the follicle that encloses it continuing to grow. It may also be caused by endometriosis (see opposite) or simply by a combination of factors, both hormonal and general. Many ovarian cysts disappear spontaneously. If they do not, they may grow, giving rise to feelings of fullness or distention across the lower abdomen and/or pain during intercourse. They may then require medical treatment, usually hormonal in nature. Surgery is not the preferred method of treatment. In some hospitals in the USA, vitamin E has been used with apparently impressive results. (See also Lump in the breast)

Dandruff

Dandruff is a common scalp disorder and it affects nearly everyone, often repeatedly, at some time in their lives. Like all other skin tissue, the outer layer of dead cells on the scalp is constantly being shed and replaced by younger cells beneath it. Dandruff occurs either when this outer layer accumulates on the scalp and fails to shed itself normally or when the process of cell division is stepped up in the basal layer of the epidermis.

If you have dandruff, treat it with the weak cetrimide solution given on page 98 before switching to one of the harsher acting dandruff shampoos. If the condition then continues unabated, buy a shampoo containing tar or zinc pyrithione, which is thought to have a slowing effect on the rate of cell turnover beneath the skin. Dandruff that is patchy or that comes away in large scaly pieces creating scabbing or bleeding is not necessarily dandruff. Some skin disorders, such as psoriasis, eczema and ringworm, can masquerade as dandruff — affecting the scalp, while often leaving the rest of the head and body quite clear. So be awake to the possibility that your dandruff may not be dandruff at all and, if in doubt, consult a trichologist or dermatologist.

Diarrhoea

Diarrhoea can be symptomatic of almost anything, from jittery nerves to food poisoning, and can be a particular hazard when travelling abroad where standards of hygiene and sanitation may be poor. While nervous diarrhoea subsides with the nerves and does not require treatment, diarrhoea produced by digestive or systemic upset can be treated with an anti-bacterial agent if severe. One of the most effective medicines for treating diarrhoea is kaolin and morphine, or straightforward kaolin, which is widely available throughout the world and in many countries can be purchased across the counter without a prescription. Take it as directed and, if the recommended dose produces no improvement in 24 hours, consult your doctor. You should also consult your doctor if you notice any significant change in your bowel habit and, particularly, if you have bouts of diarrhoea that alternate with constipation.

Dysmenorrhoea (painful periods)

Two out of every three women suffer from period pains (cramps) at some stage of their lives. Produced by strong contractions of the muscles surrounding the uterus, these pains are thought to be produced by local hormones, known as prostaglandins. In some sufferers, levels of this hormone can actually climb to eight times the normal level.

Unlike PMS, dysmenorrhoea is much more common among younger women up to the age of 25. Dysmenorrhoea usually disappears spontaneously after the birth of a baby and is often helped by the contraceptive pill, when hormone levels are 'balanced' out. Bad pains in later life should always be investigated medically.

Mild to moderate period pains rarely last more than about two hours and can often be helped by simple exercises — the pelvic rotation ('belly dancing') on page 202 is particularly good — which persuade tense muscles to stretch and relax. Other self-help methods include taking a 'shot' (1 oz) of brandy or whisky as a relaxant; taking a pain-killer, such as soluble aspirin, which is also a mild prostaglandin inhibitor, every four hours; drinking catnip or mint teas; sitting propped up with one hot water bottle against your back and another between your thighs; or pressing the small hollows by your ankles on either side of the Achilles tendon with your thumbs (an ancient Chinese remedy). Severe cases of dysmenorrhoea can be treated by the prescription of anti-spasmodic agents, such as mefenamic acid, which have an inhibiting effect on the action of the prostaglandins, to relieve the pain in over 80 per cent of cases.

Earache

Earache usually arises either as a result of a local ear infection or as 'referred' pain from an infection elsewhere, such as in a tooth. As all ear infections require medical investigation and usually a course of antibiotics to clear them, you should consult your doctor if the pain persists for more than 24 hours. In the meantime, treat it with a painkiller and leave the ear well aone.

Eczema (dermatitis)

Eczema is a general term used by dermatologists to describe a non-specific or specific (i.e. allergy-related) skin reaction that itches. The word itself derives from the Greek, *ekzeeim*, meaning to boil or bubble over, and this is particularly expressive of the red scaling patches and watery blisters characteristic of the condition known as infantile eczema — so called because it particularly affects children and usually disappears at around the age of eight. This type of eczema is particularly wretched. Because the condition itches unbearably, the child scratches and so sets up a vicious itch-scratch-weep-crust cycle. The sores themselves are not infectious and can be helped to heal by preventing the child from scratching (cut nails short and avoid putting irritant materials next to the skin), and using a steroid cream, such as hydrocortisone, to reduce the irritation and soothe the damaged skin. Zinc lotions and creams are also effective — particularly if the latter also contains coal tar which can help to relieve the itching. Cold compresses of linen or lint moistened with a watery solution of aluminium acetate (available over the counter from your chemist) may also help. Avoid over-frequent bathing and the use of soaps and detergents which can aggravate the condition by drying out the skin. Special diets have been shown to help in a few cases — particularly diets from which all cow's milk products have been eliminated and goat's milk substituted.

In adults, eczema can occasionally be an expression of an allergy (see page 214), usually but not always a 'contact' allergy to a substance such as nickel, or rubber. Treat the eczema topically as above and ask your doctor to refer you to a dermatologist for patch testing, which may determine the culprit.

Endometriosis

This gynaecological disorder is caused by patches of the uterine lining attaching themselves outside the uterus — such as on the Fallopian tubes or the ovaries — and, confusingly, continuing to behave as though they were still inside the uterus, i.e. bleeding during menstruation. The most common symptoms of the condition are bad period pains and/or pain during intercourse. If undetected, these patches may obstruct the Fallopian tubes or the ovaries and may then cause infertility.

The most effective way of controlling the condition is to stop menstruating. This can be achieved either through hormonal control or by becoming pregnant. Sometimes the pregnancy in itself turns out to be 'treatment' enough, leaving the sufferer symptom free after it. If you do have diagnosed endometriosis, and if pregnancy is not a viable option now, it is certainly worthwhile considering having children sooner rather than later in the light of possible future infertility.

Enlarged toe joints (bunions)

These almost always occur on the big toe and tend to be an inherited condition. Although they are not necessarily caused by ill-fitting footwear (some people who spend their time walking barefoot have them), they are certainly aggravated by it — particularly if the toes are too cramped.

As the enlarged joint becomes increasingly inflamed and the pressure within it rises, the traditional 'bunion' shape will begin to appear — the big toe being forced in towards the others, as the joint juts outwards to the side. If you have enlarged toe joints, or a familial tendency to them, keep your weight within limits, apply paddings and dressings to relieve the pressure, wear comfortable footwear and take the weight off your feet whenever possible. Prevention is always better than cure: choose shoes that have their widest part at the base of the toes and that allow the toes to move freely inside them. Although bunions can sometimes be rectified surgically, it is very much a last resort and results are often disappointing.

Eyes (chemicals, eyelashes, foreign bodies in)

<u>If a chemical comes into contact with the eye,</u> wash it out under cold running water by holding your head beneath a tap or shower head, letting the water flow gently and opening your eyes underwater several times. Continue for a minute or so. Keep your head tilted to one side to prevent the chemical from being washed into the other eye and be gentle; never direct the water straight at the cornea.

<u>If an eyelash or particle comes into contact with the eye</u> and the instinctive blinking and watering reaction fails to clear it, do not rub the eye. Hold the eyelids apart and gently coax the offending particle or lash out of the eye with the corner of a tissue or clean handkerchief. If you cannot see anything in the eye, it is probably lodged beneath one of the lids. Try holding the upper lid over the lower for a few moments to dislodge it. If this does not work, pull gently upwards on the upper lashes and bend the lid upwards. Someone else should then be able to spot it and to retrieve it.

N.B. If a particle scratches the cornea, the eye will feel as if it is still there for some time after it has been removed and may require antibiotic drops to help it heal.

<u>If a piece of glass or metal comes into contact with the eye, see your doctor immediately.</u>

Fainting

Fainting can be induced by emotion, shock, illness, tiredness, staying for too long in a sauna or very hot bath, not having eaten for a long time, early pregnancy and even by prolonged periods of standing. Warning signs are usually sensations of dizziness or cold and pallor in the face as the blood drains away. As loss of consciousness is caused by a reduction of blood supplied to the brain, the best possible thing you can do if you feel you may be about to faint is to sit or crouch down with your head between your knees. The action of gravity should be enough to restore blood supply to the brain.

If someone has already passed out, lie her on her side (<u>never</u> sit or prop her up in a chair) with her legs raised above the level of her head. Loosen tight clothing around the neck and the waist and, when she comes round, give her sips of cold iced water and — most important — time to recover fully.

Food poisoning

Food poisoning is caused by toxic bacteria breeding in food and infecting the intestines. Symptoms, which can be extremely unpleasant, include intense vomiting and diarrhoea, together with severe stomach pains. These can take anywhere between one and 48 hours to develop. Common sources of the bacteria are reheated meat, shellfish, rice, frozen foods that have not been properly thawed and canned fish and meat that have been contaminated during packaging.

If you have food poisoning, avoid all solid foods. It is essential, however, that you replace the fluids you are losing, so try to drink plenty of clear liquid, such as water, tea without milk, juices or consommé, even if you can only manage a mouthful or so at a time. If your stomach does not settle within 24 hours, ring your doctor and give details of everything eaten in the 48 hours before developing the symptoms.

Foot problems

See Athlete's foot, Corns and calluses, Enlarged toe joints.

Gastritis

Gastritis is a pain — often persistent — in the upper abdomen and it is caused by excessive acidity in the stomach, leading to inflammation of the stomach lining. The condition itself is usually a sign of self-abuse, and is aggravated by highly spiced foods, alcohol, very rich or acidic substances and erratic eating habits. It may occasionally be caused by metabolic disease or infection. Counteract the acidity in your stomach by drinking plenty of milk (this is preferable to stronger alkalis, such as bicarbonate of soda) and by looking after your general health more diligently. If the pain persists, consult your doctor.

Gingivitis (gum disease)

This is such a common condition that there is a greater likelihood of your having it than not. Sore or bleeding gums are the main sign and a clear indication that your tooth brushing routine needs revising (see pages 110-12).

Glaucoma

Glaucoma is an eye affliction caused by a disturbance of the fluid balance within the eyeball and a consequent increase of pressure inside the eye. If allowed to persist, glaucoma may damage vision by pressing against the optic nerve. One of the main symptoms of glaucoma is 'tunnel vision' — in other words, an increasingly restricted field of vision, even though you can still focus perfectly well. Other warning signs and symptoms, which may or may not be present, are headaches and seeing auras or 'haloes' around bright objects. Because glaucoma is an age-associated defect — it is rarely seen in people under 35 — and because it can be absolutely symptomless in the early stages (by the time it is diagnosed medically, the process has often gone so far that the sufferer can be classified as 'blind' for health insurance purposes), you should have an eye test at about the age of 45 to check that you have not got it. This is particularly important if there is a history of it in your family. Once detected, glaucoma can never be 'cured' but it can be controlled in one of three ways: medically, through prescription of certain drugs, surgically, in order to release pressure inside the eye, or through the use of prescription eye drops which use a drug called pilocarpine to constrict the pupil, so making the wearing of glasses unnecessary.

Gonorrhoea

This is extremely common and highly infectious and now second only to measles in the British league of infectious diseases (first in America, where about 20,000 people catch it each week).

Gonorrhoea is transmitted only on intimate contact by the *gonococcus bacterium* which has a rapid two- to three-day incubation period. Symptoms in men are fairly dramatic at the onset with a thick discharge and a burning sensation when urinating. They are much less dramatic in women in whom there may sometimes be a thin, yellowish discharge. Usually, however, there are no symptoms at all. Although the condition can be treated very effectively in most cases with a single dose of penicillin, follow-up is essential, both because some strains of the disease are becoming resistant to this antibiotic and because gonorrhoea, if left untreated, may lead to salpingitis (inflammation of the Fallopian tubes) which can in turn lead to infertility.

Although most clinics now aim for an immediate 95 per cent cure rate, there is increasing concern over the number of penicillin-resistant strains of the disease. In 1978, for example, out of a total of 60,000 cases in the UK, 35 were totally resistant to penicillin. In 1979, this number had risen to 100 and, in subsequent years, has continued to rise, although the total number of reported cases has actually fallen a little. In 1981, 444 cases of total resistance were reported. These figures make follow-up more important than ever. (See also Sexually transmitted diseases.)

Haemorrhoids (piles)

Haemorrhoids are dilated veins in the anus, the opening to the bowels, that may become inflamed and painful. They are caused by anything that increases blood volume in the abdomen, such as constipation or straining when opening the bowels, overweight and pregnancy. You do not get haemorrhoids from sitting on radiators. Symptoms of haemorrhoids are itching, bleeding, soreness and, often, intense pain on coughing, laughing or going to the lavatory. The best way of protecting against haemorrhoids is to make sure that you are getting enough fibre in your diet (see page 62). This can also be an effective way of treating them in the early stages, when suppositories and hot baths tend only to offer temporary relief. More advanced cases, however, may require the application of elasticated bands to cut off circulation, injections (as for Varicose veins) or surgery.

Halitosis (bad breath)

This can be caused by any number of factors, most of which do not originate in the mouth. As eliminating the problem involves eliminating it at source, mouthwashes are not on the whole a satisfactory solution or safeguard against the condition (see also page 135).

Hangovers

Hangovers have probably been around for almost as long as alcohol. In the first century AD, Pliny advised sufferers to take an elaborate morning-after concoction of owl's eggs doused in red wine and so became the first recorded advocate of the now proverbial 'hair of the dog' theory. This theory may have some substance because it helps to offset some — but by no means all — of the unpleasant effects of 'withdrawal', namely the raging headache, general malaise, gastritis caused by raised acidity in the stomach and general feelings of sickness and nausea.

As the main effects of hangover are caused by dehydration, you can help to guard against them by interspersing alcoholic drinks with water, milk or fruit juice and by drinking copious amounts of water before you go to bed. Early morning hangovers are usually accompanied by a mild form of gastritis (see page 217). Taking a mild alkali, such as a glass of milk, may help. If you want to take a painkiller for the headache, however, take paracetamol (acetaminophen in USA) in preference to aspirin, which can irritate the stomach and thus make the condition worse.

Hay fever

See Allergy.

Headache

Headaches can be caused by any number of things. These include tension, frustration, fatigue, infection, sensitivity to certain foods, colds in the head, infected sinuses, alcohol, changes in altitude, injuries or blows to the head and fluctuating hormone levels. This list is virtually endless.

About 70 per cent of all headaches are thought to be tension headaches. These are caused by a prolonged, often uneven, contraction in the muscles at the base of the neck and shoulder blades and are aggravated by poor posture and psychological stresses, such as frustration, fear or even excitement. Tension headaches commonly feel like a tight band across the head, are worse in the evening than the morning and are twice as common among women as men. As any type of headache — and this one in particular — is associated with muscle spasm around the head and neck, relieve the tension by relieving the contraction in the neck muscles. Try any of the exercises shown on pages 42-3; lie down so that the head is supported and rotate the neck gently to relieve stiffness; massage sore strained muscles by clasping one hand over the other and pressing in firmly with the heels of the hands from the base of the neck up to the skull; ask a friend to 'free' your neck: you lie on your back with your head supported by a pillow while she gently stretches it out away from the shoulders and turns it to left and right; try the Chinese acupressure point, known as *tsuan schu*, and press firmly inwards with the thumbs on the inner corner of the eye just beneath the eyebrow for the duration of a complete outbreath. If none of these works, take two soluble aspirin or paracetamol (acetaminophen in USA) and wait for the pain to subside. If this type of headache is a frequent occurrence, you should take steps to identify and, where possible, to remove or relieve the root of the problem.

The second most common type of headache is known as a cluster headache and is linked with three major factors. The first is sex. Men are eight times more likely to be sufferers than women. The second is age. It usually first appears between the ages of about 30 and 45. The third is lifestyle. Heavy drinkers and/or smokers seem to be particularly prone.

Cluster headaches can be excruciatingly painful, are often considered to be a form of migraine but can be distinguished from the normal type of migraine because they tend to be self-limiting. They last in bouts from two to 17 weeks and during that time they tend to arrive with alarm-clock regularity, sometimes as often as six times a day. Like migraine, cluster headaches tend to be unilateral (on one side of the head only). The sensation of pain is first felt around the eyes, travelling downwards to affect nostrils, jaw and mouth. Treatment usually consists in the careful prescription of drugs which will inhibit the dilation of the blood vessels. It is now also generally recognized that sufferers can help themselves enormously by avoiding alcohol. (See also Migraine.)

Herpes

See Cold sores.

Hypertension (high blood pressure)

When you have your blood pressure checked — which should be whenever your contraceptive pill prescription is renewed, if you are under the age of 35, and once a year if you are over the age of 35 — two readings will be taken. The first figure is called the systolic pressure, and represents the pressure of the blood in the arteries as the heart pumps it through. The second figure is called the diastolic, or resting, pressure and represents the pressure of the blood in the arteries between heart beats. Although 120/80 is considered classically 'normal', there are wide variations all considered to be within normal limits. However, once your blood pressure, and particularly your diastolic pressure, rises beyond a certain point, (insurance companies usually put it at 150/90), it is considered high and you are said to 'have' hypertension.

Hypertension is not a disease but it requires medical management because it is a recognized predisposing factor towards diseases such as stroke, deep vein thrombosis or coronary heart disease, which can have serious, even fatal, consequences. Although, in some cases, blood pressure can be lowered by practising relaxation and breathing techniques, it can usually only be effectively controlled through the prescription of certain drugs. If your doctor prescribes tablets for high blood pressure, it is essential that you take them <u>even if you are feeling perfectly well</u>, that you report any side-effects as the prescription may need adjusting, and that you return for regular check-ups.

An excessively high salt intake is now thought to be a major contributory factor to hypertension.

Ingrowing nails

These occur only on the feet, never on the hands, and are caused by the edge of the nail growing into the skin which then folds back over it. Ingrowing nails can be caused by a number of things, principally a blow or injury to the toe and bad cutting (see pages 116-17 for guidelines) or, more simply, an hereditary predisposition. Ingrown nails can be extremely painful and usually require minor surgery in order to remove part, sometimes even all, of the nail. If you have a tendency to ingrowing toenails or have a toenail that is digging into the flesh on either side, roll up small pipes of cotton wool and wedge them gently between the nail and the flesh to prevent irritation and inflamma- tion.

Irregular menstrual bleeding

Spotting or 'breakthrough' bleeding durinc the middle of the cycle often occurs quite normally, especially in women on the pill. As long as this is not heavy or prolonged, you have no cause for concern. If, however, you bleeding is very irregular, or is excessively heavy or if you have been through the menopause, you should consult your doc tor. In these cases, bleeding may indicate a gynaecological disorder, such as endomet riosis or the presence of a polyps (harmless growths) in the uterus, and should always be investigated.

Jet lag

Jet lag occurs because the internal clocks that help control your body temperature blood/sugar levels, hunger and sleepinc patterns are out of synchronization with the outside world — usually four or more hours in front or behind it. Normally, when movinc from place to place, these clocks have time to adjust gradually to a new schedule, but ai travel has changed all this. Such travellers are liable to become confused, disorientated hungry when no-one else is, sleepy wher the rest of the world seems wide-awake and vice versa. The mere fact of travelling so fa so fast is enough to induce any or all of these symptoms (particularly, and still inexplicably, when travelling east) but they wil certainly be aggravated by drinking alcoho 'in flight' and, it now seems, eating and drinking in ways that appear to inhibit your ability to adjust easily to a new time scale From these findings, an American physician, Charles Ehret, has devised this diet to help minimize the effects of jet lag.

<u>Three days before take-off:</u> three full meals (high-protein breakfast and lunch, high-carbohydrate supper). Tea or coffee only in the afternoon.

<u>Two days before take-off:</u> three light low-carbohydrate meals. Tea or coffee only in the afternoon.

<u>Day before take-off:</u> as for three days before.

<u>Day of flight (travelling east):</u> fast or eat very little before flying. Once on the plane, drink lots of tea and coffee, omit alcohol and evening meal, try to sleep, and eat a high-protein breakfast (if necessary take your own).

<u>Day of flight (travelling west):</u> fast on the plane, drink lots of strong coffee or tea in the morning, but none in the afternoon. Omit the lunchtime or evening meal.

<u>On arrival:</u> whatever the time, eat a hearty meal in accordance with local mealtimes, stay active and go to bed reasonably early.

Keloids

Keloids are scars that develop over wounds and that grow much larger than the original wound. Also known as hypertrophic scarring (see page 166), keloids are 10 to 20 times more common on black skins than they are on white ones and commonly appear after surgery, particularly if the scar is subject to tension. Caesarian delivery is one example, ear piercing another. The area between the neck and the nipple is particularly prone to this type of scar formation. Although keloids can be removed surgically, there is always the danger that renewed surgery will simply aggravate the problem, thus resulting in an even larger 'scar'. Most doctors prefer to leave keloids alone, although steroid injections can sometimes help to bring them down.

Lice
Lice on the hair are extremely contagious and are common among schoolchildren. These can easily be treated by washing the hair with a specially formulated shampoo, available over the counter at chemists and drugstores. Lice on the genitals (crabs) are similar, but not identical, to the ones which affect the head. These can only survive in short hair, commonly pubic hair, but may migrate to other hairy parts of the body, such as the armpits or the legs or chest in men. Symptoms of lice are, first, visual (the insects can be clearly seen, although not the eggs) and, second, itching. They can be treated by applying a lotion to remove both insects and eggs — something that shaving the pubic hair will not do.

Lumbago
See Back trouble.

Lump in the breast
Finding a lump in the breast is a traumatic event for any woman. Often unnecessarily so: of all lumps in the breast, only a small proportion (probably less than 10 per cent) are cancerous. But, even so, you must consult your doctor if you find a lump, or suspect you have found one, for the following reasons.
- It is impossible to tell merely by feeling whether a lump is cancerous or not.
- Any lump in the breast requires further investigation (biopsy or X-ray, see page 207) if its cause cannot be determined by clinical examinations.
- Most lumps should be removed surgically to guard against the possiblity, however remote, of their turning malignant or cancerous at a later date. In most cases, the surgery required to remove lumps is restricted only to that area of the breast and leaves the smallest of scars, especially if surgery is carried out below the level of the nipple.

Painful, lumpy breasts among women under the age of 30 are most commonly caused by naturally fluctuating hormone levels just prior to menstruation, causing the breasts to become extremely sore, tender and granular in texture. The condition can often be successfully treated by adjusting and regulating the hormone levels. Because there are no specific lumps — just a general feeling of lumpiness — there is no need for surgery. Other common types of breast lump are benign tumours, or fibroadenomas (these are most common between the ages of 25 and 35, may feel like hard round marbles beneath the skin and should be removed surgically), and benign fluid-filled cysts (most common in early adulthood). These may appear and disappear for no clear reason at all or may require medical treatment. Cysts may sometimes feel so hard as to seem quite solid. They can sometimes be diagnosed and treated at the same time by aspirating the lump with a needle and drawing off the fluid inside it.

You can help yourself by being aware of

any changes in the shape, size and texture of your breasts that do not normally occur over the stages of the menstrual cycle, and by reporting anything that seems abnormal or potentially abnormal to your doctor (see Breast self-examination, pages 210-11, and Cysts on page 216).

Migraine
Migraines are very common. The latest figures suggest that as many as four women out of every 10 will suffer a headache at some time in their lives which may be classified as migrainous. Classically, the condition starts with disturbances of vision caused by a constriction of the blood vessels supplying oxygen to the eye. These may include seeing bright lights, zig-zag lines, auras or 'haloes' around bright objects, or vision may be blurred or even double. Less commonly, tingling or sensations of numbness may be experienced in the hands and feet. This stage usually lasts for about 20 minutes.

The headache, unbearably oppressive in nature, often starts on one side of the head (the word itself derives from the Greek, via the French, meaning 'half a head') and, in up to 90 per cent of cases, is also accompanied by feelings of nausea, if not by actually vomiting.

Migraine seems to run in families (about 50 per cent of sufferers can trace an hereditary factor), usually arrives before the age of 40 and afflicts three times as many women as men. While the cause is not yet established — the most likely theory is that it is caused by a blood disorder causing the vessels to spasm and dilate — attacks have been fairly conclusively linked to a number of factors. Principal among these are stress (anxiety and tension are common precursors of migraine attacks) menstruation and foods containing nitrite, glutamate and other yet unidentified chemicals. Recent studies suggest that migraine sufferers may be unable to metabolize proteins present in certain foods. Higher levels of these proteins still circulating in the bloodstream are then thought to act as a stimulus or trigger for the attack. In one study on 500 migraine sufferers, the following foods were most consistently implicated:

Chocolate	75%
Cheese and dairy products	48%
Citrus fruits	30%
Alcoholic drinks	25%
Fatty fried foods and vegetables	18%
Tea or coffee	14%
Meat, especially pork	14%
Seafood	10%

Other contributing factors may include a change in routine, physical or mental fatigue, too little or too much sleep, travel, a change in climate or temperature, high winds, bright glaring sunlight, noise, sleeping tablets, oral contraceptives, hunger, head injury, high blood pressure, toothache and other pains in the head or neck.

Because migraine is triggered by so many different things and because each sufferer will have particular sensitivities to some, but not all, of these trigger factors, the best preventative course lies in working out

which ones you are sensitive to and taking steps to avoid them. Keep a diary for a period of at least three months and record your attacks of migraine together with any associated factors, such as the stage of the menstrual cycle, foods eaten, meals missed and particular stresses. You can also help yourself by recognizing the warning signals that precede an attack and taking appropriate action. Along with, or in place of, visual disturbances, you may experience dizziness, numbness, nausea, increased sensitivity to noise or light, unusual energy or hunger, yawning, trembling, changes in mood and outlook, unusual pallor or an increase in frequency of passing water. When these occur, do not soldier on. Use any of the relaxation methods detailed on pages 176-7, lie down in a darkened room and try to sleep. If you feel very sick, anti-emetic drugs, which your doctor can prescribe for you, may help. Take soluble aspirin or paracetamol (acetaminophen in USA) for the pain and, if attacks are severe, consult your doctor. Stronger analgesics may then be given or, occasionally, drugs to reduce the dilation of the blood vessels and thus to prevent, or at least minimize, the headache. But some of these, such as ergotamine, do have side-effects — over-frequent doses leading to incessant headaches, for example — and are therefore rarely prescribed.

Nail separation
Nail separation is caused by a fungal infection working its way from the tip of the nail to the lanula at the base, thus causing it to lift from its anchorage on the nail bed. A white spot at the tip of the nail is an early sign of separation. It can be extremely painful and, although it can be treated in a variety of ways, it always requires evaluation first by a doctor or dermatologist in order to establish which type of fungus is responsible.

Nail inflammation (paronychia)
This condition, also known as 'housewives' hands', is caused by a fungus and produces painful inflammation around the folds of skin that surround the nail. Treatment usually consists in the prescription of an anti-fungal ointment. You can do much to help prevent the condition by protecting your hands with rubber gloves when immersing them in warm, soapy water.

Non-specific infection (non-specific urethritis or NSU in men)
This is one of the most common of all sexually transmitted diseases. In about 50 per cent of cases, a tiny microgerm, chlamydia, has been detected.

In men, symptoms of the disease resemble a milder version of gonorrhoea (see page 217). In women, there are often no symptoms whatsoever, though sometimes there may be a thin yellow discharge and a burning sensation when passing water.

In women, there is a danger that chlamydia may migrate to the Fallopian tubes and cause an infection which may lead to permanent damage (sterility). In men, chlamydia may occasionally produce pain and inflammation and may also be a contributing factor to lowered fertility. If present in the birth canal, there is a risk of eye infection to babies together with an increased risk of pneumonia and failure to thrive.

NSI is treated with a seven- to 14-day course of tetracycline (antibiotic). This carries a cure rate of only 80 to 85 per cent. Although the other 15 to 20 per cent will often respond to a different antibiotic, the recurrence rate for both types of treatment is high. (See also Sexually transmitted diseases.)

Nosebleeds
Nosebleeds can be caused by any number of factors, from changes in blood circulation during pregnancy to a blow on the nose. Some nosebleeds start spontaneously for no clear reason and most stop just as abruptly.

What to do: lean forwards and let your nose drip for a few minutes. If the bleeding does not stop, gently pinch the nostrils together for about 10 minutes, so that you are breathing through your mouth. Release slowly. If your nose is still bleeding, repeat the procedure by pressing the sides of the nose together with an ice pack (put ice cubes in a plastic bag and wrap in a small towel). If bleeding persists, consult your doctor. If bleeding stops, help prevent a recurrence by not blowing your nose for several hours afterwards.

N.B. If you suffer from recurrent nosebleeds, you should see your doctor, as this can be symptomatic of high blood pressure.

Painful periods
See Dysmenorrhoea.

Phobias
You can be phobic to almost anything — cats, dogs, spiders, snakes, heights, thunder and lightning, eating in public, illness, death, germs, dirt, fire — anything which engenders such terrifying fears that you will go to any lengths to avoid it. Of all the phobias, the most common is agoraphobia (fear of going outside the home or 'safe' environment) and it afflicts many times more women than men.

Many phobics combine their own private and specific fear with the more general one of admitting to it or seeking help. This is a major hurdle and usually an unnecessary one. Phobias can be treated, often extremely successfully. So if you do have a phobia, help yourself by seeing your doctor or by contacting one of the excellent voluntary associations. Sometimes just 'sharing' your fear with someone who is prepared to offer help and support may make it seem less terrifying and will certainly lessen the terrible feeling of isolation.

Treatment for phobias tends to be managed either by psychiatric (behavioural) means or by medical ones. Most phobias are thought to be the result of an early conditioning experience — a comparatively trivial stimulus, such as a dog or a thunderstorm, becoming associated falsely with a panic reaction. Psychiatrists can often help patients to 'unlearn' this association by exposing them to the fear stimulus. Sometimes this is done in gradual stages, at others much more quickly. This last approach is known as 'flooding' and can have remarkable results. Because anxiety and depression can be so intense while undergoing treatment, and because some phobias and some types of patient may not respond positively to such psychotherapy, anti-anxiety or anti-depressant agents may also be prescribed.

Some types of anti-depressant have been effectively used in the management and treatment of agoraphobia.

Piles
See Haemorrhoids.

'Pink eye'
See Conjunctivitis.

Premenstrual syndrome
PMS, also known as PMT, is a blanket expression for a number of symptoms regularly experienced by some women in the days before their periods start. These symptoms may include breast tenderness and bloating (rings and shoes, for example, that are worn quite comfortably over the rest of the cycle may become tight and painful), headache, lethargy, irritability and depression. For some women, symptoms are mild and transitory and can be satisfactorily relieved by a certain amount of foresight and simple self-help. For others (about one in ten), symptoms may last for up to 14 days — actually half the cycle — or may be so severe that they seriously disrupt both their own lives and those of the people living close to them.

Although the premenstrual syndrome was first identified as long ago as 1931, the precise cause has yet to be established. It is known to be hormonally based, however, and through this finding several treatments have now emerged. The first, particularly helpful for bloating, breast tenderness and depression or tension, is to take 45 mg of vitamin B6 (pyridoxine) twice daily after meals three days before you anticipate the start of your symptoms. Increase this to 75 mg twice daily if there is no improvement but do not exceed 100 mg, as too much of the vitamin may lead to increased acidity in the stomach. A second method, particularly helpful for depression, irritability, abdominal distention and bloating, is to top up levels of progesterone using a synthetic compound which is taken over the second half of the cycle. This must be prescribed by your doctor. A diuretic, spirolactone, may also help to counteract bloating. Meanwhile you can help yourself by keeping a chart of your symptoms (see page 27), together with details of your period (heavy, light, prolonged, brief, etc) and any symptoms experienced elsewhere over the cycle. If you are suffering from PMS the cyclical nature of your symptoms will soon become apparent and should convince your doctor if he or she happens to be sceptical. You can also help yourself by getting plenty of rest, by not attempting or undertaking too much over this time, by practising relaxation, taking gentle exercise and by eating less salt (now thought to be a contributing factor).

Physical symptoms of PMS: swelling and bloating; breast discomfort (tenderness, lumpiness, pain); weight gain, headache, migraine, backache, cramps, skin disorders.

Psychological symptoms of PMS: depression, irritability, lethargy, lack of co-ordination, clumsiness, tearfulness, erratic and illogical behaviour, lack of confidence, lowered sex drive.

Psoriasis
At least two people in every 100 have psoriasis, but although it is one of the most common skin disorders, there is still much to be learnt about it. The condition itself consists of raised red patches covered with fine silvery scales. It rarely itches, is not infectious or contagious, and commonly first appears between the ages of 15 and 30. It is usually confined to the legs, knees, elbows, scalp, lower part of the back and the shoulders and it disappears and reappears with sickening regularity. The patches themselves are produced by an abnormal thickening of the top layer of the skin, which is, in turn, produced by an excessively rapid cell turnover rate in the basal layer. In severe cases, it may take the skin cells just four days to get to the surface of the skin instead of the usual 28. Nobody knows why. What is known is that there is a strong family tendency (if both parents have it, there may be about a one-in-three chance of getting it), that it is aggravated by a number of factors, such as stress, alcohol, injury, throat infection and certain drugs, and that there is no permanent cure. Although psoriasis can be effectively treated, it will always reappear. Until recently, treatment has consisted of creams and lotions, principally tar ointments and dithranol. These are both fairly effective but extremely messy to apply. A comparatively new treatment, known as PUVA therapy, has had encouraging results and seems to produce a preventative as well as a curative effect. This capitalizes on the fact that psoriasis usually responds very positively to moderate sunbathing, particularly if there is a lot of UVA in the atmosphere. This therapy combines the controlled use of ultraviolet with psoralens. These sensitize the skin to sunlight, when taken by mouth or painted on to the skin before exposure. PUVA must be administered with caution and under supervision, as it is now fairly well established that excessive ultraviolet exposure can lead to skin cancer. For this reason, it is rarely prescribed for patients under the age of 40. The depressing fact that there is still no simple and effective long-term treatment for psoriasis, together with a general lack of understanding about the condition, can make sufferers feel isolated and depressed. In Britain, the Psoriasis Association is an important source of information and reassurance. Three equivalent self-help organizations also operate in the USA. Ask your doctor or a dermatological department of a hospital for details.

Scabies
This fairly common condition is caused by a tiny mite. It is spread both by sexual contact and by contact within the family. Symptoms are a general skin rash, characterized by linear burrows in the skin between the fingers and toes, red spots elsewhere on the body and itching, especially when warm and in bed at night. Scabies can be treated with creams and lotions. It is essential to get it cleared as the spots are liable to further infection.

Sexually transmitted diseases
If you have sexual intercourse, you are at risk from sexually transmitted disease and the greater your number of partners, the greater your degree of risk. It is important, therefore, that you should be on the lookout for any signs that may indicate that you have contracted one, or sometimes more, of them. As symptoms of sexually transmitted disease in women are often undramatic and easily missed, you should also be aware of how each of these diseases and infections will affect your partner, so that in the event of his getting one or more of the symptoms listed here, you can both go to your nearest clinic for a check-up. Never be embarrassed about seeking medical attention for conditions that you may have contracted sexually. If undiagnosed, some of them can become widespread, may lead to more generalized infection and may also affect your chances of bearing children.

Symptoms of sexually transmitted disease include painful sores on or around the vagina, a discharge that may be yellow, white or brownish in colour and may be foul-smelling, and sensations of itchiness or discomfort when passing water. Sometimes, however, few or none of these symptoms may be present.

Once you are at the clinic, an investigation will be carried out. This may be uncomfortable but not painful. Smears will also be taken and sent to a laboratory for culture. Sometimes you may get an immediate diagnosis. It is absolutely vital that you return to the clinic both to receive your test results and for the follow-up checks that your doctor specifies in order to ensure that all lingering traces of the infection have disappeared.

Protect yourself against infection by observing scrupulous hygiene (see Cystitis), by asking your partner to wear a condom if you know, or believe he might have, a sexually transmitted disease or if you have recently had a baby, abortion, miscarriage, D and C or IUD fitted (all of these increase the possibility of infection for a few weeks afterwards). Have regular check-ups — at about six monthly intervals — if you are sexually active with more than one partner, particularly if you are in your teens or early twenties, as both factors increase your susceptibility to infection. Finally, wear cotton, in preference to nylon, underwear. It is more absorbent and reduces the risk of irritation in the event of your getting an infection. (See also Cold sores, Gonorrhoea, Non-specific infection, Syphilis, Thrush, Trichomoniasis.)

Stretch marks (striae)
These appear after pregnancy or as a result of large and repeated fluctuations in body weight, and are permanent, although they will fade slightly with time.

Stretch marks are caused by the skin stretching as the weight increases. Once a certain degree of strain is reached (the threshold for which varies from individual to individual and is almost certainly genetically determined), the skin breaks beneath the surface leaving transparent, long white scars on hips, thighs, breasts or abdomen. You can guard against getting these long tears in the connective tissue by keeping your weight as stable as possible and trying not to let it fluctuate within a range of more than, say, 3 kg (7 lb). You obviously cannot and should not watch your weight in this way during pregnancy when most doctors consider a gain of anything between 9 kg (20 lb) and 12.5 kg (28 lb) to be healthy. While keeping the skin supple and well moisturized probably helps to minimize the damage, it will not prevent stretch marks occurring. This is because the break happens much deeper down in the dermal layer

of the skin. Vitamin E supplements and creams have also been shown to have little or no, effect as a preventative measure — despite the many claims to the contrary. A more credible theory is that people who develop stretch marks during their teens (when most skins stretch easily to accommodate the changes occurring at puberty) or during pregnancy have lower levels of zinc than women who go through several pregnancies with no sign of a stretch mark anywhere. As zinc, along with the vitamins C and B6, is involved in the production of the collagen and elastin that give the skin its elasticity and strength, there may well be a case for eating zinc-rich foods (namely all seafoods, especially oysters and herrings) at least once a week during pregnancy.

Styes
Styes are caused by an infection in the hair follicle at the root of an eyelash. The infected area becomes sore and red, making blinking extremely painful. Later, a spot will form and the eyelid may itch. Rubbing the eyes must be avoided, however, because this will only increase the irritation and may spread the infection. Do not try to treat a stye yourself beyond bathing it gently, using cotton wool moistened in warm water or a weak solution of boric acid. There is no truth in the old 'gold' remedy, so if you do get a stye, consult your doctor instead, who will treat it with an antiseptic ointment. Very occasionally a stye may be 'blind'. That is, it develops in a gland beneath the skin and becomes blocked. This will need separate treatment, sometimes even surgery, to clear it.

Sunburn
Prevention is always better than cure and, now that there is a science to suntanning, there is little excuse for burning. So heed the warnings, take note of the SPF factors and tan safely. If you ignore all this or still manage to burn, see page 84 for notes on first aid and, if the burn is severe, take it to a doctor as soon as possible.

Syphilis
This causes 100 deaths a year in the UK. Because of the severe complications of this disease (skin ulcers, heart disease, paralysis, blindness, insanity, death), early diagnosis is absolutely essential.

Seen most commonly among homosexual or bisexual men, syphilis is transmitted sexually by a tiny germ, treponema pallidum, which has an initial incubation period of up to three months. If this early stage of the disease goes undetected, however, the disease then enters a dormant or latent stage for between five and 50 years.

Early signs of syphilis are painless and transient spots or ulcers on the genitals. While these are always visible in men, they may go completely unnoticed in women. Even if this is not the case, there is an additional risk that concern will evaporate once the sores have disappeared. At the next stage, a generalized rash appears all over the body (this is also temporary) and may be accompanied by headaches, fever and general body ache. Once these symptoms have passed and the disease has entered the latent stage, syphilis can only be diagnosed in a blood test but it can still be transferred sexually. Because of this and because babies born to mothers with syphilis may be born dead or diseased, antenatal clinics should always give blood tests to check for the disease.

In the early stage, syphilis can be completely cleared with a 10- to 14-day course of penicillin with follow-up to ensure there are no lingering traces of infection. (See also Sexually transmitted diseases.)

Thread veins

Thread veins — also called broken, spider and red veins — are dilated blood vessels in the skin. These can be caused by anything from pregnancy to injuries or blows to the skin and are also hereditary. Those ruddy faces and rosy cheeks that run in families are often the consequence of a maze of such 'veins' on the cheeks. Thread veins are also a natural 'side-effect' of the ageing process, when the thinning of the collagen makes for a lack of support so causing them to become more pronounced. Thread veins can be treated using the same method as for varicose veins (see right) in miniature. A scelerosing agent is given by injection and, on meeting the tiny blood leakages, causes them to constrict and to reform as bruised blood. They then fade away as any bruise would do. While this method can be effective, particularly on the coarser veins, it is expensive and time-consuming and it may take as long as a year of treatment before any real improvement can be discerned. A much more hopeful method is to use a laser beam which works painlessly, effectively and at the speed of light to cauterize the vessels. However, this treatment is still very expensive and not likely to become generally available for several years.

Thrush (vaginitis)

Thrush, monilia, and candidiasis all describe the same problem and it is one now thought to afflict as many as nine out of 10 women at some time in their lives. The infection itself is caused by a germ known as *candida albicans*. This yeast, which lives quite normally in the mouth, vagina and anus, can become more rampant when taking antibiotics or steroid drugs, if you are diabetic or have a thyroid disorder, if you are pregnant or take a contraceptive pill or for no clear reason at all. Other predisposing factors include wearing nylon underwear (choose cotton or silk), incorrect or lack of hygiene (always wipe front to back) and sexual intercourse when the germ is most commonly transmitted or transferred.

Symptoms of thrush are intense recurrent vaginal itching (never scratch as this will only intensify the discomfort), a thick white discharge, irritation and redness around the vulva and a burning sensation when passing water. These symptoms are not always present.

Once diagnosed, thrush can be treated in a variety of ways — with local pessaries and creams, with tablets or, more recently, with special tampons impregnated with an anti-candida agent. If you are using pessaries or creams to treat the infection, you must complete the course prescribed, even if the symptoms seem to have cleared completely. If there are any traces of the infection, the likelihood of a recurrence is high.

Thrush is one condition where household remedies can be extremely effective. These are certainly worth trying if, for any reason, you cannot see your doctor. They include douching with two tablespoons of white vinegar or lemon juice in 600 ml/1 pint (2½ cups) water, to increase the acidity of the vagina and suppress the activity of the yeast, and applying live natural yoghurt to the vagina with a blunt-ended injector tube or with your fingers. This contains a bacterium (*lactobacillus*), which is also found naturally in the vagina and is known to have an inhibiting effect on the candida bacteria. Always see your doctor as soon as you can.

Toothache

Toothache always occurs for a reason, so never sit it out and wait for the pain to subside. Make an appointment to see your dentist and, in the meantime, take an analgesic or painkiller and apply oil of cloves to the tooth and gum which has a numbing, anaesthetic effect.

Toxic shock syndrome

Toxic shock syndrome (TSS) is not a common disorder. In fact, it is more of a 'freak' phenomenon. In the whole of the USA for example, no more than 50 cases are reported a year. Alarm set in, however, following a sequence of events in 1978 in which the syndrome, which can be fatal, became linked with menstruation and, in particular, with the use of tampons. One particular high-absorbency tampon found to be recurring in case histories has been withdrawn from the market. Since then a considerable amount of research carried out indicates that toxic shock is not tampon-linked. But, as long as any doubt exists, it would be wise to follow the safeguards suggested by US doctors: change tampons frequently, use sanitary towels for night-time and avoid tampons with abrasive plastic applicators that may damage the skin on insertion.

Trichomoniasis

This condition is a common cause of abnormal discharge in women (men tend only to be carriers) and is transmitted sexually by a tiny one-celled organism, *trichomoniasis vaginalis*, which has an incubation period of less than a month.

Symptoms of trichomoniasis ('trich') can be extremely unpleasant — inflammation of the vagina together with a thick, yellowish discharge and itchiness and discomfort when passing water. Sometimes, however, there may be no symptoms at all. The main complication of the disease is that mothers may infect daughters at birth.

Fortunately, once diagnosed, trichomoniasis is easily and rapidly cured with a single dose or short tablet course of Flagyl. (See also Sexually transmitted diseases.)

Vaginal discharge

Changes in the consistency of the naturally-occurring mucus on the cervix and in the vagina over the stages of the menstrual cycle are a healthy indication of ovulation (see page 195), except when on the contraceptive pill, or pregnant when the stability of the hormones throughout the cycle results in an absence of ovulation and a minimal or non-existent 'discharge'. An abnormal discharge persists throughout the cycle, is thick, white, yellow or brown in colour, may smell unpleasant and be accompanied by itching and irritation or discomfort when passing water. If you have any of these symptoms, you may have an infection, so consult your doctor. (See also Sexually transmitted diseases, Thrush and Trichomoniasis.)

Varicose veins

Varicose veins are hard, knotty, distended veins that appear just beneath the surface of the skin and are almost always confined to the legs. They are caused by a weakness in the valve that controls the blood flow from the deep veins to the smaller, superficial ones. Once the volume of blood rises past a certain point, the smaller veins dilate and buckle under the increase in pressure.

Varicose veins are an inherited condition and can run unerringly in families for generations. This familial tendency can be allayed by taking the following common-sense measures to reduce pressure on the veins. Remember, too, that anything that increases the stress on the legs or that affects the volume of blood circulating around the lower half of the body can aggravate or even trigger the appearance of these veins.

- Avoid anything that restricts blood flow round the legs, such as tight clothes or boots or sitting with your legs crossed.
- Take some exercise daily, such as brisk walking, swimming or cycling, to stimulate the circulation.
- When sitting down, support your legs. Once horizontal, the pressure on the veins is negligible. Get into the habit of doing small foot exercises to keep the blood moving — wriggle toes, rotate ankles.
- Avoid extremes of temperature, such as excessively hot baths.
- If pregnant or standing for long periods of time, wear support tights. These offer greatest compression at the ankle, working like a tube of toothpaste, by directing the blood flow upwards.
- Get enough fibre in your diet (see page 62 for sources). A constipated digestion concentrates blood in the abdominal area of the body and increases the pressure on all surrounding veins.

Varicose veins can be treated in one of two ways. The older, more traditional and much more drastic method consists of 'stripping' and tying the vein. If the veins are not concentrated at the top of the thighs and provided that there are no contra-indications, such as a deep vein thrombosis or other obstruction of the blood vessels, they can be treated by injecting a scelerosing agent into the vein which causes it to contract and, eventually, to shrink away completely. The veins are treated one or two at a time. Aftercare consists in bandaging the treated leg for about a week and exercising gently to keep the blood circulating freely.

Vitiligo

Vitiligo is a condition in which the skin gradually loses its pigment. Almost always progressive in nature, the condition first appears at any age and on any part of the body. The white patches are usually symmetrical (i.e. on both hands or both feet) and are particularly susceptible to sunburn, as the skin no longer has any melanin to protect it. Less of a problem for fair-skinned people, who can usually camouflage the condition with cleverly applied make-up, vitiligo can be extremely traumatic for darker-skinned people because the contrast in colour is so much more apparent. PUVA therapy (see Psoriasis) can sometimes help to repigment the skin but this has the disadvantage of making the normal, surrounding skin darker too. If the white patches are very widespread, it may be worth bleaching the darker patches of skin but this can have disappointing results as it is extremely difficult to match up margins perfectly.

Warts

Warts are caused by the *papova* virus and can appear anywhere on the body, including the genitals. They have an almost indefinite incubation period, are slightly contagious and can be transmitted by intimate contact. Most warts are self-limiting. That is, if left untreated, they will eventually go. It usually takes between three months and 15 years for the body to develop its own antibodies, or immunity, to the virus — after which time the wart simply disappears. Most disappear after about two years: just about the time when disillusioned sufferers are turning to alternative remedies, such as hypnosis or charms! More conventional means of hastening the disappearance of a wart include cutting it out, freezing it (cryotherapy), passing an electrical current through it (diathermy) or applying strong organic acids to dissolve the infected tissue. All of these methods involve some degree of pain or discomfort and most leave a scar. For this reason, it is now thought preferable to leave warts to heal in their own time unless they are causing pain or discomfort. Plantar warts or verrucae on the sole of the foot are one example. Whatever you do, do not stab away at warts in the hope of 'removing the roots'. You may spread the infection.

Water retention (oedema)

In some circles, water retention is no more than a fashionable euphemism for overweight (see also Cellulite). In medical circles, however, water retention is a much rarer and, often, more serious disorder. It may, for example, be symptomatic of underlying metabolic, cardiac or kidney problems requiring immediate medical treatment in order to maintain a healthy fluid balance. If everything is running smoothly, however, the body does all this for itself — automatically and unerringly adjusting its fluid balance to accommodate for changes in activity, temperature, diet, even the time of day.

Problems, however, may sometimes set in four days or so before menstruation when falling levels of progesterone (see page 194) are thought to cause the body to retain more water than usual, producing the characteristic 1-2 Kg (2-5 lb) weight gain and, occasionally, puffiness, bloating and discomfort. This is known as 'cyclical' oedema and is a recognized clinical feature of the premenstrual syndrome. If this causes distress or discomfort, it can usually be relieved with vitamin or hormonal therapy or with a diuretic, such as spirolactone.

Hormones and diuretics should always be taken under medical supervision. Never dose yourself with diuretics if trying to lose weight as they may place an unacceptable load on the kidneys.

Index

Acknowledgments

ILLUSTRATION

Special photography by: Robert Golden: 62-5, 76-7, 162-3, 164, 188-9; Sandra Lousada: 1-5, 12-18, 20 (centre and right), 21, 22, 26-59, 74-5, 78-81, 86-103, 106-117, 121, 129, 134-7, 142-161, 176-181, 190-212; Tim Simmons: 23-5, 118-19, 126-7, 133, 170-3, 182-5; Charlie Stebbings: endpapers, 19, 60-1, 66-73, 104-5, 187.

Other photography

Werner Forman Archives: 6 (above left); The National Gallery, London: 6 (above right); The Bridgeman Art Library: 6 (below left); The Ashmolean Museum, Oxford: 6 (below right); The Metropolitan Museum of Art, gift of Consuelo Vanderbilt Balsan, 1946: 7 (above); The Trustees of the Tate Gallery, London: 7 (below); Beaton: Paula Gellibrand and Greta Garbo 8; Aquarius, London: Marilyn Monroe 8; Rutledge: Henrietta Tiarks 8; Bailey: Penelope Tree and Jean Shrimpton 8-9; Toscani: Margaux Hemingway 9; O'Lochlainin: Katharine Hepburn 9; Albert Watson: 20 (left), 83; Alan Randall: 139, 141.

Make-up for special photography by:

Christine at Image
Teresa Fairminer at Image
Maggie Hunt at Models One/Elite
Carol Hemming
Ariane

Hair for special photography by:

Ivy at Schumi
Vicky at Molton Brown
Barbara at Molton Brown
Meryl at Molton Brown
Robert Lobetta

Photographic styling by:

Alison Pollard

The publishers would like to thank the following companies for kindly lending accessories for photography:

Butler and Wilson (jewellery) 154-161, 193; A Bigger Splash (taps and basin) 109; Casa Catalan (tables, plants and pots) 28, 181, 210-11; Conran (bowls) 115, 116-17, (tray) 210-11; Courtenay (shirt) 58, (camisole) 95; Damart (vests) 20, 109, 110-11; The Dance Centre 1, 40-55, 56; Debenhams (blouse) 160; Designers Guild (cushions) 176-7, (lamp, china, rugs) 210-11; Detail (earrings) 103, (necklace) 170; Edina and Lena (pullovers) 158, 161; Fenn, Wright and Manson (suede top and shirt) 156, 159; Freeds (leotards) 33, 34, 35, 40-55; Gamba 40-55, (exercise suit) 178; Graham and Green (blinds, paper and chair) 28; Great Expectations (dress) 201; Harrods (bowls, etc) 21, (loofah) 94, (towels) 101, (bowls) 115, (towels and manicure equipment) 20, (towels) 116-17, 134; James Drew (shirt) 154-5; Jasper Conran (shirt) 190-1; Jones (earrings) 136, (necklace) 190-1; Kenzo (blouse) front cover and 3, (dress) 193; Laura Ashley (wallpapers) 28, 210-11; Liberty (shawls) 154-5, 156; Lunn Antiques (sheets) 26, (bed linen, cushions) 28, (camisoles) 98-101, (linen) 181, 197, (quilt) 201, (bed linen, cushions) 210-11; Miss O (shirt) 157; Mitsukiku (kimonos) 20, 98-101; Next (jumpers) 75, 103; Nina Campbell (glass) 109; Osborne and Little (wallpapers) 20, 109-11, 115, 116-117; N Peal (knitwear) 190-1; Paul Smith (shawl) 161; Pineapple Dance Centre 40-55; Philip Kingsley 78-9, 100-1; Piero de Monzi (shirt) 158; Sulka (pyjamas) 26, 210-11; Telephone Box 28, 181, 201, 210-11; Molton Brown endpapers.

Page 160: Mrs Desmond Preston; hair by Barbara; make-up by Teresa Fairminer.
Pages 190-1: Olive Allan and Christine Davies; hair by Vicky; make-up by Christine.
Page 193: Polly Richards; hair and make-up by Carol Hemming.
Pages 202-3, 205: Juliet Hughes-Hallet; hair by Ivy; make-up by Christine.
Pages 212-13: Mrs Ronald Hutton; hair by Simon Southall of Headlines; make-up by Christine.

Artwork by: Arka Graphics: 194-5; Russell Barnett: 42-50, 122; Lynne Riding: 112, 115, 124, 146, 174; Maire Smith: 80, 96, 108, 114, 120, 126-35; Martin Welch: 14, 16, 42 (bottom left), 82, 111, 123, 147-69.

TEXT

Page 10: John Berger quotation from *Ways of Seeing*, published by the British Broadcasting Corporation and by Penguin Books Limited © Penguin Books Limited, 1972.
Page 11: Virginia Woolf quotation from 'The New Dress', one of a collection of short stories from *A Haunted House*. This passage reproduced with the permission of The Author's Literary Estate and The Hogarth Press.
Pages 14 and 31: Weight graph devised from weight/height tables produced by the British United Provident Association (BUPA) and reproduced with their permission.
Page 19: Compulsive eating/dieting questionnaire adapted from Internal and External Components of Emotionality in Restrained and Unrestrained Eaters devised by J Polivy, CP Herman and S Warsh in the *Journal of Abnormal Psychology*, 1978, 87, page 497.
Page 23: List of Life Change Units reproduced with the permission of the British Safety Council.
Page 32: Body fat graph devised from figures produced by JVGA Durnin and J Womersley and cited in an article, 'Body fat assessed from total body density and its estimation from skinfold thickness: measurements in 48 men and women aged 16 to 72 years' in the *British Journal of Nutrition* 1974, 32, pages 77-99.
Page 35: Exercises to beware of based on recommendation by the American Medical Association's Department of Health and Education.
Page 36: Jane Fonda quotation from *Jane Fonda's Workout Book* published by Allen Lane. © The Workout Inc, 1981. This passage reproduced with the permission of Penguin Books Limited.
Page 62: Fibre values for listed foods taken from McCance & Widdowson's *The Composition of Foods* by AA Paul and DAT Southgate, published by Her Majesty's Stationary Office (London, 1978) and reproduced with the permission of The Controller Her Majesty's Stationary Office.
Page 82: Sun protection factor chart compiled from figures produced by Piz Buin Protective Tanning.
Pages 142-3: Face measurements based on material from Mademoiselle Magazine, USA.
Pages 210-11: Breast self-examination series based on method recommended by the Women's National Cancer Control Campaign (UK).